C000092667

A Political History of Ear

A Political History of
Early Christianity

Allen Brent

t & t clark

Published by T&T Clark International
A Continuum Imprint
The Tower Building, 11 York Road, London SE1 7NX
80 Maiden Lane, Suite 704, New York, NY 10038

www.continuumbooks.com

British Library Cataloguing-in-Publication Data
A catalogue record for this book is available from the British Library

ISBN: 978-0-567-03174-7 (Hardback)
         978-0-567-03175-4 (Paperback)

Typeset by Newgen Imaging Systems Pvt Ltd, Chennai, India
Printed and bound in Great Britain by CPI Antony Rowe, Chippenham, Wiltshire

Caroline Penrose Bammel, FBA
In piam memoriam

CONTENTS

PREFACE

This book traces the history of early Christianity as a political movement with serious political challenges to the Pagan Empire that pagans correctly identified and of which they did well to be aware. The hostility between Paganism and Early Christianity was not the result of an unfortunate misunderstanding but the result of a threat whether overtly or surreptitiously posed by the growth of both the order of Christian societies and the development of the theology that underpinned that order. Stoic and Middle and Neo Platonist assumptions were to produce two rival cosmologies in which Pagan and Christian social order was constructed, with imperial religion relying upon a polytheistic ordering of the cosmos and Christianity, in one form or another, upon a Trinitarian one.

The methodology in terms of which my thesis proceeds can be exemplified from two proponents of the relationship between metaphysical order and political order. The first was Peter Berger who developed a sociology of knowledge in which the metaphysical order was studied as a social construction: what people believe about the world of nature as part of a cosmic order of things external to society is in fact the reflection of social order.[1] Reality is socially constructed so as to legitimate the structure of authority within society, making patterns of authority stable and enduring, and not simply unstable and ephemeral, by anchoring social order in some putative order of nature beyond society. Berger however was to emphasize that his account was essentially a study of the role that bodies of metaphysical knowledge whether theistic or atheistic (such as the Newtonian mechanistic model of physics) functioned in the ordering of social relations: he wished in no way to deny further claims to truth that they might make. Thus a given form of society with a given set of social relations might be necessary to explain the emergence of a particular kind of cosmology but such social relations were not sufficient to explain that cosmology and its further development.

One could, for example, write an account of the development of mathematics in terms of economic groups pursuing their material self-interest in which their social interaction was seen to produce various kinds of relationships between mathematical concepts and theorems. Such an account would therefore show

---

1. P. Berger and T. Luckmann, *The Social Construction of Reality* (Harmondsworth: Penguin, 1967), pp. 122–45.

how modern mathematics (and in consequence cosmological explanations in modern physics) arose from its generation from the roots of such a social construction of mathematical and physical reality. But at the end of the day, it is quite remarkable that a system generated by such sociological roots that imply a quite different aim actually succeeds in fitting the 'real' world.[2] Nevertheless it is difficult to believe that it was purely accidentally that, at the same time that Newton propounded a view of the cosmos in terms of the combination of various individual atoms not further divisible under various kinds of physical forces, Locke articulated his view of the origin of civil society based upon a social contract entered into by individuals at some putative dawn of history. Just as nature consisted of irreducible atoms combined into molecules of various complexity to form an orderly cosmic order, so too irreducibly unique individual persons as social atoms combined under the rules of contract given in a state of nature to form molecular social institutions which in combination gave rise to social order.

Berger in insisting that social forms were necessary to scientific, religious or political ideas arising, but not sufficient, acknowledged Weber's critique of Marxist determinism in which religious or political ideas were wholly produced by social relations. Weber saw the contingencies of accidental historical events occurring chaotically at any given time as setting the agenda in which certain ideas could emeger. But for Weber ideas determined how the agenda now developed and what conclusions it reached. Any number of societies could be shown historically to have the social and economic conditions that existed historically before the rise of capitalist modes of production. But only in the Europe of the seventeenth century did this begin to take place.

Weber claimed that it was Protestantism characterized by Calvinism that carried the agenda forward in this situation in a way that similar agendas in the past could not. Capitalism required limitless production aimed at market success and this required continuous reinvestment of profits productively to continue growth and competition. Similar social and economic conditions had existed previously in other ages and continents, in, for example, ancient China, but capitalism had not emerged in a society in which those who had produced resources surplus to their subsistence requirements had simply devised ostentatious new forms of personal consumption. Popular Calvinism taught that personal choice could not determine one's personal salvation but only divine election in the inscrutable counsels of God. In order for someone to be convinced of their redemption they needed to be reassured that they had been foreordained to eternal life. But this assurance could not come from any personal and individual choice. One needed business success in order to feel that God smiled on one, and the more the success the more one could feel

2.   P. Berger, *The Social Reality of Religion* (Harmondsworth: Penguin, 1973), Appendix 2.

assured of a favourable providence that indicated one's divine election. Yet if one spent what one produced surplus to one's requirements on, as it were, wine, women and song, one would simply show that one was not among the chosen elect. So one reinvested the surplus, being prepared to live puritanically and frugally. Thus popular Calvinism fitted precisely what was required as an idea developed and pursued for the historical events in the time and place of seventeenth century Europe to issue in the capitalist mode of production.[3]

Quentin Skinner has developed such a methodology in the field of Reformation history and theology. His Weberian argument is that though the coming together of particular events determines which kind of idea is on the agenda, the ideas themselves and their logic are critical for determining why those events had the outcome that they did. Thus Luther's view on justification and his denial of the objectivity of sacramental grace became critical for the development of modern ideas of sovereignty and the nation state. If you denied any mediator between God and humanity other than the spiritual Christ with whom you treated as an individual, yourself with your God alone mediating your salvation, then the authority of an institutional and international church standing over against and challenging the nation state was entirely removed. If there was no divinely constituted, hierarchical society, which through the ministry of bishops, priests and deacons could objectively absolve and deliver salvation to the individual through the miracle of the font and the altar of the Mass, then sole political power was in the hands of the temporal ruler: there was no absolution to be had from any oath made; there was no threat to the individual's salvation from excommunication from font and altar. Lutheranism was therefore as an idea, whatever its internal logic, necessary for the rise of the sovereign nation state in which a temporal ruler would exercise absolute power within bounded territorial limits.[4]

It is my object in this book to explore such a methodology in application to the political development of early Christianity from the emergence of the Jesus movement principally in the form found in the Markan, Roman community until the post Decian and post Diocletian emergence of Constantine. My assumption is that there was clearly no inevitability, historically speaking, about the emergence of catholic Christianity as the predominant political influence in Medieval, pre-Reformation Europe from the chaos of events and ideas in the first and second century. Since political and social structure reflects the social construction of the cosmic order of the universe, then for Christianity to triumph it needed to re-order in its own terms Pagan cosmic order as represented

---

3. I cite this example for purposes of illustration of a general case about the development of historical ideas: I am aware that the particular case is not without its critics, see M. Weber, *The Protestant Ethic and the Spirit of Capitalism* (New York: Scribner, 1958), cf. R. Aron, *Main Currents in Sociological Thought*, vol. II (London: Weidenfeld and Nicolson, 1968), pp. 220–25.

4. Q. Skinner, *The Foundations of Modern Political Thought* (Cambridge: University Press, 1978).

by Middle Platonism and popular Stoicism. In executing such a task, it would
need to convert Paganism. But it could only do so by adopting for itself and
becoming convinced of the formal principles of such pagan philosophies and
using them as the tools of such cosmic reconstruction: only in such a way
would pagans be persuaded to use their tools in such a new way and so participate in the new, Christian project of cosmic reconstruction and maintenance.

Thus we argue that, for Christianity to succeed, it needed to reconstruct its
earlier construction of an apocalyptic or Gnostic cosmic universe. That earlier
construction presented a cosmic order in chaos, whether with signs and portents indicating the break up of the natural order prior to the imminent Second
Advent of Christ, or of a natural order equally in chaos as the result of a cosmic
catastrophe from which the individual and fragmented soul needed to escape.
It was such a cosmic chaos with a natural order breaking down in terms of
adverse signs and portents that was reflected in pagan Roman, Republican
political order. Augustus in bringing about the political order of the Principate
had also reconstructed cosmic order: in the new golden age the portents and
prodigies of Sibylline prophecy had come to an end in a new, golden age. For
Christianity to succeed as a political force, it needed therefore to reconstruct its
apocalyptic or Gnostic constructions in terms of a new, divine cosmic order
in which a new, Christian political order would be reflected. Thus from the
late first (St Luke) to the second and third centuries the task of reconstructing
cosmic order in terms of a monarchical and hierarchical Trinity was begun,
with corresponding claims to a Christian social and political order that would
reflect it. It is to the fleshing out of this thesis that I will shortly now turn.

My book is another product of a continuing research project, initially funded
by the British Academy (1996–1997) and Leverhulme Trust (1998–2000), and
now continuing with new, British Academy funding (2009–2011). I must
register also thanks to the Faculty of Divinity, and the Hort Memorial Fund, for
continuing support for my research and teaching activities, and for my recent
award of a Doctorate of Divinity in the University of Cambridge.

ALLEN BRENT
St Edmund's College
Cambridge

ABBREVIATIONS

Abbreviations for Journals and Standard Works of Reference

1QM	Dead sea scrolls, War Scroll found in Qumran cave 1
11QMelch	Dead sea scrolls, Melchizedek Scroll found in Qumran cave 11
ABD	David Noel Freedman (ed.), *The Anchor Bible Dictionary* (New York: Doubleday, 1992)
AGJU	Arbeiten zur Geschichte des antiken Judentums und des Urchristentums
AJA	*American Journal of Archaeology*
AJP	*American Journal of Philology*
APAW	*Abhandlungen der königliche preußischen Akademie der Wissenschaften*
ANRW	Hildegard Temporini and Wolfgang Haase (eds), *Aufstieg and Niedergang der römischen Welt: Geschichte und Kultur Roms im Spiegel der neueren Forschung* (Berlin: W. de Gruyter, 1972–)
ArcCl	*Archeologia Classica*
von Arnim	J. von Arnim, *Stoicorum Veterum Fragmenta*, vols. I–IV, (Leipzig: Teubner 1903–1905). *Abbreviations for Ancient Authors Classical Works and Epigraphy*
ATR	*Anglican Theological Review*
BMC	*Coins of the Roman Empire in the British Museum*, edited by H. Mattingly (London: Trustees of the British Museum, 1923–)
CAH	*Cambridge Ancient History*
CAH²	*Cambridge Ancient History*, 2nd edition
CH	*Church History*
CIG	*Corpus inscriptionum graecarum*
CIL	*Corpus inscriptionum latinarum*
EPRO	*Études Préliminaires aux Religions Orientales dans L'Empire Romain*, edited by J. Maarten and M. J. Vermaseren (Leiden: E. J. Brill, 1972)

ETL	*Ephemerides theologicae lovanienses*
GRBS	*Greek, Roman, and Byzantine Studies*
HTR	*Harvard Theological Review*
Horsley, *New Documents*	G. Horsley, *New Documents Illustrating Early Christianity* (Macquarie University: Ancient History Documentation Center, 1983-)
IG	*Inscriptiones Graecae*
IGRR	*Inscriptiones Graecae ad res Romanan pertinentes*
IGUR	*Inscriptiones Graecae Urbis Romae*
IL	*Inscriptiones Latinae*
JAC	*Jahrbuch für Antike und Christentum*
JbNum	Jahrbuch für Numismatik und Geldgeschichte
JRS	*Journal of Roman Studies*
JSNT	*Journal for the Study of the New Testament*
JSNTSup	*Journal for the Study of the New Testament*, Supplement Series
JTS	*Journal of Theological Studies*
LCL	Loeb Classical Library
NovTSup	*Novum Testamentum*, Supplements
OGIS	*Orientis Graeci Inscriptiones Selectae*
P. Giss	*Papyrus Giessen* P. A. Kuhlmann (ed.), *Die Giessener literarischen Papyri und die Caracalla-Erlasse-Edition*, edited by (Berichte und Arbeiten aus der Universitätsbibliothek und dem Universitätsarchiv Giessen 46; Giessen: Universitätsbibliothek, 1994)
P. Oxyr.	B. P. Grenfell and A. S. Hunt (eds), *The Oxyrynchus Papyri* (London: Egyptian Exploration Fund, 1898–)
RB	*Revue biblique*
RivArchCr	*Rivista di Archeologia Cristiana*
RIC	H. Mattingly, E. A. Sydenham and C. H. V. Sutherland (eds), *Roman Imperial Coinage* (London: Spink and Son, 1923–)
R.Phil.	*Revue Philologique*
RSR	*Recherches de science religieuse*
SEG	*Supplementum Epigraphicum Graecum*
SNTSMS	Society for New Testament Studies Monograph Series
SPAW	Sitzungsberichte der preussischen Akademie der Wissenschaften
ST	*Studia theological*
STAC	*Studien und Texte zu Antike und Christentum*
StEphAug	*Studia Ephemeris Augustinianum*
StPat.	*Studia Patristica*
Suppl. JnStJud	*Supplements to the Journal for the study of Judaism* (Leiden: Brill 2004)

VC	*Vigiliae Christianae*
VCSup	*Vigiliae christianae Supplements*
WMANT	*Wissenschaftliche Monographien zum Alten und Neuen Testament*
WUNT	Wissenschaftliche Untersuchungen zum Neuen Testament
ZKT	*Zeitschrift für katholische Theologie*
ZPE	*Zeitschrift für Papyrologie und Epigraphik*

Abbreviations for Ancient Authors

Classical Works and Epigraphy

Aelius Aristides, *Or.*	*Orationes*
Aesclepias of Mendes, *Theologumena*	*Theologumena*
Alexander Aphrodisias, *Fato*	*De Fato*
Alexander Aphrodisias, *Mixt.*	*De Mixtione*
Apuleius [Pseudo Aristotle], *Mundo*	*De Mundo*
Apuleius, *Metam.*	*Metamorphoses*
Augustus, *Res Gest.*	*Res Gestae*
Cicero, *Div.*	*De Divinatione*
Cicero, *Leg.*	*De Legibus*
Cicero, *Nat. Deor.*	*De Natura Deorum*
Cicero, *Rep.*	*De Republica*
Corpus Hermeticum, *Fragments*	*Fragments*
Chrysippus, *Fat.*	*De Fato*
Chrysippus, *Fin.*	*De Finibus*
Dio Cassius,	*Historiae*
Dio Chrysostom, *Or.*	*Orationes*
Diogenes Laertius,	*Successions of the Philosophers*
Dionysus of Halicarnassus,	*Antiquitates Romanae*
Herodian,	Herodian, *Historiae*
Herodotus,	Herodotus, *Historiae*
Hesiod, *Works*	*Works and Days*
Horace, *Carmen Saeculare*	*Carmen Saeculare*
Horace, *Odes*	*Odes*
Julius Obsequens, *Prod.*	*Liber de prodigiis*
Justinian, *Dig.*	*Digesta*
Livy	*Ab Urbe Condita*
Lucan, *Bell. Civ.*	*De Bello Civili*
Lucian, *De Dea Syriae*	Lucian, *De Dea Syriae*
Lucian, *Pereg.*	*De Morte Peregrinni*
Lucretius, *Rer.Nat.*	*De Rerum Natura*
Martial, *Epig.*	*Epigramata*
Philostratus, *Vit. Apol.*	*Vita Apollonii*
Philostratus, *Lives*	*Lives of the Sophists*

Plato, *Pol.*	*Politicus*
Plato, *Rep.*	*De Republica*
Pliny, *Ep.*	*Epistulae*
Pliny, *Nat. Hist.*	*Naturalis Historia*
Pliny, *Paneg.*	*Panegyricus*
Plutarch, *Ant.*	*Anthony*
Plutarch, *De Comm. Not.*	*De Communibus Notitiis*
Plutarch, *Mar.*	*Marius*
Plutarch, *Tit. Flam.*	*Titus Flamininus*
Polybius, *Hist.*	*Historiae*
SHA, *Aurelian.*	Scriptores Historiae Augustae, *Diuus Aurelianus*
SHA, *Elagab.*	Scriptores Historiae Augustae, *Elagabalus*
SHA, *Gordiani Tres*	Scriptores Historiae Augustae, *Gordiani Tres*
Seneca, *Ep.*	*Epistulae*
Seneca, *Trag. (Octavia)*	*Tragoediae*
Simplicius *in Arist. Phys.*	*Commentarius in Physicam Aristotelis*
Statius, *Silv.*	*Silvae*
Stobaius, *Eclog.*	*Eclogae*
Suetonius, *Aug.*	*Augustus*
Suetonius, *Nero*	*Nero*
Suetonius, *Titus*	*Titus*
Suetonius, *Dom.*	*Domitian*
Suetonius, *Tib.*	*Tiberius*
Suetonius, *Vesp.*	*Vespasian*
Tacitus, *Annal.*	*Annales*
Tacitus, *Hist.*	*Historiae*
Ulpian, *De officio proncon.*	*De officio proconsulis*
Valerius Maximus, *Fact.*	*Factorum et Dictorum Memorabilium*
Velleius Paterculus,	*Historiae Romanae*
Vergil, *Aeneid*	*Aeneid*
Vergil, *Ec.*	*Eclogae*

Early Christian and Jewish Writers

Acta Justini	*Acta Sancti Justini et Sociorum*
Acta Callisti	*Acta Sancti Callisti Papae Martyris Romae*
Ambrose, *Ep.*	*Epistles*
AmbroseSerm, *Contr. Auxent.*	*Sermo contra Auxentium*
Anselm, *De Fide Trinitatis*	*De Fide Trinitatis*
Athenagoras, *Leg.*	*Legatio pro Christianis*
Augustine, *City of God*	*The City of God Against the Pagans*
Barnabas,	*Epistula*
Clement of Alexandria, *Exerpt. Theod.*	*Excerpta de Theodoto*

Clement, *Cor.*	*Letter to the Corinthians*
C.A.	*Constitutiones Apostolicae*
Cyprian, *Demet.*	*Ad Demetrianum*
Cyprian, *Donat.*	*Ad Donatum*
Cyprian, *Mort.*	*De Mortalitate*
Cyprian, *Ep.*	*Epistulae*
Cyprian, *Laps.*	*De Lapsis*
Cyprian, *Unit.*	*De Unitate Catholicae Ecclesiae*
Did.	Didache
Dionysius of Alexandria,	*Ad Fabianum*
Dionysius of Corinth,	*Epistula ad Romanos*
Eusebius, *H.E.*	*Historia Ecclesiastica*
Eusebius, *Oration*	*Oration on the Tricennalia of Constantine*
Eusebius, *Vit. Const.*	*Vita Constantini*
Gelasius, *Ep.*	*Epistulae*
Gos. Pet.	*Gospel of Peter*
Gos. Thom.	*Gospel of Thomas*
Gos. Phil.	*Gospel of Philip*
Gos. Truth	*Gospel of Truth*
Hermas, *Sim.*	*Similitudines*
Hermas, *Vis.*	*Visiones*
Hippolytus (Pseudo), *Ap. Trad.*	*Apostolic Tradition*
Hippolytus (Pseudo), *Ref.*	*Refutatio Omnium Haeresium*
Ignatius, *Ephes.*	*Letter to the Ephesians*
Ignatius, *Magnes.*	*Letter to the Magnesians*
Ignatius, *Philad.*	*Letter to the Philadelphians*
Ignatius, *Pol.*	*Letter to Polycarp*
Ignatius, *Rom.*	*Letter to the Romans*
Ignatius, *Smyrn.*	*Letter to the Smyrnaeans*
Ignatius, *Trall.*	*Letter to the Trallians*
Irenaeus, *Adv. Haer.*	*Adversus Haereses*
John of Salsbury, *Metalogicus*	*Metalogicus*
Josephus, *Antiqu.*	*Antiquitates*
Josephus, *BJ*	*De Bello Judaico*
Justin, *1 Apol.and 2 Apol.*	*Apologiae* 1 and 2
Justin, *Dial.*	*Dialogus cum Tryphone*
Minucius Felix, *Octav.*	*Octavius*
Odes of Solomon	*Odes of Solomon*
Orac. Sibyl.	*Oracula Sibyllina*
Origen, *Celsus*	*The True Word, Against Celsus*
Philo, *Aetern. Mund.*	*De Aeternitate Mundi*
Philo, *Incorrupt. Mund.*	*De Incorruptione Mundi*
Philo, *Opif.*	*De Opificio Mundi*
Philo, *Rer. Div. Her.*	*Quis Rerum Divinarum Heres Sit*

Philostratus, *Lives*	*Lives of the Sophists*
Polycarp, *Philip.*	*Letter to the Philippians*
Pseudo Clement, *2 Cor.*	*2 Corinthians.*
Pseudo Clement, *Homilies*	*Homilies*
Pseudo Clement, *Ep. Ad Iacob.*	*Epistula ad Iacobum*
Tatian, *Orat.*	*Oratio ad Graecos*
Tertullian, *Apol.*	*Apologia*
Tertullian, *Pudic.*	*De Pudicitia*
Theophilus, *Ad Autol.*	*Ad Autolycum*
Trad. Ap.	*Traditio Apostolica*

Chapter 1

THE JESUS OF HISTORY AND HIS MOVEMENT, AND THE POLITICS OF HIS DAY

Apocalyptic literature is a literature dealing with an ultimate and final settlement of human affairs. Whether its principal concern is with the end of human history in which the Day of the Lord will set in blood and fire, or whether it rather seeks the hidden eternal realm beyond the veil of sense and sight, its objective is a final end in which the transient and imperfect present will be subsumed into an eternal and perfect divine order of things. Whatever the true and essential character of apocalyptic, its use in at least some of the earliest communities of the Jesus movement undoubtedly was as a prophecy of imminently future events. We shall argue that it was from such communities that the later Church developed that was to confront the Roman Empire.

We shall see, in our second chapter, how that the Christianity with which the Roman state first came into conflict was one with an apocalyptic vision of its destiny and of the significance of its founder. Both the Roman Christian community to whose tradition Mark's gospel (A.D. 65) bears witness as well as that of the Seer of the book of Revelation (A.D. 79–95) represented such an apocalyptic view of Christianity. But what connection did such apocalypticism have to the Jesus of history?

It is my argued conviction in this book that the apocalypticism of early Christianity, and the conditions that it posed on the relationship between that form of Christianity and the Roman state, underwent a radical, historical transformation. In place of the radical disjunction between the coming kingdom of God and the Pagan Roman empire on its way to destruction arose, in a way generally characteristic of ultimately successful political movements, the view that existing social structures of the *status quo* could be transformed by the values of the movement that opposed it, rather than simply uproot and replace it. I am aware that some might regard my discussion regarding the development of the apocalypticism of Jesus' followers as a resurrection of what might be regarded as an old argument about the 'delay of the parousia' that they consider *passé*. Some prominent contemporary, New Testament scholars would, as we shall see, be sceptical of such an argument regarding the development of Christian theology and church organization.

I must, therefore, emphasize that my argument will not be dependent on such a view. Rather it will be based on the fact that historically the first recorded conflict in early Christianity with the Roman Empire was, as can be inferred from Mark and from Revelation, a clash between an apocalyptic form of Christianity, and a Roman Empire that I shall argue to have had its own political legitimation in terms of a popular, Stoic eschatology. Mark, on the Q hypothesis that I accept, was incorporated with that document almost wholly into Matthew and Luke, the former of whom heightened his apocalypticism and the latter of whom softened it. If John were dependent on Mark too, this would also imply a transformation of apocalyptic not only by Luke but also by John. My account will therefore stand regardless of what the Jesus of history might have originally claimed about the kingdom of God.

My discussion will not be dependent, therefore, on whether the Jesus of history proclaimed either an apocalyptic or an eschatological message, or whether, alternatively, an apocalyptic or eschatological form has become imposed upon traditions of Jesus' words and acts with originally a wholly different import. My discussion regarding the subsequent transformation of the apocalyptic of Mark or of John the Seer in interaction with the political ideology of the pagan Roman Empire will thus stand separately from such a discussion of whether or not their apocalypticism represented the claims of the Jesus of history, his character, and in what sense he shared in the expectations of his followers. But since it would appear strange to write a political history of a movement without any account of the views of its founder, I will argue very briefly here my position regarding the Jesus of history, and his relationship to the political and social structures of his time, and in inevitable conflict with many scholars in a complex debate.

1. *Modern Rejections of the Eschatological Jesus in Criticism of the Canonical Gospels*

Some recent work has sought to deny any connection between the teaching of the historical Jesus and apocalyptic, considering instead that he was a wisdom-sage attacking, like a Cynic philosopher, accepted religious conventions. Some scholars such as Mack and Downing have explored the alleged relationship between the Jesus movement and Cynic philosophy through an analysis of Jesus' sayings and the structure of the Cynic diatribe.[1] Borg, with whom, as we shall see Schüssler-Fiorenza agrees, sees the Jesus of history as a Jewish Wisdom teacher rather than a Cynic. The latter, however, stresses more the metaphysics of Wisdom that leads her to a 'high' Christology with which other

---

1.   B. L. Mack, *A Myth of Innocence: Mark and Christian Origins* (Philadelphia: Fortress, 1988); F. G. Downing, *Christ and the Cynics* (Sheffield: Academic Press, 1988). See also M. J. Borg, *Jesus in Contemporary Scholarship*, (Valley Forge, Pennsylvania: Trinity Press International, 1994).

writers in the North American school would not necessarily follow if such a Christology is regarded as true to the claims of the Jesus of history about himself.

Borg was to develop further his non-eschatological picture of Jesus in terms of a figure that attacked the religious basis for the social stratification of his time in terms of holiness codes. His picture stresses the purity of ruling groups and the uncleanness of groups excluded from power and prestige. It is in such a context that Borg sees Jesus' acts such as welcoming 'tax-gatherers and sinners', or his words about the prodigal son who becomes unclean when he feeds swine, or his attack on the Pharisees for 'cleansing the outside of the cup', or his parable of the Good Samaritan.[2]

Mack and Downing's picture has been further developed by Horsley and Crossan. For both Jesus was a social revolutionary, a peasant who represented the interests of a downtrodden rural peasantry against urban, ruling elites who included the high priestly establishment as instruments of Roman, colonial oppression.[3] Crossan takes up Borg's point about holiness codes and develops it. The miracle of the feeding of the 5,000, repeated some five times over our four Gospels, has at its core the notion of 'commensality' or table-fellowship as central to the movement of the historical Jesus. At such a common meal, all social boundaries of race, sex and class were abolished. Jesus, by means of such an institution within his community, was directly challenging hierarchy and the patron–client relationship employed by the Pagan Roman, Imperial Power as the instrument of its domination.[4] It is in such a social and political context that the Jesus of history is to be located rather than as an eschatological prophet of the end-time.

Schüssler Fiorenza and Borg have rather sought a more Judaistic and less Graeco-Roman context than the Cynic movement in which to place the sayings of Jesus. Both writers see Jesus as the wisdom sage. Schlüssler Fiorenza's perspective is that of a radical feminist who regards the Jesus of history as claiming to be 'the prophet and child of Sophia'.[5] Thus she focuses upon the Q saying the form of which in Matthew she considers most original. Jesus is criticized for eating and drinking with tax-gatherers and sinners, whereas John is condemned for asceticism. Jesus opponents therefore are not wise because

---

2. See e.g. Mk 2:15-17; Lk. 19:7-10; 15:25-32; Mk 7:5-15; Lk. 10:29-37, cf. M. Borg, *Conflict, Holiness and Politics in the Teachings of Jesus* (Lampeter: Edwin Mellen, 1984), pp. 87–103, and *Contemporary Scholarship*, pp. 26–28.

3. R. Horsley, *Sociology and the Jesus Movement* (New York: Crossroad, 1989) and *Jesus and Empire: The Kingdom of God and the New World Disorder* (Minneapolis: Fortress 2003); J. D. Crossan, *The Historical Jesus: The Life of a Mediterranean Jewish Peasant* (Edinburgh: T. & T. Clark, 1991).

4. Crossan, *Historical Jesus*, pp. 396–99, and Borg, *Contemporary Scholarship*, pp. 34–36.

5. E. Schüssler Fiorenza, *In Memory of Her: A Feminist Theological Reconstruction of Christian Origins* (New York: Crossroad, 1983), pp. 134–135; Borg, *Contemporary Scholarship*, p. 25.

their different judgements are self-contradictory. But Jesus in his words and miraculous acts displays wisdom, and 'wisdom is justified by her deeds'.[6]

Jesus will then identify himself directly with the figure of Wisdom in Judaic tradition in the lament over Jerusalem, also in Q:

> Jerusalem, Jerusalem, who murders the prophets and stones those who have been sent to you, how often I desired to gather your children as a hen gathers her chicks under her wings but you were unwilling. Behold your house is left desolate to you and you will not see me from now on until you say: 'Blessed is he who comes in the name of the Lord'.[7]

Here we find the female imagery of hen and chicks reminiscent of the hovering of the (feminine) Spirit who so behaves when it (she) 'hovers (or broods) over the face of the waters' like, as one Rabbi says, 'a hen over her chicks'. We read Joshua ben Hananiah's statement:

> The Spirit of God was brooding over the face of the waters like a dove, which broods over her young but does not touch them.[8]

The dove in Philo is used as the symbol for Wisdom and Logos, and it was the Holy Spirit that descended on Jesus at his baptism 'as a dove'.[9]

Thus Jesus emerges from a Judaic tradition in which Wisdom, identified with spirit, is a divine principle. Wisdom designed the 'structure of the world'. As one writer claims: 'All that is hidden, all that is plain, I have come to know, instructed by Wisdom who designed them all.'[10] Wisdom is spirit, 'she is a breath of the power of God, pure emanation of the glory of the Almighty.'[11] Like the Stoic logos-Spirit, she is 'almighty, all-surveying, penetrating all intelligent, pure, and most subtle spirits'.[12] Jesus thus implores Jerusalem like Wisdom raising her voice and calling on 'simpletons' to 'learn how to behave' and 'fools' to 'come to their senses'.[13] This was the Wisdom that claimed 'the Lord created me, first-fruits of his fashioning . . . from the beginning, before

6. Mt. 11:7-19 with which Lk. 7:24-35 agrees while substituting 'all her children' for 'deeds'.

7. Mt. 23:37-39; Lk. 13:34-35. Matthew's position of the saying late in Jesus' Ministry before his prediction of Jerusalem's destruction is its obvious place: Luke places it at the beginning of his last journey to Jerusalem in an artificially constructed 'Travel Narrative'.

8. Cited in C. K. Barrett, *The Holy Spirit in the Gospel Tradition* (London: SPCK, 1947), p. 38.

9. Philo, *Rer. Div. Her.*, 126 and 134, cf. Mk 1:10. See also Mt. 3:16 in contrast to Lk. 3:22: 'in bodily form as a dove'.

10. Wis. 7:17 and 21-22.
11. Wis. 7:25-26.
12. Wis. 7:23.
13. Prov. 8:1-5.

the earth came into being . . . I was beside the master craftsman, delighting in him day after day'.[14]

The 'Wisdom of God' proclaims his prophetic message in the first person, according to Luke's version of Q, whereas according to Matthew 'Jesus' is recorded as the speaker.[15] 'She makes all things new; age after age she enters holy souls, and makes them God's friends and prophets.'[16] Wisdom is also associated with acts of healing, and the physician is praised.[17] Thus we read in Mark the consternation of the crowds who say: 'What is this wisdom given to him and such miraculous powers transmitted through his hands!'[18] Matthew reads this statement as one in which wisdom implies power to heal: 'Whence comes to this man this wisdom and miraculous powers?'[19]

Schüssler Fiorenza propounds therefore a 'high' Christology claimed by the Jesus of history: she represents Jesus as not simply a teacher of wisdom but of its embodiment or incarnation as the cosmic principle upon which the universe has been established. Clearly she is not concerned about claiming that the Jesus of history used images of 'himself' that implied 'his' pre-existence as a divine principle so long as that principle is feminine: Sophia (σοφία: Wisdom) is a 'she' and not a 'he'. Thus the case for feminist claims is supported and the Jesus of history can be shown to be the opponent of patriarchal structures of society as opposed to the divine plan. As such we may see a trajectory with the Fourth Gospel, at least if we consider that gospel as parasitic upon the synoptic tradition. The synoptic 'wisdom' strikingly parallels John's logos made flesh, even though the cause of patriarchy may be advanced by the use of λόγος as a masculine term.[20]

One basic theme of this book is that the Logos as a cosmic principle proved later to pose a fundamental question for the nature of the political order of a Christian society. If such a 'high' Christology was claimed by the Jesus of history himself, it will be seen in our later chapters that it was this element that was to develop into the Christian political philosophy espoused by Eusebius and used in support of Constantine and his place in salvation history as the first Christian emperor. Whether intended by the Jesus of history or not, once Christianity entered the mainstream of Graeco Roman culture, any Logos Christology was bound to raise political questions. In that culture, political authority was regarded as a reflection of the natural order, and the Logos as the rational order of a nature in metaphysical harmony and peace within itself.

14. Prov. 8:22-31.
15. Lk. 11:49, cf. Mt. 23:34
16. Wis. 7:27.
17. Sir. 38:1-3.
18. Mk 6:2
19. Mt. 13:54
20. Jn 1:1-14.

The earthly ruler was the mediator between that metaphysical order found in nature and human political order. The issue was, therefore, who was the particular human, authority figure, who could represent Christ as Logos, and therefore as the ground plan of the cosmic order.

The non-eschatological picture of Jesus that has so far emerged has arisen from selecting the supportive passages cited in the canonical gospels and distinguishing them from other, apocalyptic passages in which Jesus claims that his purpose is to bring to an end this order of space and time and to establish in its place an eternal and supernatural order of things. These apocalyptic passages are then regarded as later additions by certain groups in the early church. But let us now look at to what extent non-canonical gospels, principally those found in the Nag Hammadi documents, can be used to support such a case.

2. *The Nag Hammadi Library and the Eschatological Jesus*

The argument for such a high Christology for Christ as Wisdom has been furthered by studies of the Nag Hammadi and other documents, which can be seen as a trajectory from such a core Christology, as Koester and others have argued.[21] We have several representatives of Sethian Gnosticism with its theories of emanations, the principal one of which is Sophia. In the *Hypostasis of the Archons* it is Sophia (or Pistis Sophia) who reveals to the creator of the lower world, Sakla or Yaldabaoth that he is not the supreme creator of everything. This work represents a developed system considered heretical by the later church and coming from the third century. Indeed a similar consideration holds regarding the Gospel of Judas following the publication of the fragments from the Codex Tchacos. The reversal of Judas' normal role in the gospel story so that he becomes the favoured disciple is so that he can receive the revelation of the true 'kingdom' of the twelve aeons, and of Adamas and Barbelo that prefigure in the speculations of later, Sethian Gnosticism. Such a 'kingdom' is clearly not one of future eschatology but of an already present, unseen and eternal world beyond the veil of sense.

The issue with the newly discovered Nag Hammadi corpus is not whether it contains gospels capable of giving us a more reliable history of Jesus than our canonical four. The texts of the former present clearly similar problems to the canonical gospels in that they represent material that has been recast and reformulated in terms of the developing tradition of distinct faith-communities. But can we find early accounts in the corpus, less developed, and appearing comparable to the sayings of Jesus and his claims to represent Wisdom in our canonical gospels? Two principal candidates present themselves, namely the

---

21. H. Koester, *Ancient Christian Gospels: Their History and Their Development* (London: SCM, 1990), p. 86, citing J. S. Kloppenborg, *The Formation of Q: Trajectories in Ancient Wisdom Collections* (Studies in Antiquity and Christianity; Philadelphia: Fortress, 1987), and D. Lührmann, *Die Redaktion der Logienquelle* (*WMANT*, 33; Neukirchen: Neukirchen Verlag, 1969).

Gospels of Thomas and of Peter, though the latter, not from Nag Hammadi, survives in Greek fragments discovered at Akhmîm and at Oxyrhynchus.[22]

The *Gospel of Thomas* undoubtedly forms the centre of the stage in which arguments for Jesus as the Cynic sage on the margins of Judaeism in Hellenized Galilee are played out. This gospel is also used to support arguments for Jesus as the Wisdom teacher, whether or not accompanied by the high Christological claim about Jesus as the unique representative of Sophia. *Thomas* is a sayings source with no Passion narrative. For the author or authors it represents a community that treasured Jesus' saving words rather than saving acts. As such it bears some resemblance to some sayings of Jesus such as that of Matthew, in which a wise and a foolish man build houses respectively on rock or on sand, whose prefix is: 'Every one who hears these discourses of mine will be likened to a wise man who . . .'.[23]

In *Thomas* we find parallels with the parables of Jesus in the synoptic gospels, but sometimes we find examples of this genre that are unique. An example of a parallel is the parable of the Sower found in *Thomas* without the elaborate interpretation of Mark that has made it specifically an allegory of the developing Christian mission, with setbacks and successes depending upon the individual qualities of the prospective converts.[24] The question thus raised is whether *Thomas* has a more primitive version that clearly lacks the interpretation added by Mark's community. Furthermore, in many instances eschatological outcomes of what Jesus says are not given. For example, the parable of the Drag Net according to *Thomas* reads:

> The man is like a wise fisherman who cast his net into the sea and drew it up from the sea full of small fish. Among them the wise fisherman found a fine large fish. He threw all the small fish back into the sea and chose the large fish without difficulty. Whoever has ears to hear, let him hear.[25]

The parallel is to be found in Matthew's special material, which informs us that 'the kingdom of heaven is like a net', and that the catch consisted of good fish that were kept, and the bad thrown away, as a parable of the final judgement at the end of the present age. Koester argued that both Matthew and Thomas have used a common tradition, but that Matthew has imposed upon this tradition an eschatological interpretation:

> So it will be at the close of the age. The angels will come and separate the evil from the righteous and throw them into the furnace of fire; there men will weep and gnash their teeth.[26]

---

22. J. K. Elliott, *The Apocryphal New Testament: A Collection of Apocryphal Christian Literature in an English Translation* (Oxford: Clarendon Press, 1993), p. 150.

23. Mt. 7:14.

24. *Gos. Thom.*, 9, cf. Mk 4:1:9 and added, 10-20 (= Mt.13:1-17; Lk. 8:4-15).

25. *Gos. Thom.*, 8.

26. Mt. 13:47-50.

Thomas' logion is one of several that have led to the argument that the Jesus of history preached a kingdom of God or the 'kingdom of my Father' in a purely spiritual and present sense.

In support of such a contention, we might appeal to the *logion* from Luke's special material:

> Being asked by the Pharisees when the kingdom of God comes he answered them and said: 'The kingdom of God is not coming with openness, nor will they say "Behold, here or there!" For behold, the kingdom of God is within you. '[27]

Here we might argue that *Thomas' logion* testifies to a shared tradition that takes us back behind the eschatological editing of the writers of the canonical gospels:

> Jesus said: 'If those who lead you on say to you: "Behold, the kingdom is in the sky", then the birds of the sky will take precedence over you. But the kingdom it is inside of you and it is outside of you. It is when you will know yourselves that then you will be known. And you will understand that it is you who are the sons of the living Father. But if you do not know yourselves, then you exist in poverty and you are the poverty.'[28]

Koester, on the basis of this absence of such eschatology, has argued, along with Kloppenborg and others, that *Thomas* represents a more primitive testimony to the historical Jesus, who himself made no such eschatological claims.

Thomas would then take its place with Q as one of the two very early and primitive expressions of the sayings of Jesus many of which were incorporated in more developed and redacted forms in the later canonical gospels. But in Q, unlike *Thomas*, there are additions to claims that the kingdom is present that are clearly eschatological. There is no mention of Jesus as the apocalyptic Son of Man in *Thomas* but in Q, for example, we have: 'As the lightening flashes and radiates from one part of the sky to another, so will be the Son of Man in his day.'[29] Luke places such apocalyptic items in Q, incorporated by Matthew into his version of the Markan apocalypse, separately in his own *logia* apocalypse. On this basis both Kloppenborg and Koester claim that Q circulated originally without the *logia* apocalypse that formed part only of its final edition: originally Q had not this later apocalyptic focus for the kingdom sayings.[30]

It should however be noted how *Thomas* functions in their account as the prime witness whose testimony is used to establish that Q is primitive when it is non-eschatological. Thus one can conclude that, when Luke records the

---

27. Lk. 17:20-21.
28. *Gos. Thom.*, 3.
29. Lk. 17:23 (= Mt. 24:27).
30. Koester, *Ancient Christian Gospels*, p. 86, citing Kloppenborg, *Formation of Q*, pp. 154–65.

saying susceptible of an apocalyptic interpretation: 'I have come to cast fire upon the earth and how I wish it were already kindled,' of which Matthew too has a version of this saying in which 'peace' is substituted for fire, both testify to a Q that continued with the language of bringing division and setting sons and fathers, mothers and daughters and other such familial relatives against each other. Such a context in Q can only be explained away with difficulty as without an apocalyptic context: such language of divisions in human relationships was the common stock of apocalyptic expectations.[31]

In the light of a *Thomas* parallel, it is possible to claim that such an apocalyptic context is a contamination from the final edition of Q influenced by the *logia* apocalypse. The parallel version thus reads: 'Jesus said: "I have cast fire upon the world, and see, I am guarding it until it blazes."'[32] Thus the original meaning of Luke's Q saying, preserved in an allegedly more primitive condition in *Thomas*, might have been: 'The fire of saving wisdom is already present so follow me in nurturing it in your heart until it blazes and transforms you.'

But there are, I believe, fundamental objections to these arguments for a primitive, non-eschatological edition of Q. These have been well rehearsed by Catchpole and Tuckett. The principal objection is that Q agrees with Mark in its own, original material that the ministry of Jesus begins with John the Baptist, and that the message of John was an apocalyptic message.[33] Jesus was baptized into John's movement. We need therefore to be able to support a hypothesis that Jesus self-consciously departed from John's apocalyptic context, to which the early church was to return after the crucifixion.[34] It is an objection to which Borg responds in a fashion that I find somewhat cavalier.[35]

The real problem that I find with the argument is that the evidence that is held to expose the two versions of Q and to determine a non-eschatological original version is found in *Thomas logia* themselves. Q of itself, even if we were to concede the two versions, would not by itself enable us to say that the non-eschatological was the original rather than the eschatological. We could argue, as indeed the generation after Schweitzer argued, that the non-fulfilment of eschatological expectations lead to the reinterpretation of the text. It is a form of this argument that I shall be expounding in this book.

In order to establish the primitive character of an allegedly non-eschatological core version of Q, we need first to establish the primitive character of the Thomas *logia* regarding an inner and spiritual kingdom. But in order to do that, we must show that the Thomas *logia* themselves are untouched by eschatology

---

31. Lk. 12:49-53 = Mt. 10:34-36, cf. Mk 13:12.
32. *Gos. Thom.*, 10.
33. Mt. 3:7-10 = Lk. 3:7-9.
34. C. M. Tuckett, *Q and the History of Early Christianity: Studies on Q* (Edinburgh: T & T Clark 1996), pp. 107–63; D. R. Catchpole, *The Quest for Q* (Edinburgh: T & T Clark, 1993), chapter 5.
35. Borg, *Contemporary Scholarship*, pp. 77–80.

that only appears later in the tradition. If we cannot do this, we have no way of determining whether the process of what we may call de-apocalypticization is in fact not the work of the final editor and rather, instead, the apocalyptic *logia* are themselves the primitive strand in the tradition. *Thomas* must present us with uncontaminated wisdom or Cynic-sage tradition about the Jesus of history. Only then can we connect the non-eschatological strand in Q, and pronounce this the original primitive strand. But this is alas impossible. We must now examine this case critically.

3. *The Case for a Suppression of the Eschatological Jesus in* Gospel of Thomas

Let us look again at the first *logion* on the kingdom. Putting the kingdom in places like sky or sea more suitable for birds or fish may look like the cleverness of an original Cynic-sage, but note that the words of Jesus are introduced in answer to 'those who coax you on' in a deceptive manner.[36] Clearly the Thomas *logion* is polemical and directed against 'false' leaders of the Christian community, who are locating the kingdom in heaven and predicting its coming to earth like the New Jerusalem, though for the author it might just as well have been in the sea. Thomas is setting himself self-consciously against an eschatological interpretation of Jesus that he knows rather than testifying to a wisdom tradition of alternatives of which he is ignorant because his *logia* come from an early and primitive phase in the tradition where eschatology was unknown.

Furthermore the writer attempts to privilege the alleged tradition of Thomas against that of Peter and Matthew of which he clearly has knowledge.[37] When the latter two try to compare Jesus respectively to a righteous angel or to a wise philosopher, their answers are rejected in the light of Thomas' affirmation of his inability to answer. These descriptions of Jesus could well be parodies of both canonical Mathew, characterized in terms of the Sermon on the Mount, and canonical Mark and the Petrine tradition of 'my son Mark', where the heavenly Son of Man (the 'righteous angel') is to return with his angels. Not simply the later Papias, but also the tradition of the pseudonymous 1 Peter, locates Mark with the greeting of the Roman church, 'she who is elect in Babylon'.[38]

The community of *Thomas* clearly knew of other Christian communities with leaders claiming the authority of tradition since the author, immediately

---

36.   *Gos. Thom.*, 10: where ⲥⲱⲕ ϩⲏⲧ ⲑⲎⲨⲦⲚ̄, usually translated 'those who lead you'. When the meaning 'lead' is given by not adding xht, see *Pistis Sophia*, 368. For more usual expressions for 'lead' (ⲣ̄ ⲁⲡⲉ) see Prov. 24 and Deut. 28:44. See also ⲣ̄ ⲛⲟϭ in *log.* 12.

37.   For a further discussion of this point and its implications, see N. Perrin, *Thomas, the other Gospel*, (London: SPCK, 2007), pp. 107–112.

38.   1 Pet. 5:12, cf. Papias apud Eusebius, *H.E.*, III.39.15 and Mk 13:26-27.

before this claim for *Thomas*, has preserved one saying with which it is clearly at variance:

> The disciples said to Jesus: 'we know that you will depart from us. Who is to become a great man over us?' Jesus said to them: 'The place where you have come, [there] you shall go to James the Just, the one for whom both heaven and earth came into existence.'[39]

As Valantasis points out, this saying is not part of the overall texture of the picture of Jesus that emerges in *Thomas*.[40] Jesus is 'the living one' who continues in a present and active dialogue in which the readers share with the disciples and, at one point, Mary. In this *logion* Jesus is not present having departed. James is almost a rival for that living, present and cosmic Jesus. But they do not need a great leader, whose claims to leadership are surely parodied in the exaggerated claim ('for whom both heaven and earth came into existence'). In the *logion* that follows Thomas is not the leader but the example of one who ponders the mystery of the living one himself, and need not communicate this to fellow members of his community who can join in the dialogue and discover it for themselves, much to the chagrin of community leaders like Peter and Matthew.

Thus Thomas is told three things which he cannot reveal to his companions for their own safety.[41] Here we have clearly what is the tradition of a group that sets its revelation against other Christian communities, and which imposes its own interpretation upon early Christian tradition, like those various groups labelled 'Gnostics' did. The figure of Thomas and his record of the sayings of Jesus are being set against those of other apostles, whom the author claims were wrong or deficient in what they said about Jesus. We cannot therefore privilege the sayings of Jesus in Thomas nor claim that they are any more exempt from the process of redaction than those of the canonical gospels. And we do find traces of eschatology in Thomas that may well indicate the author's desire to repress or recast this theme.

Indeed, if we consider that the author is pursuing a theme, we may well be sceptical about the common claim that there is no purposeful arrangement in the collection of the *logia* in *Thomas*.[42] It is not simply that *logion* 3 is directed at an eschatological and spatio-temporal view of the kingdom. Indeed, many others of the *logia* with which *Thomas* begins can be read, not as simply an assertion of an inner and mysterious spiritual kingdom which the individual realizes and becomes like it, but rather as the assertion of such a concept against

39. *Gos. Thom.*, 12.
40. R. Valantasis, *The Gospel of Thomas* (London and New York: Routledge, 1997), pp. 73–74
41. *Gos. Thom.*, 13.
42. Koester, *Ancient Christian Gospels*, p. 81.

an eschatological notion. We have in *logion* 3 the notions of a goal ('Let him who seeks continue seeking until he finds') that leads to the eschatological notion of ruling over the whole universe after 'much tribulation': 'When he finds, he will become troubled. When he becomes troubled, he will wonder, and will rule over the All.' In some *logia* the revelation is to be in the future and not in a present dialogue with the 'living Jesus'. Whereas *logion* 5 makes the claim 'there is nothing hidden that will not become manifest' the result of present and willed recognition, in *logion* 6 the reason for not telling lies and doing what is hateful is about future judgement:

> Do not tell lies, and do not that which you hate, for all things are plain in the sight of heaven. For there is nothing that has been hidden that will not be revealed and nothing that has been covered that will remain without being uncovered.

The contention that in the 'realized' *logia* are to be found the original words of Jesus the wisdom teacher ignores the parasitic nature of the claims about the kingdom spiritually realized in interaction with the words of the 'living Jesus'. Such realized claims presuppose a reinterpreted eschatology rather than ignorance of any eschatological context to the claims of the historical Jesus.

Koester and Valantasis consider all attempts to see *Thomas'* isolated *logia* as assembled purposefully into an interrelated interpretative pattern to have failed. But clearly there is a claim being made at the very outset in the context of a dispute with other Christian communities, such as those identified with Matthew, Peter and James, as we have seen to be the case in *logia* 12–13. At the very outset 'Didymus Judas Thomas' is privileged as the author who 'wrote down' what were 'the secret sayings' of 'the living Jesus'. (Praef.) The literary device of declaring that Jesus' words are thus 'secret' or 'hidden (ⲉⲑⲏⲡ)' is to privilege these words with authority even though unknown to other Christian groups. Readers are to engage as individuals with the text in order to 'find' their 'interpretation' so that 'they will not taste of death'. (*logia* 1–2). There then follows the warning that we have seen against 'those who lead you on'.[43]

What then if we were to see a continuing pattern from *logion* 4 in which the juxtaposition of *logia* can be seen to be not accidental? In that case the focus of our interpretation would be of groups of *logia* and not on a single *logium* in isolation? We may prescind from our discussion *logia* whose original context we have lost and therefore their meaning, such as the meaning of the lion that becomes human by eating it, or the fisherman who keeps only one large fish from his catch (*logia* 7–8). We may focus firstly on *logia* that might be given a non-eschatological interpretation, like the parable of the Sower can be given, as recorded in *Thomas*, or has certainly been given in its Markan version.[44] But if the sayings form a pattern in terms of which they are to be interpreted, they

---

43. See above, footnote 31 and associated text.
44. *Gos. Thom.*, *logion* 9 and Mk 4:1-9 as interpreted in 10-20.

cannot thus be interpreted as a stand-alone item. We must interpret them in relation to the *logia* that precede and follow them so that, if they are not to be interpreted eschatologically, then at least their interpretation is parasitic upon an eschatological claim thus being refashioned and reinterpreted.

With regard therefore to the non-eschatological interpretation, implicit in *Thomas logion* 9, we may rather appeal to the interpretation parasitic upon eschatology of the preceding *logion* 4 that reads:

> The man old in days will not hesitate to ask a little small child that is seven days old concerning the place of life and he will live. For there are many first who will become last and they will become one and the same.

We have here an image of the future state in which role-relations are reversed and in which 'a little child will lead' an old man into the paths of life.[45] The general principle of the reversal of first–last is thus preserved. The non-eschatological *logion* (6) follows, but then *logion* 7 immediately comes after that we have argued to be explicable as parasitic upon an eschatological example. Then, following the enigmatic *logia* 7–8, regarding the lion and the great fish, we find in 9 the non-eschatological parable of the Sower. But immediately following it we have *logion* 10 on fire in contrast to its Q parallels that we have considered. Though, as we have said, in a Thomas context, this might be interpreted as the 'fire of wisdom',[46] more normally, as in the case of both Mark and Q on John the Baptist, 'fire cast upon the world' has an apocalyptic relevance. We may say therefore that, even if the *logion* will bear such an inner and spiritual interpretation, that interpretation is nevertheless parasitic upon an eschatological claim now refashioned.

So too is the case with *logion* 88, where we have angels as well as prophets who are yet to come:

> Jesus said: 'The angels are coming to you with the prophets and they will give to you those things that are (or will be) yours. And you yourselves, yes you, give them what is yours and say to yourselves "When will they come and take their own possessions"'?[47]

The community of Thomas may have a Gnostic and mystical interpretation of this coming, and of what the disciples already possess in terms of the spark of divinity within them. But the originally apocalyptic form of the saying is sufficiently preserved as to glower through such a reinterpretation. What surely

---

45. Cf. Isa. 11:6.

46. See above, footnote 27 and associated text.

47. *Logion* 88 is difficult to construe but it seems to me that NneteuNt htNse ('those things that belong to you (or that are yours)' should be construed as future in association with a future verb, sena + nhtN ('they will give you').

the disciples originally possess of the prophets is the interpretation of their words as prefiguring Christ's coming, which they will come to receive back?

Furthermore, that this is the case the immediately following *logion* 11 will now demonstrate. The interpretation imposed on the initial statement is one that later Valentinianism, among other forms of Sethian Gnosticism, will find favourable, namely it is about becoming two, namely being joined again to one's original angelic other self. But the first lines reflect eschatological imagery:

> This heaven will pass away and the one above it will pass away. The dead are not alive and those who live are not dead. / In the days when you consumed what is dead you made it what is alive. / When you dwell in the light, what is it that you will do on the day when having become one you make yourselves two?

Valantasis is surely correct when he claims that we have probably three originally distinct *logia* here that I have demarcated with '/'. The Thomas community gathers to meditate upon the saving words that it experiences first with perplexity, with the feeling of 'disturbance' promised in *logion* 2. The three sayings appear initially unrelated, like the antithetical terms of a *via negativa*, until the individual in conversation with the living Jesus resolves the antithesis and finds mystical knowledge. But as Valantasis points out, the first *logion* is clearly a response to an eschatological claim that is there as a backcloth to a tradition that is being reshaped.[48]

According to traditional eschatology, 'heaven and earth will pass away' but Jesus' words will abide forever. In Thomas' Sethian universe, there is more than one heaven and the earth has no reality such that its passing away is in any way significant. In traditional apocalyptic, at the scrolling away of heaven and earth, the dead will rise and those that are alive will join them. This *logion* expressly contradicts such a claim: those made alive by the saving words of the living Jesus will not 'taste of death', (*logion* 1) and the remainder of humanity will remain dead. The interpretation here bears witness to an eschatological tradition such as that owned by the Q apocalypse so that Thomas cannot be used to identify an earlier stratum of Q uncontaminated by such apocalyptic. We could make a similar case for several other *logia*.[49]

Let me now draw some conclusions for my discussion so far.

First, let me say that I would not wish in any way to deny many features of the picture of Jesus that emerges from the North American, Jesus Seminar approach to the Jesus of history, in terms of the revolutionary character of Jesus' sayings and their formation in a Wisdom or even Jewish Cynic tradition. Furthermore, I have no reason to deny the argument that many of the unique

48. Valantasis, *Thomas*, pp. 70–73.
49. For example, *Gos. Thom.*, *logia* 16, 19, 38, 51, 57, 65, 111.

Thomas sayings may go back to the historical Jesus, and many of those with synoptic parallels may be preserved in *Thomas* in a more primitive form. But that said, I would nevertheless deny that we are justified in privileging the reformulation of such sayings or the interpretive context in which they appear against what we find in the synoptic or Johannine traditions. The Thomas *logia*, just like those of our canonical gospels, have undergone a process of selection and transmission in a distinct community with its own cultural and historical perspective. That perspective bears all the marks of its own social and historical development in the course of the two centuries or more before it assumed its present, fixed literary form.

Secondly, given that Thomas stands on the same critical and interpretive ground as the canonical gospels, there is, I believe, more reason for seeing the trajectory from an originally eschatological context for the *logia* to one of reinterpreted and realized eschatology compatible with the mystical individualism that is the context in which such *logia* have now been set. I have shown grounds for regarding certain *logia* as parasitic for their meaning on eschatological imagery. We have seen that their realized versions are set self-consciously against Jacobean, Matthaean and Petrine traditions, and those of others 'who coax you on'.

Statements about the 'kingdom', or 'the kingdom of my Father' are: 'The kingdom of my Father is inside of you and it is outside of you' (*logion* 3), that remove any eschatological context from such sayings and make the 'kingdom' a spiritual concept to do with the heart of the individual are as much community interpretations and reformulations as those of the canonical gospels with which they are nevertheless properly compared. It is surely significant that the one example that Thomas gives of the kingdom as described specifically in something like synoptic terms, namely the enemy sowing weeds among the good seed, ends with exhorting to wait until the weeds are grown:

> For on the day of the harvest the weeds will be plainly visible and they will be pulled up and burned. (*Logion* 57)

Clearly these words can be given a spiritual and mystical interpretation about the attainment of the divine through self-knowledge, but it is equally clear that such an interpretation is a forced interpretation of an eschatological text.

Even if any of the so-called 'wisdom' sayings had emerged in a form that was not parasitic for their reinterpreted meaning on an original eschatological context, the Wisdom tradition of their putatively original and non-Gnostic form would not have excluded eschatology as the accounts of Borg and Schüssler Fiorenza appear to imply. The putative existence of Wisdom sages who had no concept of an eschaton is a post-Enlightenment construction of those who seek refuge from the implausibility of traditional apocalyptic in the context of a closed, mechanical universe of material cause and effect driven by the blind forces of nature. As John Sweet pointed out, there are significant parousial elements in, for example, the *Wisdom of Solomon* in which the souls of the 'just' are thus promised:

> In the moment of God's coming to them they will kindle into flame, like sparks that sweep through stubble; they will be judges and rulers over the nations of the world, and the Lord will be their king forever.[50]

Furthermore it should be remembered that Daniel itself, while prophesying the future in apocalyptic terms, is nevertheless in the Wisdom tradition. Of Daniel and his companions it is said:

> To all four of these young men God had given knowledge and understanding of books and learning of every kind, whilst Daniel had a gift for interpreting visions and dreams of every kind.[51]

Of the wisdom that 'Solomon' sought he can say:

> She knows the past, she can infer what is to come; she understands the subtleties of argument and the solving of problems, she can read signs and portents and can foretell the outcome of events and periods.[52]

As Rowland has pointed out, it is a mistake to see those texts that we describe with the general description of 'Gnostic' as negating an apocalyptic world-view. Both apocalyptic and Gnostic texts are about revealing the hidden 'furniture of heaven'.[53] Thus it is false to separate Wisdom sayings of Jesus from apocalyptic expectation.

Thirdly, however insightful both Crossan and Horsley may be on the social and political radicalism and the Jesus of history, their accounts have the tendency to simply excise all imminent apocalyptic as a context of the sayings of Jesus whose authenticity, with the aid of *Thomas*, they will allow. They must then defend the Wisdom context for the sayings, only to find that they cannot excise from such a context the apocalyptic framework that we have mentioned: a Wisdom tradition without apocalyptic is in terms of a strictly historical analysis a pure illusion, as our reference to Daniel at very least makes clear. The Cynic context makes some historical sense, but only by excluding the Wisdom tradition with its apocalyptic assumptions also from the earliest *stratum* of sayings. But the whole point of introducing such a perspective was to privilege the sayings in *Thomas* as the key to recovering the Jesus of history. Without the Wisdom tradition, the whole point is lost of invoking *Thomas* as prior to the

---

50. Wis. 3:7-12.
51. Dan. 1:17.
52. Wis. 8:8.
53. C. Rowland, *The Open Heaven: Study of Apocalyptic in Judaism and Early Christianity* (London: SPCK, 1985), pp. 9–14.

apocalyptic section of Q and guaranteeing the primitive character of non-eschatological Q sayings. A context of pagan Cynicism does make historical sense and is clearly historically defensible, but I fear that once we add the epithet that makes the Jesus of history a 'Jewish Cynic sage' the background becomes less plausible to draw in strict historical terms. Similarly, North American attempts to interpret Jesus as primarily a figure with relevance to post-Enlightenment politics appear to fail as reconstructions that are properly historical.

Let us now consider further such a case outside the specific context of a discussion of the *Gospel of Thomas*.

4. *The Case for a Suppression of the Eschatological Jesus in Post-Enlightenment Social Theory*

Horsley and Crossan would explain the sayings of Jesus shorn of any serious or immediate historical apocalyptic claim as witnessing to a radical revolutionary Galilean peasant challenging hierarchical and patriarchal power structures in urban political and religious elites. Their explanation of the significance of Jesus words and acts and his fate at the hands of the authorities is thus expressed in terms of theoretical models in the social sciences that have been developed in the course of, and subsequent to, the eighteenth-century European Enlightenment. Marx exemplified one such fundamental model in his theory of dialectical materialism.

Marx held that the driving forces of history were economic and the course of events historically determined by such material causes. Thus the reasons that human beings gave in terms of alleged non-economical and immaterial realities were illusions created by the superstructure of society, consisting of such agents as the judiciary, the church, the press and other mass media, parliamentary democratic ideology, etc. The superstructure creates therefore a gigantic social illusion about the legitimacy of the arrangements for 'inequality' and 'repression' that blinds subjects to the real, economic base of their suppression in the real substructure of society. The legitimating function of the superstructure is thus to palliate the massive force of resentment that would otherwise result in instability and revolution. That illusion pretends that the present social order, and the economic order on which it is based, is the only kind of social order that there is and can be without the chaos that would deny such order. Social hierarchies based upon class, race and sex, are all that there can ever be, and have an irrefutable moral base. But such a consciousness of things is a 'false consciousness', and its justification is, in fact, a 'legitimation' that blinds participants in the social order to the real, economic and exploitative foundations on which capitalist society rests.[54]

---

54. R. Aron, *Main Currents in Sociological Thought* (London: Weidenfeld and Nicolson, 1968), I, pp. 118–126.

A second post-Enlightenment feature of the discussion is the language of rights implicitly or explicitly introduced. The historical Jesus is identified with the 'rights' of peasants over landowners, of slaves over masters, of clients over patrons. But the language of rights in such a context of moral protest, particularly expressed in terms of 'human rights' from the twentieth century onwards, comes from Locke in the seventeenth century.[55] Here, unlike in the case of Marx, natural reason, rather than material causes determining the course of history, was to prefigure with reference to a primitive contract upon which society was based. Put simply, perhaps over simply, trade negotiations with North American Indians on the part of those who were settling there were seen to be the model of how human societies had originated. Without a shared language in which to conclude the contract, the settlers pointed to beads and the natives to skins, and each side gestured in agreement to the exchange of such goods.

At some putative dawn of history, individual human beings existing in a state of nature had concluded a contract by such means in consequence of which civil society was founded, the aims of which was for the individual to achieve his own private ends better than if he had remained in a state of nature. Human beings had thus formed societies, not because they were driven by economic forces to which they were partially or wholly blind, but because they were reasonable and following their natural reason about what was in their best interests. But if the contract were to be morally binding, or even legally so, then there had to be certain preconditions to entering into the contract.

For a contract to be morally or legally binding, then it had to be freely entered into. No rational agent would freely enter into a contract that involved the taking away of his life, nor the removal of his property unless he so consented to do so in exchange for a larger increment of benefit. Thus there existed certain natural rights that the contract never gave and which it could not take away, fundamental to which were 'life', 'liberty' and 'property'. The first two of these were to appear in the Declaration of Independence, and Franklin would have included the third had not Jefferson insisted on its replacement by 'the pursuit of happiness'.

In such a context it becomes possible for such writers as Borg, Crossan, Horsley and Schüssler Fiorenza to understand the ethical imperative of the Jesus of history as concerned with 'justice' for the 'oppressed' within a paradigm of explanation that looks for a readjustment of social relationships in terms of a putative contractual agreement between members of a society that has been disregarded. Indeed such a Lockean claim can be cashed in favour of

---

55. J. Locke, *The Second Treatise of Government (An Essay Concerning the True Original, Extent and End of Civil Government)*, edited, with a revised introduction by J. W. Gough (Oxford, Blackwell, 1966), chapter 2, sections 6-8; M. Cranston, *John Locke: A Biography* (New York: Arno Press, 1979), pp. 208–13.

more 'hard headed', 'socio-scientific' terms and seen as economic deprivation as the driving force of what 'really' went on in the ministry of Jesus. To cite an example from Crossan, using Lenski's model, we have to do with the priestly hierarchy as

> the preserver of an ancient Redistributative Ethic of primitive societies in which the accumulation of goods in private hands served as a form of communal insurance rather than as private property.[56]

In the all-pervasive patron–client relationship, which defined for example the relations between the Herods and Rome, the subservience of client to patron can be understood, and justified in terms of such a 'communal insurance' relationship in contrast with master–slave relationships.

We may find a second example in Crossan's explanation of Palestinian unrest expressed by various Messianic movements from 4 B.C. to A.D. 70. Here he invokes Gurr's cross-cultural model of political violence. Here the concepts of 'relative deprivation', in which people become conscious of a gap between the 'is' of their present advantages and the 'ought' that they believe with justice that they are due. The driving force that leads to the political movement whose violence is aimed at closing the gap is 'a biologically inherent tendency, in men and animals, to attack the frustrating agent'.[57]

Gurr then describes three kinds of perceived deprivation, (i) decremental deprivation in which the gap is closed because aspirations decrease, (ii) aspirational deprivation, in which these increase or intensify thus widening the gap, and (iii) progressive deprivation in which, though the gap has become narrower at one time, nevertheless present advantages decline but expectations continue to increase. Progressive deprivation (iii), according to Crossan, best marked the situation in Galilee up until the war of A.D. 66:

> For there to have been a *perceived* deprivation, the peasants must have been pushed below the subsistence level, not into poverty, which was 'normal', but into indigence and destitution. In Lenski's stratification, large numbers of the *peasant* class were being pushed down amongst the *unclean, degraded,* and *expendable* classes.[58]

It was such a peasant class that Jesus defended seeking to negate their unclean and degraded status with his practice of commensality. Horsley, who follows such a sociological analysis, is nevertheless against the discussion of Brandon

---

56. Crossan, *Historical Jesus*, p. 45, quoting G. E. Lenski, *Power and Privilege: A Theory of Social Stratification* (New York: McGraw-Hill, 1966), p. 266.

57. Crossan, *Historical Jesus*, p. 219, quoting T. R. Gurr, *Why Men Rebel* (Princeton: U. P., 1970), p. 33.

58. Crossan, *Historical Jesus*, p. 221.

that the Jesus of history and his first followers were Zealot sympathizers, and insists instead that Jesus was essentially non-violent though not pacifist in his approach.[59]

There is however a fundamental problem with the deployment of such a social-scientific model the articulation of which will now introduce one of the fundamental themes of this book.

When we use such terms as 'decremental deprivation' or 'rights', 'oppression', economic 'inequality', etc., we are clearly using concepts that derive their meaning and explanatory force from forms of discourse that have arisen, as we have indicated, in the wake of the seventeenth-century European Enlightenment. The context in which we understand such specific expressions is that of contractualist theories inspired by Locke, or by mechanical and causal theories that have their origins in Marx. These are the terms in which 'we', or many of us particularly in North America, have come to understand the role and mission of the Jesus of history. Indeed such a social-scientific project may help us, or some of us, to adapt the message and ministry of Jesus to our own time, and thus to produce what Ernst Bammel called, critically, a 'mythistory' of a new kind.[60] But such an approach does not tell us what the participants in those events themselves understood as their significance.

It is my contention that we need to explain those events in terms of what the participants themselves understood as their significance, which was clearly not the language of rights, inequality and social deprivation that come from our Enlightenment discourse. If the Jesus of history were a social revolutionary, then that does not mean that he was a this-worldly figure rejecting apocalyptic but rather that he saw the significance of his own words and acts in terms of an apocalyptic imagery of the coming kingdom of God. Our tendency to think that when we have found the social implications of Jesus acts in terms of our discourse of rights and inequalities, and a post-seventeenth century, mechanistic universe of cause and effect, then we can exclude the significance of the apocalyptic dimension. We have seen how defective such an analysis is when we create the notion of Wisdom teachers with no eschatological consciousness of the significance of their claims.

In the light of this conclusion, it is interesting to see how even Borg is troubled by such a stark criticism. Borg now claims that he does wish to include eschatological expectation within the worldview of the Jesus of history as

---

59. R. Horsley, *Jesus and the Spiral of Violence: Popular Jewish Resistance in Roman Palestine* (San Francisco: Harper and Row, 1987), pp. 318–26, cf. S. G. F. Brandon, *Jesus and the Zealots* (Manchester: University Press, 1967) and E. Bammel and C. F. D. Moule, *Jesus and the Politics of His Day* (Cambridge: University Press, 1984).

60. E. Bammel, 'The Revolution Theory from Reimarus to Brandon', in Bammel and Moule, *Jesus and Politics*, pp. 64–67.

either Jewish-Cynic or Wisdom sage. But this must be highly qualified so as not to obscure the 'real' reason:

> One could argue that John's language of judgment (along with much apocalyptic language) can be read in a more socio-political way . . . I think that Jesus probably had some eschatological beliefs. It seems likely that he believed that God's promises to Israel would someday be fulfilled . . . I do not mean that Jesus never said anything about eschatology. I mean, rather, that imminent eschatology is not to be the interpretative context for reading the Jesus tradition.[61]

But here we find only the emergence of the social-scientific model in a new form. We know the real explanation for the events of Jesus ministry in terms of the Galilean peasant protesting the rights of the dispossessed and excluded and negating patriarchal, religious, sexual and class hierarchies: the cause and effect of Gurr's 'biologically inherent tendency, in men and animals, to attack the frustrating agents', expressed and refined in operational terms as 'perceived deprivation'.[62]

Horsley too accepts the historical orientation of his account in a similar fashion:

> Jesus' proclamation and practice of the kingdom of God indeed belonged in the milieu of Jewish apocalypticism. But far from being an expectation of an imminent cosmic catastrophe, it was the conviction that God was now driving Satan from control over personal and historical life, making possible the renewal of the people of Israel. The presence of the kingdom of God meant the termination of the old order.[63]

Clearly for Horsley the apocalyptic vision is peripheral and super-structural—a 'spin' assisting though in some sense masking the underlying social and ultimately economic realities that were the real forces creating the conflict and tensions of the ministry of Jesus. Thus Horsley claims of late Second Temple Jewish society:

> . . . apocalyptic traditions and literature carried the crucial liberative functions of the imagination or 'fantasy' or 'vision' . . . especially under conditions of systematic injustice and forcible repression and, occasionally, of special provocation . . . In placing the then-current situation in historical perspective the apocalyptic imagination thus also involved a critical demystifying of the pretensions and practices of the established order . . . The apocalyptic imagination thus had a strengthening effect on the people's ability to endure, and even a motivating effect towards resistance or revolt.[64]

61. Borg, *Contemporary Scholarship*, p. 77 and p. 88.
62. See above, footnote 56 and associated text.
63. Horsley, *Spiral*, p. 160, cited also by Borg, *Contemporary Scholarship*, p. 93, his footnote 35.
64. Horsley, *Spiral*, p. 143 and 144.

Thus once again the worldview is regarded not as integral to the explanation of what moved events but as convenient political rhetoric, the 'spin' behind which there is a different kind of substance.

I cannot however subscribe to this kind of historiographical method. I believe, with Weber, that the process of a true historical inquiry needs to be marked by what he described technically as *Verstehen*.[65] Weber claimed that the social scientist is not to be viewed as we might view a natural scientist, as an objective observer with no part in the phenomenon that he observes. The social analyst must account for his own role in changing the phenomenon that he is observing and compensating for this as a means to securing objectivity. I believe the same holds for our attempts to observe and analyse past history.

In order to understand what motivated events in terms of ideas, it is necessary for the historian to become a kind of participant observer in the historical events that he seeks to discuss from literary and other remains. A modern historian will bring with him in his search the post-Enlightenment conceptual apparatus of Lockean philosophy and Marxist and other attempts at a scientific sociology. But the historian must appreciate that these are not the perspectives within which first-century participants in the events that he describes would have interpreted those events.

The motivational force of the belief systems within which they operated must be acknowledged and not simply disregarded as 'mere spin'. To use a term from the sociology of knowledge developed by Berger and Luckmann, we must enter their social construction of reality and examine how their symbolic universe of meaning accounts for how they behaved. If we do so, we must take those symbolic universes seriously and examine closely the operation of the logic of their discourse within its own terms if we are to truly 'understand' those events and produce anything resembling a historically objective account of what took place. We cannot simply describe those beliefs and then dismiss them as epiphenomenological 'spin', as does Borg by implication in the passage that we quoted.[66]

It will be important therefore for my account to indicate briefly the position that I am taking in relation to the frequent rhetorical and journalistic device of commenting on 'spin' and 'substance' in political discussion. My conclusion would be that these terms cover a variety of devices in political argument. The first is that sometimes and perhaps too often politicians may be said to 'spin' when they are simply placing a false gloss on something the real nature of which they wish to conceal. One example of this, shortly before our time, was Harold Wilson who led a British Labour Party with a very strong, democratic Marxist Left Wing, seeking an economic revolution in terms of nationalization, of 'public ownership of the means of production, distribution and exchange'.

65. M. Weber, *Basic Concepts in Sociology*, trans. H. P. Secher (Peter Owen: London, 1962), pp. 18–19, and pp. 30–33; Aron, *Sociological Thought*, II, pp. 197–202.

66. See above, footnote 59 and related text.

Wilson was reported as having said at a private lunch with a newspaper jour-nalist regarding his opponent and Conservative Prime Minister, Harold Macmillan, 'He's a political genius. Whilst boasting of Suez he is leading his party back from Suez. I would like to do that with the Labour Party regarding nationalization.'[67]

Clearly Wilson's use of the 'spin' of socialist phraseology was therefore a means of concealing, by his own admission, his real intention to produce a market economy capable of raising productivity with the government control-ling at most 'the commanding heights of the economy'. It was a 'spin' that convinced many of his radical left wing that really he was on their side, until the collapse of Eastern European and Russian forms of socialism showed the inability of centrally controlled economies to deliver either social equality or rising living standards. Wilson's real programme was not represented by the way that he chose to 'spin' it.

The advent of Blair, however, revealed a different kind of 'spin'. When for example, welfare handouts in the form of unemployment benefits, particularly youth unemployment benefits, were slashed, or those for disability or one-parent families, any conservative notion that this was because the recipients were 'sponging' on society and simply needed to be starved back to work were rejected. Instead the policy, supported by counsellors trained to advise those whose benefits were cut, was to assist those now regarded as their 'clients' to undertake retraining in order to find a satisfying place in the work force and to lead the kind of fulfilled life that they really wanted and that was their social right. Political opponents of such a policy might well claim that it was typical of New Labour in that it represented 'all spin and no substance', that what was really the true motive was to disregard the poor and the oppressed and to save welfare money for the Exchequer. But note that in this case 'spin' was simply a hostile gleam in an opponent's eye: the New Labour politician really did believe in the grounds that he gave for his actions. 'Spin' rather than 'sub-stance' was a hostile opponent's way of dismissing a political case: those whose policy was under attack never saw things in that way.

Let us now turn, therefore, to our final account of the Jesus of history, and one that takes his eschatology seriously, as the moving force of the movement that he initially founded.

5. *Eschatology and Jesus' Acts*

We examined in a previous section (3) eschatological fragments in the *logia* of *Thomas* that imply a reinterpreted eschatology of the historical Jesus in which the inner and personal, spiritual kingdom has been substituted for a future and transcendent one in the primitive tradition. The question thus posed was: why

---

67. P. Foot, *The Politics of Harold Wilson* (Harmondsworth: Penguin, 1968).

cannot we hypothesize a trajectory in that tradition that goes from original eschatological claims through those parasitic on eschatological claims and then finally to non-eschatological claims such as those of the Gnostic saviour dialogue whose words produce present salvation? Certainly Mark evidences such a trajectory when he takes the parable of the Sower and adds a reinterpretation of the seed as the story of personal conversions and backsliding in the early church to a parable that his community at least saw originally in terms of the coming again of the Son of Man.[68]

We will argue that the production of a realized eschatology in which claims about Sophia or Wisdom, shorn of eschatological elements, was an essential prerequisite if the early Christianity of the Markan community was to achieve the kind of interaction with contemporary pagan society that was to affect political structures in the here and now before the hoped-for Eschaton. We shall argue (Chapters 3 and 4) that Luke's was the prime example of a realized eschatology that claimed the peace of Christ for Theophilus and his group as the true goal of what Augustus and his contemporaries sought in attempting to secure the *pax deorum*. Augustus' claim was based on its own, realized pagan eschatology of the inauguration of the new, golden age. Second-century Christian writers were to propose the refashioning of a pagan cosmology in terms of a Christian one based upon a Logos Christology adapted to a Stoic and Platonic metaphysics, as we shall see in Chapter 6. Since political order is a reflection of metaphysical order, such a refashioning would prove the essential pre-condition of the emergence of a Christian political order under Constantine and his successors. The success of the project was not to be achieved without a source of tension and modification resulting from an ongoing apocalyptic tradition, as we shall see in Chapters 4 and 7.

But Mark and his apocalyptic community existed before the development of such a political project and its ideological transformation. And so finally in this chapter we turn to a consideration of the understanding and intentions of the Jesus of history, as established by the work of E. P. Sanders.[69]

So far we have discussed the Jesus of history in the work of scholars who have expressed extreme scepticism regarding the narratives of the Synoptic Gospels. The focus rather has been upon the sayings of Jesus, divorced from the allegedly artificial, narrative setting in which the Synoptic evangelists have been accused of fictitiously placing them. The *Thomas logia* have, as we have seen, been often questionably claimed as earlier versions of the Synoptic *logia*, and superior because his gospel, along with other, non-canonical gospels, has no or little narrative context. Scholars used to ask, as the primary question of Gospel criticism, about what we can learn from the Jesus of history from Jesus' sayings that those scholars privileged as being of superior and primary

68. See above, footnote 24 and associated text.
69. E. P. Sanders, *Jesus and Judaism* (London: SCM, 1985).

historical worth over against what is recorded of the events and actions of Jesus' alleged Life.

Sanders' great achievement has been to pose a new way of looking at the Gospel material that concentrates rather on the significance of the few but significant events of Jesus' life of which we can be sure. We can begin by ruling out the Birth Stories, since there are none in Mark, and those of Matthew and Luke are so divergent. Both agree that Jesus was born at Bethlehem, with Matthew insisting that this must be so in fulfilment of Micah's prophecy, but they give entirely different accounts of why this is so in the case of a historical person who is known as 'Jesus of Nazareth' and not 'of Bethlehem'.[70] According to Matthew, the holy family had always lived originally in Bethlehem and Christ was born in their house: they only came to Nazareth as a result of Herod's hostility. According to Luke they had lived in Nazareth always, but travelled to Bethlehem to be enrolled in a universal census of all people in the Roman Empire that required Joseph to return to his birthplace and to be enrolled there with Mary.[71] Thus they were to return with the Christ Child born in the stable to Galilee.[72] We shall be examining in detail Luke's paralleling of the beginnings of Christ's reign of peace with that of Augustus in Chapter 4. But for now, the recovery of any firm historical details from these two conflicting accounts is fraught with difficulty and conjecture.

The same is true for the accounts of the resurrection. The earliest text of Mark bears witness to the absence of a body in the empty tomb and the promise of a future, eschatological appearance of the risen body, as I shall argue in the next chapter, as Son of Man. Matthew, Luke and John each have different accounts of the risen Christ appearing to different persons and groups, with no agreement: the text of their common source, Mark, clearly had no appearances for them to follow. In Matthew the appearance is to the women after they have run from the empty tomb, and then to the eleven disciples on a mountain in Galilee where they receive their universal mission.[73] In Luke the empty tomb is witnessed by the women, and confirmed by Peter, with a subsequent appearance to two disciples on the road to Emmaus, and subsequently to the eleven and others with a demonstration that the resurrection was physical.[74] In John it is Peter and the Beloved Disciple who witness the empty tomb, only the latter of whom initially grasps its significance 'and believes'. Subsequent appearances then take place to Mary of Magdala, then to the disciples at the Johannine Pentecost when the insufflation takes place, and then to Thomas, and finally, in

70. For 'Jesus of Nazareth', see e.g. Mt. 21:11; Mk 1:9; Jn 1:45-46; Acts 10:38. For Bethlehem, see Mt. 2:5-6 citing Mic. 5:1; Lk. 2:4; Jn 7:42.
71. Lk. 2:1-5.
72. Lk. 2:39.
73. Mt. 28:8-19.
74. Lk. 24:9-43.

an appendix, to Peter again and the Beloved Disciple.[75] Here our ability to corroborate one account against another is as difficult as with the birth stories.

There is a similar problem with the details of the trial of Jesus in the Synoptic gospels, critical as the trial scene is to the question of the Jesus of history's claim to be the Son of Man.[76] Since Peter was to deny Jesus 'in this night',[77] and the Sanhedrian met in formal council 'early', before light, a serious question regarding the legal standing of such a 'trial' is clearly raised: how formal and indeed legal was such a 'trial' as opposed to a less formal hearing.[78] Furthermore, as only Jesus, forsaken by his disciples, was there, can we rely on any credence in the account. We shall in a moment be arguing further that we can be sure of certain features, the source of which we can only speculate, reassured by the consideration that in all conspiratorial meetings there will be those nevertheless sufficiently on the fringes to leak to those on the fringes of the group being conspired against, with a certain inevitability of the information working its way through to those in the centre.

But nevertheless there are historical features of Jesus' life of which we can have some measure of historical certainty. Working backwards, we can be reasonably certain, thanks to Josephus and Tacitus, that

a.   Jesus of Nazareth met his death by crucifixion under Pontius Pilate and as a result therefore of a charge accepted, and a sentence executed by a Roman magistrate and not a Jewish court, which, if allowed to do so under Roman rule, would have ordered stoning.
b.   Jesus was involved in a controversy about, leading to a particular act in, the Temple that led to his arrest.
c.   Jesus called twelve disciples with a mission to Israel, and preached and healed.
d.   Jesus was baptized by John the Baptist.[79]

Beginning with (d), an event testified to both by Mark and by Q, we can therefore conclude that the movement into which Jesus was baptized was an apocalyptic movement, looking for the imminent future judgement of the world by fire.[80]

75.   Jn 20-21.

76.   Mk 14:53-64 (= Mt. 26:57-66; Lk. 22:66-71).

77.   Mk 14:30, cf. 48-49.

78.   Sanders, *Jesus and Judaism*, pp. 297–301 sets these out in detail. See also S. G. F. Brandon, *The Trial of Jesus of Nazareth* (London: Batsford, 1968), chapter 6; D. R. Catchpole, *The Trial of Jesus: A Study in the Gospels and Jewish Historiography from 1770 to the Present Day* (Studia post-Biblica 18; Leiden: E. J. Brill, 1971); E. Bammel, 'The trial before Pilate', in Bammel and Moule, *Jesus and Politics*, pp. 415–51; P. Winter, *On the Trial of Jesus*, second edition, revised and edited by T. A. Burkill and G. Vermes (Studia Judaica 1; Berlin and New York: De Gruyter, 1974), chapter 3.

79.   See also the list of historical facts in Sanders, *Jesus and Judaism*, p. 11.

80.   Mk 1:1-11 (=Mt. 3:1-6; 11-17; Lk. 3:1-6; 15-16; 21-22). For Q see Mt. 3:7-10; 12; Lk. 3:7-9; 17. Sanders, *Jesus and Judaism*, pp. 91–93.

Indeed, hypotheses are frequently advanced to circumvent this conclusion that suggest that the Jesus of history broke with John's movement over eschatology. Sometimes such hypotheses are related to attempts to identify the Jesus movement with that of the Dead Sea Scrolls, with Jesus as the 'Teacher of Righteousness' and John as the 'Wicked Priest'. I cannot here do justice to Sanders' complex analysis of these points but his general criticism of such a view is that it is highly improbable in the light of Paul's testimony that Christianity began with an apocalyptic movement that Jesus rejected, only to be ignored, and eschatology resurrected by Paul and his other followers.

More specifically (c), the specific number of disciples as 12 is indicative of Jesus' restoration eschatology in creating a New Israel with a new temple. Sanders is able to document such an eschatology as a contemporary Jewish hope, and relate such a hope to Jesus' ministry as described in the Synoptic gospels.[81] In this respect, we may see that this is the proper context in which to set the account of the miracle of the Feeding of the Five Thousand on which Crossan was to base what we have argued to be an anachronistic and Post-Enlightenment account of the Jesus of history. The Feeding was understood in the later, Sibylline oracle, not as embodying a principle of 'commensality' with the outcast and unclean, but in the context of the restoration of Israel. The 'twelve basketfuls' of bread and fish left over gave such a clue, and connected it with the mission of the Twelve whose number therefore bore such a restoration message.[82]

Jesus' ministry was closed by a journey to the Temple at the time of the Passover, and his subsequent crucifixion at the hands of the Roman power (a). A hearing before Pilate records the accusation that Jesus claimed to be 'King of the Jews'. Thus Crossan might argue that the Jesus movement was primarily, in post-Enlightenment categories, a political rather than a religious movement: to the charge that there was no religious–political distinction in Jesus' day, he will reply that the religious eschatological message is simply spin and the real motivation is social justice. Jesus was not simply and essentially a religious prophet or apocalyptic visionary, ultimately deluded, who genuinely believed that with the cultus ended, this order of space and time was about to be transcended by the coming of God's eternal reign. But as we have asked, are these post-Enlightenment alternatives really, in terms of first-century Palestine, bogus as alternatives? A political revolutionary, in such a context, would not express himself in terms of economic equality delivered by the construction of a new, egalitarian and properly functioning, machine of government. Rather, the reign of God and his angels would be the terms in which such a transformation of present social inadequacies would be expressed and passionately believed.

---

81.   Sanders, *Jesus and Judaism*, pp. 61–119.
82.   Mk 6:42 (=Mt. 14:20; Lk. 9:17); Jn 6:13.

The reason for Jesus' crucifixion rests upon the grounds for his condemnation by both Jewish and Pagan authorities, however formal or informal the process that led to this result may in fact have been. If we cannot be certain about the Trial, we can be certain about the act of Jesus on the temple (b), and in the light of those suggestions about the meaning of this act that may have become reformulated into an account of a formal judicial process (that may be fictitious) with charges formally made. Let us turn therefore now to how we are to understand the brute fact of Jesus' history that is the event described interpretively as the 'Cleansing' of the Temple.

6. *The Cleansing of the Temple and the Grounds for the Execution of Jesus of Nazareth by Crucifixion*

The canonical gospels for their part are adamant that if we insist on distinguishing a political charge, however religiously based, from a purely religious charge of sacrilege, then it was the latter that was the case with Jesus. We must therefore now examine in greater detail the issue as to whether the 'real' charge was treason rather than sacrilege, and that for this reason Jesus was executed by the Romans by crucifixion rather than by a Jewish court by stoning. It can be argued that the latter had the right to order capital punishment, despite suggestions in the canonical gospels to the contrary.[83]

In the act that Jesus performed in the Temple, the so-called 'Cleansing' of the Temple, the tables of the moneychangers were overthrown. The act can be regarded as that of a political revolutionary, representing the protest of the Galilean underclass to its exploitation by the political and hierarchical elites of the cities, in particular Jerusalem: the sale of animals at extortionate prices to those who could not transport safely from their own from distant villages without blemishing them was a symbol of exploitative repression. Thus we have the Jesus of much of contemporary North American scholarship as liberation theologians would like to depict him, a political revolutionary championing the cause of oppressed Galilee against a Jerusalem Jewish elite in collaboration with the occupying Roman, imperial power.

But as an act of political revolution, the overturning of moneychangers' tables at extortionate exchange rates in order to purchase doves from those who sold them would have required the violence of which there is no trace in the Synoptic records. There was no intervention either of Jewish Temple police or of Roman soldiers from the neighbouring castle of Antonia, with the kind of armed force that a violent act would have attracted. Jesus was subsequently arrested while alone with a small group of disciples, one of whom attempts a violent self-defence. If Jesus' correction of this disciple is an invention of the Gospel writers in favour of an allegedly non-historical picture of 'the peaceful

---

83. Brandon, *Zealots*, pp. 3–8; pp. 246–49.

Jesus',[84] then we may well ask why Jesus was crucified alone?: if there had been a violent struggle, we should have expected some if not many of his followers to have been apprehended on the spot or rounded up and crucified with him. Either therefore the so-called 'Cleansing of the Temple' was the complete fabrication of the gospel writers, or it cannot have the revolutionary and politically violent implications in which Crossan believed.

But the act recorded need not bear, and cannot bear, in view of the lack of intervention by the authorities, the interpretation that it was a violent act of insurrection. At all events, it was an act that Jesus is recorded as performing alone when 'he entered the temple courtyard and cast out those who bought and sold in the temple courtyard, and threw over the tables of the moneychangers and the chairs of those who sold doves. And he allowed not that anyone should carry a vessel through the temple courtyard.' The ascription of a purely individual act to Jesus is made by all four-gospel writers.[85] It was hardly then an act of insurrection in which his disciples would also needed to have been involved. There is however another interpretation in terms of a restoration ideology prophetically proclaimed. There was a tradition in the Old Testament prophets of performing 'prophetic signs', and Jesus here is acting as a prophet performing such a sign.[86] Jeremiah on one occasion smashed a jar in a prophetic pre-enactment of the fate of Judah and Jerusalem, Ezekiel made a model of the city and smashed down the walls of his model as a similar prophetic sign, as did Isaiah when he walked naked for three years in anticipation of the captivity to come.[87]

But that Jesus performed the act upon the Temple in which he cast out the moneychangers and, for a short space of time, brought, by these means, the temple cultus to a halt, cannot be doubted. What, Sanders asks, can be inferred from this indisputable fact about the intentions of the Jesus of history? Jesus was performing a prophetic sign enacting mimetically the fate of the Temple.

Support for the historicity of Jesus' act can be demonstrated from how it is described according to the author of the Fourth Gospel. Jesus had challenged his contemporaries with the claim:

Destroy this temple and in three days I will raise it up.[88]

The author, embarrassed by such a claim, assures us that this was commonly misunderstood and that Jesus had meant, not the actual temple at Jerusalem,

---

84.   Brandon, *Zealots*, chapter 6, cf. M. Hengel, *Victory over Violence, Jesus and the Revolutionists*, translated by David E. Green, with an introd. by Robin Scroggs (Philadelphia: Fortress Press, 1973), and Sanders, *Jesus and Judaism*, p. 68.
85.   Mk 11:15-16 (=Mt. 21:12; Lk. 19:45-47; Jn 2:14-17.
86.   Sanders, *Jesus and Judaism*, pp. 61–71.
87.   Isa. 20:2-4.
88.   Jn 2:19.

but 'the temple of his body'.[89] The gospel of Mark denied that Jesus had ever said such words: they are produced at his trial scene by 'false witnesses' who say:

> I will destroy this temple made with hands and in three days I will build another not made with hands.[90]

But you never need to deny what has never been seriously asserted, nor do you need to make up the claim of a historical personage that you wish to deny.

The Jesus of history had made this assertion, whether at an actual trial or otherwise, in connection with his act of 'purifying' the temple. Jesus' act of overturning the tables of the moneychangers, and those who provided animals for sacrifice, his preventing movement through the temple, etc., was not that of a violent revolutionary. Neither he himself, nor the disciples who accompanied him, had provoked by that act the intervention of the temple police or of the soldiers of the imperial power. The act is not that of a violent band of revolutionaries but of players who mime prophetically a future scene or indeed perform a prophetic sign that signifies what it effects and effects what it signifies. Jesus' expectation of the imminent destruction of the 'temple made with hands' and its replacement by an eternal and spiritual temple ('not made with hands') means that he believes that by his act this order of time and space was coming to an end and being transformed into God's eternal temple.

Mark (followed by Matthew and Luke) were to record a trial of Jesus before the Jewish High Priest in which the latter had replied in answer to a question about his Messianic claim:

> I am; and you will see the Son of Man seated on the right hands of the Power and coming with the clouds of heaven.[91]

The 'Son of Man' was not 'a man amongst men' as we so often read these words outside their original historical and literary context. In Daniel, albeit as perhaps a corporate and collective figure, but as an individual figure in *Esdras* and *Enoch*, the Son of Man, existing before creation, was destined to appear as a heavenly figure at the end of the world.

Mark's gospel believes both that Jesus was that kind of 'Son of Man' and that he would be revealed as such, after suffering and death, within the lifetime of the first disciples. After the Transfiguration, Jesus begins to teach that the 'Son of Man must first suffer before entering his glory', and that 'there are those standing here who will not taste of death until they have seen the kingdom of

---

89.   Jn 2:21.
90.   Mk 14:57-58.
91.   Mk 14:62 (=Mt. 26:63-64; Lk. 22:68-69), cf. Dan. 7:13.

God having come in power'. The form in which that coming will take place for Mark is purely an apocalyptic one:

> Then shall they see the Son of Man coming on the clouds of heaven with great power and glory. And then he shall send his angels and he shall gather together his elect from the four winds, from the end of the earth to the end of heaven.[92]

Indeed it may well be that, according to Mark, this was the form and the moment in which Jesus, after he suffered, would appear as a resurrection body. I will return to this argument in the next chapter where I will discuss the implications for Mark's community of the narrative of the Empty Tomb, and the angelic announcement of a 'seeing' again of the risen Jesus, in all his physical facticity, in an eschatological context at his coming again as Son of Man with power and great glory at the end of the age soon to come, amidst all the events of the apocalyptic drama.

But at this juncture we must ask what this implies for the original meaning for Jesus of the character of his ministry.

The political charge alleged by the Jewish authorities in order to secure Jesus' crucifixion was therefore a fabrication that concealed rather than revealed the nature of the prophetic sign, which had caused no disturbance that would otherwise have led to an arrest by the Roman authorities themselves, and perhaps summary execution. This fact alone, and not the assumed Markan apologetic of a fictitious 'pacific' Jesus, clearly supports such a conclusion. The Jesus of history was condemned on the charge of blasphemy in which he claimed that, by his prophetic act, this order of time and space was near its conclusion, and that a new temple would replace the old one with a new cultus in a transformed and eternal order. It is this Jesus, with the claim to be Son of Man as an eschatological figure that may flow from what his act implies, that it is the task of Christian theology to interpret and seek in what sense such a claim is true. It is a view of Jesus with which the political position of the Jesus movement within the Roman Empire would have to grapple, as it sought to pass from apocalyptic opposition to the present to accommodation with the Roman Empire. It is to a description of early Christianity's imperial accommodation that we now turn, which we shall see as being both transformed by and in turn transforming the Jesus movement.

---

92. Mk 13:27-28.

Chapter 2

THE FIRST CONFRONTATION WITH PAGANISM
UNDER NERO AND THE MARKAN COMMUNITY

In the year A.D. 64, the emperor Nero set in train the first persecution of the early Christian Church. Thus, for the first time, a confrontation took place between Christianity and the pagan imperial power that now recognized Christians as a named, hostile group. From the Christian side we have almost contemporary records that allude to those events that are reflected in Mark's Gospel. From the Roman side we have Tacitus' account, written under the emperor Trajan some 50 to 60 years later (A.D. 110–120). From these two different sources we may now endeavour to reconstruct the issues, as they were perceived from the opposing points of view of both sides.

1. *Pagan Hostility and the Peace of the Gods (*Pax Deorum*)*

Christianity was seen by the Romans as a malign force disturbing the metaphysical peace of nature and of society, and witnessed in criminal behaviour and sexual depravity. According to Tacitus, a fire had broken out in the capital for which this writer would sorely love to blame the emperor. His description of the fire follows his claim that Nero 'was defiled by every natural and unnatural lust' and had celebrated a mock homosexual wedding dressed as a female.[1] His own court chamberlains had with impunity rushed through the streets of Rome with burning torches setting houses on fire, while their inhabitants fled for shelter to monuments and to tombs. Nero watched the conflagration that lasted for seven nights from the tower of Maecenas and, while dressed as an actor, he sang his poem describing the burning of Troy.[2]

Nero now began to rebuild the city in fine style, with indeed provision for more water points and fire appliances, and public guards appointed to protect these against criminal action that had clearly also acerbated the situation by preventing adequate supply of water to quench the blaze. The emperor was clearly going to great lengths to cover his tracks if indeed he had made any,

---

1. Tacitus, *Annal.*, XV.37.
2. Suetonius, *Nero*, 38; Dio Cassius (Xiphilinus) LXII.17–18; Pliny, *Nat. Hist.*, XVII.1.5; Seneca, *Trag. (Octavia)*, 851–855.

as Tacitus and others have suggested. But such acts that to us in our post-Enlightenment world seem the practical and utilitarian tasks of government were not the only acts required by an Emperor in the face of such a disaster. The Sibylline books had to be consulted in order to discover whether such disasters had been part of the divine plan. The deities, such as Vulcan, god of fire, and Ceres and Proserpine had to be propitiated along with Juno with sacrifices and prayers. It was, as we shall see in greater detail, the function of government to secure the *pax deorum*, the 'peace of the gods' in place of their anger that had produced such a disastrous event. It will be important for us to understand that such a sacerdotal function of government was taken seriously by the Romans, and was part of their metaphysical understanding of the character of political arrangements within the cosmos as a whole.

Tacitus will insist, in his determination to vilify and damn Nero, that his subsequent action against the Christians was a personal subterfuge in order to cover his own responsibility for the fire. We shall see shortly that it was far more than this, and reflected the metaphysical means that was believed to be the essential response of good government to such disasters. But for now let us record how Tacitus describes the events of the persecution proceeding.

'Christians', named after their founder 'Christus', executed in the reign of the emperor Tiberius when Pilate was procurator of Judaea, were accused of the arson. They were not however hunted down by Nero's personal staff and summarily executed. There was a due process, presumably before the praetor's courts that heard criminal cases. Under torture, those examined had implicated a large number of other persons who were arrested and duly convicted. After guilty verdicts they were used, as criminals condemned to capital punishment could be used, in order to participate in a spectacle in an arena.

The arena was Nero's own, his circus to be found on the Vatican hillside near to an area in which later, around A.D. 160, a monument was to be built over arguably a grave that had been there from Nero's time and was identified as that of Peter the Apostle.[3] According to one account, a simple monument was erected close by Nero's circus to mark the place where Peter suffered, to be built over and monumentalized in the second half of the second century. The Roman community was experiencing horrendous persecution. In A.D. 65 it had seen, according to universal tradition, the martyrdoms of Peter and Paul. Tacitus informs us of Nero's garden party in the following passage:

> Nero . . . subjected to the most extra-ordinary tortures those hated for their abominations by the common people called Christians . . . So an arrest was made of all who confessed; then on the basis of their information, an immense multitude was convicted, not so much of the crime of arson as for hatred of the human race . . . They were covered with wild beasts' skins and torn to death by dogs; or they were fastened on

---

3.   J. Toynbee and J. Ward Perkins, *The Shrine of St. Peter and the Vatican Excavations* (London: Longmans Green, 1956), chapter 6.

crosses, and, when daylight failed were set alight to serve as lamps by night. Nero had offered his gardens for the spectacle and gave an exhibition in his Circus, mixing with the crowd in a charioteer's clothing or mounted on his chariot. Hence though being guilty and worthy to be made most pertinent examples, a sentiment of pity was roused on their behalf because they were being eliminated not for the welfare of the state but for the cruelty of on single man.[4]

But though Tacitus insists that the need for scapegoats for the fire was the true reason for the persecution, the charges that he reports as actually raised against the Christians are not those of arson. This itself is curious, and leads us to suspect that he has been so carried away by his desire to use the gratuitous cruelty to the Christians to damn the memory of Nero that he has overlooked the real charges that would have stood, even if there had been no fire along with other disasters of Nero's reign. They were convicted, Tacitus has to admit, 'no so much on the charge of arson, but for their hatred of the human race'. But what were these charges?

Tacitus informs us that what 'Christus' had begun under Tiberius in Judaea and had now spread to Rome itself was a 'superstition bringing destruction (*exitiabilis superstitio*)'. Christians were 'hated for their outrageous conduct (*per flagitia inuisos*)'. What were the practices that were so outrageous and how did they constitute not only 'superstition', but also a superstition 'bringing destruction'?

The word '*superstitio*' refers, not to general irrational and pathological forms of religion as in our sense, but to alien and foreign religious practices.[5] Such practices did not only 'bring destruction (*exitiabilis*)' upon those who perpetrated them themselves, but upon their fellow members in society. There were people so perverse who practised black magic and so caused a breakdown in the natural order that was reflected in breakdown in the social order: they had upset the 'peace of the gods'. Those, like the early Christians who refused to participate in the polytheism that was the religion of the Roman state were one of many such mainly eastern cults, and their true religion, it was concluded, was depraved and involved black magic. They could well be described as needing to be suppressed because of their 'hatred of the human race'.

The suppression of a cult suspected of having such a malign effect on the metaphysical order (both of nature and of society) was no new event. In 186 B.C. the cult of Dionysus had been suppressed by the consul Postumius with the claim:

Nothing is more deceptive in appearance than a depraved rite (*praua religio*). When the presence (*numen*) of the gods is put forward as a defence for crime, there steals upon the mind a fear lest in punishing human misdeeds we may violate something of divine

4. Tacitus, *Annal.*, XV.44.4-5.
5. L. F. Janssen, '"Superstitio" and the Persecution of the Christians', in *VC*, 33, 2 (1979), pp. 131–59.

law that had become mixed up with them. From this religious scruple innumerable edicts of the pontiffs, decrees of the senate, and finally responses of the *haruspices* free you. How often from the time of your fathers and ancestors have the magistrates concerned themselves with forbidding foreign sacred rites being performed, their sacrificing priests and prophets they excluded from the forum, the circus, and from the city itself. They searched out and burned the books of those prophets. They banned every practice of sacrificial performance unless according with the Roman customary performance. Those wisest of men constantly made the judgement that in every matter of both divine and human law nothing could cause more religious practice to lose strength than when sacrifices were being celebrated by a foreign ritual and not by our ancestral one.[6]

The occasion for the suppression had been the so-called 'Dionysiac riot'. As a result of the particular crimes that had been committed by members of this cult, the gods were angry that 'their own divine presence (*numen*) had been profaned by crimes and sexual immorality'.[7]

The evidence before the consuls had concerned what was described as a 'conspiracy (*coniuratio*)'. We from our post-Enlightenment perspective would tend to confine this term to a group actually bearing arms against the state and plotting by such means to overthrow a government of which they disapproved. But 'conspiracy' had a far wider meaning. A group that, abstaining from traditional Roman religion, was held to practise secret magical rites that could provoke the anger and upset the peace of the gods, was considered to be a conspiracy.

We must remember that before the European Enlightenment, nature was not distinguished from society, with the latter regarded as an artificial machine constructed by human beings in order to secure their personal and individual ends. Nature and society were one, and the same supernatural forces that determined events in the one were believed to determine also events in the other. The peace of society reflected the peace of nature and *vice versa*. Social divisions and upheavals would be represented and foretold by strange and unnatural occurrences in nature that were portents and prodigies. A magical act in nature also affected society and *vice versa*. A secret society practising such magic was, therefore, as much a conspiracy (*coniuratio*) as one that took up arms and practised violence against the state.

Livy gives us an account of the detailed accusations made against the Dionysiac group in Rome that bear striking resemblance to those made against the early Christians. An unnamed figure came originally from Greece and then from Etruria to Rome shortly before 186 B.C. He is described as 'a priest of hidden rites performed by night', and as a 'pretended priest (*sacrificulus*)' and 'frenzied prophet (*uates*)'.[8] Initiatory rites included feasting and drunkenness so that, under cover of the night, 'males had enjoyed intercourse with women,

---

6. Livy, XXXIX.16.6–9.
7. Livy, XXXIX.16.11.
8. Livy, XXXIX.8.3–4.

those of a tender age with their elders' and 'corrupt practices of every kind were commenced . . . and poisonings and secret murders so that no bodies remained for burial'.[9]

The grounds given for suppressing the Dionysiac cult were those that would have entitled Tacitus to describe Christianity as a *exitiabilis superstitio*. Tacitus has been accused of inventing the fire as the reason for Nero's attack upon Christianity for without it the suppression of a sect like Christianity would have seemed otherwise thoroughly justified.[10] It was a 'depraved rite (*praua religio)*' that was performed 'by a foreign ritual and not by our ancestral one (*non patrio sed externo ritu)*', and thus a *superstitio*.[11] Despite the views of some scholars to the contrary, it would thus appear that the magistrates at Nero's instigation were proceeding, not on the basis of a law of Nero specifically banning Christianity, but because of their sacred responsibility to secure through the ritual of the augurs as through their power in law (*coercitio*) the *pax deorum* against any foreign cult of this kind.[12]

Though Tacitus gives us no specific information about alleged early Christian practices, he does speak of 'all things horrible and shameful' coming from Judaea and infecting the Capital. The charge on which they were convicted, however, was 'not so much on account of arson as of hatred of the human race (*odium humani generis)*'.[13] But Tacitus' near contemporary, Pliny expressed some perplexity about whether someone who was a Christian should be prosecuted simply for bearing the name of Christ, or whether rather because of 'crimes connected with the name'.[14] Following his investigation of what occurred at one Eucharistic rite, he had to admit that they 'took food of an ordinary and harmless kind'. He nevertheless decided, as consuls had in the case of the Dionysiac cult almost two centuries before, that Christianity was 'a depraved and immoderate superstition (*superstitio praua et immodica)*'.

Athenagoras a few years later explains for us at what Pliny was hinting. Three charges were current, namely 'atheism, Thyestian banquets, and Oedipopean intercourse'.[15] Having seduced his brother's wife, according to the myth, Thyestes attended a banquet and ate a meal in which his children were served as a dish. Oedipus murdered his father and married his own mother. Thus the accusations against the Christians were incest and cannibalism. Furthermore, 'atheism' was linked with 'sorcery', and Celsus accused Christians of

---

9. Livy, XXXIX.8.7–8.

10. P. Keresztes, 'Rome and the Christian Church I', in *ANRW*, II.23.1, pp. 247–315 (252-57).

11. Livy, XXXIX.16.6 and 9–10.

12. P. Garnsey, *Social Status and Legal Privilege in the Roman Empire* (Oxford: Clarendon Press, 1970), p. 6.

13. Tacitus, *Annal.*, XV.44.4.

14. Pliny, *Ep.*, X.96.8.

15. Athenagoras, *Leg.*, 3.1.

practising black magic.[16] The charges against the Dionysiac cult of frenzied and abandoned dances in forests by night were associated with their re-enactment (*mimesis*) of the Dionysiac myth, as a kind of sympathetic magic.

The Oedipus and Thyestes stories were believed to be the mystery play enacted as part of Christian initiation rites, as Caecilius says in the dialogue of Minucius Felix:

> An infant, cased in dough to deceive the unsuspecting, is placed beside the person to be initiated. The novice is thereupon induced to inflict what seem to be harmless blows upon the dough, and unintentionally the infant is killed . . . the blood they lap up greedily; the limbs they tear to pieces eagerly; and over the victim they may league and covenant, and by complicity in guilt pledge themselves to mutual silence . . . On the day appointed they gather at a banquet with all their children, sisters, and mothers, people of either sex and every age. There, after full feasting, when the blood is eaten and drink has enflamed the passions of incestuous lust, a dog, which has been tied to a lamp, is tempted by a morsel thrown beyond the range of its tether to bound forward with a rush. The tale-telling light is upset and extinguished, and in the shameless dark, lustful embraces are indiscriminately exchanged; and, all alike, if not in act yet in complicity, are involved in incest.[17]

Thus the charge was brought against the early Christians of actually eating the flesh of new born babies and engaging in incest with mother or sister, in re-enactment of the myths of Oedipus or of Thyestes, in an attempt to achieve sinister, magical consequences, witnessed in portents in the heavens of a violated natural order or indeed in disorder, conspiracy and insurrection within human society. Thus the themes of uncontrolled and frenzied cult activity with unspeakable immoral acts found in Livy's description of the Dionysiac rite are continued in this description of Christianity. Caecilius emphasizes again both Livy's and Pliny's term: we have here a *religio* (rite) or a *superstitio* that is *praua* (depraved).[18]

As Tertullian was to describe the pagan reaction as that of those who

> use as a pretext to defend their hatred the absurdity that they take the Christians to be the cause of every disaster to the state, of every misfortune of the people. If the Tiber reaches the walls, if the Nile does not rise to the fields, if the sky makes no movement with rain or the earth does with quaking if there is famine, if a plague, then at once the cry goes up: 'the Christians to the lion'. So many Christians, all to one lion.[19]

Regarding charges of incest and cannibalism, Tertullian mocks the picture of secrecy and darkness that prefigures both with Livy's picture of the Dionysiacs

16. Dio Cassius, LII.36.2; Origen, *Celsus*, 1.6.
17. Minucius Felix, *Octav.*, 9.5–7.
18. Minucius Felix, *Octav.*, 10.1, cf. Livy, XXXIX.16.6; Tacitus, *Annal.*, XV.44.3; Pliny, *Ep.*, X.96.8.
19. Tertullian, *Apol.*, 40.1–2 (1–9).

reproduced in broad outline in the general pagan view of early Christianity. If the extinguishing of the lamp was so necessary, how could one be certain if the person that you were mounting were your mother or sister, and supposing you had no relatives anyway?[20] Regarding devouring infants:

> For us murder is once for all forbidden; so even when the child has been conceived in the womb, while yet the mother's blood is still being drawn on, it is not lawful for us to destroy. To forbid birth is only quicker murder. It makes no difference whether one takes away the life once born or destroys it as it comes to birth. It is a human being who both exists and who shall exist.[21]

But despite all such Christian protests, a picture begins to emerge of how Pagan Romans regarded the early Christians.

Tacitus' general description of an *exitiabilis superstitio* has now been fleshed out in finer details. Tacitus may have considered such specific features irrelevant as he tries to treat Christianity sympathetically in order to heap blame upon Nero for the fire. But even without the fire, Christianity was regarded as one of a number of eastern cults, such as Babylonian astrologers and magicians or indeed members of the cult of Dionysius that were a conspiracy (*coniuratio*). To be such a *coniuratio* such religions need not lead to actual physical disorder within Roman society though well they might. It was enough to incur the charge that they refused to participate in Roman religious practices whose intention was to secure and perpetuate a benign cosmic order, namely the *pax deorum*.

The classic example that arguably parallels the legal status of early Christianity was the *senatusconsultum* of A.D. 14 against the Magi and Chaldeans. Under this legislation, the practice of magic or of divination in which the future could be seen and foretold was made illegal. As with Pliny, the question arose as to whether merely professing knowledge or, rather and in addition, more positive public 'profession (*professio*)' was to be punished. *Professio* as well as practice was ruled out in a series of rescripts issued to individual governors, who complained of 'insolence (*contumacia*)' or boastful self-assertion in public displays of adherents to such religious practices.[22] As Barnes pointed out:

> Pliny, when trying the Christians before him, had no need to rely on any law that made Christianity a capital crime: indeed he appears not even to know whether there was one.[23]

20. Tertullian, *Apol.*, 8.3 (10–12) and 7–8 (28–36).
21. Tertullian, *Apol.*, 9.8 (31–36).
22. Ulpian, *De officio proncon.* VIII, cf. Dio Cassius, LVII.15.8; Tacitus, *Annal.*, II.27–32; Suetonius, *Tib.*, 36. See also A. N. Sherwin-White, 'The Early Persecutions and Roman Law Again', *JTS*, 3.2 (1952), pp. 211–12.
23. T. D. Barnes, 'Legislation against the Christians', *JRS*, 58 (1968), pp. 32–50 (36).

Barnes claims that it was a *mos maiorum* that the gods of the Roman state should be worshipped, and that practitioners of magic arts who did not do so would disturb the *pax deorum*. It was this that was the source of persecution.[24]

Thus early Christians, like the Dionysiacs, appeared as 'a secret race that shuns the light'. Their public refusal to participate in the state religion was seen as theatrical obstinacy deliberately flaunted (*contumacia*). They were practitioners of secret magical rites involving incest and cannibalism that would produce portents indicative of an upset nature as stars moved from their natural order in the form of comets, or lakes turned to blood, or young women gave birth to serpents, etc. These were the images evoked when one such Christian family refused to burn the sacrificial flame on their household altar when everyone else's was illuminated, as the crowds gathered for the festal holiday with religious processions circulating their cities in honour of the gods of the Roman state with which were being increasingly combined those of the dead and deified Roman emperors.

This, we may, say, was the picture of the Christians as pagan Romans saw them. But how did the Christians see the Romans?

2. *A Christian View of the Romans in Nero's Reign*

The answer to the question of the early Christian view of the Romans will depend upon of which Christian group one will ask this question. Scholars in recent years have long acknowledged the diversity of early Christian groups so that we have come to speak of the 'Jesus Movement', in which there occurs a variety of understandings of the aim of the founder. How a group views those outside will inevitably depend on the self-consciousness of the group regarding its religious character and purpose. In our first chapter we have already mentioned such divergences stemming from traditions of the Jesus of history, and of the kind of community that he intended to create.

Was the Jesus of history a social and therefore political revolutionary, or a prophet expecting the imminent and in some sense apocalyptic transformation of the present age into an eternal order of things? Or was he a wisdom sage like a cynic philosopher parodying and satirizing the social and religious practices of his contemporaries, whom his followers took too literally and seriously? Or was his 'kingdom' a mysterious inner and personal, Gnostic spiritual world?

Prescinding from all such discussions regarding the Jesus of history, my focus here will be on how the community of St Mark's Gospel saw their pagan contemporaries in the Roman situation in the time that Tacitus has described.

2.1 *Mark's Gospel and the Roman Community*
An ancient tradition that goes back to Papias in the second century, whose fragmentary lost work has been preserved in quotations found in Eusebius,

---

24. Barnes, 'Legislation', p. 50.

describes Mark as author of the second gospel and as 'the interpreter of Peter'. From this it has been deduced that Mark was commissioned by the Roman community to write the freshly remembered discourses of Peter after the latter's recent death in Nero's persecution. But doubts can be raised about such a deduction.

One fundamental problem is that Mark's Gospel bears all the marks of an oral transmission throughout at least a generation, in which specific names have, for the most part, dropped out and specific details been lost as words and acts are strung together in a quite artificial framework. But such a view, traditional among scholars in the late nineteenth and first half of the twentieth century, has been challenged. Mark may not read to us like a modern biography with details of dates, named characters with whom the principal character came in contact, etc. But accounts of ancient lives (*Bioi*) of philosophers and religious leaders bear many of the features of Mark's narrative. At all events, the association between Peter and Rome seems secure, in view of New Testament and other evidence.[25] 1 Peter would appear to be a pseudonymous document whose contents refer to Domitian's persecution, yet it is written in Peter's name with a salutation from 'those in Babylon', which is a clear early Christian cipher for Rome. Even if the relationship between Mark's narrative and Peter's reminiscences cannot be closely drawn, the association of Mark with Peter by Papias is at least indicative of the plausibility of Mark as a Roman gospel in the consciousness of early Christians.

Mark's narrative appears to reflect the situation that Tacitus and Josephus describe in Rome and Judaea around A.D. 65. Mark believed that Jesus would return as Son of Man within the lifetime of the first disciples. Jesus, after his exhortation to his disciples to lay down their life 'for my sake and the gospel's', assures them that whoever is ashamed of him and his words in this present world 'of him shall the Son of Man be ashamed when he comes in the glory of his father with his holy angels'. Jesus then according to Mark says:

> Truly I say to you that there are certain of those who have stood here who shall not taste of death until they shall see the kingdom of God having come in power.[26]

Though it is possible to read the story of the Transfiguration that immediately followed as the spiritual realization of the promise made here, clearly Mark has located these words in a future, eschatological context.

If such a realized eschatology was the original focus of these words, Mark has reshaped that focus. The author's own, apocalyptic perspective is seen in Mark 13, where Jesus' prophecy of the destruction of Jerusalem is followed by far the longest discourse that occupies 33 verses of his gospel that is the writer's own attribution to the Jesus of history. There indeed it is claimed that

25.   1 Pet. 5:13 cf. Rev. 18:2-3. See also Clement, *Cor.*, 5. 3–5.
26.   Mk 8:34–9:1.

Jesus foresaw in further detail what his words had promised in the following passage:

> While he was leaving the temple, one of his disciples said to him: Teacher, see what magnificent stones and buildings. And Jesus said to him, do you see these great buildings? Not one stone upon another will be left which shall not be destroyed.[27]

Mark has inserted following Jesus' words a long prediction at the conclusion of which, following the darkening of the sun and moon, and the falling of the stars from heaven and the shaking of the heavenly powers:

> And then they shall see the son of man coming on the clouds with great power and glory. And then he shall send his angels and they shall gather the elect from the four winds from the end of the earth up to the end of heaven.[28]

Certainly the Markan apocalypse would have been read with a mixture of fear, awe, and bewilderment by the Christian, Roman community around A.D. 69.

Mark's Roman community clearly believed that they were experiencing the events of the last time. The Roman Christians were being 'brought before the magistrates' or, as in Paul's case as a Roman citizen, before the emperor's tribunal ('before kings'). Apocalyptic plays an important role in the way in which such communities understand the events of their history and react to them. In Nero's persecution, of the pagans it could be said that

> They will betray you to the Jewish courts (*sunedria*) and you will be flogged at their synagogues and you will stand before governors and kings for my sake, as a witness to them, and the gospel must first be preached to all the pagans. . . . and you will be hated by all because of my name.[29]

James the Just had suffered before such a *sunedrion* presided over by Ananus the Sadducean High Priest.[30]

If not, therefore, as we have seen that some doubt, the Jesus of history himself, then certainly early Christian communities, such as that of Mark, identified Jesus with this figure, and with the corresponding apocalyptic drama. Mark's community, during the persecution of Nero at Rome and hearing news from Palestine and the East regarding the fate of Jerusalem and its temple, responded with awe and fear regarding the drama of the last things unravelling before

---

27. Mk 13:1-2.
28. Mk 13:24-27.
29. Mk 13:9-13.
30. Josephus, *Antiqu.*, 20.197–200; A. Brent, *Cultural Episcopacy and Ecumenism: Representative Ministry in Church History from the Age of Ignatius of Antioch to the Reformation, with Special Reference to Contemporary Ecumenism* (Studies in Christian Mission 6; Leiden: E. J. Brill, 1992), pp. 135–37.

their eyes. They sought anxiously the news from Jerusalem, now at the centre of the Jewish Revolt that was to be crushed in A.D. 70. Titus was in process of surrounding Jerusalem, and something horrendous was to take place, the 'abomination of the desolation' mentioned by 'the prophet Daniel'. What could this be? No one as yet knew. Such was the unfolding mystery of evil presaging the immediate reappearance of the suffering and dying Jesus as the glorified Son of Man.

But when precisely were these events to take place?

2.2 *The Effect of Events in Judaea on Mark's Community*

In answer to this question we have two indications, namely, a general persecution which for the readers would be in Rome, and events in Judaea. Christians would be brought before Jewish courts and be beaten, as indeed happened to Paul in the Acts of the Apostles, where finally he was tried before the Roman magistrate Portius Festus and by Herod Agrippa, but appealed to Caesar and thus pre-empted any verdict.[31] Thus Mark's words had been fulfilled when Jesus prophesies: 'You shall stand before governors and kings for my sake as a witness to them.'[32] In Rome too, as we have seen from Tacitus' account, Christians were brought before the praetor's court.

Josephus illuminates for us the situation in Judaea under Festus' pro-consulship. In Acts, James, the brother of Jesus, appears at the head of the Jerusalem presbyterate, who collectively persuaded Paul to conform to their version of Jewish Christianity by taking a Nazirite vow because of his Christian flock's zealousness for the law.[33] James then disappears from the scene, leaving Paul to face his accusers alone.

Acts, however, does bear witness, albeit partially, to the tinderbox political situation, although from reading this text we could conclude that Paul alone, having brought Trophimus and other gentiles in his entourage into the inner court of the temple, had been the cause of a near riot and his own arrest.[34] Josephus' account leaves us no doubt in concluding that James must have needed like a sore head the appearance of Paul in Jerusalem claiming to be the 'apostle to the nations', and accompanied by his uncircumcized gentile converts, who did not adhere to Jewish food laws.

James was to suffer martyrdom shortly after Porcius Festus had despatched Paul to Rome. It was subsequent to his death (A.D. 62), and while his successor, Albinus, was on the way from Rome a few months later, that the Sadducean High Priest, Ananus, engineered James' illegal execution by stoning.[35] As a

---

31. Acts 25:6-13.
32. Mk 13:9.
33. Acts 21:18-24.
34. Acts 21:28-29.
35. Josephus, *Antiqu.*, 20.197-200.

result, Albinus forced Herod Agrippa, the Jewish king, to depose him,[36] having been urged to do so by a Jewish faction that Josephus describes as 'fair-minded and strict in their observance of the law'.[37]

Thus, in Mark's words, James too had been delivered up 'to *sunedria* and to synagogues' in a martyrdom (in A.D. 62) that had taken place just a few years before the outbreak of the Jewish War against Rome in June A.D. 66. Paul had departed previously under guard to Rome to stand before the emperor's tribunal, or in Mark's words 'before kings'. Tacitus' fire was to break out in Rome in July A.D. 64. If the deaths of Peter and Paul were connected with the fire and the judicial process that followed it, we can date their deaths in about A.D. 65.[38] Mark's apocalypse, in that case, was read by his Roman readers as applying to their own situation as well as to events in Judaea.

Tacitus records that, in the course of the judicial process that followed in the aftermath of the fire, those first arrested were to betray others, as a result, we may assume, of the customary examination by torture. Mark's apocalypse, placed in the mouth of Jesus, accordingly informs us that 'brother shall betray brother unto death, and father child, and children shall rise up against parents and slay them'.[39] Thus starkly, and in terms of a break up in family relations, we find here the customary description of widespread betrayal in the customary language of apocalyptic literature.

Nero's persecution in fact was local and confined to Rome, and against a *superstitio* threatening the *pax deorum*: there was to be no general persecution of the Church before Decius. Yet Mark's apocalypse will imaginatively generalize that persecution so as to make it part of the drama of the last things. Nature was breaking down in disorder, and, as both Pagans and Christians were to maintain, nature and society are one, with events in the one reflecting events in the other. Earthquakes and famines, in the great 'time of trial ($\theta\lambda\hat{\imath}\psi\iota\varsigma$)' or 'tribulation', were indications of the last and final collapse of the fabric of things, when sun and moon failed and the stars fell. These portents in nature thus reflected the general collapse in society, with not simply friends and Christian brothers betraying one another in Nero's Rome, but also throughout the world and even in the most fundamental of human relations that is the family. The plausibility of the universality of what the Roman community was suffering in these particular, Roman events was enhanced by the news that was coming from Judaea and Galilee, and from Jerusalem.

Jesus, whom Mark believed to have claimed to be the Son of Man, the supernatural being who was to wind up the scroll of history, would return as such,

36. Josephus, *Antiqu.*, 20.202-203.
37. Josephus, *Antiqu.*, 20.201.
38. Reservations have been expressed regarding this connection though it seems difficult to deny the deaths of both apostles in Rome, see G. W. Clarke, 'The origin and spread of Christianity', in *CAH²*, XII.3.18b (870–71).
39. Mk 13:12.

no longer in obscurity and known only by his disciples but seen by all. But when, according to Mark, was Jesus last seen by his disciples?

It is well known that Mark's Gospel originally appears to have lacked any resurrection appearances. Mathew and Luke, though showing substantial similarities that imply that Mark was one of their common sources for the Passion Narrative and earlier, both diverge with quite different series of narratives of Jesus' post resurrection appearances. The most ancient manuscripts record the story of the empty tomb, with no visible body, and the 'young man . . . dressed in a white robe', who, tells the women who have come to the tomb to 'tell his disciples and Peter that he goes before you into Galilee, there shall ye see him, even as he told you'.[40] The original text of the Gospel records the response of the women who

> Went out from the tomb and said nothing to anyone because they were afraid (or in awe).[41]

R. H. Lightfoot, notoriously, endeavoured to produce what many saw as a non-miraculous account of the resurrection as a spiritual event in which the community in Galillee would meet with Jesus as they met for worship. But his own insightful observations should have led him to treat matters in a better and more historically critical way.

Lightfoot pointed out that though the Markan Jesus had said 'I go before you into Galilee', he had never added 'there shall you see (ὄψεσθε) (me)', as the young man in white had said 'there shall you see (ὄψεσθε) (him)'.[42] But the Markan apocalypse had promised that 'they shall see (ὄψονται) the Son of man'. The 'seeing' promised at the empty tomb was therefore an 'eschatological' seeing. The disciples, Lightfoot thus inferred, would have an eschatological vision when they met for the Eucharist in their Galilean community, where they would be 'gathered together' like the elect gathered together by angels from the four winds and the four corners of the earth. But this account of 'reinterpreted eschatology' was not Mark's reinterpretation in his community and in terms of his first century background, but rather of Lightfoot's twentieth century pre-occupation with the nature of the miraculous.

Lightfoot had proposed a highly anachronistic reading of the passage: Christ's resurrection was spiritual and involved witnessing a spiritual presence in the Church and a realized eschatology. I would reject such a reading as unhelpful in unravelling Mark's historical context, however valuable as a contribution to systematic theology that seeks to understand the Christ event. When Jesus had promised that, having been 'smitten': 'After I have risen again, I will go before you into Galilee,' Mark's interpretation of these words must be that that his

40. Mk 16:7.
41. Mk 16:8.
42. Mk 16:7.

appearance there would be as Son of Man at the close of history within the lifetime of the first Christian generation.[43] The three other gospel writers no doubt regarded things differently with their accounts of bodily resurrection appearances before the *eschaton*, but Mark, I submit, did not.

The authentic Mark had, indeed, contrary to later scribal additions, ended his Gospel with Jesus physically raised (the tomb was empty and there was no body), but making no physical appearance. But when would they 'see' him in Galilee? Mark, on such a reading of the narrative of the Empty Tomb, has indicated one time only, namely when, according to the Markan apocalypse, 'you will see the Son of Man coming on clouds' at the close of history.

Mark, arguably, was writing in A.D. 67 or 68. That he wrote even though he believed that the continuity of this age was not to be long may be indicative that he wished for his message to circulate beyond the confines of the city of Rome. Paul, probably, had been tried and condemned and executed, as had more probably Peter in A.D. 66, though neither Tacitus, nor indeed any other pagan writer, names either of them. Peter's putative remains, re-housed in a small shrine or *Aedicula* on the Vatican Hillside in around A.D. 165, were arguably there before the erection of this monument in a marked, pauper's grave near Nero's circus in which he had suffered. A future pagan charioteer was also to be buried as part of a complex of pagan mausolea gradually developed there, whose epitaph expressed his wish to be buried in a mausoleum *in uaticano ad circum* or 'on the Vatican hillside up against [Nero's] circus'. Nero's freedmen had also mausolea in the immediate vicinity. But other events were now following the deaths of Peter and Paul beginning to develop in Judaea.

It was those events that were to add plausibility to Mark's account of Nero's persecution as part of the worldwide, apocalyptic drama of the end.

James, as head of the church in Jerusalem, following Paul's departure for Rome, had tried to maintain the standing of Jewish Christianity as it had appeared in the eyes of Josephus. 'The brother of Jesus who was called the Christ' was the head of a Jewish Christian synagogue in Jerusalem, and part of the diversity within Judaeism permissible before the imposition of a uniform definition of Judaeism at Jabneh (*c.*A.D. 95) at which the 'curses on those who separate (*bircoth ha minim*)' were imposed. Just as there were Greek speaking synagogues at Alexandria and those at Dura who would permit no image of God, but would not extend the prohibition to biblical scenes, as well as Hebrew ones, so there was a synagogue consisting of Jews otherwise 'zealous for the law'[44] and following food laws and even the custom of circumcision but who believed the Messiah had come, and, having been crucified under Pilate and having risen again, was to return in glory.

---

43. Mk 8:38-9:1; 13:26; 14:27-28; cf. 16:7.
44. Acts 21:20, cf. above, footnote 30 and related text.

It was in the context of the situation in Judaea in A.D. 62, with factionalism between Sadducees, Pharisees, and the more extreme Zealots and Sicarii, heightening tension and increasing the possibility of a breakdown in order, that James' presbyters persuaded the 'apostle to the nations' to shave his head and take a Nazirites' vow and offer a sacrifice in the temple with them. It was an act of compromise that would prove to be of no avail for James' purpose, and he was to perish before Paul in the developing turmoil brought on by Ananus the maverick Sadducean High Priest.

Though there was no actual connection between Nero's limited persecution of the Christian Roman community and these events, nevertheless Mark integrates them into the pattern of his apocalyptic narrative, as we shall now see.

2.3 The Roman Community and Judaean Apocalyptic Expectations
Around the time that he is writing, in the summer of A.D. 66, riots broke out at Caesarea Maritima between Jews and Gentiles, the latter of whose pagan temples were prominent in a city that owed to Herod a temple to the imperial cult. In that year, the successor to the mercenary Albinus, Gessius Florus (A.D. 64–66), marched upon Jerusalem and crucified some of the leading citizens. Despite the intervention of Herod Agrippa II, in May or June some priests refused to sacrifice *pro salutate imperatoris*. Jews were being slaughtered as they rose against their gentile neighbours. Josephus, in his other and earlier life as rebel commander in Galilee, was to lose that province and, by late summer of A.D. 67, Ananus, deposed High Priest and responsible for James' death, was found defending Jerusalem against the onslaught of Vespasian whose son, Titus, was finally to take and burn Jerusalem to the ground along with the temple in August A.D. 70.[45]

These were the reports reaching Mark in a community overwhelmed by hope and fear, as he composed his Gospel, imposing on his narrative the view of his beloved apocalyptic discourse. Wars and civil unrest appeared to them now as universal and not merely local, with the fate of their community in Judaea and Jerusalem increasingly, since James' martyrdom, appearing dire in the deepening catastrophe there. One tradition that comes from Eusebius is that the Jewish Christian community were warned prophetically to flee to Pella, which would have been, if it happened, around A.D. 67 and before the final siege of Jerusalem.

The Markan apocalypse focuses on the plight of refugees as a feature of the tribulation woes that ensue when what it calls the 'desecrating sacrilege (βδέλυγμα τῆς ἐρημώσεως)' is set up in the Jerusalem Temple.[46] It is at this point that the writer betrays his incorporation of a written document intended to be read rather than the express words of Jesus before his Passion. In the

45. Josephus, *BJ*, 6.229-66.
46. Mk 13:14-21.

midst of the persecuted Roman community feeling the effects of 'being hated by all'[47] or, as Tacitus had described them, 'for the crimes' associated with the 'disease' of a *exitiabilis superstitio*, the writer of the original apocalypse addressed to Judaean Christians informs them that

> When you shall see the desecrating sacrilege standing where it ought not (let the reader [*sic*] understand), then let those who are in Judaea flee to the mountains . . .[48]

This phrase (βδέλυγμα τῆς ἐρημώσεως), so strange as an expression in Greek, was highly enigmatic. It was taken from the Old Testament apocalypse, Daniel.

Here is a document whose words are placed in the mouth of a fourth century B. C. wisdom sage in Babylon, but which is in fact to be located in its final form in the Hellenistic period and in the reign of Antiochus IV Epiphanes (175–164 B.C.). The Temple was destined to be recaptured by Judas Maccabeus in 165, a year before the former's death in his war against the Armenians. But previously the Temple had been desecrated by Antiochus sacrificing swine's flesh upon the altar before converting it into a temple of Zeus (B.C. 168). It is to this act of sacrilege that Daniel refers when he speaks of the 'prince who is to come' in the words:

> He shall make a strong covenant with many for one week, and for half of the week he shall make sacrifice and offering cease; and in their place shall be the desecrating sacrilege.[49]

The writer of the apocalypse that was to be incorporated by Mark and put on the lips of Jesus in order to comfort the Roman community in its trials in or around A.D. 68 knew nothing of the tools of historical and literary analysis that have recovered the original context of 'Daniel's' words.

The writer of the Markan apocalypse leaves us in a state of nervous shuddering about what precisely the 'desecrating sacrilege' would be, and Mark himself does not add any more precision to his enigmatic description. Indeed he does not know what it means more clearly since it has yet to happen. For Mark the event is imminent, but has not yet occurred. Matthew and Luke write subsequently and know the temple has been destroyed, with the result that the latter simply records that fact without including in his account any mention of Mark's enigmatic 'desecrating sacrilege'. Instead he records:

> When you see Jerusalem encircled by armed camps, then you should know that its desolation (ἐρήμωσις) has drawn nigh . . . Jerusalem will be trodden down until the times of the gentiles are fulfilled.[50]

47. Mk 13:13.
48. Mk 13:14.
49. Dan. 9:27.
50. Lk. 21:20 and 24.

Thus the events of the destruction of Jerusalem in A.D. 70 are separated from the coming of the Son of Man, and the signs of his coming are relegated to an indefinite future.

Matthew adds apocalyptic detail on apocalyptic detail, and assures us that the event will still take place, in some indefinite future in some unspecified 'holy place'. What had not happened in A.D. 70 he assures us will still happen, and what it might be was still a mystery, but the 'desecrating sacrilege' whatever it was, would be something truly terrible, a 'desecrating sacrilege', standing, not in the Jerusalem that is no more, but in some unspecified 'holy place (ἐν τόπῳ ἁγίῳ)'[51] But for Mark the event was imminent in a temple still standing in Jerusalem in A.D. 66. Where the sacrilege would take place he could not specify: it would simply be 'standing where it ought not'.[52]

The Markan community at Rome may have received news of Gessius Florus' crucifixions, or of the siege of Vespasian and Titus, and they connected these events with those of their own persecution by Nero. That the Roman community should have connected its own persecution with these events, and seen them in such an apocalyptic context, should come as no surprise when we consider that the Jewish rebels also thought in such terms.

Josephus refers disparagingly, at the time when he had been reconciled to Rome, to the activity of Jewish 'false prophets (ψευδοπροφῆται)' in the course of the rebellion against Rome, just as Mark's apocalypse refers to 'false christs and false prophets (ψευδοπροφῆται)' who will 'perform signs and wonders in order to lead into error if it is possible the elect'.[53] Josephus lists some of the actions of such false prophets in his description of the siege of Jerusalem.

One false prophet had proclaimed during Jerusalem's final destruction by fire God's command to go up into the one remaining portico of the outer Temple Court in order to receive 'miraculous signs (σημεῖα) of their deliverance (τῆς σωτηρίας)'. Thus a crowd of 6,000, including poor women and children, were engulfed in the spreading flames.[54] Numerous such prophets were enlisted by the rebel leaders.

Josephus himself nevertheless believes in 'wonders (τέρατα)', which he claimed that the false prophets had misinterpreted. A star resembling a sword had, before the siege, stood over the city and also a comet, continuing for a year.[55] Earlier, in March–April (A.D. 70), during the festival of unleavened bread, 'at the ninth hour of the night, so brilliant a light shone round the altar and the sanctuary that it seemed to be pure daylight'.[56] A cow on this occasion

51. Mt. 24:15.
52. Mk 13: 14.
53. Mk 13:22.
54. Josephus, *BJ*, 6.285.
55. Josephus, *BJ*, 6.289.
56. Josephus, *BJ*, 6.290.

brought for sacrifice gave birth to a lamb.[57] The massive bronze eastern gate of the inner court of the Temple opened of its own accord in the sixth hour of the night.[58]

On 21st May before sunset 'chariots were seen in the air and armed battalions hurtling through the clouds and encompassing the cities', to which Tacitus also adds his witness as to some of Josephus' other examples.[59] At Pentecost the priests heard at night from the inner court of the temple, 'first a commotion and a din, and after that a collective voice: "we are departing hence"'.[60] But there was also an apocalyptic framework into which these portents could be fitted.

Four years previously at the outbreak of the rebellion (A.D. 66), during the feast of Tabernacles, a certain Jesus son of Ananias, suddenly began crying 'Woe to Jerusalem', and then repeatedly:

> A voice from the east, a voice from the west, a voice from the four winds, a voice against Jerusalem and the sanctuary, a voice against the bridegroom and bride, a voice against all the people.[61]

At one point he was to add: 'and to the temple' with fatal consequences.[62]

Josephus also claims that his fellow countrymen were also deceived by 'an ambiguous oracle (χρησμὸς ἀμφίβολος)', found in their sacred writings, that at that time someone from their country would rule the world.[63] His 'oracle' is even more 'ambiguous' when one compares it, as we shall see, with clearly equivalent parallels in Tacitus and Suetonius. Scholars usually plump for the 'oracle' to be that of Balaam in Numbers (24:17–19). Here:

> A star shall arise out of Jacob, and a man shall arise out of Israel, and he will shatter the rulers of Moab and he will plunder all the sons of Seth . . .

But the claim here is not that the 'star' will 'rule the world' but simply will be successful over 'Israel's' and 'Jacob's' enemies, not 'Judah's' and therefore of the land of Judea whence Josephus' ruler is to come.

Although this passage is sometimes referred to in English as 'Balaam's oracle' (and therefore χρησμός), this word is not used in the Septuagint of any prophetic oracle. Josephus attacked the Zealots for scoffing at 'the oracles (χρησμοί) of the prophets'. But the 'oracles' to which he refers here are those prophesying the burning of the Temple, which Josephus invariably finds in

---

57. Josephus, *BJ*, 6.292.
58. Josephus, *BJ*, 6.293, cf. Tacitus, *Hist.*, 5.13.
59. Josephus, *BJ*, 6.298-299, cf. Tacitus, *Hist.*, 5.13: 'eo ipso tempore fore ut ualesceret Oriens, profectique Iudaea rerum potirentur'.
60. Josephus, *BJ*, 6.299-300, cf. Tacitus, *Hist.*, 5.13.
61. Josephus, *BJ*, 6.301.
62. Josephus, *BJ*, 6.309.
63. Josephus, *BJ*, 6.312.

Daniel.[64] There is again a reference to 'the records of the old prophets and the oracle (χρησμός) that threatens this long suffering city' in Josephus' speech to John on Titus' behalf urging the surrender of Jerusalem before the final destruction of the Temple and its cultus.[65] A rough allusion has been found here to a Sibylline oracle contemporaneous with Josephus (A.D. 80).[66] But as we shall now see, Josephus associates the destruction of the second temple with the destruction of the first under Nebuchadnessar, and associates the prophecy of Daniel with the destruction of both. In consequence, we shall find the basis for Josephus' prophecy regarding Vespasian in this source.

Both Josephus and Tacitus are agreed, as we shall see, that the real object of that prophecy would be Vespasian, who as king on Judaea's soil would reign over the Roman Empire. Let us now see how many of the features of the Markan apocalypse are also reflected in Josephus' account, whose focus is also upon Daniel's apocalyptic visions in explication of the scenes witnessed in the events of Judaea from A.D. 66 onwards.

With regard to Mark's reference to the 'desecrating sacrilege (βδέλυγμα τῆς ἐρημώσεως)', yet but shortly to take place, we have Josephus' statement, after the event, connecting Antiochus' destruction of the Temple with that of Titus: 'It came about that the desolation of the temple took place (ἐρήμωσιν τοῦ ναοῦ) according to the prophecy of Daniel.'[67] As Josephus also had commented, after referring to Antiochus:

> In the same manner Daniel also wrote about the empire of the Romans and that Jerusalem would be taken by them and the temple laid waste (ἐρημωθήσεται).[68]

Both Mark and Josephus are citing Daniel's account of Antiochus' desecration described as follows:

> . . . he will put an end to sacrifice and drink offering and there shall be upon the holy place desecrating sacrileges (βδέλυγμα τῶν ἐρημώσεων) until the end, and an end will be made to the desecration (τὴν ἐρήμωσιν).[69]

Daniel's book is also to end with a reference to 'the desecrating sacrilege (τὸ βδέλυγμα τῆς ἐρημώσεως)' as part of the 'fulfilment of the times.[70]

Josephus therefore shares with the Markan apocalypse a belief in Daniel's visions as a key to interpreting the Fall of Jerusalem (A.D. 70), in addition to the portentous signs 'in the heavens' that witness the supernatural character of

64. Josephus, *BJ*, 4.386-388.
65. Josephus, *BJ*, 6.109.
66. *Orac. Sibyl.*, 4.115.
67. Josephus, *Antiqu.*, 12.322.
68. Josephus, *Antiqu.*, 10.276.
69. Dan. 9:27.
70. Dan. 12:11.

what is taking place. There are the false prophets (ψευδοπροφῆται), per-forming σημεῖα and τέρατα in a situation of fear and hopelessness. There are also 'signs and wonders' in the heavens as the stars fall and sun and moon withdraw their light. But Josephus will not connect the 'desecration (ἐρημώ σις)' of Jerusalem with a 'sacrilege (βδέλυγμα)', not because he does not share Mark's Danielic focus, but because to go that far would not serve his apologetic purpose in making Daniel's final kingdom the victory of Vespasian and the Roman Empire, whose ἐρημώσις could never therefore have been a βδέλυγμα.

Thus in the picture that he gives us of Jerusalem under siege, we have many of the features of what the Markan apocalypse tells the Christians at Rome. But for Mark it is the Son of Man who comes 'with power and great glory' to deliver the elect from their persecuting trial, and to bring 'the kingdom of God having come with power'.[71] That figure, 'one like unto a Son of Man', comes in Daniel as the arguably angelic representative of the 'kingdom of the saints of the Most High' in succession to four beasts representing four succeeding empires. It will be interesting to ask if this too formed part of the Judaean view of the events of A.D. 70 in the Christian perspective in which Nero's persecution appears.

2.4 *Josephus on the Universal Kingdom and Its Ruler in the Light of Daniel*

Josephus, as we have said, mentions 'someone' who should 'rule the world' in 'an ambiguous oracle' in the Old Testament that he wishes to apply to Vespasian.[72] These words of themselves are rather imprecise, and seem to conceal rather than reveal the lack of uniformity in Jewish religion, before the inevitable and later reaction to Christian claims on that score, over the expectation of an indi-vidual Messiah, let alone any specific characteristics that the Messiah would possess. Indeed one form of this common tradition, shared by Josephus with Tacitus and Suetonius, who were unlikely to have read him directly, did not mention an individual but several individuals.

Sharing Josephus' by now Roman view that the Jews had incorrectly inter-preted unfavourable omens as favourable, Tacitus states:

> There was an unshakable conviction with the majority that was contained in the ancient writings of their priests that it would take place at that time that the East would grow strong and that men would starting from Judaea possess the world. This ambiguous allusion had predicted Vespasian and Titus . . .[73]

It may be therefore that Josephus only imposed an individual on this common tradition in order to sharpen the interpretation that it was Vespasian, proclaimed

---

71. Mk 13:26, cf. 14:62 and 9:1.
72. See above, footnote 54 and associated text.
73. Tacitus, *Hist.*, 13.

emperor on Jewish soil, but we shall show grounds for doubting such an infer-
ence as the sole grounds for the Josephan form of this claim. Suetonius
preserves Tacitus' form of the story when he speaks of '*men* starting from the
East . . .'.[74] Where in the Old Testament, we shall need to ask, is this ambiguity
between an individual figure and a group of individuals represented?

Can the statement both of Josephus and Tacitus and Suetonius be specifically
tied to Daniel's vision of 'one like unto a Son of Man', whose 'kingdom is an
everlasting kingdom' and 'the kingdom of the saints of the Most High' that this
figure seems to represent?[75] How close, in other words, are the Judaean expectations, recorded in both Josephus, Suetonius and Tacitus, directed to a common
tradition that illuminates the events of A.D. 70 in which Mark shares? We shall
argue that Josephus reflects, with the source also of Suetonius and Tacitus, a
particular focus upon the visions of Daniel in Jewish claims that are also
reflected in the Markan apocalypse.

The Old Testament originally had no uniform description of a uniquely
Anointed One or 'Messiah', since the term is used of any holder of sanctified
office such as priests and kings.[76] Isaiah prophesies that 'a king will reign in
righteousness' with reference to good governance of Israel, and where 'a child
has been born for us' with 'authority . . . on his shoulders' it is for the 'throne
of David and his kingdom' not for a universal empire over the whole world.[77]
Likewise in other Old Testament passages, particularly in Micah and Jeremiah,
the hope is for an ideal king who will gather, restore and protect Israel and
Judah in their own land.[78] His reputation may spread to the ends of the earth so
that kings shall come to Jerusalem and pay him homage and reverence Israel's
God. But he will not reign over all the earth.[79] The Psalms of Solomon, on
which Simon son of Gioras (the Zealot) had perhaps built his case for his
revolt in A.D. 68,[80] looked for the true king of David's line who would 'purge
Jerusalem from the nations that trample her down in destruction', and would
place (some) nations under his yoke, but would not 'starting from Judaea
possess the world'. Rather 'nations shall come from the ends of the earth to see
his glory'.[81]

Unlike such 'Messianic' passages, Josephus' figure, who shall reign over the
earth, and the plural and collective group of Tacitus and Suetonius, represent a
universal empire that actually replaces a present one. Nor can, with exception

74. Suetonius, *Vesp.*, 4.5: 'Iudaea profecti rerum potirentur'.
75. Dan. 7:13, cf. v. 22.
76. For a full discussion, see M. de Jonge, 'Messiah', art. in *Anchor Bible Dictionary*, IV.777 ff.
77. Isa.9:5-7; 11; 32:1-8.
78. Ep. Jer. 23:1-4; Mic. 5:1-3.
79. Isa. 2:3-4.
80. Josephus, *BJ*, 4.503-565.
81. *Pss. Sol.* 17.4, 23, 26-27, 30, translated and discussed in K. Atkinson, *I Cried to the Lord:
A Study in the Psalms of Solomon's Historical Background and Social Setting* (*Suppl. JnStJud*, 84;
Leiden: Brill, 2004), p. 129.

of the vision of 'one like unto a Son of Man', any other passage in Daniel indicate an actual person or persons who shall take over a sovereignty over all the world formerly possessed by others. Daniel, it is true, does use the term 'Anointed' (Messiah or χρίστος) who will come, but he means simply an anointed king. Furthermore, this Messiah or anointed king will not rule over a universal world empire that replaces those before it. Rather under him Jerusalem is rebuilt, but then 'his anointing (χρίσμα) will be removed and a kingdom of pagans will destroy the city and the holy place along with the Anointed (μετὰ τοῦ χριστοῦ)', following which calamities strike and the desolating sacrilege takes place.[82] We cannot therefore identify Josephus' single universal ruler or the 'certain persons' of Tacitus and Suetonius with this particular Danielic figure.

Universal empires are the subject of two visions in Daniel to which Josephus makes guarded and very reserved reference, and one that his reserve leads him to omit. We shall find the real reference of Josephus' claim in the very vision that he purposely omits. As Horbury has pointed out, whatever the original meaning of Daniel regarding the figure of 'one like unto a Son of Man', Josephus' Jewish contemporaries certainly regarded this figure as Messianic.[83] But let us consider the candidacy of the two explicitly Danielic references for Josephus' 'ambiguous oracle'.

The first is Josephus' detailed description of Nebuchadnezzar's dream of a statue with a golden head, 'its chest and arm of silver, its middle and thighs of bronze, its legs of iron, its feet partly of iron and partly of clay'. A stone struck and shattered the statue. Each of the four metals, gold, silver, iron, and bronze referred to four kings with four empires, each in succession to one another.[84] Originally the meaning of the text was that God would replace this succession of empires universal throughout the world with his own, represented by the stone: 'The God of heaven shall set up a kingdom that shall never be destroyed, nor shall this kingdom be left to another people.'[85] But Josephus refuses to give any meaning to the 'stone', quitting as it were while he is ahead with his Flavian readers and patrons.[86] His conclusion is that it is the last kingdom that is the one that 'will have dominion forever through its nature of iron'.[87] Thus the last, Roman empire is to be the universal and eternal one. In so expounding Daniel's vision, Josephus was clearly suppressing the views of his fellow

---

82. Dan. (LXX) 9:25-27.
83. W. Horbury, 'Messianic Associations of the "Son of Man"', *JTS*, 36.1 (1985), pp. 34-55; W. Horbury, *Jewish Messianism and the Cult of Christ* (London: SCM, 1998), pp. 33-34; pp. 85-86.
84. Josephus, *Antiqu.*, 10.205-208.
85. Dan. 2:36-45.
86. Josephus, *Antiqu.*, 10.210.
87. Josephus, *Antiqu.*, 10.208-209: 'I have not thought it proper to relate this. If anyone wants to know the future more closely, he must read Daniel for himself.'

countrymen in A.D. 68. But Josephus once again can see the Roman empire in this passage but no individual ruler.

The second is the vision at Susa of the ram with many horns signifying 'the kingdoms of the Medes and the Persians, and the goat with four horns indicating Alexander and the kings that were his successors (Seleucids and Ptolemies) and finally Antiochus, who anticipated the Roman desecration of Jerusalem, as we have seen. But there is no ruler or rulers as such mentioned. [88]

Thus we come to Daniel's sole mention of a human-like figure who shall establish an everlasting kingdom which Josephus knows but dare not mention, namely the vision of Daniel 7. Josephus' reference is surely to the vision that Daniel does not refer to directly, namely that of the three beasts and a monster, where the everlasting dominion is given to 'one like a Son of Man'. It is here alone that we have a universal empire actually replacing its predecessors, with reference to an actual person or persons effecting this. It is here and here alone that we can read of either an individual or of individuals collectively who 'starting from Judaea possess the world'.

Josephus' actual words do not help us to connect his claim very closely with this vision when he says: 'at that time from their country someone will rule the world (τις ἄρξει τῆς οἰκουμένης)'. But if we look at both Tacitus' and Suetonius' Latin we find a phrase which shows considerable equivalence to the vision of Daniel 7. Both cite almost identically the phrase *Iudaea profecti rerum potirentur*.[89] If we compare this phrase with the LXX version of the meaning of the rule of the 'one like unto a Son of Man' we read:

> And the holy ones of the Most High will receive the kingdom (καὶ παραλήψονται τὴν βασιλείαν ἅγιοι ὑψίστου) and they will have mastery over the kingdom forever (καὶ καθέξουσι τὴν βασιλείαν ἕως τοῦ αἰῶνος).[90]

Κατεχειν (καθέξουσι) τὴν βασιλείαν is the precise equivalent of Tacitus' and Suetonius' *rerum potiri* (*potirentur*). The oracle that they cite is therefore grounded in Daniel 7 and therefore shares a similar cultural ambience also with Mark 13, and the apocalyptic expectations to which Josephus testifies.

Those Jews who continued Daniel's apocalyptic hope, even though the four original kingdoms to which he had referred had not been superseded by any eternal kingdom, could well believe in A.D. 68–70 that this was now to take place, and that the last of the four kingdoms had been in fact Rome and not Macedon as was the original intention of the author of Daniel. But after Rome, despite Josephus' desire to deny his co-religionists that hope, men 'starting

---

88. Josephus, *Antiqu.*, 10.274–276, see also above, footnote 57 and associated text.
89. Suetonius, *Vesp.*, 4.5, cf. Tacitus, *Hist.*, 5.13: 'eo ipso tempore fore ut ualesceret Oriens, profectique Iudaea rerum potirentur'.
90. Dan. 7:18.

from Judaea' would, under God's hand, 'possess the world'. Or would it be a single man who accomplished this or a divine figure?

It is this particular vision of Daniel that is clearly part of the background to Mark 13 in its reference to the Son of Man coming at the end of time. In Daniel four beasts arise from the sea, one 'like a lion' but with eagles' wings, a second 'like' a bear, the third a leopard, but the fourth monstrous and terrible, 'with iron teeth'.[91] The writer makes it clear that these wild beasts and a monster refer to successive earthly kingdoms.[92] Originally the little horn that sprang from the last monster represented Antiochus IV Epiphanes, whose smaller, Hellenistic kingdom had sprung from the Macedon of Alexander the Great, the fourth empire. But in the wake of the non-fulfilment of the future anticipated, the text was invariably reinterpreted with the last empire being that of Rome.

In the vision, what replaces the wild beasts and monster arising from the sea is the coming of a figure described as the 'Ancient of Days', seated on a throne with wheels of fire, streaming fire before him with thousands of the heavenly host. 'The court sat in judgement and the books were opened'. In consequence:

> The beast was put to death and its body destroyed and delivered to be burned with fire. As for the rest of the beasts, their dominion was taken away but their lives were prolonged for a season and for a time.[93]

Thus the anticipated destruction of Rome (instead of Antiochus) would not lead immediately to the destruction of the remaining world empires. But the Jews could hope that very soon these would go the same way.

The writer continues that what succeeds the end of Rome (instead of Antiochus) will soon be what the vision symbolizes next:

> I saw one like a Son of Man, coming with the clouds of heaven. And he came to the Ancient One and was presented before him. To him was given dominion and glory and kingship that all peoples, nations and languages should serve him. His dominion is an everlasting dominion that shall not pass away and his kingship is one that shall never be destroyed.[94]

I translated the Aramaic term as 'Son of Man' in this passage, though this can be an idiomatic expression for 'human being'. If that is the case, as seems plausible, its reference appears at first sight to be clear. The four preceding empires and what sprung from the last were described symbolically as 'like' animals and a monster: these were collective ciphers representing nations as

---

91. Dan. 7:2-8.
92. Dan. 7:23-27.
93. Dan. 7:9-12.
94. Dan. 7:13-14.

collectivities. Thus the 'one like a human being (or son of man)' is also a symbol of a collectivity, namely Israel. As Daniel explains the symbolic details of his vision, after the end of Rome's (instead of Antiochus') kingdom by divine judgement:

> The kingship and dominion and the greatness of the kingdoms under the whole heaven shall be given to the saints of the Most High: their kingdom shall be an everlasting kingdom, and all dominions shall serve and obey them.[95]

If we compare Josephus's actual text with the LXX version, his wording does not help to establish any equivalence to Daniel's language when translated into Greek. It is the account that Suetonius and Tacitus follow that seems to have got this Jewish text right: it is not an individual but a group of individuals, when 'the East would grow strong', who collectively would 'starting from Judaea possess the world'.[96]

Why then should Josephus write instead that this prophecy referred to an individual, that 'someone from their country would rule the world'?[97] Why indeed should the Markan apocalypse see the Son of Man as an individual figure 'coming on clouds with great power and glory' sending his angels to gather the elect from a nature collapsing into its ruinous end?

I cannot enter many of the details of the debate regarding whether the Jesus of history used this as his personal title, and whether therefore Jesus' declaration to the High Priest that he was this figure led to his crucifixion on the charge of blasphemy.[98] Whether or not this were so, Mark's apocalypse does not come from a discourse heard from the lips of the Jesus of history on the Mount of Olives. Mark records first a bald statement predicting the dismantling of the temple stone by stone that could hardly be fulfilled by its destruction by fire.[99] But then he inserts an apocalyptic text that clearly Jesus did not speak so that it was to be heard. Rather the text of his apocalypse was to be read: it is 'the reader' who is invited to understand.[100] Mark has inserted this written text as if it had been in Jesus' original words.

Mark's apocalypse, as a free-standing text composed by someone else, does not introduce Jesus as identical with the individual that it calls 'the Son of Man': it could therefore be the kind of Jewish apocalypse based upon the exegesis of Jewish Scripture to which Josephus bears witness. If Mark therefore derived his general attribution of the term Son of Man from that source, it was from a Jewish source whose central figure Josephus confirms against Tacitus and Suetonius to be an individual figure: the title 'Son of Man' as an individual is not therefore of purely Christian, post-resurrection derivation. If it is claimed

95. Dan. 7:27.
96. See above, footnote 74 and associated text.
97. See above, footnote 72 and associated text.
98. Mk 14:62.
99. Mk 13:1-2.
100. Mk 13:14.

that 'Q' before Mark uses ambiguously 'Son of Man' of Jesus as an apocalyptic figure, it might be that 'Q' also was dependent upon such a Jewish exegesis of Daniel's text. If conversely the Jesus of history used this term of himself, then clearly he was not the only Jew to interpret Daniel's figure as an individual. It may also of course be the case that Mark found the originally Jewish apocalypse attractive precisely because the Jesus of history had also in parallel interpreted the Danielic figure as an individual, as did 1 Enoch, whether earlier or later.

Josephus, as well as Mark and his apocalyptic source, may constitute good evidence that Daniel's Son of Man never was interpreted purely as a symbol (a human being rather than a beast or monster), for the collective 'kingdom of the saints of the Most High'. It is important in any case to note that Daniel sees angelic beings as more than literary symbols for nations and kingdoms and rather as individual heavenly beings that represent their collective essences.[101] The conflict between nations mirrors the conflict between the heavenly beings who represent them, as when the archangel Michael, 'protector of your people' (Israel)[102] acts against the angelic 'prince of the kingdom of Persia' as well as that of Greece.[103]

Thus, when Daniel speaks of the 'holy ones of the Most High (ἅγιοι ὑψί στου)', he is using an expression that usually refers to angelic beings (ἅγιοι), and therefore to an angelic court and not to an earthly kingdom.[104] And among Josephus' contemporaries in A.D. 68 must be reckoned also the community at Qumran, whose monastery was to be demolished and razed to the ground in A.D. 70 along with Jerusalem. The War Scroll describes God as raising up 'amongst the angels the authority of Michael and the dominion of Israel amongst all flesh', leading an army of both angels and men. More close to the image of 'one like unto a Son of Man', the Melchizedek scroll describes him as the 'heavenly man': 'the heavenly man stands in the congregation of God, amongst the heavenly ones he judges'.[105] Furthermore, as Horbury has pointed out: 'The angelic deliverers, therefore, can be associated with the line of Israelite rulers which is central to messianic expectation.'[106]

Thus we find that Josephus and Mark's apocalypse share a similar perspective from a source, also known to Suetonius and Tacitus, about the supersession of the Roman empire by a person or persons from the East, a perspective in terms of which there is no contradiction involved between a heavenly individual figure representing mystically collective institutions such as nations on earth. Thus Suetonius and Tacitus can think of a group of individuals, in a description

101.   For a fuller discussion, see J. J. Collins, *The Apocalyptic Vision of the Book of Daniel* (Harvard Semitic monographs 16; Missoula, Mont.: Harvard Semitic Museum, 1977), pp. 115–17; Horbury, *Jewish Messianism*, pp. 33–34.

102.   Dan. 12:1.

103.   Dan. 10:13 and 20.

104.   Dan. 4:11, 20, cf. e.g. Ps. 89:6-7

105.   1QM 17.7-8; 11QMelch. 13 col.2, see also Collins, *Apocalyptic Vision*, p. 145.

106.   Horbury, *Jewish Messianism*, p. 86.

closer to Daniel's text ('the kingdom of the saints of the Most High'), but Josephus of a single person. We can further trace the text to which they specifically appeal, as does Mark, to Daniel, and to an exegesis of Daniel that predicts imminently future events. To Christian exegetes of that text the figure of the Son of Man will be Christ returning, but to Jewish ones a king in David's line but with angelic features as the heavenly merges with the earthly in the moment of apocalyptic vision. Before and even after the illegal execution of James the Just such a perspective could be shared between Jewish Christians and their counterparts in a Judaeism with a variety of synagogues that lacked the later uniformity of its Rabbinic form.

Mark's community in Rome originated from such a Judaean base, as Tacitus bears witness: the acts and sayings of Jesus recorded witness clearly to such a Palestinian base. But we must now attempt to describe more fully their relation at Rome to their origins as they reflected with horror both upon Nero's persecution that they were suffering, and the reports and rumours that were coming to them of a Jerusalem under siege.

2.5 *Mark's Community, the Twelve, and Its Apocalyptic Traditions*

Writing around A.D. 68, the author of Mark's Gospel represents a community that, at the height of Nero's persecution, fell back upon the traditions of Judaean Christianity with which it reidentified itself. The persecution of Nero was part of a pattern of events unfolding in the East in which Christ would return as Son of Man and deliverer of the New Israel, the 'elect' of the Markan apocalypse, not simply from their dispersal in regions of Judaea, but from the 'four winds' including Rome where they themselves were located. Such a view involved some backtracking for a community that had migrated originally from the East and from Judaea, albeit with their original, fragmentary accounts of the words and acts of Jesus, either written or oral, from the congregations there from which they hailed.

Some elements in the traditions that they had brought had undergone some modifications in the light of their interaction with non-Jewish culture. The authority of one form of Jewish Christianity presided over, not by the twelve apostles, but by James and the Lord's brothers had been rejected by them. James and his group they considered their equals under Christ, but not in any position of authority. The claim of Mark's community was that when his mother, brothers and sisters had sought access to him while teaching a crowd, Jesus had replied:

> 'Who are my mother and my brothers'. And looking at those who sat around him he said, 'Here are my mother and my brothers! Whoever does the will of God is my brother and sister and mother'.[107]

---

107.   Mk 3:31-34.

It is not my intention necessarily to deny that these might have been the words of Jesus, but to point to, as a principle of redaction criticism, the reason why Mark's community remembered and recorded them.

They did so not out of any antiquarian interest that did not exist until the European Renaissance, but because they embodied something important to the continuing life of Mark's community. The recording of this incident indicates a rejection by Mark's community now in Rome of the status that other Christian communities in Judaea continued to give to the Lord's brethren as particular leaders of the Christian community.[108] It is to be noted that Mark does not express the hostility of the Fourth Gospel to James' community when it makes the chilling observation 'neither did his brethren believe in him'.[109]

At one point, in engagement no doubt with their Roman, pagan mission, one remembered *logion* had led them to claim that by his words Jesus had 'cleansed all food' so that Jewish food laws no longer needed to be maintained. The *logion* read:

> The Pharisees and the scribes . . . asked him: 'Why do your disciples not conduct themselves in accordance with the tradition of the elders, but eat bread with unwashed hands? He replied to them [the disciples]: '. . . Do you not grasp that everything that enters from without into a person cannot defile him because it isn't entering into his heart but into his stomach and is excreted into the drain'.[110]

Matthew includes this passage, but not with the extensive explanation afforded by Mark of Jewish eating rituals.[111] He also omits Mark's telling addition: '[Thus he said] cleansing all food.'[112] If Mark's community had thus rejected the authority of James and his group solely to lead the Christian community, they clearly acknowledge the authority of another, Judaean group, that of the Twelve (apostles). Thus unlike the Christian Jewish group under the authority of James and 'the Lord's brethren', the Markan, Roman community had not required pagan converts to adhere to Jewish food laws, though it had felt the need to give a lengthy explanation of ritual washing of hands and their abrogation by Jesus.

That the 'Lord's brethren' were a group possessing authority because they were in the blood line of Jesus is recorded in a fragment from Julius Africanus, an early third century chronographer, who discusses what he claims is a custom characteristic of Hebrew families who traced their families to patriarchs or distinguished proselytes.[113] Most of these genealogies had been destroyed by Herod the Great out of jealousy but:

> Now a few of those concerned about this, had in their possession private enrolled lists having remembered the names by themselves or otherwise from copies. These gloried

108. Acts 1:14; 21:7; Gal.1:18–2:14.
109. Jn 7:5.
110. Mk 7:5 and 18-19.
111. Mt. 15:1-20. Luke omits these words altogether.
112. Mk 7:19.
113. Julius Africanus, *apud* Eusebius, *H.E.*, I.8.12–13.

in the preservation of the memory of their noble descent. Among these were the aforesaid so called 'Lord's brethren (δεσπόσυνοι)' on account of their connection to the Saviour's kindred, and from the Judaean villages of Nazareth and Cochaba they wandered the rest of the land, expounding, as far as they reached, the preceding genealogy and from the Book of Days.[114]

It is moreover clear from the New Testament canon itself of the authority over certain communities of the 'Lord's brethren', since the pseudonymous epistles of James and Jude have been preserved. The final canon, surreptitiously including various authority groups in the early church within its catholic whole, thus made sure that the traditions of groups superintended by 'the Lord's brethren' were included with the Apostles (Peter and (putatively) John), as well as St Paul who had claimed a disputed apostolicity. Certainly a tradition preserved in the third century Pseudo Clementine *Homilies* regard James as 'bishop of bishops, who presides over the Holy Church of the Hebrews, as all churches well founded everywhere by God's providence', whose author imagines Clement so addressing him in a letter written at Peter's instruction. After Peter's death, Clement must send his written declaration to James of his consecration as Roman bishop at Peter's hands.[115]

James' group had subscribed to the apocalyptic expectation of Christ's return as their contribution to the general Jewish expectation of deliverance from the occupying Roman power. Indeed we have a famous fragment from Hegesippus, a second century writer who records:

> Now there still survived of the family of the Lord grandsons of Jude, who was said to have been his (Jesus') brother according to the flesh, and they were delated as being of the family of David. These the prosecutor led before Domitian Caesar, for, like Herod, he was afraid of Christ's *parousia*, just as Herod had been. He asked them if they were of the house of David and they confessed. Then he questioned them about the extent of their possessions or the extent of funds under their control.[116]

Having given him an account of their meagre possessions:

> They then showed him their hands as evidence of their self-employment, showing that they were physically hardened and the skin tough on their very hands from continuous hard labour. Questioned about the Messiah and the nature of his kingdom and where and when it was destined to appear, they explained that it was neither of this world nor earthly but it would be heavenly and angelic, that it would exist at the end of the age whenever he would come and judge the living and the dead and he would render to each person according to his deeds.[117]

---

114. Julius Africanus, *apud* Eusebius, *H.E.*, I.7.13–14.
115. Pseudo Clement, *Homilies*, Clement: *Ep. Ad Iacob.*, Praef.
116. Hegesippus *apud* Eusebius, *H.E*, III.20.1–2.
117. Hegesippus *apud* Eusebius, *H.E.*, III.20.3–4.

Domitian's retort was not that of Ananus to James the Just. He dismissed the 'Lord's brethren' with contempt.[118]

This description can hardly be ranked as history: it is apologetic. But what gives the apology its point is the clear association, that the writer wishes to avoid, between the Lord's brethren as authority figures in a community making claims about a Davidic kingdom over which, as sharing with Jesus a Davidic blood line, they would rule. Though the community of Mark may dissociate itself from the 'Lord's brethren' as supreme leaders of the Church in Jerusalem or at Rome, nevertheless that community in the Markan apocalypse hardly dissented from apocalyptic expectations associated with the figure of the Son of Man.

What figures of authority, then, did the Markan community respect in their early Christian heritage in Judaea? Those in authority in the original community according to Mark were the twelve which other writers, notably Luke, calls 'apostles' as their special title:

> And he went up to the mountain and summoned whom he willed to him and they came away to him. And he made twelve of them with the purpose of their being with him and for sending them (ἵνα ἀποστέλῃ) to preach, and to have authority to cast out the daemons and he made them 'the Twelve'.[119]

Mark then proceeds to give them their twelve names, beginning with the name 'Peter' given to Simon.[120] It is this inner group to whom Jesus gives instruction in private apart from the crowds regarding 'the mystery of the kingdom of God'.[121] It is further this group to whom Jesus, according to Mark, entrusts the 'messianic secret' that the 'Son of Man must suffer before he enters his glory', and that his glory will be seen as the returning Son of Man within their lifetime when they see 'the kingdom of God having come with power'.[122] It was to the inner circle of the Twelve, Peter, James (apostle and not brother), and John that Mark describes his apocalypse as having been addressed by Jesus after he had predicted the destruction of Jerusalem to his disciples generally.

Thus though Mark's Roman community may have rejected the authority of James and the Lord's brethren, they did not reject the apocalyptic expectations of that group. Theirs may have been a more supernatural expectation of Jesus as Son of Man rather than Jesus coming as a David ruler, although Horbury has pointed out that the two were associated in literature contemporary with the gospels.[123] Mark's Roman community may have believed in Jesus as

118. Hegesippus *apud* Eusebius, *H.E.*, III.20.5.
119. Mk 3:13-16.
120. Mk 3:16.
121. Mk 4:10-12.
122. Mk 8:38; 9:1, 9, 31-37.
123. W. Horbury, *Herodian Judaism and New Testament Study* (WUNT, 193; Tübingen: Mohr Siebeck, 2006), pp. 6–7. See also Horbury, *Jewish Messianism*, pp. 86–93.

abrogating Mosaic ritual and food laws when he 'cleansed all food' in its gentile mission symbolized at the cross by the pagan centurion who cried 'surely this man was a son of God'.[124] But that community nevertheless held fast to its apocalyptic traditions about Jesus. It was perhaps inevitable that it should fall back upon those traditions when a persecution by the pagan Roman power in Rome itself was combined with an Eastern campaign set to destroy the Jerusalem temple itself.

Those apocalyptic traditions were, however, associated with the ministry of the Twelve, and with Peter, James (the deceased apostle), and John rather than with James the Lord's brother and his family. Mark indeed will call the Twelve 'apostles' on their return from a mission on which Jesus has sent them:

> And the apostles gathered together with Jesus and proclaimed to him everything that they had done and taught.[125]

But Mark may be using 'apostle (ἀπόστολος)' here, not as a title but simply as a description of them as missionaries 'sent out (ἀποστελλειν)' by Jesus.

Though Luke tries to confine these terms to the Twelve, par excellence, he also witnesses to another use of the term in which an apostle is, as in the *Didache*, a late first century document, a wandering missionary: Barnabas and Paul, though not members of the Twelve, are called 'apostles' after their 'sending out' by the church of Antioch on the first missionary journey. Furthermore in the late first century *Didache* 'apostle' is also used in the sense of 'travelling missionary'.[126] 'Apostle' is therefore used in the early church in a wider sense than that of Luke who tries to confine the term to the Twelve as witnesses to Christ's life, death and resurrection.[127] Indeed Paul claims both himself and James the Lord's brother as witnesses to the resurrection, even though neither of them are members of the Twelve, and also includes 'over five hundred brothers', including 'all the apostles' other than the Twelve also as witnesses of this event.[128]

We are witnessing in the earliest documents tensions between various groups claiming various persons as authorities in the earliest Christian communities. Even Luke, who has clearly not been successful in imposing his view of apostleship confined to the Twelve on the material that he has incorporated into his account, has nevertheless to include the Lord's brethren when he says of the apostles after the Ascension in the Upper Room:

> These all continued steadfastly of one accord in prayer with the women and Mary the mother of Jesus and with his brothers.[129]

124. Mk 15:39.
125. Mk 6:30.
126. Acts 14:4; Rom. 16:7; *Did.*, 11–12.
127. Lk 6:12; 9:10; 17:5; 22:14; 24:10; Acts 1:2, 16-26; 2:37, 42-43, etc.
128. 1 Cor. 15:3-8, cf. 2 Cor. 1:1, etc.
129. Acts 1:14.

And Paul in his genuine letters shows a constant strain in his relations with those whom he claims were 'apostles before me'.[130]

Mark reveals his community as favouring the view that the Twelve were the central authority figures of the original Judaean community from which they had come as offshoots to Rome. He, as we have seen, credits them with the knowledge imparted to them, and especially to Peter, James, and John with whom Paul had clashed, of the messianic secret and of the kingdom of God and the Son of Man, and indeed of the Markan apocalypse. There was in his tradition, however, more material about the apocalyptic significance of Twelve that was to surface in what Matthew and Luke from their sources have combined with his account. If this material was known to him and his community as seems likely, then it was not its apocalyptic character that led him to ignore it but its exclusively Jewish emphasis on the events of the end-time and the implicit exclusion of gentiles in the divine plan.

Matthew calls the Twelve 'disciples' the 'apostles' when he sends them forth in the following words:

> And having summoned the twelve disciples (μαθηταί) he gave them authority over the unclean spirits . . . The names of the twelve apostles (ἀποστόλοι) are these . . . These the Twelve Jesus sent forth (ἀπέστειλεν) having exhorted them saying: 'Do not go into the way of the pagans, and do not enter into a city of the Samaritans; but go rather to the lost sheep of the house of Israel'.[131]

According to Matthew, persecution will follow them as they perform the miraculous signs of the coming kingdom of God that they will preach, and

> For truly I say to you will definitely not have completed the cities of Israel until the Son of Man shall come.[132]

The apocalyptic mission of the Twelve, according to this particular source of Matthew, did not extend beyond the borders of Israel.

Mark will not allow that 'his' Jesus could have only come as Son of Man to deliver a persecuted Jewish Christian community. Indeed Matthew will not allow this either, since he will insist that, despite the traditional material of this nature that he includes in his gospel, at the beginning the pagan Magi did the Christ child homage, in contrast to the Jewish king Herod, and that the risen Christ would command the eleven 'disciples' to 'baptise all nations'.[133] But his traditional material as it stood came from a Jewish Christian group in the early Church that believed that Jesus had commissioned a ministry to Israel alone,

130. Gal. 1:17-2:10; 1 Cor. 9:1 and 5.
131. Mt. 10:1, 2 and 5-6; cf. 11:1: 'When Jesus had finished instructing his twelve *disciples*', i.e. before they were 'sent forth' so that they could be described as '*apostles*'.
132. Mt. 10:23.
133. Mt. 2:1-2; 28:19-20.

which would result in his coming to them alone as Son of Man at the close of history.

At the Last Supper Mark (whom both Matthew and Luke follow) records Jesus' promise that

> I will certainly no longer drink of the fruit of the vine until that day when drink it with
> you new in the kingdom of God.[134]

For Mark, as we have seen, the 'kingdom of God come in power' is the people that the Son of Man is about to gather with his angels from the four winds. His reference clearly is to a heavenly banquet at which the gentiles will sit with the Son of Man in the kingdom of God, as in the Q logion, apparently unknown to him, attached to Matthew's version to the faith of the pagan centurion:

> I must certainly say, I have not found so great faith with anyone in Israel. And I tell you
> that many shall come from the east and west and will sit down with Abraham and Isaac
> and Jacob in the kingdom of heaven.[135]

Luke too preserves traditional material that clearly associates the Twelve and their significance with the final judgement of Israel.

Also there is a Q logion, not so supportive of the gentile mission, in which Jesus promises to his disciples, according to Luke's version after the institution of the Eucharist, that

> And you are those who have endured with me in my trials. And I confer upon you
> even as my father has conferred upon me a kingdom, that you shall eat and drink at
> my table in my kingdom, and you will be seated on thrones judging the twelve tribes
> of Israel.[136]

Matthew's variant, placed in a discussion with Peter following the *pericope* of the Rich Young Man, will also repay full quotation:

> I must certainly say that you who have followed me, in the Rebirth (παλινγενεσία),
> when the Son of Man will sit upon his throne of glory, you also will be seated upon
> twelve thrones, judging the twelve tribes of Israel.[137]

It matters not for our purpose what was the more original form of the Q logion, whether it is 'the Son of Man' in the 'rebirth' (Matthew) or 'me' and the 'kingdom of God' (Luke). What these variants of a common, Q tradition inform us is that, as part at least of early Christian tradition, if not about the Jesus of

134.   Mk 14:25.
135.   Mt. 8:11 cf. Lk. 13:28 placed in the context of the question about 'how few can be saved'.
136.   Lk. 22:28-30.
137.   Mt. 19:28.

history, the Twelve were associated with the Last Supper (Luke) as a foretaste of the heavenly banquet. Here the 'Son of Man' would sit upon a 'throne of glory' (Matthew), along with the Twelve also on thrones in judgement of Israel (Matthew and Luke).

Luke, as we shall see in detail later, in a major accommodation to the pagan Roman power, was to create the age of the Church and the Holy Spirit, divorced from what thus becomes the final, Second Advent of Christ in the indefinite future. But even he has been unable to suppress the original, apocalyptic significance of the institution of the Twelve. He records the apostles asking the risen Jesus if he would 'at this time restore the kingdom to Israel'. Jesus replies:

> It is not for you to know the times or the seasons that the Father has placed in his own authority, but you will receive power when the Holy Spirit has come upon you and you shall be my witnesses both in Jerusalem, and in Judaea and Samaria and unto the earth's end.[138]

They had been instructed by the risen Jesus 'not to depart from Jerusalem but to wait for the promise of the Father which you have heard from me'.[139]

What originally was this 'promise' to be? Peter, in the sermon attributed to him on the day of Pentecost, makes the apocalyptic significance of the realization of this promise quite clear. The presence of the Spirit with the Twelve was the arrival of the end of the age, as prophesied by Joel:

> And it shall be in the last days, says the Lord, that I will pour out my Spirit upon all flesh, and your sons and your daughters will prophesy . . . I will give prodigies (τέρατα) in the heaven above, and signs (σημεῖα) on the earth below, blood, fire, vapour of smoke. The sun will turn into darkness and the moon into blood before the coming of the great and spectacular day of the Lord. And everyone who will invoke the name of the Lord shall be saved.[140]

Thus the 'promise of the Father' and the 'coming of the Spirit' was far more like what was expected in the imminent future in Mark's apocalypse by the suffering Roman Christian community rather than an event in past time that had inaugurated the age of the Church, with Jerusalem 'trodden down by the pagans' but with no apocalyptic prodigies until 'the times of the pagans are fulfilled'.[141]

It is in this light that we can see why there originally needed to be twelve apostles who should 'not depart from Jerusalem'. It was here they must wait for where, on the Mount of Olives, Jesus 'will thus come in the manner in

---

138. Acts 1:7-8.
139. Acts 1:4.
140. Acts 2:17-21.
141. Lk. 21:24, cf. Mk 13:24-26, cf. above footnotes 43 and 45 and associated text.

which you have seen him going into heaven'.[142] It was here that they were to wait, in Jerusalem and its environs, for the last things to take place, as Mark's community believed that they were, as they heard the news from Judaea in A.D. 68. If one of their number had died, deservedly they might think in the case of Judas' suicide, a Mathias must replace him, not to pursue a mission to the pagans at the earth's end, as both Matthew and Luke, in revisionist mode, assert, but to ensure that there are twelve occupants for twelve thrones to judge the twelve tribes of Israel when the Son of Man came, preceded by the apocalyptic τέρατα and σημεῖα.

It is thus no wonder that, in the account that the revisionist Luke will give us, the Twelve did not depart from Jerusalem. One tradition had been, after all, that they would not complete the cities of Israel until the Son of Man be come. Luke makes them responsible for the ordination of the seven deacons, who were perhaps originally created to serve Hellenistic Jewish Christianity. Stephen certainly is represented as a Platonic and allegorical exegete of the Old Testament, reminiscent of Philo, but one whose allegorism leads him to attack the temple itself as an act of a Judaism that understood the account of the Tabernacle in the wilderness as literal rather than allegorical. Stephen insists that

> The tent of witness was made for our fathers in the wilderness even as he who spoke with Moses commanded it to be made as an image of the real form (κατὰ τὸν τύπον) which he saw . . . David asked that he might discover the tent for the God of Jacob. But Solomon built for him a house. But the Highest certainly does not dwell in things made with hands even as the prophet says: 'Heaven is my throne, and the earth the footstool of my feet. What kind of house would you make me, says the Lord or what is the place of my rest'.[143]

Thus the Jews had failed to understand that the Tabernacle was an accurate representation (τύπος) in the world of sense and sight of the eternal and transcendent of Plato's noumenal world. When Solomon built the temple 'made with hands' he and his fellow Jews had utterly failed to see the true character of the Mosaic revelation as an allegory of Christ who was to come. Such themes were to be continued in groups such as are represented by the epistle to the Hebrews in the New Testament.

Luke here has woven another fragment relating to the history of the early church on which he has sought to impose his historiography. He will however note a persecution of such Hellenists by the Jewish authorities, which, in view of such a direct attack upon the temple cultus, was not surprising. But he also mentions that, although the 'church at Jerusalem', which may mean simply Hellenistic Jewish Christians in Stephen's Platonizing or Philonizing

142. Acts 1:11.
143. Acts 7:44-49.

group, was 'scattered throughout Judea and Samaria', the apostles remained in Jerusalem.[144] Even in this eventually, the Twelve could not leave Jerusalem, and certainly did not 'go in the ways of the Samaritans'. It was Philip, one of the deacons, who was to do this. Peter goes to Caesarea, where he encounters Cornelius the centurion who is converted, but this was still in Judea, the focus of the mission to the 'lost sheep of the house of Israel'.[145]

The mission at Antioch in Syria, where 'the disciples were first called Christians', was also the accomplishment of those scattered, and it is Barnabas and Saul (Paul), who then prefigure in Luke's account, with his records telling him that in Antioch the order of ministers appeared to have been 'prophets and teachers', as in the late first century *Didache*.

We know what a challenge pagan converts presented in early Christian history, and why, since things were not intended to happen in this way: the conversion of the pagans was to be eschatological and subsequent to Israel, duly converted to Jewish Christianity, being saved by being gathered from the four winds from the tribulation woes. This appears to have been the position of James' community, in the views placed in his mouth by Luke at the Council of Jerusalem:

> Simeon has narrated how first God made preparations to take from the pagans a people for his name. And with this the words of the prophets agree, even as it is written: 'After these things will return and I will rebuild the tabernacle of David that is fallen, and I will rebuild its scattered fragments and will set it up again, in order that the remnants of mankind might seek the Lord and all the nations upon whom my name has been named upon them'. Wherefore I judge we do not agitate against those from the pagans who are turning to God.[146]

It is therefore only after the restoration of Israel (the 'tabernacle of David that is fallen') that the pagans will be invited to join the gathered people of God and not before. Thus the original dispute with Paul over the gentile mission has been nicely glossed over by Luke in his carefully crafted, late first century account of a formal discussion in council in which everything was once and for all nicely resolved.

Luke's account conceals a whole history of tensions between early Christian communities on this issue, as Paul's primary evidence (in Galatians) shows.[147] The views identified by Luke with James community here holds that the gentiles will become 'a people for his name', and over this there was no real argument. But the Jacobean community will insist that this will be in future, eschatological time, and not in the present: it will be only after the 'tabernacle

144. Acts 8:1.
145. See above, footnote 130 and associated text.
146. Acts 15:14-19, quoting Jer. 12:13 and Amos 9:11.
147. Gal. 1:18-2:

of David that is fallen' will be built up again. In the meantime, the Christian mission is confined to 'the lost sheep of the house of Israel'. Paul, having simmered down in the years following his apparently radical rejection of Israel as part of salvation history, in his letter to the Galatians, in writing to the Romans was prepared to modify his position while reconstructing Jacobean eschatology. It would be that 'all Israel would be saved' but after, in eschatological time, and not before, in ordinary time, 'the fullness of the nations shall come in. And thus all Israel will be saved'.[148] But this was clearly Paul's revisionism.

The original significance of the Twelve as an institution, whether by Christ himself, as the gospels say, or in the early church, was by association with the twelve tribes of Israel in eschatological time. It was not to constitute the apostolate that founded the church for a future and lengthy history in ordinary time. Their purpose as leaders in the community was therefore an eschatological one: they looked forward to the coming of the Son of Man and as leaders of the community would sit on twelve thrones of judgement with him. It is this eschatological significance to which Mark with some qualification bears witness: his Jesus would come as the Son of Man within the lifetime of the first generation of followers and they themselves possessed his apocalyptic teaching that this was so and that their inner group, Peter, James and John, had handed on. But Mark will not allow that their apocalyptic mission was confined to Israel and its twelve tribes, rather than to the gentile converts who were now members of his Roman community and also enduring Nero's persecution.

It is at this point that we arrive at the probable reason why Mark should have committed his gospel to writing. Such action in this context does not imply a future history in ordinary time for which to write because eyewitnesses such as Peter had been martyred in Nero's circus. Rather with Peter having been martyred (A.D. 65), along with James the apostle far earlier, and James the Lord's brother so recently (A.D. 62), he needed to preserve the message of his gospel and its crucial apocalypse. Mark mentions no member of the Twelve now surviving, and if they still existed in Jerusalem, the events there were beginning to overwhelm them. Mark needed to obscure their original purpose in view of the gentile members of the Roman congregation: he does not mention their original role as guarantors of the twelve thrones on which they would judge the twelve tribes of Israel. But the apocalyptic dimension to both the persecution of Nero and the impending destruction of Jerusalem needed to be preserved to the very last.

We are now in position to assess both the pagan Roman Empire as the Christians saw it and the Christian community as the pagan Romans saw it.

---

148.   Rom. 11:25-16.

3. *The Christian Church and the Pagan State*

The Markan community hardly confronted the Roman state as a state with which constructive engagement was either appropriate or to any purpose. Neither Roman political institutions nor Roman society were there to be reformed: the natural relationship was one in which one endured 'being hated by all for my sake'. There was no question of active and violent resistance to the hatred of the civil power such as that in which other Jewish rebels had taken part. As such the attitude was that of the Pharisees and indeed the book of Daniel: the kingdom of 'one like unto a Son of Man', the archangel Michael and his court of the angelic beings who were the 'saints of the Most High', was a case of the transcendental angelic world merging miraculously with the present as an act of the divine will and power. It was a Pharisaic and Hassidic tradition that the Roman community was pursuing in its Christian form.

We have argued that early Christianity, in the form in which we find it in Mark's Gospel, was not persecuted by the pagan, Roman power because it threatened revolutionary violence. But we have seen that, from the Roman, pagan perspective, the threat of overt violence was not the only grounds for calling a sect a *coniuratio* or 'conspiracy'. The suppression of the Dionysiacs had been because they were considered to be practising magical rites that would threaten the *pax deorum* in a nature and in a society that were both considered to be bound together into a common, metaphysical reality. It was this threat that constituted it as a *coniuratio*. An index of this attack through magic upon the metaphysical order was the accompanying Dionysiac frenzied rites and processions, and orgies in which it could be claimed that incest and cannibalism took place in contravention of the 'natural' order of things, both in nature and in society.

In the case of early Christianity, incest and cannibalism were also claimed. But the language of the Markan apocalypse, as well as its Jewish counterparts to which Josephus alluded, also contained predictions and accounts of portents in the sky, with falling stars and a natural order whose 'powers' were 'shaken'.[149] Tacitus claims that Judaism was unable, by contrast with Paganism, because of its opposition 'to all propitiatory rites', to deal with such portents in the rites of augury that could restore the *pax deorum* in the breakdown of the order of nature to which they bore witness.[150] But it was quite likely that a different conclusion might be reached from such predictions or obsessions with present portents, namely that the sect itself welcomed the metaphysical collapse both of nature and of society and was actively promoting this by magical means.

Although Early Christianity pointed to God and his purposes worked out in human history as the reason for such portents marking the end of secular

---

149.   Mk 13:24-25, cf. Lk. 21:26.
150.   Tacitus, *Hist.*, 5.13.

history, they clearly did not deny that such portents were the 'signs and wonders' of Christ's second coming as glorified Son of Man for which they yearned.
Early Christianity as a political movement as such was therefore quite uncompromising towards the pagan political society that it opposed. This order of
time and space, that included with the political and social order the natural
order as well, was not there as something with which to seek any accommodation or *modus uiuendi*.

There could be no compromise with the present age on which God's sentence
had been passed. The present age was the kingdom of Beelzebub, the prince
of daemons, whose empire could be seen particularly in the sick whose bodies
his daemons controlled.[151] Jesus was bringing about through his healing the
kingdom of God, and although the powers of darkness appeared to triumph in
Jerusalem where he performed no miracles of healing, though one of destruction on a fig tree,[152] the cross was not the end but the beginning since Christ
risen and exalted was to reappear as glorified Son of Man.

As such, early Christianity, in the form represented by Mark, is formally
comparable with other political movements and stances, whether founded on
religious or secular assumptions. Let us examine Marxism as such a case.

3.1 *Marxism as Secular Apocalyptic*

Marxism was a secular movement that nevertheless was formally comparable
with previous, religious apocalyptic movements. History was remorselessly
moving towards a final end or goal not completely within human control, and
to resist the forces propelling human society towards that end was irrational.
Thus there could be no compromise or accommodation with capitalist society
such as social democratic attempts to modify its extremes of wealth and poverty: the only real solution to the human predicament was a 'root and branch'
replacement of existing social and economic relations by a new social order.

The dynamic of historical development had been, previously and with Hegel,
the world spirit working in historical events by analogy with the movement of
a human argument. Human beings in dialogue with one another (or the human
mind in dialogue with itself) begin by stating a thesis. A counter thesis is then
proposed challenging the 'thesis' and this may be termed the 'antithesis'. As the
argument or dialogue progresses, each disputant now modifies their original
position so that at the last neither thesis nor antithesis is seen to be wholly true
but a third position that combines or synthesizes the original claims now
emerge as the true one: this Hegel described as the 'synthesis'.

Thus he was to argue that, historically, we begin with the thesis that is feudal
society characterized by love and belonging, but no freedom. Looked at in an
admittedly romantic fashion, in feudal society one experiences, as the thesis,

151. Mt. 12:25-37: Lk. 11:17-23; 12:10, cf. Mk 3:23-30.
152. Mt. 21:18-19; Mk 11:12-14.

the protecting warmth of one's liege lord in serfdom, to whose estates one is inextricably bound and so has no freedom. The antithesis to this situation is capitalist society in which there is freedom but no loving bond between human beings: we serve our managers as the result of a contract whose terms enable us to resign or be dismissed whenever the object of the contract is at an end. But as history progresses, this kind of rational argument working its way by thinking its way out in actual events now produces a synthesis, which for Hegel was the Prussian state. Under 'our father the Kaiser' we experience the state (and society that is at one with it) as a family in which there is love but also the service that is lovingly and freely given. This was Hegel's dialectical view of history.

The early Marx at least was to take over this dialectic from Hegel but deny anything spiritual about it such that it could be regarded as the product of a divine mind. In this respect, Liberation theologians, in taking over Marx's dialectic but attributing it to the purposes of a personal and rational divinity, are not strictly the Christian heirs to Marx's alleged quest for justice and equality that they claim to be. Marxist dialectic was purely materialist and even mechanical: there was no element of a divine mind in what he described as 'dialectical materialism'. The process that propels historical events is a purely material one resulting from a natural equality that has been upset, and the correction of that disequilibrium is what drives history to the goal of a classless society in which all are to be equal.

The late medieval weaver purchased his wool and mixed his labour with it by spinning out on the loom, which he owned, the cloth, which he then sold. But with the rise of capitalist society the loom that was the 'means of production' in respect of the cloth is now owned by the capitalist mill owners who now contract the weaver as the price of his survival to produce cloth from the looms that they own, at a fraction of the price that their labour will in fact produce. Workers, 'alienated' from the 'means of production' will also feel psychological alienation in hatred for the system that exploits them and helplessness in the face of it. But the stimulation thus to overcome the alienation also produces the urge to revolt and seize back the means of production and achieve the equality to which the disequilibrium of their own inequality is thus driving them.

If we turn to the specific example of the ideology of the old Soviet Union we may express the dialectic, driven by the material fact of inequality that we have described, thus. Capitalist society now represents the thesis where the few rule the many through their possession of the means of production. But the antithesis now arises to challenge this situation, namely socialist society in which the many rule the few: the 'dictatorship of the few' has become the 'dictatorship of the many' or the 'dictatorship of the proletariat'. In the film of Dr Zhivago the question was raised at one point whether Lenin was the new Tsar. But a proponent of the Soviet system at least in its Stalinist form would not wish to deny that fact. Lenin was the new Tsar at the head of the old Tsarist apparatus of oppression, the secret police, press control, etc. His was rule in the

Tsarist sense, only in the latter case it had been rule by the few of the many, but in his case it was rule by the many of the few. But as history progressed, there would emerge the synthesis in which neither the few (thesis) nor the many (antithesis) rule, but with the withering away of the state true communism and complete equality would come.

The same underlying economic and material forces driving events in Soviet society would also according to such a hypothesis be operative in other Western societies which had experienced industrial revolutions. Finally all societies would achieve true communism and be united in a world order that was a universal brotherhood. For the moment, the antithesis must prevail with the state exercising its coercive and dictatorial power on behalf of the many also protecting its fledging socialism externally against the 'aggressive Nato alliance' and other reactionary, capitalist powers.

As with Markan expectations of the apocalyptic events, no one individual or group of individuals, by the exercise of their own, human free will, could hasten or determine how events would develop. One could learn from the parable of the fig tree how:

> . . . when its branch has become supple and it burst forth into leaf you know that the harvest is nigh. Thus with you, when you see these things taking place, know that the end is nigh at the doors.[153]

So also with the Marxist future. One needed to discern the 'signs of the times', to recognize the antithetical forces creative of change towards equilibrium after the disequilibrium of the thesis, not to be a 'reactionary', maintaining the thesis and reacting against the antithesis, and thus being crushed by the latter's forces, etc. 'Praxis' meant active engagement with the antithetical currents of history and swimming with the tide that was coming in despite all obstacles, but not theorizing or producing academic blueprints: one could not determine history: one needed to be guided by one's experience of it so as to accept its final form.

Marxist theory does not necessarily see itself as comparable with apocalyptic but clearly it shares a similar form to it in its political expectations and approach to existing society. But there are closer parallels to be drawn. Not only has history a beneficent goal towards which it is proceeding through the action of forces beyond human control, but also Marxism shares an attitude to the present order that bears comparison with the Judeo-Christian apocalyptic that Mark's community exemplified.

The present order is unstable and cannot therefore be trusted to deliver to human beings the justice that is their final due or their final state. Those who are heirs to the future will be downtrodden, whether the Christian Roman community in the tribulation woes that are necessary to achieving history's final

---

153. Mk 13:28-29.

goal, or the downtrodden proletariat awaiting the historical conditions for the reversal of the condition of their inequality. The essential character of present nature or present society (or both in metaphysical unity) is unstable and chaotic: the stars fall from heaven, the sun is darkened: the present order is chaotic and the system is riddled with contradictions: when the company for which one works is almost bankrupt, the boss requires salary reduction as the price of avoiding unemployment, but when the company is profitable, he keeps the profits.

It matters not if labour unions secure increases in wages above the rate of inflation with the resultant economic chaos because the system itself is unstable and can never achieve the end of disequilibrium so long as present conditions remain. Not transformation of the present but the realization of a future trying to be born was the object of the Markan community in awaiting their gathering together with the elect at the coming of the Son of Man, or of the Soviet community building socialism and awaiting the historical conditions for the withering away of the state and the achievement of communism. Each makes metaphysical assumptions regarding the transient and unstable present reality, which is unsusceptible to remoulding but requires radical replacement.

But such an approach to politics can only endure so long the non-fulfilment of its future hope, and cannot survive the long endurance of the corresponding empirical reality, the enduring stability of which refutes the conviction of transient instability on which the expectation of a different future is based. In the case of Marxism in the course of the second quarter of the last century, what was called 'capitalism' proved, with its free market solutions, to be the only economic system capable of lifting individuals and nations out of poverty. The old Soviet Union collapsed, as did the very command economies on which it was founded, with the state unable to fulfil its pension commitments or its health or educational responsibilities. Thus Marxism as an apocalyptic, all or nothing, approach to politics failed and those who lived under political regimes that understood society with such assumptions had to radically revise them and come to terms with forms of social and economic organization with which they had sought to dispense on the ground that these would fail under the weight of their instability.

In Eastern Europe the apocalyptic political vision collapsed, as it did in those social democratic parties with groups supporting versions of its thesis that they sought to advocate within the constraints of parliamentary democracy. Their rapprochement with free market economics and how this might nevertheless lead to removing social disequilibrium created by unacceptable inequalities lead generally to movements throughout Europe and internationally, characterized by the phenomenon of New Labour in the United Kingdom. Those committed to apocalyptic perspectives had now to engage with what they believed to be transient and passing in order to achieve the ends towards which their values had led them.

A formally similar situation was to be found in early Christianity and Judaism around the events of A.D. 70. The kingdom of the archangel with appearance 'like unto a Son of Man', consisting of angelic beings who mingled with the earthly elect that they gathered from the four corners of the earth, had not come about either in Jewish or in Christian experience. Rome as the fourth empire had not been miraculously replaced. Thus the political perspectives of the majority of adherents to such apocalyptic worldviews began gradually to alter.

Josephus' response was to depart from the politics of revolution that he had followed as a Jewish commander, and to rewrite Jewish history under the patronage of the Flavian dynasty in Rome. Revisionist history, readjusting interpretations of political events on the part of those who participated in them, now was on the agenda of those who realized that the cosmos had shown no conformity with previous expectations. Josephus proceeded to explain to his Roman, pagan patrons that throughout Jewish history Romans and Jews had respected one another and lived amicably under a political rapprochement that had been understood to exist between them. Pompey, had been the first Roman commander to annex Judaea to the Roman Empire in pursuit of a policy of ringing the Mediterranean with Roman provinces or client kingdoms in order to keep out pirates. Rome, the kingdom of iron, had replaced the Macedonian of bronze. But this had not been decline but rather the achievement of an unbreakable and eternal kingdom.[154] This had no doubt been yet another 'ambiguous allusion' that 'had predicted Vespasian and Titus'.[155]

Pompey had besieged and taken Jerusalem, and entered the temple and had committed a sin through ignorance that was 'not light' in that 'he saw what it was unlawful for any but the high priests to see' in the innermost sanctuary, the Holy of Holies:

> But though the golden table was there and the sacred lamp stand and libation vessels . . . he touched none of these because of his religious devotion, and in this respect also he acted in a manner worthy of his virtuous character. And on the morrow he instructed the temple servants to cleanse the temple and to offer the customary sacrifice to God, and he restored the high priesthood to Hyrcanus . . .[156]

Here was a model of the ideal, Roman ruler, led by 'religious devotion (εὐσέβεια)' to preserve the temple cultus, and of the ideal, moderate Jewish High Priest, Hyrcanus, who had not supported the fanaticism of Aristobulus, being allowed to continue sacrifices.[157] The subsequent Jewish War against Rome had similarly been led by extremist Zealots or *sicarii* commanded by

154. See above, footnote 80 and associated text.
155. See above, footnote 71 and associated text.
156. Josephus, *Antiqu.*, 14.72–73.
157. Josephus, *Antiqu.*, 14.73.

Eleazar, son of Simon and John of Gischala, from which the erstwhile rebel commander in Galilee now disassociated himself.[158]

The epistle of Barnabas opposes an agenda for rebuilding the temple at Jerusalem, thus revealing the real existence of such a movement in the years subsequent to A.D 70. The letter appears datable from an allusion either to Vespasian or Nerva (A.D. 96–98), again in the context of an interpretation of Daniel's vision of the four empires.[159] Josephus published the *Antiquitates* in around A.D. 93 with the original version of the *Bellum Judaicum* in Aramaic, his native language, around A.D. 75. It may well be that he entertained hopes that the sacrifices and cult of the Jerusalem temple might be restored and the temple be rebuilt as had happened in 516 B.C.

But if Josephus had entertained specifically the hopes that his account implies regarding the rebuilding of the temple, he certainly prescinded from that event any form of Messianism that was opposed to Rome. As we have seen, Vespasian fulfilled for him the prophecy of the ruler with universal dominion. Rabbinic Judaism was to some extent to pursue a rapprochement in which, though formally committed to a Messiah in some form, the apocalyptic threat to the present order of things was omitted from the picture: the present order of things was not so unstable that its disorder would be reflected in the break up of nature with falling stars, etc. But Josephus' rapprochement was far more radical: it made the end of all prophecy about a universal rule to be the Roman emperor ruling over a Roman Empire, with the possibility of Judaism proceeding as a world religion with the possibility of a restoration of the temple cultus.

Such a rapprochement is always highly flexible and requires time to evolve. Furthermore, Josephus was to prove to be a writer with more interest from Christians than his fellow Jews: his rapprochement was too radical. Furthermore, in Christianity's case, there were to be spasmodic but frequent outbreaks of persecution, in which the apocalyptic interpretation of Church-state relations could always resurface. Such will always be the threat to rapprochements that replace a previous apocalypticism.

The retreat from Marxism and an 'all or nothing' interpretation of political imperatives, accompanied by great confidence in the reformability of present circumstances without radical transformation will work while the present exhibits a stability that soothes and cancels any social-psychological fears that it is too unstable. While free-market economics appear to deliver stable inflation and rising prosperity, it is possible for former socialist apocalypticism to see the possibility of recasting the value system of the present political order in a more reconciled form. Thus the rapprochement of 'New Labour' involves agreeing that welfare needs to be 'better targeted' (rather than 'reduced'), that

---

158. Josephus, *BJ*, 2.564; 4.128; 7.262–274.

159. For Bar. 4:45 with versions of Dan. 7:8, see J. Carleton Paget, *The Epistle of Barnabas: Outlook and Background* (WUNT, 2.64; Tübingen: Mohr Siebeck, 1994), pp. 9–17.

welfare payments when restricted are not done so in order to be punitive but to educate for the person's own good, etc.

But should environmentalists and 'Greens' be correct in their predictions, or indeed a war with militant Islam lead to the cutting off of oil, etc., in the face of such natural or political catastrophes an apocalyptic approach may well again inform some political movements. Such movements might again believe that the instability of the present order of nature and of society rules out any rapprochement with the status quo, and that after that instability has produced its final, chaotic breakdown, a new order will emerge and with it the new roles to be played by individuals within it. Similarly, with early Christianity at least before Constantine, such rapprochements, though, as we shall see, eloquently proposed, were to prove fragile.

In such situations, the Western church at least was to read again Mark's apocalypse as applicable to its own situation, and as though it was the common experience of anyone truly Christian that they would 'stand before pro consuls and kings for my sake for a witness to them'. Cyprian, in the Decian persecution (A.D. 249–251) as we shall see, was to so read these lines.[160] Indeed, in Josephus' own time, as we shall see, the author of the Revelation (Apocalypse) of St John the divine in the New Testament, was, in the face of a persecution of Domitian that may have been more threatened than real, to continue apocalyptic distrust of the stability of the present and hope for 'the kingdom of this world' becoming 'the kingdom of our God and of his Christ' in a scene of the radical replacement of the former by the latter.[161] But also and contemporaneously with Josephus, we have the production of Luke-Acts in the New Testament.

We have already mentioned how Luke divorces the events of Christ's second coming from the destruction of Jerusalem and places these in an indefinite future when 'the times of the gentiles will be fulfilled'.[162] Luke's revisionist history has created a church age with its fundamental ministry founded on the Twelve as witnesses to the resurrection and the forty days till the Ascension. References to the original significance of the Twelve as awaiting their twelve thrones in judgement of the twelve tribes of Israel have been duly suppressed.[163]

We shall argue that Luke's revisionist history here is part of an overall plan, paralleling that of Josephus and contrasting with John the Seer, to suggest a rapprochement with the imperial, political ideology. In seeking such a rapprochement, he was joined in his own generation by Clement of Rome and, in the subsequent generation, by Ignatius of Antioch. Each in their own way

---

160.   Mk 13:9, cf. Cyprian (Moyses et Maximus et ceteri), *Ep.* XXXI.4.1 (71-72); LXXIII.16.2 (271–273). See also, Cyprian, *Laps.*, 20.403–405, quoting Mt. 10:32-33.

161.   Rev. 11:15.

162.   See above, footnote 49 and associated text.

163.   See above, footnote 130 and associated text.

took on and incorporated into a Christian perspective the values of the pagan Roman Empire, which they sought to reform and to transform rather than supersede.

But before we embark upon a detailed discussion of such a thesis, we must first examine the political theology of the pagan, Roman state.

Chapter 3

The Political Theology of the Augustan Revolution: Cosmic Reconstruction

The empire to which Nero, Vespasian, and Domitian had succeeded had been itself the result of a major political upheaval with its own ideological transformation. Augustus had refashioned the Roman constitution and with it had refashioned the narrative of Rome's past. Basically Augustus' political theology, by means of which he sought to legitimate his exercise of power, might reasonably be described as 'realized eschatology', in parallel with the Lukan and Johannine writings, and parts of Q and the *Gospel of Thomas*, that claim that the last things of apocalyptic expectation have been mysteriously realized in the present.

Let us now therefore sketch the origins of the pagan status quo with which Roman Christianity had clashed with such contrary visions in the time of Nero.

1. *The Republican Constitution and Its Supersession*

Rome's early constitutional history at its beginnings is obscured under a haze of legends that Livy records before his historically more reliable account begins. Rome's story is of a city-state on the banks of the Tiber that spread its influence through an alliance of equal, Italian city-states that was to undergo transformation into an alliance of unequals that produced empire. 'Democracy' is an elastic term and difficult to apply historically with exactness, but during the Republican period, before Octavian changed his name to Augustus (27 B.C.), there existed a system whereby leaders competed with each other for power, with their success or failure determined by a popular vote. Voting in the citizen body, the *concilium plebis,* did not proceed by secret ballot, and deeply written into the social if not the constitutional and legal fabric was the institution of patron–client relations. But nevertheless, despite such influence and control, potential rulers, despite their connections with the political establishment considered normal, still needed to win the popular vote for office and to carry legislation. It was a system that Augustus was to end, while allowing its features to remain in an enfeebled form for the purposes of political 'spin'.

The city-state was at first ruled by kings, the last of whom, named in legend as Tarquinius Superbus, was expelled in 510 B.C. From that time the Republican constitution was gradually to develop. First of all two consuls were to succeed those kings with similar powers with the exception of the sacerdotal role that was exercised by the *rex sacrorum*. The consuls' period in office was limited normally to one year. Their power, called *imperium*, was absolute at this time when exercised conjointly, but as one consul could veto the other, there was thus a constitutional check to absolutism. In course of time other limitations upon their power resulted, as when the office of censor was created (443 B.C.), with responsibility for citizen roles, taxation and public morality removed from the consuls' jurisdiction. The consuls were to lose their judicial powers to the praetors.

The office of a single praetor was established as a patrician post in 367 B.C. as a third holder of *imperium* after that of the two consuls, which was considered the greater (*maius imperium*). His powers were more than purely judicial, since he performed the role of consul in Rome during the consul's absence. Their number was increased around 244 B.C., one of them, the *praetor urbanus*, who conducted judicial cases in the case of citizens, and the other, the *praetor inter peregrinos*, who did the same for non-citizens. By Julius Caesar's time their number had become sixteen.

The early centuries witnessed a conflict, also obscured in legend, between patrician and plebeian clans in Rome. Before Canuleius' legislation in 445 B.C., plebeians were not allowed to intermarry with patricians. Not all senators were patricians or *patres*, but also there had come to be added to their number *conscripti* who were plebeians. But before 300 B.C. all offices, particularly religious ones, had been monopolized by the patricians. Even until 172 B.C. one of the consuls had to be a patrician. During this conflict of orders, a new office of tribune had been created, who were to be ten in number by 449 B.C. They did not have *imperium* like the higher magistrates, but their power came from their election by the people, who swore an oath to protect the inviolability of their office. From 145 B.C. they addressed the people directly, and were elected by secret ballot from 139 B.C. From a very early time they had acquired the powers to veto legislation from the senate, and over acts of other magistrates.

The role of the tribunes as guardians of the interest of the people against the political establishment arose, according to legend, from events during the conflict of orders in the fifth century B.C. The plebeians were oppressed by moneylenders to whom they were in debt following successful wars against the Volsci, Sabines and Aequi. They in desperation withdrew from the city en masse in a kind of general strike, with the Senate afraid that with the army thus disbanded, Rome was now at risk of invasion (494 B.C.). The Senate now sent Menenius Agrippa, who narrated the fable of the head and the body, claiming that the head without the bodily members could not function, but neither could the bodily members without the head. The solution was the election of (initially two) tribunes of the people, who swore an oath that they would protect to death the inviolability of the office thus conveyed.[1]

---

1. Livy, II.32.6–12.

To the number of magistrates we should add the quaestors, responsible from 427 B.C. for the Roman treasury and for record keeping, and aediles (after 421 B.C.), as superintendents of public works and the staging of spectacles such as the games. The praetors and consuls possessed *imperium*, but not the tribunes, quaestors or aediles. Their insignia of office were the 'rods and axes (*fasces securesque*)' carried in procession before them by the lictors. After a gradual evolution had led to an equilibrium in the struggle between the patricians and plebeians, with the latter having equal access to magistracies, etc., the constitution itself settled down with contenders for the magistracies competing in a *cursus honorum* that began with a quaestorship and ended for the successful with a consulship. By the late second century all ex holders of offices were enrolled in the Senate, where they exercised power and influence as part of Rome's executive government.

By 264 B.C. Rome was emerging as head of a developing Italian confederacy that had liberally awarded members of the component cities citizenship. But as an emerging and dominant military power, she was to clash with Carthage in the Punic Wars (264–241 B.C.; 218–201 B.C.; 149–146 B.C.). In consequence of her victory, she had now to add to the system of making treaties with (semi) independent allies and Hellenistic monarchs the practice of direct rule over provinces (*prouinciae*) through the appointment of proconsuls or in some cases propraetors.

Rome had acquired four such provinces between 241 and 200 B.C.: Sicily, Sardinia, Spain (and subsequently Gaul), and Macedonia. Others were to follow such as North Africa itself after Carthage's final destruction (146 B.C.), Pontus and Bithynia, Egypt, etc. Each province represented a territory within the boundaries of which *imperium* would be exercised by a Roman governor or pro-consul (or pro-praetor) sent out for this purpose. Such governors were drawn from consuls and praetors who, after their periods of office, would be awarded provinces to govern by the Senate for a fixed period, typically twelve months.

Since it was the Senate that allocated one's province, the senators exercised some real control over the consuls and co-operation was thus in the interest of both sides. But clearly the military functions of magistrates exercising *imperium* were being increased, as well as the numbers of men whom they would command in the legions who were no longer a mere citizen army. Bonds of loyalty and, even stronger, of patronage united the pro-consul or pro-praetor, now military commander (*imperator*), with his men.

It had nevertheless been the constitutional rule that once a military commander had left the sphere of his legitimate authority (*imperium*), and had re-entered the *pomerium* or city boundary of Rome, he re-entered as a private citizen without military *regalia*. Thus the ability of the power-hungry to coerce by display of force either the senate or the citizen assemblies was considerably reduced, and the commander reminded by the ceremony of the due limits of his legal authority. But another custom had been that a general would be voted by the senate a triumphal procession through the streets of the city up to the temple of Juppiter Capitolinus, in full military regalia with his armed legionaries, and displaying the spoils of war, captured notable prisoners destined for execution, prisoners of war to be released and dressed as the triumphator's freedmen, etc. Such imagery, belying the constitutional principle, projected a confusing message in times of civil conflict, despite the legitimacy given by a senatorial vote, that the requirements of remaining within one's *imperium* could be overridden for a specific purpose.

Senatorial government, whose influential, political members had entered through a mainly non-violent *cursus honorum* run by competitors for the popular vote, was to experience from the tribunate of Tiberius Gracchus (133 B.C.) the stresses and strains that were the cause of its replacement over the next 100 years in the Augustan revolution. The replacement of the small farmer by *latifundia* that were reducing him to poverty led Tiberius as tribune to propose a program of land reform, in which he had clearly infringed, in many eyes, the constitutional position of the tribune's office. When he tried unconstitutionally to stand for office a second time, riots broke out in which his opponents, including many senators, accused him of aiming for tyranny. Three hundred of his followers were clubbed to death, and their bodies thrown into the Tiber. Tiberius fell at the door of the temple of Juppiter Capitolinus near to the statues of the kings.[2]

Gaius Gracchus was to follow his brother in his election as tribune in 123 B.C., and to succeed in a second election to that office in 122 B.C. He re-enacted his brother's land bill, and other populist measures. He also proposed extending Roman franchise to the Latin allies. He sought to strengthen his power base by creating a distinction between the senatorial and equestrian order. Originally this order was distinguished by its cavalry status, but now it was to be politically distinguished from that of senator by the fact that the Equites were to control jury courts at Rome, and also began their right of tax farming in the provinces. Although he tried without success to add 300 Equites to the senate where individual Equites had nevertheless sat in the past, senators could not sit in jury courts. He also sought to reduce their influence upon the consuls by legislating that the *patres et conscripti* assign them their proconsular provinces before their year of office and not in course of it.

The result was that we have a popular party (*populares*) and one of the nobility (*optimates*) that clashed with each other again in the Forum. This time the senators did not join the fracas but passed a resolution, the *senatus consultum ultimum*, calling on the consuls to intervene. The consul Opimius, thus armed with constitutional moral support, called citizens to arms and executed some 3,000 men.

---

2. H. H. Scullard, *From the Gracchi to Nero: A History of Rome from 133 B.C. to A.D. 68* (London: Methuen, 1982), pp. 25–28.

Although the decline and fall of the Roman Republic was to take another 90 years or so, we see many of the features that were to lead to the collapse of the Republican constitution in the events of the Gracchi. We have, in the Equites, the formation of a 'third estate', separate from the Senate and developing, independently of the latter's constitutional authority, their own interests and personal power in the accumulation of wealth and influence. Offers of status had been made to the Latin allies that the senate had not allowed to be fulfilled. Furthermore, the issue of land both for the poor and for veterans from the legions had been raised with the idea of creating colonies. Who was to fulfil the desire for financial independence or for a military pension? Was it to be the Republican state, providing these on behalf of the community, or was it to be individual generals acting as patrons, and acquiring power and support of their personal clients in return?

Differences with Rome's Italian allies were to lead to the disastrous war begun when the tribune Drusus was murdered the evening before the vote for their enfranchisement (91 B.C.). Marius, with support of the populus and *ordo equester* had won his first consulship in 107 B.C., and subsequently was awarded command over the war in Africa against Jugurtha by the *concilium plebis*, despite senatorial opposition using their accustomed prerogative. He was given the credit for the victory over Jugurtha, and not the senatorial generals Metellus and Sulla (104 B.C.). Marius was now involved in the defence of Italy against the invasion of the Cimbri and Teutons, but in his absence was elected consul for the second time, quite unconstitutionally since the legal requirement was a 10-year gap between the holding of a consulship. He was to hold six successive consulships (from 107–100 B.C.), thus creating a tradition that threatened to upset the balance between powers that Polybius had admired in the Roman constitution.

Marius had, as a military reformer, recruited landless peasants to the army whose numbers needed increasing, but who became dependent on him personally for the fulfilment of the promise of a plot of land from which to survive following their retirement from active service. It was troops personally loyal to him who under his leadership crushed a popular riot following the murder of Memmius during the elections of 99 B.C., in compliance with the a *senatus consultum ultimum*.

In the social war with the Italian allies in 92 B.C. it had been his old associate and then rival in the popular cause, Sulla, who for services in the Social War was elected to the consulship of 88 B.C. and subsequently granted the province of Asia and the command against Mithridates in the East. However the tribune Publius Sulpicius proposed distributing the newly enfranchised Italians over the 35 tribes. But opposition from the senatorial optimates was to be bitter, and in his defence he appealed to Marius, whose price for support was the illegal tranference of the Mithridatic command from Sulla to himself. An armed clash in the Forum resulted. Marius was in Rome for the transfer of power but had no legions with him. Sulla then with his legions marched upon and took Rome, and the Senate and popular assemblies (Comitia) implemented his wishes partly or wholly under duress. Marius and Sulpicius were declared outlaws.

Marius had escaped and returned with an army raised in Etruria. Marius took Rome and Ostia in a bloodbath of murder and pillage. Marius and Cinna were then elected consuls, and Sulla was driven into exile with his legislation repealed. Sulla however defeated Mithridates and Sulla landed at Brundisium to be joined among others by M. Licinius Crassus and Cn. Pompeius, who raised legions at their own expense. The Republican Constitution, strained by irregular consular elections and with legislation frequently being overthrown by force, was now being shaken by the spectre of private armies, and not simply by forces personally loyal to the general that could persuade Senate and People to remunerate them. Sulla now advanced upon Rome defeating two consular armies and proceeded to mop up surviving Marian governors in the provinces. Pompey won a triumph for his success on Sulla's behalf, though with some resistance from the latter.

Sulla re-entered Rome with his *imperium* having lapsed. Under duress the Senate now pased all his passed acts as consul and as pro-consul. Legitimacy was now to be acquired by force and not proper and due constitutional process. Finally Sulla was appointed dictator *legibus scribundis et reipublicae restituendae* (dictator for the purpose of prescribing laws and restoring the republic) without any time limit: supreme power was now in his hands for as long as he chose to exercise it. As we shall see, Augustus too was to claim as the restoration of the republic his own military autocracy that was to prove long-lasting. The tribunes' powers of initiating legislation and their right of veto was brought effectively to an end. But Sulla curiously was to retire in 79 B.C. and, on his death, he was accorded a public funeral in Rome (78 B.C.). Thus senatorial administration was able to recover and the constitution given a new opportunity to function effectively.

M. Aemilius Lepidus was to lead the counter revolution following his election to the consulship in 79 B.C. on a platform opposed to Sulla's revolution, including restoration of the Marian exiles and full powers to the tribunate. But he fell out with his colleague for 78 B.C. Q. Lutatius Catulus over an attack in Etruria on Sullan colonists. Lepidus was reported to be marching upon Rome (77 B.C.) with the result that the senate passed the *senatus consultum ultimum*. But in order to deal with the situation, Pompey was given first *propraetorium imperium* and then, having defeated Lepidus, he refused to disband his army and the Senate legimated his position by making him pro-consul of Spain along with Metellus who was already in proper constitutional possession of this command.

While Pompey was engaged in this military action in Spain, the slave revolt lead by Spartacus broke out. Both consuls were sent out against him, but separately, and then united, they were defeated by him (72 B.C.). The Senate turned to Crassus but the People voted for Pompey to be associated with him in a military command. With Spartacus defeated, both advanced towards Rome and settled their differences, mutually agreeing that both should be consuls together. The Senate was forced to grant Pompey a dispensation from Sulla's law under which he was 6 years below the required age for a consulship. It was for this reason that Pompey had insisted on being given a triumph: with his troops still under his command in full battle regalia he was able to coerce the Senate. Now both, being able to disregard constitutional proprieties themselves, proceeded to deprive the Senate of Sulla's safeguards that could have enabled it to govern effectively. They restored all the tribunician powers as well as the office of the censor. With their extra constitutional power over their veterans, and skilled in the art of persuasion by displays of force, they were well able to control the tribunate as they had done the Senate (69 B.C.). Well might they now retire without taking immediately pro-consulships that might have led to them confronting each other in a civil war.

In 67 B.C., in the wake of the threat of piracy to the corn supply of Rome, the tribune A. Gabinius, using the renewal of the powers that Pompey and Crassus had restored, moved that an extraordinary command be created for someone of consular rank. This person, (undoubtedly Pompey was intended), was to be given *imperium* which would, contrary to due constitutional theory, be *infinitum* or 'without limits' by sea. Moreover, his authority would be equal to that of all provincial governors within 50 miles inland, with money, infantry, and the right to appoint his own legates. A weakened Senate protested, with only Julius Caesar favouring the proposal, but the measure was passed in scenes of riot in the Forum. The restoration of the tribunician powers had well served Pompey's extra-constitutional ambitions.

It soon became obvious that the need for an extraordinary command against the pirates was the pretext that the Senate had suspected. With the pirates defeated, Pompey's extraordinary command was extended to Cilicia, Bithynia and Pontus with the campaign against Mithridates. Julius Caesar supported the bill, and Cicero as praetor delivered his speech in support, *Pro lege Manilia*. In the east Pompey was now monarch in all but name. It was as a result of this campaign that he was to ring the Mediterranean with a continuous line of Roman provinces from Pontus on the Black Sea to Syria, with adjacent client kingdoms. It was in connection with these events that Pompey was to intervene, as we mentioned in our last chapter, in the affairs of Palestine under a Seleucid Hellenistic monarch. Syria was now annexed by Rome (64 B.C.). Pompey was to recognize John Hyrcanus as High Priest and Ruler, and to enter the Holy of Holies but without further desecration or despoliation, as Josephus claims (63 B.C.).

Not to be outdone by Pompey, Crassus, who had returned from retirement to become censor in 65 B.C., had proposed full citizenship for the Transpadane Gaul, opposed by his other censor colleague, in consequence of which both resigned their office. But future willing troops were thus won over to his side by such a demonstration of concern for their interests. He then put up a tribune to propose the annexation of Egypt. But both the Senate and Cicero, as defender of Pompey's interests, managed to defeat the proposal.

Crassus now put up a tribune to propose an agrarian bill setting up a commission of 10 men for 5 years with *imperium* to allocate land for colonies in Italy and the provinces. This can be read, rightly, as a defensive measure against Pompey's return and his need to reward his veterans with grants of land. Cicero's oratory in defence of Pompey's interests helped to defeat this measure too. At this point Catiline, failing to achieve office by constitutional means, staged an uprising. Cicero denounced Catiline in his famous orations, prosecuted 5 of the ringleaders, and obtained the death penalty that he had carried out by troops under his command. In the year of his consulship (63 B.C.) he had managed to persuade a reluctant Senate to pass a *senatus consultum ultimum*, and the military powers thus reluctantly awarded to Pompey's agent were used to defeat Catiline himself, who fell with his forces at Pistoria in Etruria (62 B.C.).

At this point Pompey returned, his path prepared by Q. Metellus Nepos a tribune who had attacked Cicero and proposed a bill to summon him home. Pompey was to be allowed to stand for the consulship *in absentia*. Riots followed, and Metellus left Rome for Pompey's camp. Cicero had clearly lost Pompey's complete trust in his appeal for a *concordia ordinum* that would preserve constitutional government. Pompey was now to shatter Cicero's dream by entering into the concordat that we know as the 'First Triumvirate', in which Pompey, Caesar and Crassus were to carve up republican government between themselves in pursuance of their private interests. All three were thrown together in an alliance of convenience due to senatorial rebuffs.

Crassus had wanted the Senate to set right a bad bargain made by a group of *publicani*, or tax-collectors that were his clients, over the collection of taxes in the province of Asia. Pompey was denied his Eastern settlement and land for his veterans. Caesar, after his Spanish campaign as propraetor, wanted both a triumph and a consulship. In order to be granted the former, he needed to be allowed to stand for the latter in *absentia*, which the Senate declined to allow him to do. The program of the triumvirate was a program in which all three pooled their wealth and patronage in order to secure what Senatorial government had refused them, and to use constitutional procedures to these ends. Thus Caesar became consul in 59 B.C. and secured for the three what the Senate had refused them. In reward Caesar was granted Cisalpine Gaul and Illyricum for 5 years, the senate having previously determined that his pro-consular province should be the *siluae callesque* of Italy that was little more than a forestry commission. Transalpine Gaul was subsequently added at Pompey's instigation.

After some stresses and strains, the Triumvirate was to survive in order to extend Caesar's proconsular command for a further 5 years (55–50 B.C.). As a *quid pro quo*, the tribunes were induced to block consular elections and so secure second consulships for Pompey (the Spains) and Crassus (Syria). These then proceeded to secure pro-consulships for 5 years, with Pompey resident near Rome and administering his Spanish provinces through a legate. In 53 B.C. Crassus as pro-consul in Syria fell in battle at Carrhae against the Persians. Thus an uncertain peace was left to the two duumvirs Pompey and Caesar.

Pompey proceeded to take supreme power into his hands when rioting prevented consular elections taking place before the end of 53 B.C. The Senate passed a *senatus consultum optimum* and gave him as pro-consul residing in Rome a military command. The senate voted that Pompey should be sole consul so that he had now both consular and pro-consular *imperium*, without any colleague with equal powers as a counterbalance and with the Republican constitution thus now further shredded. Caesar had been the beneficiary of a bill to allow him to stand for a consulship *in absentia* that he could take up immediately following his pro-consulship in Gaul. But Pompey now exposed his fellow duumvir's unconstitutional position by carrying a measure that all candidates for magistracies should appear in person, with Caesar being the exception. Furthermore, another of his measures was that there should be an interval of 5 years between a magistracy and a pro-magistracy, thus debarring others from the power enjoyed by himself. Notwithstanding, his Spanish command was extended for a further 5 years. He then accepted the election of a consular colleague from August onwards.

Pompey, with considerable Optimate support, now moved against Caesar. Consular elections had resumed for 51 B.C. One consul moved that Caesar lay down his command and challenged the validity of the law allowing him to stand as consul *in absentia*. On December 1st, following the chaos caused by tribunician vetoes on these proposals, there was a further proposal, also promptly vetoed, from Caesar's agent, C. Scribonius Curio, that both Pompey and Caesar give up their commands. Caesar's request for an extension of his Gallic command until the end of 49 B.C. had already been rejected. Claudius Marcellus now called upon Pompey to save the Republic.

Metellus Scipio now proposed that, if Caesar did not disband his armies by a fixed date, he should be declared an enemy of the state. The two tribunes who had vetoed this proposal, Anthony and Cassius fled, under threat to their lives, to Caesar at Ravenna. Caesar now advanced across the Rubricon, where by a strict constitutional definition his geographically bounded *imperium* had ended, and marched successfully on Rome, forcing Pompey's withdrawal to Brundi-sium. Pompey's forces were finally to be defeated at Pharsalus, with Pompey's escape to Egypt resulting in his death by order of the young king Ptolemy. It was here that Caesar was to be found three days after Pompey's murder, who so antagonized his erstwhile supporters among Ptolemy's advisors that he was besieged in the palace quarters of the city through the winter (48–47 B.C.). Cleopatra, estranged joint-ruler of Egypt, smuggled herself in, and, on Ptolemy's death in battle against Caesar's troops, was restored as joint ruler with Ptolemy XIV, a younger brother.

Caesar returned to Rome in 47 B.C. He had been elected dictator in 49 B.C. to an office that lasted 11 days, but which enabled him to be elected to his second consulship for 48 B.C. Both offices were theoretically constitutional, although extra constitutional forces were now clearly influencing and determining such appointments. A dictatorship was originally an extraordinary appointment with powers to be used to restore constitutional government in periods of anarchy. He went through the formal constitutional motions of having a consular colleague, though he himself was now elected again dictator, this time for a year. He enjoyed a break from consular office in 47 B.C., but returned in 46 B.C. to a third consulship, and a third dictatorship to last for 10 years. In 45 B.C he became dictator for life, ending his fourth consulship in the October of that year.

At this point rumour and innuendoes abound, and the truth of their origins become difficult to establish. When hailed as 'king' by those whom two tribunes had threatened to punish, Caesar replied 'I am not "King" but "Caesar"' (non sum Rex sed Caesar), since 'king' was used as a person's name (*cognomen*) as well as a title in Latin as it is in English as a surname. Ambiguous religious honours were paid to him, such as the erection of his statue in the temple of Diuus Romulus (Quirinus) with another near those of the kings of Rome. He had received divine honours from Greek city-states in the east, but so had Roman generals for some 150 years before him. Thus an inscription at Ephesus hailed him as 'god manifest and common saviour of the life of man'. But unlike his predecessors, he was to have a cult after his death to *Diuus Julius*.

A Sibylline oracle was interpreted as meaning that the Persians who had triumphed against Crassus at Carrhae could only be defeated by a king. If this was the production of his propaganda machine, this might indicate, along with the ready acceptance of his cult after his death, that he had been profoundly influenced by his mistress, Cleopatra, and the prospects of his son Caesarion. But any such ambitions for him personally were to be ended by his former supporters, who saw finally the tyranny that was developing around them. Brutus, who claimed descent from his namesake who had slain Tarquinius Superbus, the last kind of Rome in 510 B.C., led the conspiracy which, on the Ides (15th) of March, 44 B.C., were to assassinate the dictator, who fell in the Forum at the foot of Pompey's statue.

The consuls Mark Antony and the Magister Equituum, Aemilius Lepidus, now emerged as the official heads of the state. Lepidus was governor of Narbonese Gaul and Hither Spain, and thus had troops at his disposal with which to support himself and Antony. A deal was struck following the hostile reception of the conspirators by the general population that they would be pardoned but Caesar's will would be honoured. The will favoured his great nephew, Octavian, against Antony but was brim full of popular benefactions that enabled Antony in his funeral oration to whip up mob frenzy against Brutus, Cassius and their followers.

Octavian, learning from the will that he was Caesar's adopted son, and with three quarters of his estate, landed at Brundisium with the name C. Julius Caesar Octavianus, inheriting his clients and veterans. Thus with this private army he was growing stronger against the threat of Antony, Brutus, and Cassius and the legions that they commanded by virtue of their pro-consular appointments. Antony was now declared a public enemy, and the conspirators granted command, Brutus and Cassius in Macedonia and Syria with *maius imperium* in the East, with Pompey's son, Sextus Pompeius in command of a fleet, and Decimus Brutus in command of the consular armies. Octavian by this time had eight legions at his disposal with which he marched upon Rome where he was elected *consul suffectus*. Lepidus failed to support the senatorial government, and joined Antony, being also now declared a public enemy.

Meanwhile in Rome both Octavian's adoption by Julius Caesar was confirmed, and the amnesty granted to Caesar's assassins was revoked. At the same time Antony and Lepidus ceased to be public enemies by a senate decree, thus paving the way for their meeting with Octavian that was to result in the Second Triumvirate. On 27th November 43 B.C., by due constitutional process, in contrast with the private agreement that had created the First Triumvirate, they were appointed for 5 years with extraordinary powers to make laws and nominate magistrates and governors. They proceeded to divide up the provinces between them, with the armed forces that were thus placed at their increasingly personal disposal.

The hope for the preservation of senatorial government now rested with Brutus and Cassius and their commands. But Octavian's strength was growing, and in the direction of a Hellenistic monarchy as may be seen in the senate's recognition of him as *filius dei* (son of a god), son of Diuus Iulius, on 1st January 42 B.C. At Philippi on the Via Egnatia, in combination with Antony, Brutus and Cassius were defeated. In consequence, the virtual division of the empire, with Octavian in control of the West and Antony of the East, with Lepidus ignored, now took place.

Antony's forces were to 'liberate' Syria from a Parthian invasion, and to install as Tetrarchs Herod and his brother in Judaea in place of Hyrcanus (37 B.C.). It was in the midst of such eastern consolidation that Antony sent Octavia, Octavian's pregnant sister, back to Italy, while he tried to contract an eastern marriage with Cleopatra, giving her Coele Syria, Cyprus, and part of Cilicia, and recognizing their children, Cleopatra Selene and Alexander Helios. In the spring of 36 B.C., Cleopatra who was by then expecting their third child, Ptolemy Philadelphus, returned to Egypt. That year had also seen the removal of Lepidus from the Triumvirate and Octavian granted the *sacrosanctitas* of a tribune. The ancient plebeian oath to protect to the death the life of a tribune who would guard the subject's liberty against consular autocracy was now servicing an advance towards absolutism.

Following his success in Armenia, Antony now in Egypt with Cleopatra (34 B.C.), staged a pageant in the Gymnasium in Alexandria. Antony and

Cleopatra sat enthroned, the former portraying Osiris-Dionysus and with the latter in the robes of the goddess Isis his goddess consort. Antony proclaimed that Ptolemy Caesar (Caesarion), Cleopatra's child by Julius Caesar, was Caesar's true heir and not therefore by implication Octavian. Rome's eastern provinces were now assigned to his dynasty with Cleopatra. Caesarion was 'king of kings' and Cleopatra 'queen of queens', and joint monarchs of Egypt and of Cyprus. Under them different parts of the empire were assigned to the children of Antony and Cleopatra, Alexander Helios (Armenia, Parthia, and Media), Ptolemy Philadelphus (Syria and Cilicia) and Cleopatra Selene (Cyrenaica and Libya).[3]

In 33 B.C. the limit beyond which the Triumvirate could no longer exercise constitutional power had been reached. Antony sent Octavia formal letters of divorce. Octavian now read out Antony's will to the Senate as evidence, along with reports of the pageant at Alexandria, of the latter's attempt along with the Hellenistic (Egyptian) queen to set up an oriental, imperial monarchy.[4] Not only was Caesarion his heir, but Antony was to be buried in Egypt at Cleopatra's side. Antony, who had crossed into Greece with Cleopatra, was now deprived of his consulship.

In the tension now actively nurtured by Octavian's agents, Italian municipalities and many others in the Western provinces took a personal oath of allegiance to him as he himself describes:

> The whole of Italy, by its own wish, swore an oath to me and implored that I lead it in the battle in which I was victor at Actium. The provinces of Gaul, Spain, Africa, Sicily, Sardinia swore the same oath.[5]

Octavian's propaganda machine, with some justification, was able to characterize Antony as in the thrall of a foreign queen, seeking to impose an oriental despotism upon Rome. He, on the other hand, was the representative of true, Roman values. From the details of the Will, now read out by Octavian in the Senate, it could be inferred and proclaimed by his enemies that if Antony was successful 'he would grant the city of Rome to Cleopatra, and dominion would be transferred to Egypt'.[6]

In the light of this event, duly crafted in the worst possible form by Octavian's propaganda machine, Octavian could thus encourage all Italy and many provinces to vow a personal oath of allegiance to him as his clients. Under his patronage they would join in his movement to deliver Rome from the threat of eastern and Egyptian despotism under a foreign queen who had fashioned a pro-consul after her own, perverse image. We shall need to consider further the

---

3. Dio Cassius, XLIX.41.1–3.
4. Dio Cassius, L.3.4.
5. Augustus, *Res Gest.*, V.25.
6. Dio Cassius, L.4.1.

character of the scene at the donation of Alexandria, and what it really represented in the discourse that Octavian shared with Antony in the legitimation of their rival claims to power. For now let us record that they came finally to Actium in 31 B.C., in which battle Octavian prevailed, and was to pursue Antony and Cleopatra to Alexandria in the following year where both were to commit suicide, and Caesarion to forfeit his life.

Octavian was now to claim to have restored the republic but in fact created a military dictatorship and provided for an autocratic succession. As such he could claim to be the true heir to the Caesarean party, having outmanoeuvred Antony in his ambitions for that position. Caesar had been life dictator *rei publicae resituendae* and not, like Antony with his Egyptian queen and her progeny, an oriental and despotic monarch. Accordingly, Octavian's own claims place divinity firmly in the background. His claim in the *Res Gestae*, originally inscribed on two bronze pillars in Rome in front of the mausoleum of Augustus (A.D. 14), was

> When I was nineteen years of age, by my decision and at my own expense I provided an army by means of which I claimed back the liberty of a republic oppressed by the tyranny of a faction.[7]

Augustus then proceeds from what he began in 43 B.C. to list the constitutional offices that he had occupied, beginning with the Senate's vote of the imperium of a propraetor and his compliance with the Senate's *consultum ultimum* of that year.[8]

The Senate had acknowledged the constitutional character of his wars against his rivals by granting him triumphs and saluting him as imperator 21 times. When both the senate and the people offered him the office of dictatorship, he had declined, as he had initially a life or yearly consulship (22 B.C.).[9] At the time of writing (A.D. 14), he had been consul on 13 occasions and had exercised *tribunicia potestas* for 37 years. By now of course his extra constitutional power with the backing of soldiers wedded to him by the personal ties of patronage meant that his was a military dictatorship in all but name: he could well decline these offices in a display of constitutional subservience.[10] But he claimed only the legitimacy of apparent constitutional office:

> When the Senate and Roman people unanimously agreed that I should be elected overseer of laws and morals, without a colleague and with the fullest power, I refused to accept any power offered to me that was contrary to the traditions of our ancestors.[11]

---

7. Augustus, *Res Gest.*, 1.1.
8. Augustus, *Res Gest.*, 1.1.
9. Augustus, *Res Gest.*, 1.5.
10. A point not lost on contemporary commentators, see Dio Cassius, LIV.4; Velleius Paterculus, II.89.5.
11. Augustus, *Res. Gest.*, 1.6.

It was his *tribunicia potestas* that enabled him constitutionally to perform these functions.

But when we reconsider the development of the constitution and its purpose, following the expulsion of Tarquinius Superbus that we have sketched, we see how hollow were Augustus' claims to constitutionality. Liberty, which in human affairs is ever limited to a certain degree, was allowed by the separation of powers that had emerged in the third and second century B.C. between consuls and tribunes, praetors and censors and lesser magistrates that were subject to time limits within which second terms could be enjoyed. The *cursus honorum* had allowed an open competition for office and political power that was umpired by popular election. Now offices that were separated in pursuit of human liberty were held by Augustus together, as when he chose to hold several consulships against the backcloth of an enduring *tribunicia potestas*. It was as if, with ourselves, the Orwellian nightmare of his novel, *1984* had been fulfilled, and we were confronted by a head of state whom we accused of destroying parliamentary democracy. We might find the dictator responding to our accusations: 'I have not abolished constitutional monarchy, nor the offices of Prime Minister or Leader of the Opposition under the crown. I am the Monarch, the Prime Minister, and the Leader of the Opposition. I combine all these constitutional functions and powers in my own person.'

We confront the fact of the rise and fall of the Roman Republic, however, with a perspective that we have received from the eighteenth-century, European Enlightenment. We understand matters in terms of the state as a machine, and the machinery of government collapsing in the context of certain historical and economic events. The collapse of the Republican constitution we understand to be due to the growth of the Equites as a third estate deprived of political power commensurate with their economic power as *publicani*, etc., as the result of the claims upon the growing imperial structures in the form of directly governed provinces regarding legionaries who required pensions that senatorial government refused them when led by a pro-consul of whom they had come to disapprove, the groundswell of Italian allies demanding citizenship, etc., the personal ties and loyalties created by the deeply imbedded patron–client relationship in the social structure of Roman society, etc. That is how the social reality of the Roman Republic and its collapse confronts our Enlightenment view of history. But it is not how that social reality was perceived (or constructed) by those who participated in it, and which confronted them. We may believe that we understand the 'real' causes of the failure of Republican government at Rome in the first century before Christ. But our understanding was not that of those overtaken by such events in their historical and social context.

So far our historical account has been highly revisionist in that we have excluded from it such religious offices as *pontifex maximus*, as *augur*, etc., granted, to a greater or lesser extent, depending on the particular individual. The omision of a discussion of these offices as peripheral to the Roman constitution thus reflects our Enlightenment rejection of the metaphysical backcloth to political events in which Roman paganism believed. Augustus in the *Res Gestae*, in his assertion of the constitutional propriety of his position in terms of ancestral custom, also included among offices vital to his position such religious priesthoods as *pontifex maximus*, augur, etc., and indeed the Senate changed his name from Octavian to Augustus when he had performed an act of augury.[12] His adoption by *diuus* Julius he asserted had given him divinity too, and the divine title *diui filius*. As he himself recalls, the Senate at the conclusion of the Parthian war (29 B.C.) had decreed that his name be included in the Salian hymn, and was therefore included in the list of the gods.[13] But we must now see that these terms and political offices were part of the perceived, metaphysical reality that confronted both paganism and early Christianity.

2. *Stoicism, Myth and Historiography*

Our post-Enlightenment definition of reality regards society operating by analogy with a machine that can malfunction in a particular historical and economic context. Those who participated in the events of the decline and fall of the Republican constitution did not understand what was happening to them and their society in such terms as these, which I have chosen to use in the previous section, in the light of our Enlightenment heritage. Let us return for one moment to Polybius' account of Roman history (220–145 B.C.), written in the years following 144 B.C.

In the years immediately following the third Macedonian War (172–168 B.C.), Polybius was taken as a prisoner to Italy. Here he was to become tutor to the adopted son of Aemelius Paulus, P. Scipio Africanus, at whose side he was later to stand when he was pro-consul and Carthage was burning (146 B.C.). Aemelius' household had also contained the Stoic philosopher, Panaetius.

Polybius describes three kinds of political constitution, kingly rule, aristocracy and democracy. But each of these good kinds of government has its pathological counterpart in tyranny, oligarchy and mob-rule. Each tends to change into its opposite as history unfolds:

> We should therefore assert that there are six kinds of governments, the three above mentioned . . . and the three that are naturally allied to them, I mean a tyranny, oligarchy, and mob rule. Now the first of these to come into being is rule by a sole person (μοναρχία), its growth being natural and unaided; and next arises kingly rule (βασιλεία) derived from rule by a sole person following its due arrangement and setting right. Kingly rule first changes into its inherent pathological form, tyranny; and next naturally develops aristocracy from the destruction of both forms. But then of course democracy is produced from the natural development of aristocracy into

---

12. Augustus, *Res. Gest.*, 6.34.
13. Augustus, *Res Gest.*, 2.10; cf. Dio Cassius, 51.20.

oligarchy, and when the general population prosecutes in rage the injustices of the authorities. The development is then completed by mob rule (ὀχλοκρατία) in consequence of the violence and lawlessness of democracy.[14]

Polybius' understanding of nature here is what we would describe as 'empirical'. As he appeals to Plato, we might see Polybius focusing here upon Plato's phenomenal world of change and decay and its behaviour.[15] Thus he appeals to 'the actual history of the facts and the common intelligence of mankind'. Thus, prescinding from Plato's metaphysics, Polybius endeavours to give an account of the movement and change of good constitutional forms into their pathological opposites in terms of human passions and emotions, herding together for protection, failure of descendents to follow the moral pattern of their ancestors, jealousy and rivalry arising from surplus energy when basic security has been achieved, etc.

But Polybius believes that such an empirical account, prescinding from what we would describe as metaphysics, nevertheless points to a cyclic development. The history of human constitutions does not finally end with mob rule and anarchy but, from the latter, a master and monarch arises once again, and from rule by a single person kingly rule and subsequently tyranny once again develop, and so things turn in a full circle and so endlessly continue:

> This is the cycle (ἀνακύκλωσις) of constitutions, this is the plan of nature (οἰκονομία) according to which states change, pass on, and again turn into their opposites. Anyone who clearly perceives this change may indeed in speaking of the future of any state be wrong in his estimate of the time the process will take, but if his judgement be not tainted by animosity or jealousy, he will very seldom be mistaken as to the stage of growth or of decline it has reached and as to the form into which it will change. And especially in the case of the Roman state will this method enable us to arrive at a knowledge of its formation, growth, and greatest perfection, and likewise of the change for the worse that is sure one day to follow.[16]

The wise framer of a constitution would, therefore, like Lycurgus at Sparta, provide for a constitution that was not unambiguously one or an other of the three best, but would be a mixture of them all. Although decline and rebirth were inevitable, nevertheless one could, as a wise statesman, make the good form of government, if present, last by producing an equilibrium in which kingly rule, aristocracy and democracy were finely balanced. The Romans similarly, in their Republican constitution, had achieved the same result, and for the reasons with which we began.[17]

Such was Polybius' account in which the Republic would inevitably decline, but for reasons to do with the instability and change inherent in Plato's account

14. Polybius, VI.4.6–11.
15. Polybius, VI.5.1–2.
16. Polybius, VI.9.10–12.
17. Polybius, VI.10.

of the phenomenal world for which no real and metaphysical account was appropriate. But his commonsense and empirical account of the development and decline of political structures was not to be shared in this form by his contemporaries. Let us remember that his contemporary was the Stoic philosopher, Panaetius, at Rome with him in the late second century B.C. in the household of Aemelius.

Panaetius shared Polybius' desire to remove the mythical backcloth to philosophy, and any concomitant metaphysical explanation and justification of the myth. Already in mythology there had existed a myth of the four ages, gold, silver, bronze and iron that we have seen had recurred in Daniel's Jewish apocalypse. Hesiod regarded history as declining from a golden past through five races of human beings, the golden race, the silver race, the bronze race, the heroic race, and then the race of iron.[18] Every good feature of the golden race has now become its evil mirror image, destined to be destroyed by Zeus 'when they come to have grey hair on their temples at their birth',[19] unlike the golden race in its time which 'lived like gods without sorrow of heart, remote and free from toil and grief; miserable age rested not on them'.[20] In a theme reminiscent of Mark's apocalypse:

> The father will not agree with his children or the children with their father . . . nor will brother be dear to brother as afortime. Men will dishonour their parents as they grow quickly old, and will carp at them, chiding them with bitter words, hard-hearted they, not knowing the fear of the gods.[21]

Thus we have a myth of decline, but not one that is due to human defect: the races are as they are by decree of Zeus, according to whose decree all things necessarily develop. There is but the barest hint in Hesiod of a return to a golden age when he says:

> Thereafter, would that I were not amongst the men of the fifth race, but either had died before or been born after.[22]

But there is no further indication given that history moves cyclically.

It is Plato, to whom Polybius has expressed his indebtedness, to whom we owe the notion of a historical cycle in the myth of what for him has become four ages in place of five races.

> During a certain period God himself goes with the universe as guide in its revolving course, but at another epoch, when the cycles have at length reached the measure of his

18.   Hesiod, *Works*, 110–176.
19.   Hesiod, *Works*, 179–181.
20.   Hesiod, *Works*, 109–115.
21.   Hesiod, *Works*, 182–187, cf. Mk 13:12.
22.   Hesiod, *Works*, 174.

allotted time, he lets it go, and of its own accord it turns backward in the opposite direction, since it is a living creature and is endowed with intelligence by him who fashioned
it in the beginning. Now this reversal of its motion is an inevitable part of its nature . . .
The fact is that at certain periods the universe has its present circular motion, and at
other periods it revolves in the reverse direction.[23]

If nature behaves in such a way, then so does the movement of human social
history, since no distinction is made by ancient philosophers in general between
nature and society. The universe, which is a living thing, cannot be unchanging
because only the Forms are unchanging and eternal. It however does the next
best thing, and tries to emulate the eternal Forms by moving in a circular
motion thus imitating without realizing their unchanging nature. Plato relates
his view specifically to the myth of the golden age and its decline.[24]

Chrysippus (280–207 B.C.), in more than the generation before Polybius,
had been the latest in the line of the Stoic philosophers, preceded by Zeno
(333–264 B.C.) and Cleanthes (331–232 B.C.), to produce a philosophical
account justifying the theology presupposed by the myth of historical decline
and renewal. Basically they were opposed to Plato's dualism between matter
and spirit in which matter was part of an unstable, phenomenal world, poised
between existence and non-existence, and not being knowable, and the transcendental world of Forms or essences of things. The soul in the body was akin
to the transcendental world, but caught in this world of sense and sight from
which it could escape only by a hard-won mystical vision.

To the contrary, these Stoics taught that there was no final distinction between
matter and spirit, and the universe was a monistic whole and ultimately divine.
The λόγος spirit was the divine breath pervading all matter, and giving to it its
coherence and order. If one might be allowed to put it that way, the physical
world was not a domain set apart from divine transcendence, but rather it was
the inseparable clothing of God. Forms and essences of things were of the
same ontological status as the material objects in which Plato had said that they
participated, or in which they were reflected. The Stoics instead argued for
a hylomorphism in which, in an inseparable whole, there were to be found
two principles, the active (τὸ ποιοῦν) and the passive (τὸ πάσχον), corresponding to the form or essence of a thing, and the receptivity of matter to be
informed by it.[25]

We can now see how a Stoic metaphysic of political change also enabled to
be taken seriously religious practices such as divination and augury that discerned the process of such change, and was to play a major role in Augustus'
religious reformation that was part of his transformation of the political
constitution.

23. Plato, *Pol.*, 269 C–D and 270 B.
24. Plato, *Pol.*, 271 D–274 A.
25. Diogenes Laertius, 7.134.

3. *Stoic Cosmology, Determinism and Divination*

From such reflections a Stoic cosmology was to emerge consistent with the monism that I have described. In the beginning all was fire, not the empirical fire that we observe, but an aetherial, refined fiery breath – the divine λόγος or reason, whose spiritual designation represents a difference in degree but not in kind in comparison with matter. The cosmic process begins with the λόγος, as refined fire which congeals into phenomenal fire, air, water and earth. These four, primary elements then combine to form the substance of the world which, by a cyclic process, is fated to break up and change once again into the primeval fire from which the world had originally arisen. This process is called the ἐκπύρωσις. Then the cyclical process begins again.[26]

We may characterize this doctrine as a 'Stoic eschatology' in that it deals with the close of history and its beginning again. Such an eschatology deals with how all things come to an end, but unlike in Judeo Christian eschatology, history has no final goal but is cyclical. Sometimes when the (re)ordering of the world (κοσμοποιία) after the ἐκπύρωσις is called the 'rebirth (παλιγ γενεσία)'.[27] This is the very term used by Matthew of the age to come:

> Truly I tell you that you who have followed me, in the rebirth (παλιγγενεσία) when the Son of Man shall sit on the throne of his glory you also shall sit upon thrones judging the twelve tribes of Israel.[28]

Furthermore, a pseudepigraphic, mid-second century text in the New Testament, attributed to Peter, describes the end of the world in such terms as:

> The day of the Lord will come as a thief in which the heavens shall pass away with a rushing motion and the elements shall burn up and melt away and the earth and all the works in it will be uncovered.[29]

The Christians addressed are described as:

> . . . hastening the coming of the Day of the Lord on account of which the heavens will be on fire (πυρούμενοι) and the elements burnt up and melted. But we expect new heavens and a new earth according to his promise, in which righteousness dwells.[30]

---

26. See I. von Arnim, *Stoicorum veterum fragmenta*, vol. II, *Chrysippi fragmenta logica et physica* (Leipzig: Teubner ,1903), frag. 596–632.

27. Simplicius *in Arist. Phys.*, p. 886.11 (= von Arnim, frag. 627; Philo, *Incorrupt. Mund.*, 235.13B (= von Arnim, frag. 613).

28. Mt. 19.28.

29. 2 Pet. 3.10.

30. 2 Pet. 3.12-13.

Not only will the heavens 'be on fire (πυρούμενοι)' as in the ἐκπύρωσις, but the process of order and stability and its loss is due to the immanent λόγος which pervades all things:

> The heavens of old and the earth out of water and through water were held together (συνεστῶσα) by the λόγος of God through which the then world was deluged with water and perished. But the present heavens and the earth are stored up by the same λόγος being preserved by its fire for the Day of Judgment . . .

Thus the λόγος Spirit, the ground plan of the world and its immanent reason, has therefore the nature of fire. Stoic and early Christian eschatology are to this extent in 2 Peter at one.

But as we have seen, there are extraordinary signs or portents described in early Christian apocalyptic, as in Mark 13, though not in 2 Peter. Stars would fall from heaven, the moon turn to blood, and unspecified fearful and deceptive 'signs' and 'wonders' (σημεῖα and τέρατα) would wreak havoc.[31] Such 'signs' were normal part of the conceived reality of Roman paganism from the first, and were part of the constitutional arrangements of Rome that we have so far ignored in following our European Enlightenment perspective that rules out such arrangements as unimportant and superstitious. We must now see what role these played both in Roman political practice and in Stoic theory.

Such signs were called in Latin *portenta* or 'portents', and *prodigia* or 'pro- digies'. Examples of them were showers of stones from the sky, the birth of an hermaphrodite that the *haruspices* had put to death, heads of statues of gods turning around during an earthquake, two suns appearing in the sky, birth of a mule with three feet, appearance of a meteor, etc.[32] It was the function of the *pontifices*, *augures* and *haruspices* to advise the consul in performing the religious rite known as an *augurium*. By means of measuring with a wand (*lituus*) patterns in nature the future could be divined and whether a proposed course of action would be accompanied by the 'peace (*pax*)' or the 'anger (*ira*)' of the gods. Thus we may say that the command of duly constituted authority (*imperium*) needed to be combined with the taking of the auspicial in an act of augury (*augurium*).[33] We saw in our last chapter the role of the magistrate in seeking the *pax deorum* led to the persecution of early Christians.

Some scepticism regarding portents has been noted on the part of both Livy and Cicero. But we should note that the practice of ancient religion was not a matter of private choice in the private sphere. Whatever the rational justification of an augural act and its credibility with a given individual or

---

31. Mk 13.22-23.
32. Julius Obsequens, *Prod.*, 2(= Livy, XXXVIII.36.4); 3(= Livy, XXXIX.22.3–5); 7(= Livy, XL.45.3 and 59.7–8).
33. Livy, XL.52.5.

group of individuals, religious ritual of this kind was what Durkheim would describe as a 'social fact'. Social actions for Durkheim were facts in that a social action was any pattern of behaviour, more or less general throughout society, exercising constraint upon the individual.[34]

As a modern example of ritual as social fact, exercising constraint apart from the particular belief of a participant, I take from one experience of serving Mass on one occasion. After communion, as I assisted the priest in washing the chalice that had held consecrated wine, I proceeded to pour water first from one cruet as I held back the unconsecrated wine in the other. There was a muffled protest as the chalice was snatched away in alarm. Afterwards my apology was met with a relaxed bonhomie from the priest in question. He explained that it should be wine first and then water, because traces Christ's blood in the chalice needed to be washed with unconsecrated wine first before the water could be applied. 'At least', he said with a chuckle and a shrug, 'if you believe in consubstantiation and all that sort of thing'. The point is that, standing back from the ritual and reflecting on it he might well appear to have been sceptical about it. But while involved in the act itself, he responded with the passion and emotions of a 'true believer' even if he was not prepared to articulate any precise justification of what he had done. Any ritual system that objectifies belief systems in such a form gives them a facticity in some sense independent of any one participator. They are general patterns of behaviour exercising constraint upon the behaviour of individuals.

And this is precisely the case reflected in Cicero's work, *De Natura Deorum*. This is a dialogue between an Epicurean (Velleius), a Stoic (Balbus), and a fellow member with Cicero of the Academy (Cotta) on what constituted religion. But we should note the context that Cicero has constructed in order to initiate the discussion. Cotta has just been elected a *pontifex* and Lucilius Balbus proceeds to argue a Stoic justification for augural rites to which Cotta was now obliged to give attention. Balbus is quick to point out before he has given any metaphysical justification that, during the second consulship of the elder Tiberius Gracchus (163 B.C.), father of the tribunes Tiberius and Gaius (133 and 123–122 B.C.), the election of the new consuls (P. Cornelius Scipio Nasica and C. Marcus Figulus) had been declared null and void. Tiberius as consul had crossed the city boundaries and then returned without taking the *auspicia* for a second time before attending a meeting of the Senate. A returning officer had been struck dead while reporting the names of the consuls elect.[35]

Gracchus had initially protested the validity of the election, but it is important to note on what grounds: it was clearly not a question of the validity of the People's choice in exercise of their liberty. He clearly acknowledged that

---

34. E. Durkheim, *The Division of Labour in Society*, introduction by Lewis A. Coser; translated by W. D. Halls (New York: Free Press of Glencoe, 1997).

35. Cicero, *Nat. Deor.*, II.4.10.

the constitutional nature of the deposition depended upon augury to secure divine approval but objected to the means of consultation when the Senate had recourse to the soothsayers (*haruspices*) in order to test the validity of proceeding with a consular election:

> Thereupon Gracchus . . . burst into a rage. 'How now', he cried, 'was I not in order?' I put the names to the vote as consul, as augur, and with the *auspicia* taken. Who are you, Tuscan barbarians, to know the Roman constitution, and to be able to lay down the law as to our elections?'[36]

Clearly his argument with the Senate was not on the principle of *augurium* itself, but because they had preferred the opinion of the Tuscan *haruspices* over his own, who as consul had the right to perform the augural rites.

Indeed, the forced resignation of the two consuls elect only followed when Tiberius himself had remembered his lapse, and owned up to the college of augurs, who referred the matter to the Senate, who in consequence ordered their resignation. Thus in classical Durkheimian terms they were confronted by a social fact as a thing, a pattern of behaviour, more or less general in their society, exercising constraint upon them. It was better for Cotta to act according to the ancestral customs and discipline rather than break from them: consuls elect had lost office because of consuls who had done no less.

There existed a college of augurs who were there to be consulted but whose pronouncements had no force in law unless asked for by the Senate. The augurs in 57 B.C. publicly pronounced that Caesar's laws (59 B.C.) had been flawed at a meeting called by a magistrate (*contio*), but because the Senate had not consulted them, the laws in question remained in force.[37] When the tribunes during the conflict of the orders began taking the *auspicia* before holding assemblies, passing decrees, and electing magistrates, in a sense they were mimicking the consuls' and the Senate's patrician role in doing the same. Any magistrate could consult the *auspicia* and use his observations as grounds for calling off an assembly, and thus delaying or even vetoing legislation.[38] As North says: 'For early Rome it does not need proving that there was a close connection between the *auspicium*, the right to take the auspices, and the magistrate's legitimate authority; it is quite specifically part of the legal structure of the republic.'[39]

Cicero himself had personally reached no final conclusion on the truth of portents, yet he recognized them as part of the Roman political tradition that

36.   Cicero, *Nat. Deor.*, II.4.11.

37.   J. North, 'Diviners and Divination at Rome', in *Pagan Priests. Religion and Power in the Ancient World*, edited by M. Beard and J. North (London: Duckworth, 1990), p. 52.

38.   For several examples and Cicero's views, see L. Ross Taylor, *Party Politics in the Age of Caesar* (Berkeley and Los Angeles: University of California Press, 1964), pp. 78–85.

39.   North, 'Diviners', p. 68.

had to be followed. He reproduced the arguments on both sides of the question in a dialogue in the *De Legibus* between Atticus and Marcus. The latter replies to the former, who raises the possibility that the *auspicia* may have been invented for purely political purposes, which perhaps represents Cicero's own doubts. Marcus replies:

> I think that the art of divination, which the Greeks call μαντική, really exists, and part of this which concerns birds and other signs is part of our discipline. For if we concede that the gods, and the universe is ruled by their will, that they are mindful of the human race, and that they have power to give indications of the future, then I do not see any reason for denying divination.[40]

Thus Balbus will be able to reassure Cotta that the social fact that presents itself to him, constraining his performance as a magistrate in order to secure his political ends, has a justification in the philosophical theology represented by Stoicism.

We may now reflect on how such an account will justify divination. If the fiery spirit that permeates all things is rational, all things are determined by providence in a rational order. As Chrysippus said:

> Fate is the reasoning of the world (ὁ τοῦ κόσμου λόγος) or the reasoning of the things in the world that are governed by providence (λόγος τῶν ἐν τῷ κόσμῳ προνοίᾳ διοικουμένων . . .).[41]

Thus, if all things are rationally determined, then it will be possible for the trained eye of the augur or of the haruspex to see in the flight of birds and in the entrails of a sheep the providential pattern of imminently future events, whether for good or for harm, whether expressing the 'peace (*pax*)' or the 'anger (*ira*)' of the gods. As Balbus says regarding divination:

> Many observations are made by those who inspect the victims at sacrifices, many events are foreseen by augurs or revealed in oracles or in prophecies, dreams, and portents, a knowledge of which has often led to the acquisition of many things gratifying men's wishes and requirements and also to the avoidance of many dangers.[42]

Thus Cotta could be well assured as a *pontifex* that the taking of the auspicia were not simply the requirement of custom and tradition, but also supported by philosophical reasoning.

But we have seen that the logic of Stoic metaphysics went further than simply justifying the seeking of divine approval for a course of action through

---

40. Cicero, *Leg.*, II.13.32.

41. Chrysippus, *Fin.*, 2 and *Fat.* (apud Stobaeius, *Eclog.* I, 39, 1 = von Arnim, II, 264, 18). See also (apud) Alexander Aphrodisias, *Fat.* 22 = von Arnim, II, 273, 26).

42. Cicero, *Nat. Deor.*, II.65.163.

acts of augury. We have seen from the logic of such metaphysics an eschatology in which all things were destined to return to the primeval fire and be reborn into a new world order in ever recurring cycles (the ἐκπυρωσις). Individual Stoics such as Panaetius might have denied that eschatology, but its core logic was sufficiently enduring for his pupil and contemporary of Cicero Poseidonius to reaffirm the doctrine. In such a context *portenta* that were adverse were not simply signs of divine disapproval of a certain course of action: they became, the more they increased, signs of the last phase of the sunset of the world moving towards its fiery consummation. When Stoic metaphysics was joined in explanation with a myth of the four ages, in which the last age of iron would be replaced by the age of gold in a new historical cycle, then adverse portents would herald the final collapse before the rebirth of all things. Thus the magistrate seeking or performing an augural act was seeking to discern a new age, a *saeculum nouum* in process of coming into existence.

Cicero for his part shared in such an eschatological explanation of the historical events that were unfolding in his own time as the Republican constitution was collapsing. Although Polybius understood history as proceeding in a cycle, he did not look to the kind of metaphysical explanation of the Stoics to explain the dynamic of that process as we have seen. But Cicero is influenced by the more metaphysical account of Poseidonius and his traditional Stoic predecessors, and says:

> For one thing in particular I had learned from Plato and from philosophy that certain transformations in the state are natural so that at one time the state is controlled by princes, at another time by the people, then at another time by individual rulers by themselves.[43]

He claims that this last state had befallen his country in the form of the first Triumvirate. His preferred state was that of a mixed constitution, which would enjoy a longer stability than any of Polybius' three good and three corrupt forms of government. As he makes Scipio Africanus assert:

> The kingship, of the three primary forms is in my opinion by far the best. However, even to kingship a kind of government is preferable that is moderated and balanced from the three best forms of state . . . Such a constitution, in the first place, offers a high degree of equality, which is a thing free men can hardly do without for an considerable length of time, and, secondly it has stability. For the primary forms already mentioned degenerate easily into the corresponding perverted forms, the king being replaced by a despot, the aristocracy by an oligarchical faction, and the people by mob and anarchy; but whereas these forms are frequently changed into new ones, this does not happen in the case of the mixed and evenly balanced constitution, except through great faults in the governing class.[44]

43. Cicero, *Div.*, II.2.6, cf. Plato, *Rep.*, VIII.2.545.
44. Cicero, *Rep.*, I.45.69.

Despite his previous appeal to Plato, Cicero is therefore under the influence of a Stoically conceived cyclic view of history. Cicero has reached the conclusion that the historical fate of free constitutions cannot be avoided but only retarded in a cyclical view of history controlled by a fate beyond human control.

It was to be the role of Augustus and those who wrote his narrative of political theology, to refocus such a Stoic perspective into a justification of his transformation of republic into empire, and to replace Cicero's claims for a mixed constitution with one of the absolute monarchy of a *princeps*. We shall now see how Lucan expresses to the generation after Augustus this fundamental shift of perspective.

4. *Lucan and the Inevitability of the Principate*

Lucan was to write in Nero's time his great epic of the civil war, and to place in stark relief the occurrence of portents and the collapse of the natural order of the world. For Lucan, as we shall now see, portents and prodigies occur when nature loses its order and comes to be at variance with itself: they are signs of the ἐκπύρωσις when the λόγος is in process of becoming once again the primeval, aetherial spiritual fire that it was at the first. The stars would move from their courses, as can be witnessed in the case of portents, because, as Cleanthes had said:

> Cleanthes, striving to justify the ἐκπύρωσις, asserts that the sun will assimilate the moon and the remaining stars to itself and will change them into itself. So then the stars, though they are gods, will co-operate with the sun in their own destruction making their contribution to the ἐκπύρωσις.[45]

Here, once again, we note a convergence in eschatological expectation between the late Republic and early Empire, and the Jewish apocalypticism of the Markan, Christian Roman community, albeit on differing religious assumptions. The clearest example of the use of such a Stoic perspective in the interpretation of the events of political history we find in Lucan's great but unfinished epic of the civil war, written in Nero's time. Here we find the change from Republic to Empire described in terms of a Stoic understanding of nature and historical development. Lucan himself, nephew of Seneca, died as a result of his involvement in a conspiracy to take Nero's life. But the conspirators had not the object of restoring the Republic, but simply replacing him with a more benign emperor. Fate had determined the development of the monarchy, and to resist it was clearly useless.

The gods play no role in Lucan's account, but there are the divine forces of Stoicism duly demythologized and laid bare by the augurs and *haruspices*.

---

45.   von Arnim, I.114.26–30 (= Plutarch, *De Comm. Not.*, 1075D).

The civil war begins with Julius Caesar's conflict with the senate following the collapse of the first Triumvirate. But when Lucan looks for the causes, he finds these in Stoic metaphysics:

> My spirit is moved to set forth the causes of these events. The hugeness of the task lies open, to set forth what drove a people to fly wildly into armed conflict, what thrust forth peace from the world. It was the malevolent procession of the Fates and its forbidding the high and great long to stand and Rome not bearing under so great weight her deep collapse. For, when the framework of the world is unravelled, then the final hour compresses so many ages, reverting to primeval chaos, stars clash with stars in confusion, fiery constellations fall towards the sea, the earth refuses to extend her shores and will shake the ocean, the moon will march in opposition to her brother and will drive her chariot along in a zig-zag curve. In her anger she will demand the day for herself, and the total, discordant fabric of the shattered world will throw into disorder the bonds of its association.[46]

Thus Lucan was to set the social and political chaos in the context of a Stoic cosmology, with its underlying metaphysical assumptions about nature and change. Nature and society were one, and disorder found in the one would be reflected in the other.

The stage of the world in its cycle of decline and rebirth could be discerned by augury. Caesar, having crossed the Rubicon in 49 B.C., was approaching a Rome abandoned by Pompey. A noiseless thunderbolt from an unclouded sky smote the capital of Latium. The sun eclipsed. The fire on the altar of Vesta was suddenly extinguished. Women gave birth to creatures of monstrous sizes. Sibylline oracles were disseminated prophesying doom. A Fury was seen shaking her hissing hair with a flaming torch:

> Trumpets sounded; and dark nights witnessed a din like armies engaging in fight. The shade of Sulla was seen to rise from the midst of the Campus Martius, and to chant prophecies of woe and Marius raised his head at the cool waters of the Anio and burst forth from his tomb, putting to flight the peasants.[47]

For such horrendous portents Lucan now seeks an explanation in terms of a Stoic metaphysics, placed in the mouth of a *haruspex*.

Arruns is sent for and he duly acts:

> First, he bids the destruction of monsters, which nature, at variance with herself (*natura discors*), had brought forth from no seed, and orders that the abominable fruit of a barren womb shall be burned in flames of evil omen.[48]

---

46. Lucan, *Bell. Civ.*, 1.67–80.
47. Lucan, *Bell. Civ.*, 1.580–583.
48. Lucan, *Bell. Civ.*, 1.589–591.

Next he enlists the entire state cult. The pontiffs, augurs, *flamines*, vestal virgins, the *quindeciuiri* (college of fifteen priests), and other sacred functionaries join in solemn procession around the *pomerium* or city boundary to perform a *lustrum* or purificatory sacrifice.[49] Arruns now sacrifices a bull and consults the *exta* of the victim, and finds them to be horribly deformed. He therefore prophesizes a dire future.

Nigidius Figulus now intervenes in the epic in order to give a philosophical explanation of these events:

> Either . . . the world strays for eternity governed by no law, and the stars move to and fro with a movement that cannot be determined; or else, if Fate is the cause of motion, for Rome's city and the human race a corruption (*lues*) in its final form (*matura*) is being brought about. Will the earth gape and cities be swallowed up? Or will burning heat destroy our temperate clime? . . . What kind of disaster are the gods preparing? What form of ruin will their anger assume?[50]

Thus with 'nature at variance with itself (*natura discors*)' the universe is losing its coherence in the rational spirit or λόγος. Fate is the cause, which is destiny and thus the product of the λόγος that infuses all things with its personal plan. The result is the kind of situation that one Christian writer was to describe as 'the powers of nature will be shaken',[51] and another 'the elements will burn up and melt away'.[52] Figulus concludes:

> This frenzy will last for many years. What profit in asking those higher beings above for an end? That peace (*pax*) comes with a lord and master (*dominus*). Continue, O Rome, the unbroken succession of your ills, and extend the carnage for many ages. You will only be free while the civil war lasts.[53]

Thus, in Tacitus' words, for *pax* one needs a *princeps*: the peace of the gods 'peace (*pax*)' will only replace their 'anger (*ira*)' when a free republic that has become, in Polybius' and Plato's words, mob-rule, will be transformed into monarchy.[54] At that point too nature will act in concert and itself be transformed into a renewed state of order.

We have thus seen that portents that formed part of Stoic eschatology played a role too in political theology, and the operation of the Roman constitution, as they did in the early Christian, Markan apocalypse. Indeed Tacitus implies that, even if the prodigies that occurred immediately prior to the destruction of the temple in A.D. 70 had not been interpreted favourably to the Jewish cause, the

---

49.   Lucan, *Bell. Civ.*, 1.592–607.
50.   Lucan, *Bell. Civ.*, 1.641–650.
51.   Mk 13.26.
52.   See footnote 30 above, and associated text.
53.   Lucan, *Bell. Civ.*, 1.670–672.
54.   Tacitus, *Annal.*, IV.32–35.

Jews would have been in a hopeless condition regarding them since they lacked the ritual resources for controlling them:

> Prodigies (*prodigia*) had indeed occurred, but a race subservient to superstition (*super-stitio*) held it to be a sacrilege to avert them by sacrificial victims or by means of votive offerings in its opposition to ceremonial rites (*religiones*).[55]

It is interesting to observe from this passage that Judaeism is not considered a depraved form of religion (*superstitio*) because it practises rites of aversion (*religiones*), but because it does not, and cannot therefore secure the *pax deorum*. We can see therefore why Tacitus also, unreflectively because he is otherwise unimpressed by portents, describes Christianity as a 'deadly super-stition (*exitiabilis superstitio*)', not because it believed in rites of aversion, but because it appeared to do so in depraved rites, and therefore did not share in the concern to achieve the *pax deorum* through the relevant ritual of augury. Pliny, as we saw in the last chapter, had used similar language when he described Christianity as a *superstitio praua et immodica* ('a depraved and immoderate superstition').[56] But there is more.

When Octavian claimed the title of Augustus, he was making a claim to stand at the centre of the cosmic process that had secured the *pax deorum* both in nature and in society. We shall see in the next section how this claim is expressed visually in the iconography of the *Ara Pacis*. But first let us look at some other indications of this claim and its cosmic context.

We have a relief panel depicting Augustus with his augur's wand (*lituus*) from an altar of the Lares. Indeed, in his *Res Gestae* he claims the office of augur along with that of *pontifex maximus* and other priesthoods, and indeed it was his first sacerdotal appointment (41 B.C.).[57] He claims furthermore that his military achievements have been made 'under my favourable omens (*auspiciis meis*, in Greek οἰσίοις οἰωνοῖς)'.[58] But literary sources and the continuity of features of this image on the *Ara Pacis* itself suggest that his depiction as augur was not simply the incidental representation of one office among the many that Augustus had held.

Suetonius lends no support to the claim that Octavian renamed himself as Augustus as a divine title. Rather it was to do with his claim to be re-founding Rome for a second time. At the beginning of 27 B.C., in a carefully choreo-graphed spectacle, Octavian had before the Senate formally relinquished all powers. The Senate responded by granting him a vast *prouincia* (Spain, Gaul, Syria and Egypt), and was granted also the title of 'Augustus'. Thus began the second founding of Rome. But rather than call himself 'Romulus' Octavian

55. Tacitus, *Hist.*, 5.13.
56. Pliny, *Ep.*, X.96.8.
57. Augustus, *Res Gest.*, 7.
58. Augustus, *Res Gest.*, 4.2.

now preferred 'Augustus' because it associated him with an unusual act of augury, the augury by means of which Rome had originally been founded. As Suetonius claims:

> He preferred to be called Augustus, not only with a new but more significant surname, but also because religious places which are consecrated by an augur's ritual are called 'august', either from the increase or from the movement and feeding of birds, just as Ennius informs us when he writes:
>
> Afterwards Rome had been founded by an august augury (*augusto augurio*).[59]

Thus Suetonius regarded the title *Augustus* as implying Augustus' office of augur and the practice of *augurium* specifically in connection with the second founding of Rome.

If Suetonius does not directly associate the second founding of Rome with the return of the golden age after the cosmic decline and collapse into an age of iron, Dio Cassius certainly does, and reflects directly Lucan's description of Augustus' principate as the remedy for a 'nature at variance with itself (*natura discors*)'. Livy, on whose lost ending Dio Cassius may have been dependent, records regularly the ritual involved in the *auspicium*. Frequently, in Rome's earlier period, the *pax deorum* is sought for and found in the ritual, and sometimes not found, as when during the first Punic War, the consuls failed to expiate the gods for the portents that had occurred.[60] But there is clear evidence that Livy and others believed that such unsuccessful expiations in the light of adverse portents increased greatly towards the end of the Republic.

We do not have Livy's lost ending, but we do have extracts and fragments, and a text representing the Livian tradition known as the *Julius Obsequens*. Here we find that every military and political disaster is accompanied by adverse omens. If this tradition is faithful to Livy's lost account, then, despite Livy's personal scepticism about portents, his account testified to the general social construction of events in which nature was reflected in society and society in nature, and that the epoch of history was one of cyclic decline and breakdown awaiting renewal. Not only portents, but their control through augury, can now be placed in the context of a Stoic political theology.

For Dio Cassius, Augustus' name refers to his divine qualities.[61] But the significance of an act of augury performed by Augustus as the foundation of the Principate is not lost on him. Dio refers to a special augural rite, the *augurium*

59.   Suetonius, *Aug.*, 7.

60.   Livy, XXVII.23.1, for other examples see Brent, *The Imperial Cult and the Development of Church Order: Concepts and Images of Authority in Paganism and Early Christianity before the Age of Cyprian* (*VCSup*, 45; Leiden: E. J. Brill, 1999), pp. 28–35.

61.   Dio Cassius, LIII.16.8.

salutis as the appropriate rite on the occasion of universal peace.[62] But the rites were to record the continuing anger and not the peace of the gods:

> Nevertheless it was in some way possible at that time for the divination to be held (τὸ οἰώνισμα), but it was impure. For certain birds flew from the unlucky quarter, and for this reason they repeated the augury. Other unlucky omens too occurred . . . Amongst these were thunderbolts from a clear blue sky, earthquakes, and ghosts.[63]

The significance of the second founding of Rome for Dio is that Augustus was to succeed where Republican magistrates had failed, not simply in what we would regard as their functions as secular magistrates, but in their religious duties as well. The rites of *augurium* and *haruspicium* exercised by them had failed, and it was their duty to employ the appropriate sacramental means of seeking the order of a cosmic peace in tandem with the civil peace.

Augustus was to close the doors of the temple of Janus to show that peace had been secured by land and by sea. It had been closed once before under Numa, and then after the first Punic War. Accompanying this act was an extraordinary act of augury, which this time was successful:

> Nevertheless the action which pleased him more than all the decrees was the closing by the senate of the gates of the temple of Janus, implying that all their wars had entirely ceased, and the taking of the *augurium salutis* (τὸ οἰώνισμα τῆς ὑγείας), which had at this time fallen into disuse for the reasons that I have noted.[64]

Augustus' representation of himself in the *Res Gestae*, and iconographically on the altar of the Lares, was of the performer of the *augurium salutis*, only possible in a particular and special moment in the cycle of history. The returning *saeculum aureum*, with all its metaphysical justification in Stoic terms for which Lucan was to call, would therefore have, as its agent and harbinger, the figure of the emperor as augur. The imperial coinage, even as late as Constantine, was to reflect this ideology of the Principate, particularly under Hadrian, and then Decius Trajan and his contemporaries.

The depiction of Augustus as augur on the altar of the Lares had included an image of Gaius or Lucius Caesar on the left, and Julia on the right with features reminiscent of the goddess Venus, albeit with a *patera* in her hand suggesting that she too was a participant in a sacrificial rite in which incense was burned or wine poured out as a libation. Julia was Augustus' daughter, and married to Agrippa, and their children as his grandsons, Gaius and Lucius were the heirs apparent. The significance of Augustus as augur is his successful performance, almost uniquely in Rome's history, of the *augurium pacis* that can

---

62. Dio Cassius, XXXVII.24.1.
63. Dio Cassius, XXXVII.25.1.
64. Dio Cassius, LI.20.4.

now inaugurate the second founding of Rome. But dynastic implications also now follow.[65] There is hint of divinity in the depiction of Julia, particularly as Vergil had made it plain that the divinity of the gens Julia was the result of the union of the divine Venus with the earthly Anchises. But divinity is not at the forefront of the imagery where Augstus' power is represented as sacerdotal and augurial, and not emphatically divine. Such observations might also be made of the *Ara Pacis*, as we shall now see.

5. *The Refounding of Rome and the* Ara Pacis Augustae

Augustus records that on his return from Gaul and Spain:

> . . . the Senate voted in honour of my return the consecration of an altar to Pax Augusta in the Campus Martius, and on this altar it ordered magistrates and priests and Vestal virgins to make annual sacrifice.[66]

The Senate's decree was passed on 4th July, 13 B.C. Three and one half years later (30th January, 9 B.C.) the altar was completed and dedicated.

As we have seen, for over a century the Roman republican constitution had been in crisis and the Republic engulfed in a number of civil wars that marked the gradual collapse of that constitution. That collapse, we have argued, was not simply understood in utilitarian terms of the 'machinery' of government ceasing to function as its political engineers had so designed it. The collapse was viewed as a metaphysical collapse of a nature at variance with itself (*natura discors*) that needed to be set right by the appropriate sacrificial and sacramental means. The art and iconography of the *Ara Pacis* was to witness to the completion of the Augustan revolution that was both political and religious. The *Ara* is an artefact that expressed the political theology legitimating Augustan autocracy.

The purpose of the altar and its inauguration seems clearly to celebrate the *augurium pacis*, and to renew its effects each year, in hope for the continuance of 'peace by land and sea', even when the opposite appeared to be the likely case, and the gates of the temple of Janus opened once more. The outer wall of the altar displays both upper and lower friezes on both its longer sides. The lower frieze exhibits vegetation represented as acanthus scrolls unfolding from a luxuriant tuft of acanthus, interleaved with various kinds of plants bearing fruit. Lizards and scorpions sometimes appear eating some of the leaves, or snakes threatening nests of birds. There are full-grown swans also depicted.

On the upper frieze we have depicted a procession of priests (pontiffs, *flamines* and augurs), along with members of the imperial family, with Augustus

---

65. P. Zanker, *The Power of Images in the Age of Augustus*, translated by A. Shapiro (Ann Arbor: University of Michigan Press, 1990), p. 172, fig. 135.

66. Augustus, *Res Gest.*, 12.2.

leading the procession accompanied by lictors, in view of his rank as a magistrate with *imperium*, and by augurs indicative of the sacrifice that he is to offer with the assistance of the Camillus also depicted. Augustus is veiled for sacrifice, as is Agrippa, at whose side and dragging on his robe is Gaius the grandson and son of both respectively. The juxtaposition of the two friezes portrays a symmetry between the natural and the social order: the harmony of nature is reflected in the orderly political succession of Augustus' heirs guaranteed by the sacerdotal figures, who mediate the *pax deorum* to nature as to society: the harmony of civil society arises out of the harmony of nature.

The processional scene is probably not a literal depiction of what happened at the *inauguratio* of the altar, but rather an ideal and composite picture, as are some other scenes, each of which depicts some aspect of the legitimation of Augustus' power. Drusus, Livia's son and Augustus' stepson, already dead, is depicted. There is a scene of what appears to be a *suouetaurilia*, or the sacrifice of a pig and a bull, depicted on the crowning slab of the sacrificial table within the outer walls. Such a rite was usually conducted with a census, but no census was taken in 9 B.C. Augustus and Agrippa as censors had carried out the first census for 40 years in 28 B.C., in which they filled a Senate that had become depleted by the carnage of civil war. The general citizen population now numbered over 4 million persons. A census was fundamentally a religious act, as its other Latin name, *lustrum* ('cleansing sacrifice') makes clear. A pontifical procession, at whose head was a pig and a bull, circled around the boundary or *pomerium* of the city of Rome in a rite that 'cleansed' the sacred space, and therefore the individuals who were contained within it, and sanctified political authority, *imperium*, exercised within that bounded space. Augustus' revolution was a religious as well as a political revolution.

Augustus and his spin-doctors clearly, therefore, wished to perpetuate the image of the census with its related images of the consecration and cleansing of sacred space within which power is legitimated, and to universalize the image as a general claim to Augustus' metaphysical accomplishment. They may also have, by means of this *suouetaurilia* panel, been anticipating the census that followed in 8 B.C., only one year after the completion of the *Ara* and its dedication (9 B.C.). The second founding of Rome is celebrated on the *Ara Pacis* and associated with a number of events that give the appropriate metaphysical character to the Principate. Augustus with an act of augury is not simply founding Rome a second time, but successfully performing an augury that as a sacrament can effect the return of the golden age. The predestined course of a cyclic history is centred on his person alone.

The interpretation of the two friezes on the south and north panels is reinforced by the iconography of those of the east and west. As one approaches the opening onto the steps that lead up to the sacrificial table, two scenes meet us on the right and the left upper panels below the continuing vegetative frieze. On the left of the east façade we have depicted a mother with two children on her lap. The children are well fed and blossoming in health, and around the head of the right hand child we observe a bouquet of poppies, ears of wheat, and lilies in gigantic and supernatural size. It is a pagan millennium in which 'earth shall yield its abundance'. On the mother's right and left are the two *Aurae uelificantes* or the nymphs of the winds of land and of sea. The *Aura* on her right is born by a flying swan, with earth yielding crops at her feet, and that on her left by a sea dragon with representations of waves beneath her.

The central figure was originally identified by Petersen and Moretti as *Tellus* or the earth mother goddess, or by Spaeth as of Ceres, the goddess of harvest and fertility.[67] Certainly such imagery is evoked by the garland crown of fruit and flowers that peeks out from under the veil that covers her head, as well as the sheep and oxen that lie in peaceful pose at her feet. The *Ludi Saeculares* or 'centennial games' had been celebrated 4 years earlier (17 B.C.). But these games were clearly an advertisement of Augustus' *saeculum aureum*, and Horace in the ode composed for the occasion, the *Carmen Saeculare*, celebrates 'Mother Earth (*Tellus*), fertile in fruit and cattle' and Ceres too 'crowned with wheat' and the 'fertility of the land'.[68] Clearly the imagery applies to Ceres as well as to *Tellus*, and given such ambiguity, Zanker sees the image as depicting the goddess *Pax,* which he relates to the opposite panel (eastern façade) where we find the fragmentary remains of the goddess *Roma* seated on a trophy of weapons. The goddess *Pax* is thus brought into quite visual connection with the *pax Augusti*. But given the fluidity of images here evoked, we might also include a further image and one related to Augustus' divinity, however repressed in this particular artefact.

At the opposite end of the altar there is a further relief preserved, depicting Aeneas and the *Penates* (gods of hearth and home). On the opposite side, the corresponding panel depicted Romulus and Remus, suckled by the she-wolf (*Lupercalia*), as Mars, god of war, looks on. Thus there is represented Vergil's narrative of Rome's origins in the *Aeneid*, in which the traditional account of Rome's ancestry is subsumed into that of Aeneas, a refugee from the Greek Trojan Wars, led by destiny to found the city (Rome). The *Penates* or household gods are housed in a small, portable temple or *aedicula*, and stand in the background. In the foreground is Aeneas, an elderly figure, veiled for sacrifice, with what was originally a *patera* in his right hand, pouring a drink offering. In offering the rite, he is assisted by a *camillus*, a sacerdotal assistant. But behind him we can trace in a mutilated figure the presence of Iulus Ascanius, Aeneas' son, and founder of the *gens Julia* from his father's union with the goddess Venus. It is this that was to make Augustus 'son of god' through Julius Caesar's line, and it is as 'son of god, who shall found the golden age' that Vergil describes Aeneas as saluting in the underworld the shade of Augustus yet to be

---

67. E. Petersen, *Ara Pacis Augustae* (Wien: A. Hölder, 1902) and G. Moretti, *Ara Pacis Augustae*, (Rome, 1948), cf. B. S. Spaeth, 'The Goddess Ceres in the Ara Pacis Augustae and in the Carthage Relief', *AJA*, 77 (1994), pp. 65–100.

68. Horace, *Carmen Saeculare*, 29–32 and O. Rossini, *Ara Pacis*, (Rome: Eclecta, 2006), p. 39.

born as the 'offspring of Iulus'.[69] Augustus' claim to be of the *genus diuorum* would moreover succeed even against a sceptic that might point out to his status as the adopted son of Julius Caesar, and not an immediate blood relative. We should remember that his father, the original Gaius Octavius, though of provincial stock from Velitrae, married Octavian's mother Atia as his second wife. Her mother was Julia, wife of Julius Caesar.

If we now return to the *Tellus/Pax* panel, we can detect here images of Venus that therefore continue the theme of the *gens Iulii*, and the divinity of Augustus' imperial line. Lucretius, the great Epicurean poet, began his *De Rerum Naturae* with the lines:

> Begetter of the sons of Aeneas, desire of men and of the gods, nursing mother Venus, under heaven's gliding stars you guide their ships and you fill to abundance the whole earth with fruitful crops . . . At your presence the winds take flight, from you and at your advent heaven's clouds, for you the richly patterned earth sheds forth its scented flowers . . .[70]

Thus the central figure, therefore, as Galinsky has pointed out, evokes both Venus imagery and Augustan dynastic imagery.[71]

We see the winds of land and sea represented by the *Aurae uelificantes*, and the earth's abundance with fruitful crops, 'the richly patterned earth' and 'its scented flowers'. We see Venus associated through the continuing iconography around the altar, with Aeneas and, therefore, with Venus' divine offspring. But Venus' features bear a striking resemblance to those of Augustus' daughter, Julia, who had borne to Agrippa Gaius and Lucius, who became Augustus' heirs. The two children tugging at the breasts, or seated on the lap of Julia/Venus, can be identified with Gaius and Lucius, who also appear in the procesional frieze (south) where Julia is following the little Gaius who is tugging on the hem of the tunic of Agrippa his father, veiled for sacrifice and preceded by a *lictor*.[72]

The message of the *Ara Pacis* is that Augustus, as augur, had performed the *augurium pacis*, which Republican magistrates, under a republican constitution with time limits on the holding of offices, including sacred ones (with the exception of the *Pontifex Maximus*), had been unable successfully to perform. So superabundant were the consequences of his sacral act that 'peace by land and by sea' had been accomplished, together with the earth flourishing in all its fruitfulness. The *pax deorum*, the 'peace of the gods', had been achieved, not simply in terms of one society in one geographical territory but universally

69. Vergil, *Aeneid*, 6.789–790 and 792–793.
70. Lucretius, *Rer. Nat.*, 1.1–8.
71. K. Galinsky, 'Venus, Polysemy, and the Ara Pacis Augustae', *AJA*, 96, 3 (1992), pp. 457–75.
72. See Rossini, *Ara Pacis*, pp. 56–57, cf. p. 38, 40 and 69.

throughout the world, both in nature and in the new, imperial order in society. Thus the golden age had replaced the age of iron in the fated cycle of human history, and Augustus stood as the agent of a destiny, whose reality the arguments of a brilliant, Stoic philosophy were well able to authenticate along with the way in which divination and augury could rationally be held to discern that destiny. Augustus marked a restoration of the order of society rooted in the order of the cosmos, a setting right of what Lucan described as 'nature at variance with itself (*natura discors*)'.

But the imagery of the *Ara Pacis* did not lack allusions to the divinity of the Augustus, who, as Octavian, had claimed to be Caesar's heir, and who had gained from a reluctant Senate the dedication in the Forum of the temple of *Diuus Iulius* (42 B.C.). He had done so as part of the second Triumvirate in which Antony, continuing to claim leadership of the Caesarean party, had become *flamen* of Julius' cult. Caesar during his lifetime had, according to the tradition of Dio Cassius, surrounded himself with some of the accoutrements of divine honours. His chariot stood in front of that of Juppiter at the Capitoline temple, his statue placed among those of the gods, with Mark Antony acting as his *flamen*. During games and theatrical performances his statue was displayed on a *puluinar* or couch of the gods.[73]

Since therefore both Caesar and his claimed heirs, Octavian and Antony, began by sharing a belief at least in his divinity, we must now ask why Octavian as Augustus approached the subject of his divinity apparently so circumspectly.

6. *The Divinity of the Roman Emperor*

Two factors appear to have been at work, the first the course of his propaganda campaign against Antony. Octavian had assailed the pretentiousness of Antony's claim to possess divinity with Cleopatra, so that he could not plausibly now claim it directly for himself. But even here there was the counter propaganda that assumed that claims to divinity were not what had been wrong, but rather claim to be the wrong divinity. Antony as Dionysus was morally the wrong kind of divinity for a Rome, in which Augustus (somewhat hypocritically) was to enforce the restoration of morals. Atia, presumably before Vergil's narrative legitimating power in terms of the descent from Venus, had apparently reported that Octavian had been the result of sleeping in the temple of Apollo, and being impregnated by the god in the form of a serpent.[74] Octavian could well trace his divine descent from Apollo as well as having Venus in his bloodline.

The fundamental reason for the reluctance appeared to be the absence of personal divinity in legitimating the exercise of specific political powers in

---

73. Dio Cassius, XLIV.6.
74. Aesclepias of Mendes, *Theologumena*, (= Suetonius, *Aug.*, II.94.4).

the tradition of Republican Rome. Roman patrician families might claim the prestige of divinity in their bloodlines, but this did not make them divine representatives in the offices that they held. Well might therefore Octavian work more circumspectly than either Antony or Caesar before him.

Augustus' claims to divinity were made by implication, as on the *Ara Pacis*, and by a careful insinuation of the imperial into the pattern of traditional cults. *Pax* was one of many cults of abstract qualities personified as divinities, along with *Concordia*, *Salus*, *Fides*, and duly celebrated with sacerdotal offerings. But the altar was not simply the *Ara Pacis* but, to give it its full name, was the *Ara Pacis Augustae*, which is more properly translated 'the altar of the Augustan Peace'. Fears has pointed out how, by the addition of Augustus' name used adjectively, the abstract divinities were associated with his own, and focused upon his person.[75] *Fides* becomes *Fides Augusta*, *Salus* becomes *Salus Augusta* and so on. Indeed, this gradual and cunning assimilation of emperor worship with existing cults were to form a general feature of the development of the imperial cult.

We shall later see how Domitian insinuated his own image worn as a medallion in the *coronae* or crowns woven and gilded from laurel leaves on the heads of the priests (*Flaviales*) who presided over the religious ceremonies of the Capitoline games (A.D. 86). Thus his image could be venerated along with but clearly not instead of those of the Capitoline Triad, Jupiter, Juno and Minerva.[76] In Hadrian's time, we have the example of Julius Demosthenes bequest for a music festival at Oionanda (A.D. 125) in which the images bearers (θεοφόροι) of the traditional god of the city (Apollo) are joined with those who bear the images of the imperial household (σεβαστοφόροι).[77] Thus the divinity of the imperial house is joined with that of the tutelary deities of the city in a celebration of the unity of the city-states of Asia Minor within the power structure of the imperial whole.

The gradual acclimatization of the Roman social consciousness to ruler-worship was however assisted by some deep-seated tendencies in traditional Roman religion. The pouring of wine or offering of incense to the gods of hearth and home by the *Paterfamilias* or patriarchal head of the Roman household at meals and other times is a well-attested practice. Thus one might say that there was a private cult, potentially in every Roman household, in which the spirits of one's ancestors were afforded religious devotion.

Augustus was portrayed as a *Lar* on one panel of an altar whose remains are in the Capitoline Museum.[78] His identification with the Lar is indicated by the

75.   J. R., Fears, 'The Cult of Virtues and Roman Imperial Ideology, in *ANRW*, II.17, 2 (1981), pp. 827–948; Brent, *Imperial Cult*, pp. 64–67.

76.   Suetonius, *Dom.*, 4.4 and Brent, *Imperial Cult*, chapter 4.

77.   *SEG*, XXXVIII.1426.C. See also Brent, *Ignatius of Antioch and the Second Sophistic* (*STAC*, 36; Tübingen: Mohr Siebeck, 2006), p. 165.

78.   Brent, *Imperial Cult*, p. 63 and Plate 11.

laurel bay leaf held in the figure's right hand. This was a symbol of Augustus and appeared at the entrance of his house in the forum. The picture suggests a small statue, an example of some 235 others, carried in procession and deposited in *aedicula* or shrines in the form of a house. On another panel of the altar we find depicted the offering of a pig, which was the usual sacrifice to the *lares et penates*. The *Lar*, originally protector god of one's house and home had now become superintendent of a *uicus* or district of the city. Different *vici* or districts of the city were foci of unrest during the republican period, and thus we find the imperial cult assisting the social mobility of new magistrates by making them both rulers and priests of the *uici* of the city.

On another panel there are four *uicomagistri* or superintendents of districts of the city.[79] They, wearing togas indicative of their rank, are conducting a sacrifice at the head of a procession with two of them in the foreground holding a *patera* in their hands and pouring wine or incense into the flames. Their names occur in the background. These were freedmen with a cult that gave them a new status, with slaves as *ministri* of the sacrifice.

A further development within traditional Roman religion that was to assist in the growing conception of the emperor's divinity was the cult of *genius*. A person's *genius* was their true self, bearing the impress of their enduring character and existing on a spiritual level. When concepts of an afterlife in a distinctly personalized form gained what appears to be general acceptance, the *genius* came to refer to one's continuing existence after death of the body. *Genii* could haunt a specific place with which they had been associated, as *genii loci*. But given the formation of a concept of individual survival, the *genii loci* could now be associated with the *lares et penates*, who were no longer amorphous entities without personality, lingering ghostly shadows of their former selves, but now distinct and enduring personalities. The *genii* of one's ancestors lingered in specific shape around their graves or homes.

Thus it became possible to honour with cult the emperor's *genius*, by which military oaths were to be sworn. Indeed, perhaps in 12 B.C., reference to his *genius* was made in all official oaths after the names of Jupiter and the *Di Penates*.[80] It was by the *genius* of Caesar that early Christians were ordered to express conformity with the state religion. In the Acts of the Scillitan Martyrs (A.D. 180), when Speratus asserts: 'I do not recognise the empire of this age, I recognise my master, the king of kings and emperor of all nations',[81] Saturninus the pro-consul replied: 'We are religious, and we swear by the

---

79. Brent, *Imperial Cult*, p. 62 and Plate 8.
80. Scullard, *Gracchi to Nero*, pp. 234–35.
81. J. Armitage Robinson (Ed.), *Passio Scilitanorum*, in *Passio Perpetuae*, in *Texts and Studies: Contributions to Biblical and Patristic Literature*, No. 2 (Cambridge: University Press, 1891), pp. 112, 18–22.

genius of our Lord Emperor'.[82] The beginnings of such a cult we can find once again in the remains of artefacts of the *uicomagistri* in Augustus' reign.

We have a frieze from an altar located in the Vatican Museum where, though the *lares* are in view, the focus is on a sacrifice to the *genius* of Augustus. Here we find a frieze depicting an offertory procession of a *vicus* organized with its own cult. Four *magistri vici* are depicted with clear portraits of their individual faces. But here the iconography is not of a sacrifice to the *lares*. Three young men with statues of the *lares* are led by a fourth bearing a specific image of Augustus. Immediately behind the animals for sacrifice are two persons wearing togas of rank, with two lads with laurel garlands around their heads accompanying them. The togas identify them as of senatorial rank, and indeed the consuls of that year as shown by the lictors accompanying them. But the significance of the statues and their arrangement is that what is now depicted is a sacrifice to the *genius Augusti* in which the *lares* take part, but are not the objects of, the sacrifice.[83]

Thus the ground was well prepared by a set of developing assumptions for the acceptance of ruler-worship at Rome. The emperor was not normally worshipped whilst he was still alive any more than the *lares* or *genii* of one's ancestors. It was only after his death that he joined other members of the imperial family and received cultic devotion. The famous example of this was Vespasian, who when he was on his deathbed and his life ebbing away said: 'Alas, I guess I am becoming a god'.[84] Claudius and Domitian claimed divine honours during their lifetime, but suffered on their deaths a *damnatio memoriae*, which meant that they were excluded from the dead and deified emperors and their families to whom cult was offered.

Augustus was not offered cult during his lifetime in Rome, even though Horace countenanced the possibility when he proclaimed that, after Persia and Britain had been added to the Roman empire, Augustus would be held a 'god at the present time (*praesens deus*)' upon the earth.[85] But undoubtedly Augustus was so honoured in the East, particularly the Hellenistic East. It is from this source that we can identify the causes for the development of ruler-worship alone from an original amorphous and vaguely conceptualized sentiment of ancestor worship.

There was a tradition before Augustus of initiating cults to Rome personified as the goddess *Roma*. In the course of the second century B.C., we find at both Aphrodisias and Chios the beginnings of such cults that became common.[86]

82. Armitage Robinson, *Passio Perpetuae*, pp. 112, 9–11.
83. Brent, *Imperial Cult*, Plate 10.
84. Suetonius, *Vesp.*, 23.4.
85. Horace, *Odes*, III.5.2.
86. S. R. F. Price, *Rituals and Power: The Roman Imperial Cult in Asia Minor* (Cambridge: University Press, 1984), pp. 41–42.

Subsequently the name of Augustus was added to that of *Roma* in the dedication of temples in such places as Ancyra, Mylasa and Ephesus.[87] In 29 B.C. the Asians and Bithynians offered cult to Octavian, following his success against Antony, but the former refused the offer. He allowed the dedication of sacred precincts in temples in Ephesus and in Nicaea to *Roma* and Julius Caesar, his dead and deified adoptive father. But Dio claimed that only the 'Hellenes' were allowed to offer cult to himself in Pergamum and Nicomedia.[88] According to Suetonius, he insisted that any such cults be offered to *Roma* as well as himself.[89]

Temples were therefore erected to the living emperor on what appears as the initiative of the Greek cities themselves, which later generally petitioned the Senate to endorse their decrees and be allowed to offer such cultus.[90] Following the example of Mytilene on Lesbos, cities sent embassies to Rome with copies of their decrees, and had copies distributed to other cities in rivalry and one-upmanship, awaiting imperial approval in reply, as was to happen at Oioanda under Hadrian in the case of Julius Demosthenes' bequest.[91] Furthermore, though the ideological foundations of the ruler cult lay in the East, it also became a religious phenomenon in the West very shortly after its inception as we shall shortly see. When Augustus became *Pontifex Maximus* (12 B.C.), an imperial cult was inaugurated for the provinces of the Three Gauls at Condate on the occasion of the emperor's birthday, with a local chieftain of the Aeduan tribe, Gaius Iulus Vercondaridubnus, appointed as his high priest, and there were other examples soon to follow such as that of Claudius at Colchester (Camulodunum).[92] There was clearly no obstacle to Augustus being high priest of the state religion and also an object of cult worship himself.

The reluctance of Augustus to accept such cult may of course be of a piece with the character of the Octavian who, in 27 B.C., had stage managed the gesture of handing back the whole Roman State to the Senate on the lapsing of his special powers. The Senate's carefully orchestrated response granted him a vast province over Spain, Gaul, Syria and Egypt with command of legions to ensure the continuance of his autocracy. Reluctantly, faced with overwhelming senatorial protests that he should not stand down, he had accepted.

Ruler worship was unusual at Rome and had, as we have said, originated in the East. The cult of *diuus Iulius*, beginning according to Cassius Dio in Caesar's lifetime, could be attributed to the influence of Cleopatra and what

87. Price, *Rituals and Power*, pp. 166–69.
88. Dio Cassius, LI.20.6–8.
89. Suetonius, *Aug.*, 52.
90. P. Garnsey and R. Saller, *The Roman Empire: Economy, Society and Culture* (London: Duckworth, 1987).
91. See above, footnote 74.
92. Livy, *Epit.*, CXXXIX and Garnsey and Saller, *Roman Empire: Economy*, p. 166.

we shall see to have been an (Hellenistic) Egyptian political theology of divine monarchy. But too much has been laid at her feet by Octavian and his spin-doctors in their opposition to Antony. It may be argued, as Price has in part argued, that the Hellenistic East could only be governed in a form that made the city-states complicit in Roman domination by means of the acceptance of the emperor as divine ruler.

As we have pointed out, it was the city-states such as Pergamum and Nicomedia that actually petitioned to be allowed to offer cult to Octavian. The imperial cult was used by those city-states, with political institutions founded upon assumptions of liberty and autonomy, to create a kind of social-psychological space in which such liberty and autonomy could still be felt to be enjoyed. By divinizing the force of an external, imperial power they insulated their conception of their autonomous institutions from damage and confusion by making it transcendent, and not part of the machinery of the everyday and normal working of their constitutions: divine activity could be allowed exemption from the normal rules. It was a lesson that one Roman general had learned some time before the middle of the second century B.C., who was depicted naked, and in semblance of the sculptor Lysippus' portrayal of Alexander with the Spear.[93] Marius too, after his victory over Jugurtha and the Cimbri, had choreographed his triumphal procession through Asia drinking wine from a *kantheros* in imitation of the divine Dionysus.[94]

Let us look more closely at the political theology of the ruler cult, focusing particularly upon Antony and Cleopatra, and the Donation of Alexandria (34 B.C.). We shall now see that, despite the attack of Octavian's propaganda machine on Antony, both were to legitimate their claims to absolute power in terms of a common set of formal metaphysical assumptions about the nature of power and its exercise. Julius Caesar, Antony and Octavian may have found themselves adopting the style of Eastern rulers not primarily from Cleopatra's influence, but because they grasped that this was the only ideology by means of which the exercise of imperial power could be made legitimate in the Hellenistic city-states of the East.

7. *Ruler Worship in the East: Antony and Cleopatra*

Let us begin by sketching in greater detail the scene (in late 34 B.C.) in which, according to Octavian's spin-doctors, Cleopatra and Antony paraded them-selves as joint rulers from an Egyptian world capital at the event known as the donation of Alexandria. It is a scene carefully constructed by such spin-doctors, but its main elements may not be the fiction that has often been

93.   Zanker, *Power of Images*, p. 5 and p. 4 fig. 1.
94.   Valerius Maximus, *Fact.*, III.6.6 and Zanker, *Power of Images*, p. 8.

supposed. The scene in the gymnasium at Alexandria had followed Antony's successful Armenian campaign, and the capture of its king, Artavasdes, who was now paraded in Alexandria in chains of gold in a scene reminiscent of a Roman triumph. Certainly there was a great Dionysiac procession at Alexandria, which thus shared religious features in common with Roman triumphs.[95]

Under Cleopatra's influence, so ran the orchestrated rumours, Antony had acted as gymnasiarch at Alexandria, which meant that he had dispensed with the dignified, Roman attire with the insignia of the rank of a Roman imperator, and dressed instead in a purple robe and white shoes with the rods of this official. He called her 'queen' and 'lady (δέσποινα)'.[96] While Cleopatra was carried on her magisterial chair (δίφρος), it was said that Antony accompanied her on foot with her eunuchs, and he himself in public was seen reclining on a gilded couch or similar official chair. Portrait painting and statues represented him as Osiris (or Dionysus), with Cleopatra his consort as Isis. Whenever she used an oath, she would add something like 'as surely as one day I will dispense justice on the Capitol'.[97] Sometimes he was described as Dionysus and she Selene:

> In a procession at Alexandria, he had impersonated Father Liber, his head bound with the ivy wreath, his person enveloped in the saffron robe of gold, holding in his hand the thyrsus, wearing the buskins, and riding the Bacchic chariot.[98]

This was the backcloth to the scene in which the provinces of Rome's empire were distributed to Cleopatra's children, Alexander Helios, Cleopatra Selene and Ptolemy Philadelphus, as well as to Caesarion, whom she had borne as claimed heir to Julius Caesar. What of course Octavian's spin-doctors did not go on to mention was that Antony had performed a similar role immediately before the events of 44 B.C. in the nascent cult of the living *Diuus Iulius*, when he had acted as a *flamen* to Caesar who was addressed as 'Jupiter Julius'.[99]

The claim of a Pharaoh to be the incarnation of Osiris and his consort that of Isis was traditional in Egypt. The Egyptian king was the incarnation of all divinity. He is identified with Horus as the reborn god of death and life. As a Pharaoh died, he became Osiris and his son and heir became Horus. Isis was wife and sister of Osiris, and thus the king's consort at least in one version of a highly convoluted myth. As a succession myth, it indicates the rebirth of political order as integral to the natural order. Heirs to the Egyptian throne

---

95. C. Pelling, I. 'The Triumviral Period', in *CAH²*, X.1, *The Augustan Empire, 43 B.C. – A.D. 69*, p. 40, citing Versnel 1970 (A. 97), pp. 20–38; 235–54; 288–89.
96. Dio Cassius, L.5.1; Plutarch, *Ant.*, 33.
97. Dio Cassius, L.5.4.
98. Velleius Paterculus, II.82.4; See also Plutarch, *Ant.*, 36.
99. Dio Cassius, XLIV.6.4.

notoriously had to fight the chaos of rebellion on the part of groups of their subjects in events to which the frequent floodings of the Nile seemed to be natural analogues. The order of political succession was thus a divine order reflected in nature. The liturgical expression in the coronation ritual, or in the New Year festival, was on the theme of triumphing over chaos through the incarnation of divine order in both nature and in human society. As Mowinckel in debt to Frankfort pointed out:

> Therefore the king's death and his entrance into the world beyond . . . together with the accession of the new king form a 'transition' of vital significance. It is consummated in the accession festival, which has been called 'the Mystery Play of the Succession'. In it there is enacted with complete realism, and with the same result, all that took place at creation, when the world order was established, and as the historical institution of the monarchy. The god, who at one and the same time has joined his ancestors and been reborn in his son, stands there again in the fullness of divine power, holding the world order in his hand and securing life and blessing . . . World order and justice again repose securely in the divine king.[100]

Thus the belief in divine kingship as reflecting the divine order of nature permeating human society was deeply rooted in Egyptian religious and political tradition.

But despite Octavian's black propaganda, Cleopatra and her dynasty were not native Egyptian. Her ancestor, Ptolemaeius, had been a Greek general of Alexander the Great, who had succeeded to one part of the latter's empire following his death. Alexander the Great had originally been proclaimed divine by the Corinthian league after his return from India, and it is at this point in the history of Greece that the concept of a divine ruler enters Greek political thought.[101]

We have fragments of a compendium of the Pythagorean authors, Diotogenes, Sthenidas and Ecphantus, constructed later by Stobaeus, and dated by modern scholars originally around the third century B.C. These writers addressed possibly Hieron II, king of Syracuse, and a Hellenistic monarch. Diotogenes claimed:

> Now the king bears the same relation to the state as God to the world; and the state is to the world as the king is to God. For the state, made as it is by a harmonizing together of many different elements is an imitation of the order and harmony of the

---

100. S. Mowinckel, *He that Cometh*, translated by G. W. Anderson (Oxford: Blackwell, 1956), p. 30, citing H. Frankfort, *Kingship and the Gods: A Study of the Ancient Near Eastern Religion as the Integration of Society and Nature* (Chicago: University of Chicago Press, 1978), pp. 90–123.

101. G. F. Chesnut, 'The Ruler and the Logos', in *ANRW*, II.16.2, pp. 1310–32 (1311), and L. Cerfaux and J. Tondriau, *Le Culte des Souverains dans la civilisation gréco-romaine* (Bibl. de Théol., Sér. 3,5; Paris-Tournai, 1957).

world, while the king who has an absolute rulership . . . has been transformed into a god amongst men.[102]

Thus there was symmetry between the divine order and human order that, as we have seen, the Stoics described as λόγος ἐνδιαθετος.

The state was an imitation or *mimesis* (μεμίμαται), and the king therefore was a *mimesis* of Zeus, king of the gods. Sthenidas makes the point explicit that the king became a god 'by birth and by imitation (γενέσει καὶ μιμάσει)'.[103] It is a general principle of Hellenistic philosophical theology that in imitation you become ontologically that which you imitate. Ecphantus was to associate specifically the king with his version of the Stoic doctrine of the logos that permeated all things in the form of seeds that were scattered (σπερματικός λόγος). The king became bearer of the divine *logos* and thus the guarantor of a political order that was *ipso facto* moral.

It was not simply in Egypt, but in the East in general, following Alexander, that the ruler cult became of central importance. When, for example, Antiochus III of Syria extended his power over the city-states of Western Asia Minor, it was the people of a state such as Iasos that erected an altar to his divinity in thanksgiving for their liberation from Philip V of Macedon (197 B.C.). The regular sacrifices offered on behalf of new magistrates coming into office were now changed, and sacrifices made on the altar of divine Antiochus and his Seleucid ancestors, whose divine ancestor had been Apollo. Laodice III, Antiochus' queen, became associated in cult with Aphrodite, with sacrifices offered to her by couples in process of marrying.[104]

Furthermore Teos had, in revolt from the Attalid kingdom of Pergamon, submitted to Antiochus III, and, as part of that submission, had set up a cult of Antiochus and Laodice (204–203 B.C.). Their cult statues were set up in the temple of Dionysus so that 'by sharing in the temple and other matters with Dionysus, they should become the common saviours of our city'. They thus were equal in divinity to the tutelary deity of the city, and their protection was considered as equally divine as his.[105]

Roman generals were also known to have received from Greek city-states in the East cults in their honour well before Augustus. Marius is one example who, following his victory over the Cimbri at Vercellae (101 B.C.), had enjoyed offerings of food and libations with 'the rest of the gods' from family cults in Roman homes.[106] Titus Flaminius, consul in 198 B.C., had made arrangements for mainland Greece, after the defeat of Antiochus IV (194 B.C.), and Asia Minor (188 B.C.). The Chalcidians, in response, dedicated a gymasium to Titus

---

102. Stobaeus IV.7.61, quoted in Chesnut, 'Ruler', p. 1315 footnote 15.
103. Stobaeus, IV.7.63, quoted in Chesnut , 'Ruler', p. 1318.
104. S. R. F. Price, *Rituals and Power*, p. 30.
105. Price, *Rituals and Power*, p. 31.
106. Plutarch, *Mar.*, 27.5.

and to Heracles, and in another place a Delphinium to him and Apollo. The priesthood of his cult still existed in Plutarch's time (born, A.D. 45), with sacrifice in his honour and a hymn that ran:

> We revere the faith (*Fides*) of the Romans, and we guard it with great solemnity by our oaths. Sing O you maidens to great Zeus and to Rome, and to Titus and *Fides* of the Romans. Hail Paian Apollo, O Titus our saviour.[107]

Thus Titus, after his death was revered as the saviour Apollo, though previously he was associated with Heracles.

It must be noted that when a particular political rule was ended, then the cult to the particular ruler ceased. Price quotes as an example the end of the rule of Philip V of Macedon over the Athenians, who had celebrated his cult and that of his ancestors back to Antigonus 1st. Often however the cult of the new ruler was simply assimilated to that of the old, as when at Delos Ptolemaic festivals simply replaced those of the Antigonic kings, with their altars renamed and reused.[108]

When Antony therefore assumed beside Cleopatra the costume of Osiris or Bacchus, he was simply conforming to the usual processes of legitimating power by impersonating the divine order of the cosmos in a drama of replay. Such a practice, according to Mowinckel and Frankfort, had a long history in Egyptian religion, as had been witnessed in the accession festival marked by a mystery play enacting the divine drama of that succession. But it had a thoroughly Greek justification in both the Stoic philosophy of Sthenidas and Ecphantus, in terms of the cosmic order reflected through the monarch as political order.

The concept of a divine ruler had thus been made acceptable to Antony and his contemporaries in terms of the Hellenistic concept of the divine order of the universe, the immanent logos ($\lambda\acute{o}\gamma o\varsigma\ \emph{\"{e}}\nu\delta\iota\alpha\theta\varepsilon\tau o\varsigma$) of Stoicism mediating the metaphysical order of the world into human society. It was not alien and Egyptian, but was the product, if anything, of Cleopatra's Hellenistic heritage. The pageant at Alexandria was not merely a spectacle of entertainment, but a drama of replay that was sacramental in that it effected what it symbolized and symbolized what it effected. Furthermore, although there were clearly Pythagorean and Platonic versions of arguments for considering the ruler as a divinity, the clear Stoicism revealed in many expressions of the doctrine made it congruent with Lucan's world in which nature could lose the divine order of the $\lambda\acute{o}\gamma o\varsigma\ \emph{\`{e}}\nu\delta\iota\alpha\theta\varepsilon\tau o\varsigma$, and require re-ordering again by a *princeps* who could banish the prodigies and portents that were an index of *natura discors*. Thus a divine ruler, reasserting both the social, moral and natural metaphysical order, was to be as much part of Octavian's political perspective as it had been of

---

107. Plutarch, *Tit. Flam.*, 16.3–4.
108. Price, *Rituals and Power*, p. 40.

Antony's. This was message of the underlying metaphysics of the scene enacted by Cleopatra-Isis and Antony-Osiris-Dionysus.

There was an inclusive character to Graeco-Roman religion to which the technical term 'syncretistic' has been applied. And our account, ranging from the iconography of the *Ara Pacis* to that of the Donation of Alexandria, has shown that syncretism, combining both Western Roman and Eastern Hellenistic worldviews into a united and functioning whole. Let us now summarize what we have thus established.

8. *In Conclusion: Pagan Eschatology and the Divine Ruler*

From a Western perspective Augustus, as his name implied, through his office as augur, had performed a remarkable act of augury, the *augurium pacis* that had achieved the peace of the gods (*pax deorum*) in nature and society. His revolution had marked, as Lucan insists, the return of the golden age after the decline into the ages of bronze and of iron: his act had corrected the metaphysical decline into chaos of nature and of society, witnessed by the supernatural signs and portents (*portenta* and *prodigia*) that were the marks of a nature at variance with itself (*natura discors*). This was the vision that both Lucan and the iconography of the *Ara Pacis* shared.

It was also a vision that could not be dismissed as the product of mass hysteria, the ignorant ravings of the masses when convulsed by the economic and material forces that swept away the Republic and replaced it with the autocracy of the Principate. We have shown that it was reinforced by a persuasive and convincing intellectual justification in Stoic eschatology. The language of returning golden age, and the ages of iron and brass, accompanied by indicative signs and portents, was a picturesque and popular representation of the cyclic movement of history, moved by the λόγος ἐνδιαθετος, in which all things were fated to return to the primeval and aethereal fire from which they had originated, and to be restored again in the cyclical process of renewal and rebirth in a process known as the ἐκύρωσις. Within such a scheme of things the ruler, as the harbinger of the golden age, could simply act as *Pontifex Maximus* or as *augur* or both, in a refashioned constitution that was the product both of a political and of a religious reformation.

In such a scheme of things, the ruler needed to be a priest as well as an emperor, but not necessarily a divine one. Paradoxically emperors did become the object of worship in cults of which they were also high priest, a paradox in which later Christian worshippers and readers of Hebrews in the New Testament were to share.

But we have seen that the divinity of the emperor also became part of this worldview of renewal and rebirth, where it appears, somewhat surreptitiously and in an elusive fashion, through the figures of Venus and Anchises on the *Ara Pacis*. The worship of one's ancestors in the *Lares et Penates* smoothed the way for the acceptance of the emperor's divinity, but did not necessitate it. But the association of the eschatology of the returning golden age indicated by the augural act of the emperor as *Pontifex* with the emperor's divinity was not simply accidental. The eschatology of the ἐκύρωσις was connected, through the doctrine of the 'immanent logos (λόγος ἐνδιάθετος)' controlling all things by its force of destiny, to the ruler who, as λόγος, was also therefore divine. Here was the philosophical theology that underlay Vergil's claim that he who would 'found the golden age' would be 'Augustus Caesar, offspring of the gods'. The legitimacy of the emperor's acts as that divinity would be confirmed by the positive signs and portents that accompanied them, along with the positive signs seen in the patterns of flights of birds, and in the entrails of the sacrificed victim.

The message both of the *Ara Pacis* and of Vergilian political messianism was that of the restoration of the golden age. The religious achievement of the Principate had been the banishment of the metaphysical chaos of which the civil war and external disasters had been the symptoms requiring remedy, whose success was marked by the *augurium pacis*. But if these were so, positive portents were to be the norm marking the emperor's benign destiny, and prophecy must now be of a golden age of peace and plenty and not of disasters and destruction.

The source of prophecy concerning Rome's future was the Sibyl at Cumae, and indeed the written oracles purporting to come from her. There had been such an eschatological context to what was asserted in the imagery of the pageant at Alexandria, in which those who supported Octavian also shared, only in the latter case what was prophesied was to be different. The scene at Alexandria had had its counterpart in a sibylline prophecy:

> And while Rome will be hesitating over
> the conquest of Egypt, then the mighty Queen
> of the immortal king will appear among men . . .
> three will subdue Rome with a pitiful fate . . .
> And then the world under a woman's hands
> will be ruled and will give universal obeisance . . .[109]

Vergil had modelled his fourth Eclogue on a Sibylline oracle.[110] In asserting the second founding of Rome as the return of the golden age, it was necessary to shape such oracles in a form in which they would be 'on message'.

As part of his reformation of Roman religion, Augustus had constructed a temple to Apollo (dedicated in 28 B.C.), whom he had considered his tutelary deity at Actium (31 B.C.), and whom some legends had claimed as his divine father after Atia's overnight slumber in his temple.[111] An impressive building

109. *Orac. Sibyl.*, 3.46-53 and 75–77.
110. Vergil, *Ec.*, 4.
111. Above, footnote 74 and associated text.

was erected, whose surrounding colonnade featured statues of the Danaids and Apollo, with images of his mother and daughter, Atia and Julia, within.[112] It was here that the books of Sibylline oracles were transferred from the temple of Jupiter (19 B.C.), which had housed them under the Republic and where they had then been consulted by senatorial decree. It was on the occasion of the secular games (17 B.C.) that the texts of the oracles were purged.

From the picture that has emerged of a pagan eschatology, with divine rulership guaranteeing a pagan millennium such as we saw depicted on the *Ara Pacis,* we can now grasp the full effect of the apocalyptic message of the Markan, Roman community in the years leading up to A.D. 64, the first persecution under Nero. Here was not simply a sect threatening the general *pax deorum,* but specifically the *pax deorum* secured by Augustus as the foundation of his returning golden age. The Markan apocalypse proclaims that the very portents and *prodigia* that the imperial ideology claimed to have banished, at least in sufficiently huge numbers to testify to the metaphysical collapse of a *natura discors,* are about to return. The predication of a general outbreak of earthquakes, famines, nation rising against nation, a temple defiled by a mysterious 'desolating sacrilege', the darkened moon and a blood red sun, 'shaking' of the 'powers of nature' all, in Roman eyes, raise the spectre of the world before Augustus filled with such monstrous prodigies that Augustus as augur had banished with his returning golden age. To assert that these had not gone away, or that they would return, and another figure, the Son of Man, would rule the nations and produce peace in nature and in society, was a political claim that challenged the Augustan ideology written so large on the *Ara Pacis.* Christ's second coming as Son of Man would accomplish the real, in terms of Matthew's reading of his text, 'rebirth (παλιγγενεσία)' of the cosmic order.[113]

παλιγγενεσία was a term used by Stoic writers to describe the reordering of the world after the destruction of its order that was the ἐκπύρωσις, that we have argued to prefigure in Augustus' political theology. At least Matthew, as one not particularly Roman reader of Mark's text, was able, therefore, to associate the general language of his apocalyptic themes with the metaphysical and Stoic language of the ἐκπύρωσις and its aftermath. Chrysippus had used this term in this sense, as Philo records in his work *On the Incorruptibility of the World*:

> According to the Stoics, there is one universe, and God is responsible for its birth but not for its destruction. There is a force inherent in all objects of a never resting fire that dissolves all things into its own substance over long cyclic process of time. From that power a rebirth of the world (ἀναγέννησις) again finds its order by the design of its architect. According to these writers, the universe is in one sense eternal, but in another

---

112.   S.R.F. Price, 'The Place of Religion: Rome in the Early Empire', in *CAH2,* X.16, pp. 832–33.
113.   Mt. 19:28, cf. chapter 2, footnote 133.

sense perishable, perishable with regard to any continuing structure, but eternal on account of the conflagration (ἐκπύρωσις), and made undying through its rebirths and cycles which never terminate . . . Those who always gabble about conflagrations (ἐκπύρωσεις) and rebirths (παλιγγενεσίαι) amaze us . . .[114]

Cicero was to translate παλιγγενεσία as *renouatio* or 'renewal' when he expressed Chrysippus' doctrine thus:

At the last the entire universe will catch fire . . . and so nothing will remain except fire from which again through god who breathes life into it a renewal (*renouatio*) of the universe takes place and thus an ordered world arises once more.[115]

Renouatio, interestingly in view of what we have said about the *augurium pacis* in relation to Augustus' divine mission, was the term used for the renewal of sacred rites because some point of ancient ritual has been, through careless-ness or accident, omitted in order to reverse adverse portents. The early Christian claim to a παλιγγενεσία by other means seriously shattered such a pagan worldview of those who, through a conversion experience, came to accept the faith of the Markan community.

In our quoted extract from Philo, we observed that he used synonymously with παλιγγενεσία the term ἀναγέννησις. This of course is the term in its verbal form used in the New Testament for 'rebirth' experienced in Christian baptism.[116]

We saw in our last chapter what the response of pagan Rome under Nero was, according to Tacitus, to the community of Mark's Gospel and its immi-nent expectations following events in Judea. The nature of that response has perhaps been veiled from us by a Tacitus, who had little sympathy for Nero, and who delighted in blaming him for the fire, while claiming that the real reason for the persecution of the Christians was the false charge that it was they in fact who had started the fire. But as Keresztes has pointed out, Tacitus may have mislead us in his desire to demonize Nero by individualizing his act into one of personal cruelty in defence of a personal case. No other writer, whether Christian apologist (Eusebius, Jerome), or pagan writer (Suetonius, Sulpicius Severus), mentions anything other than the charge of 'hatred of the human race (*odium humani generis*)'.[117]

But, in the picture of paganism that has emerged in this chapter, the reason for Christianity and Roman paganism clashing the moment the former came to the latter's notice is not simply some vague notion of upsetting the *pax deorum*

---

114. Philo, *Aetern. Mund.*, 3.8–9 and 9.47. See also 17.85; 18.93; 19.99. For further refer-ences, see von Arnim, IV: Indices, p. 111.

115. Cicero, *Nat. Deor.*, II.46.118.

116. 1 Pet. 1:3 and 23.

117. Keresztes, P., 'Rome and the Christian Church I', in *ANRW*, II.23.1, pp. 247–315 (252–57).

through the practice of magic as was believed of the Dionysiac rioters or of Chaldean astrologers, as was the case in the *senatusconsultum* of A.D. 14. Here the practice of magic or prophetic arts was made illegal, as seen in Ulpian's commentary on its implementation.[118] Nero and his successors, in proceeding against Christianity, were not proceeding against what was for them a cult the details of whose true beliefs were in a shadowy haze and lost on them. The evidence of the Markan apocalypse, and its heightened accentuation in Matthew, provided detailed evidence of a clear threat to the religious reformation that had been established by Augustus and his heirs, and on which the legitimation of their political power had been founded.

Mark's description of falling stars, a darkened sun and bloody moon, accompanied by the shaking of the powers of nature and the collapse of both the natural and the social order was a direct negation of the millennial claims of the Principate that had expurgated the Sibylline library in 17 B.C. Apart from the swarm of bees (11 B.C.) presaging an ambush, it is with this year that the *Julius Obsequens* of the Livian school ends its chronicle of portents. Indeed, the writers' claim that 'the whole force of the Romans was crushed in an ambush' was patently false, and Drusus achieved military success.[119] It was therefore the penultimate entry that saw Livia's Apennine estate suffering an earthquake, a meteor illuminating the night sky from south to north, and Augustus gardens by the Colline gate lost a tower due to a lightning strike.[120] These were the last significant portents to be recorded. As Dio Cassius adds, Tiberius and Drusus had left the city and Augustus was away. The night following their departure, the temple of Iuventus burnt down, a wolf at large on the Via Sacra had got into the Forum and killed people, in addition to the meteor that *Julius Obsequens* mentions. But the remedy for these signs was prayer for the return of Augustus: it was not to look for the return of a crucified Messiah on the clouds of heaven as Son of Man. The *quindecimuiri* held the quadrennial celebration of Augustus' rule in his absence.[121]

Dio Cassius had dated these events in 16 B.C. following Augustus' departure and that of Drusus and Tiberius. On his return in 13 B.C., as we have seen, had followed in thanksgiving the decree of the Senate for the inauguration of the *Ara Pacis* with the *augurium pacis*. *Pax* had come, as Lucan says, both in nature and in society, with a *princeps*. The imagery of the Markan apocalypse, and its message of imminent cosmic collapse marked by portents (or 'signs and wonders'), thus represented a political statement against Augustus' millennial project and that of his heirs such as Nero. Nero's persecution was not,

---

118. Ulpian, *De officio proncon.*, VIII, cf. Dio Cassius, LVII.15.8; Tacitus, *Annal.*, II.27–32; Suetonius, *Tib.*, 36. See also A. N. Sherwin-White, 'The Early Persecutions and Roman Law Again', in *JTS*, 3.2 (1952), pp. 211–12.

119. Pliny, *Nat. Hist.*, XI.18.55.

120. Julius Obsequens, *Prod.*, 71.

121. Dio Cassius, LIV.19.7–8.

therefore, as Tacitus claims, the personal act of a shifty tyrant, but of a Roman emperor defending the iconography of his office and that of his predecessors and successors.

What response was the Roman Christian community, and other Christian communities that shared their outlook, to make to the attack by the state? One possible response they might see in that of a Jew like Josephus who, as we saw in chapter 2, ceased to be rebel commander in Galilee by A.D. 67 when he proceeded to interpret all signs and wonders observed around the fall of Jerusalem as referring to Vespasian's victory, whose coinage is marked by a star. It was a judgement with which Tacitus, as we have seen, was to concur.

One response is for the oppressed community to take up arms in guerrilla warfare on a terrain where it could be effective. There is no evidence that any early Christian group took this option, unlike some Jews whose resistance was to resurface in the Bar Cochbah revolt in designating their leader clearly as 'the star (cochab)': these particular Jews clearly did not believe in Josephus' reinterpretation of oracles, signs, and wonders to apply to the endurance of the pagan empire. But as we have seen was the case in Europe prior to 1989, those who believe in the historical inevitability of the fulfilment of the claims that they make can well rest easy over rejecting coming to power by force: social democratic Marxists were quite prepared to wait for the appointed moment in which capitalism would collapse under its own inherent contradictions, and then the resultant new order could be constructed under their leadership.

Such a pacific response, shared by Christianity with the oracles of the book of Daniel and with the Pharisaic movement in Judaism, believed equally that history, whose course was pre-ordained by God's will, would finally deliver new power relationships in which their downtrodden position would be set right. Such a response by the community of Mark, and other similar minded early Christian groups, would of course admit only a very moderate concession to the political system under which they were governed. That system, like the 'capitalism' of the Marxist and radical socialist approach of the last century, was destined to decline and to break up. The representatives of the new order needed simply to wait their moment, with their own definition of political structures for the future remaining intact and unaltered, and simply awaiting the historical moment for their implementation. And so it was that the writer of the book of Revelation in the New Testament was to set out his program of what was to 'shortly come to pass' in the Roman Empire of Domitian, and of the coming to power of those who would reign with Christ at his return.

But there are other responses of movements that become far more successful in changing history. One such response is for the movement under attack to seek ideological rapprochement with those who oppose them. The leader of that movement will claim, like New Labour, that so long as their 'values' are preserved, the way in which they see the course of their implementation – and by means of what new social structures – are negotiable with the wider society. Those who share in the wider culture with them also need convincing, and they will only be convinced if there is a synthesis between their present social reality and that which is being proposed. We shall argue that such was the response of Luke and his community, and that was continued in Clement of Rome, Justin Martyr and others up until the fulfilment of their 'project' with Constantine. Another response was a retreat from social involvement and inter-action into an individual mysticism, seeking personal redemption beyond society, and indeed the (lesser) created order. This we shall see to be the case with such groups as are labelled 'Gnostic'. But it was to be the Lukan project that was to succeed in leading Christianity's transformation of pagan culture, and to some extent its own transformation by that culture that the exponents of 'the project' would nevertheless not wish to admit.

But we turn to John the Seer, and the book of Revelation.

Chapter 4

JOHN THE SEER'S APOCALYPTIC RESPONSE: AN ATTACK
ON AUGUSTAN COSMIC RECONSTRUCTION

Titus had razed Jerusalem to the ground in A.D. 70 after Vespasian's departure for Rome, where both were to enjoy a triumph, and the former a triumphal arch in the following year. The 'desecrating sacrilege' had taken place in so far as Roman standards, adorned with images regarded as idolatrous by the Jews, had been taken into the Temple court, while the city and the Holy Places were in flames, and pagan sacrifices made with Titus acclaimed imperator.[1] But the further events of the Markan apocalypse had clearly not been realized.

One reaction was that it was still to happen. Matthew certainly believed this about Mark's apocalypse that he developed into further more lurid details: the 'desolating sacrilege' could no longer occur in the temple at Jerusalem since this was no more but it would happen somewhere else, 'in (some other) holy place'.[2] The mysterious 'sign of the Son of Man' would be seen in the sky immediately prior to his 'coming with the clouds of heaven'.[3] John the Seer and author of the book of Revelation was to predict, possibly in Vespasian's time, but more probably, in my opinion, in Domitian's, 'those things that must come to pass', immediately after what he wrote to the seven churches of Asia Minor at the very beginning of his work.[4] The writer is instructed by the angel that accompanies him in his vision that 'the time is near' for the fulfilment of his prophecies. Jesus himself promises 'I am coming quickly'.[5]

At first sight we appear to have the typical reaction of a doomed group whose expectations are unfulfilled, and will never be fulfilled. A small minority might still continue in such terms the sense of identity and purpose that constitute it as a group with a mission that makes it a movement. But lack of fulfilment of its claims will inevitably lead to a slackening of support, and a loss of very wide appeal. Its ability to engage with wider society and gain adherents will diminish the more its claims are unfulfilled. In other words, if the Jesus movement were to be able to become the world-wide religion that was Christianity,

1. Josephus, *BJ*, 6.316.
2. Mt. 24:15.
3. Mt. 24:29-30.
4. Rev. 4:1.
5. Rev. 22:10 and 20.

it had to find new ways of engaging with wider Graeco-Roman society: it required a new consensus and a new agenda that would satisfy more than a narrowly Jewish and apocalyptic perspective: it needed to combine the sensibilities of Jewish Hellenistic groups with positively pagan ones. Only if it could find the means of satisfying those other agendas could it become a universal religion capable of politically transforming the pagan society to which it was opposed, and win the ability to redefine the aspirations of that society and the acknowledgment of the legitimacy of the power of its own leadership within it.

The battle of the Jesus movement to evolve from a small cult to a universal faith that redefined and thus transformed Roman society so that it could achieve political power within it was not fought upon the lines with which we are familiar in post-Enlightenment Europe. Our contemporary European culture, from the eighteenth century until the 1980s before the collapse of Marxism and the rise of Islamic societies in the East, has been dominated by an ideology of material progress. The purpose of human, social organization became material and economic. In terms of politics, this meant the pursuit of the greatest happiness of the greatest number by the application of economic principles that were to produce material prosperity. The success and failure of individual leaders and politicians were related to their ability to maximize such ends in contrast to their opponents. Any political project defined by religious ends was ruled out, such as a moral order pleasing to God and offering salvation, preparing both society and individuals for an eternal end. Church and state were to be separated: the individual was free to seek his own salvation and follow his own moral code: civil society was solely concerned with such economic objectives as 'raising the standard of living', or maintaining the internal or external peace so that the former could be enjoyed.

In endeavouring to engage with such a politically successful, secular and materialist enterprise, Liberation theology was to spurn the religion of individual salvation and individual morality. It rejected such individualism as an acceptance of the marginality of religious belief and its irrelevance to political society. Rather it sought to show a Christianity that licensed political engagement on behalf of the poor that would do what? Satisfy the objective of Enlightenment in that by a new form of Christian praxis the material benefit of the deprived would be increased, and the 'greatest happiness of the greatest number' duly maximized. Thus the oppressed would be 'liberated'.

Liberation theology, together with the utilitarian and Enlightenment culture with which it sought to engage, was to be duly shattered by the change that found its focus in the successful attack upon the Twin Towers on 9/11. Both found themselves faced with a militant Islam that since has successfully progressed and fanned itself (or been fanned) into a growing political movement, whose sought for goal is the achievement of an Islamic society whose success is not measured by its members in material and economic terms. Any such achievement is incidental to the creation of a theocracy in which an Islamic definition of God's will is done in the due moral ordering of society by, of course, its leaders, whose power thereby becomes legitimated by such 'spiritual' and not 'materialistic' criteria.

The position faced by Mark's group was not of a civil power like that of the Enlightenment rejecting religious and spiritual goals in favour of material criteria of political aims and political success. Rather it is like a Christianity that might recover its nerve in a contemporary conflict with militant Islam, if not like that of Western materialism in search of an effective ideology against a new and different foe. The ideological conflict is not between a materialism that rules out the spiritual and religious dimension that is irrelevant within an all pervasive secular worldview, but between two conflicting religious perspectives, each claiming to be the rightful occupant of the ground of the other.

We saw in our last chapter how the paganism that early Christianity needed to confront if it were to be an effective political force did not negate its spiritual and eschatological goals for society with anything like Enlightenment, secular materialism. Rather, the movement that brought Octavian to power and made him the emperor Augustus was a spiritual movement with its own, pagan eschatology. The golden age, the *saeculum aureum*, had returned through the agency of an Augustus and his imperial cult that produced peace in nature and society, and a world of super abounding wealth, not by understanding economics as a material exchange between man and nature, but by controlling spiritual forces by a successful act of augury, the *augurium pacis* that had secured the peace of the gods in nature and in society. The *Ara Pacis* had inaugurated a pagan millennium in which the peace of the gods would be eternal under a universal, Roman Empire.

The returning golden age therefore had both a sacral and a political agent in the person of the emperor. The *princeps*, who had achieved such a *pax*, we might say was indeed the 'prince (*princeps*) of peace'. He was, furthermore, divine by virtue of his parentage both immediately by adoption by Julius Caesar, but also through other blood ancestors. The *Gens Julia* was founded, as Vergil, Augustus' court poet will never fail to remind us, as a result of the liaison of the goddess Venus with Anchises. Thus Augustus was *genus diuorum* or 'offspring of the gods'. Vergil in the *Eclogues* had prophesied the birth of a divine child as well as a new age in a transformed nature.

This then was the dominant political ideology, caste in a deeply religious, pagan mould that the Seer of the Revelation was to confront. Unlike Mark in his apocalypse, and Matthew, the continuator of his apocalyptic tradition, the Seer of Revelation was to reconstruct the pagan images of power and authority in terms of that Christian, apocalyptic tradition, as we shall now see.

Vespasian erected, in A.D. 75, a *Templum Pacis Augustae*, a temple of Augustus' Peace, magnificently adorned, according to Josephus, with paintings and sculptures on ancient themes, although the *fiscus Judaicus*, the Jewish temple tax, was now to be paid by Jews to the temple of Juppiter Capitolinus in Rome

instead of to the now destroyed Jerusalem temple.[6] The themes of the Ara
Pacis could therefore be continued by a new Augustus, and Vespasian emphasized from the first his continuity with the latter. Vespasian, like his rivals,
had adopted the Julian family name of Caesar. His coinage, moreover, celebrates the Augustan theme of *Fortuna Redux*.[7] The themes of the returning
golden age and the millennial peace could thus be continued. Dio records that,
in A.D. 70 at Alexandria, Vespasian had healed a blind person, and one with
a withered hand. The blind person received the emperor's spittle in his eyes in
a scene reminiscent of a scene from Mark's Gospel, not repeated in Matthew
and in Luke, where Jesus spits into the eyes of a blind man in process of
healing him.[8]

The author of Revelation was to challenge that millennial and Augustan
claim to have achieved the *pax deorum* in nature and in society. In broad terms
he confronts the imperial power with the continuing themes of the Markan
apocalypse. What is 'to come to pass' is in effect the collapse of the natural
order into its primeval chaos. The prodigies and portents, the signs and the
wonders, that according to Lucan had marked in nature its loss of order, were
now to return, despite the recent assertion of Vespasian in the iconography of
the *Templum Pacis Augustae*. When the lamb opens the seventh seal:

> There was a great earthquake, the sun became black like hairy sackcloth, the full moon
> became like blood, and the stars of the heaven fell to the earth like a fig tree drops its
> winter fruits when shaken by a great wind. The sky was opened up like a scroll rolled
> open and every hill and island was shaken from its place.[9]

Subsequently the inhabitants of the world, from kings to slaves, flee to the hills
and mountains. The rider who had appeared at the opening of the second seal
had 'taken peace from the world'.[10]

Such pagan portents had occurred in the political chaos that preceded
Vespasians's accession, in the camp of his enemy and rival, Vitellius (A.D. 69),
where the sight of the moon eclipsed in blood had caused consternation in his
camp.[11] The restoration of the *pax deorum*, with the accession of Augustus'
true heir, is thus a common feature of the legitimation of imperial succession.
The supersession of Macrinus by Elagabalus (A.D. 218) was also accompanied
by an eclipse of the sun and a comet.[12] In Revelation, when the fourth angel
sounds his trumpet, a third part of the sun, moon and stars is affected, so that

---

6.   Josephus, *BJ*, 7.158–60; 216–18, cf. Dio Cassius, LXV.7.2.
7.   M. Griffin, The Flavians, in *CAH²*, IX.1.1, pp. 13–14.
8.   Dio Cassius, LXV.8.1.
9.   Rev. 6:12-14 cf.; Mk 13:24-25.
10. Rev. 6:3-4.
11. Dio Cassius, LXV.11,1.
12. Dio Cassius, LXXIX.30.1.

a third of the day and night are darkened.[13] Other angels produce prodigies familiar to Graeco-Roman paganism.[14]

Hail would fall mixed with blood, grass and trees are scorched, a third of fish in the sea die when the water becomes blood, a blazing mountain falls into the sea, water in rivers becomes bitter, etc.[15] For a later example, at the outbreak of the struggle between Septimius Severus and Albinus (A.D. 196), a great fire was seen in the northern sky at night, and a fine rain resembling silver fell from the sky on the Forum of Augustus.[16] In Revelation: 'The fourth angel poured his bowl over the sun and it was given him to burn men in fire'.[17] In the second plague, the sea 'became blood as from a dead man and every living things in the sea died'. In the third plague, the rivers and fountains of water became blood.[18]

When the fourth seal was broken, the Seer saw 'another horse appear, deathly pale, and its rider was called "Death" and Hades followed at its heels'. Thus in the collapse of nature the underworld disgorges itself in what emerges as a Christian version of Lucan's 'nature at variance with itself (*natura discors*)'. Arruns the *haruspex* discerns in the entrails that the anger and not peace of the gods is witnessed and claims:

> Not with mightiest Jupiter has my sacrifice found favour; but the infernal gods have entered the body of the slaughtered bull.[19]

Figulus now introduces his more philosophical and metaphysical explanation, with the order of nature collapsing in earthquake and fire, and with the gods 'speedy destruction preparing for Rome and all mankind'. Lucan continues:

> 'Either' said he, 'the universe strays forever governed by no law, and the stars move to or fro with course unfixed. Or else, if guided by destiny, speedy destruction preparing for Rome and all mankind. Will the earth gape and cities be swallowed up? Or will the burning heat destroy our temperate climate? . . . Will water everywhere be tainted with streams of poison? What kind of disaster are the gods preparing? What form of ruin will their anger assume? The lives of multitudes are doomed to end together. If Saturn . . . were not kindling his black fires in the zenith, then Aquarius would have poured down such rains as Deucalion saw, and the whole earth would have been hidden under a waste of waters. Or if the sun's rays were now passing over the fierce lion of Nemea, then fire would stream over all the world, and the upper air would be kindled and

---

13.   Rev. 8:12.
14.   K. Berger, 'Hellenistisch-heidnische Prodigien und die Vorzeichen in der jüdischen und christlichen Apokalyptik', in *ANRW*, II.23.2, pp. 1428–69 (1442).
15.   Rev. 8.
16.   Dio Cassius, LXXVI, 4.6–7.
17.   Rev. 16:8, cf. 8:7-8.
18.   Rev. 16:3-4.
19.   Lucan, *Bell. Civ.*, 1.633–634.

consumed by the sun's chariot . . . Why have the stars fled their courses? The madness
of war is upon us'.[20]

Previously Lucan had claimed that, among the portents that had called for the
act of augury:

> The ghost of Sulla was seen to rise in the centre of the Campus Martius, and to chant
> sad oracles, while Marius burst forth from his grave and put to flight the peasant
> farmers when his head was raised over the cool waters of the Anio.[21]

Clearly the underworld, like the Seer's 'Death and Hades', were involved in the
collapse of cosmic order that had led to the disorder in nature and in society
that Augustus' *augurium pacis* had addressed. The 'beast' of Revelation had
been disgorged from the Abyss, like the ghosts of Marius and Sulla, as part of
the general break up of the cosmic order.

When, therefore, John the Seer writes the vision that he does, it cannot constitute anything other than a challenge to the imperial ideology of Augustus
and his successors to have achieved the *pax deorum*. In direct denial of what
Augustus and Vespasian as his actual and ideological successor had claimed,
the order of nature and society was not at peace, with all harmful portents
banished in a cosmos in which the ruler, as logos, had reasserted order over a
disordered chaos of natural and social events. Rather that cosmos was about to
collapse, with signs and wonders indicative of that collapse, in seals on nature
broken to release them, in powers from the nether world released and demanding universal worship for the beast that arises from the abyss.[22] The beast, if not
Satan himself, is he who is the earthly representative of the dragon or Satan
cast out of heaven by Michael and his angels.[23] There is to be a 'battle' between
the saints, whose foreheads are sealed in baptism with the seal of God,[24] and
those who wear the mark of the beast, as the former vanquish the latter by their
witness to Christ in the persecution with which they are afflicted.[25] And Christ
will deliver them by bringing them in his newly created cosmos to 'a new
heaven and a new earth'.[26]

The Seer of Revelation will indirectly identify Rome as the object of his
oracle by using the cryptogram of 'Babylon', in the tradition of the Jewish
Sibylline oracle that attacks the Roman power:

> And from heaven a great star shall fall on the dread ocean and burn up the deep sea with
> Babylon itself and the land of Italy, by reason of which many of the Hebrews perished,

20. Lucan, *Bell. Civ.*, 1.641–659.
21. Lucan, *Bell. Civ.*, 1.580–683.
22. Rev. 11:7; 13:1-10.
23. Rev. 12:8-9; 20:10.
24. Rev. 9:3.
25. Rev. 13:17; 16:2; 19:20.
26. Rev. 21:1 and 5.

holy and faithful, and people of the truth . . . Woe to thee, thou city of the Latin land, all unclean, thou maenad circled with vipers, thou shalt sit a widow on thy hills, and the river Tiber shall bewail thee, his consort, with thy murderous heart and ungodly mind. Knowest thou not the power and design of God? But thou saidst: 'I am alone, and none shall despoil me'. Yet now shall God who lives forever destroy both thee and thine, and no sign of thee shall be left any more in the land, nor of the old time when the great God brought thee to honour. Abide thou alone, thou lawless city: wrapt in burning fire, inhabit thou in Hades the gloomy house of the lawless.[27]

John the Seer represents such a tradition without directly equating Babylon with Rome, but making clear, in his vision of the Great Harlot, that this was in fact the case:

I saw a woman riding a scarlet beast which had seven heads and ten horns and had blasphemous titles written all over it . . . on her forehead was written a cryptic name: 'Babylon the great, the mother of all the prostitutes and filthy practices on the earth'. I saw that she was drunk, drunk with the blood of the saints, and the blood of the martyrs of Jesus . . . The seven heads are the seven hills on which the woman is sitting.[28]

It is thus the city on seven hills, Rome, which is described with her subsequent fall announced.[29]

In this vision, therefore, unlike in the Markan apocalypse, Rome and its empire that embraces Asia Minor is clearly identified. But the context in which its fall is set makes the vision, unlike its Sibylline counterpart, not simply a denunciation of Rome in an oracular outburst. John the Seer's apocalyptic context, with all the portents and prodigies, the signs and wonders, of a 'nature at variance with itself', would have made his work a refutation of imperial claims to effect the *pax deorum*, even if no specific reference had been made, albeit in the form of a cryptogram, to Rome itself. Both Vitellius (A.D. 69) and his successor Vespasian (A.D. 70) issued edicts banning astrologers from Rome.[30] Domitian was to follow suit (A.D. 89). We have seen precisely why they needed to do so if they were to maintain the ideology of the *Pax Augusta* as the act of augury that had banished the anger of the gods, and replaced this with a universal and enduring peace.

Domitian was to succeed Vespasian (A.D. 81), and arguably, in his reign, John the Seer saw his vision on the island of Patmos in Asia Minor. John was not simply to challenge the absence of prodigies and portents in an imperial order in which the order of nature was reflected in the order of human society. He was also to produce alternative images to those of the imperial ideology transformed into the early Christian hope for Christ's Second Coming: there was to be no possibility of compromise and symbiosis so that imperial structures

27. *Orac. Sibyl.*, 5.155–75.
28. Rev. 17:4-7 and 9.
29. Rev. 18:1-3.
30. Dio Cassius, LXIV.1.4 and LXV.9.1.

themselves in this world could be transformed into the Christian renewal of imperial society.

We shall now examine how John the Seer is to further challenge the *Pax Augusta* celebrated in Vespasian's *Templum Pacis Augustae* with reference to specific features of the imperial cult in Asia Minor, and the refocusing of that cult under Domitian.

1. *Domitian's Refocusing of Ritual on the Emperor's Divinity*

Irenaeus claimed that John saw his vision in the time of Domitian.[31] That Revelation was produced in Domitian's reign seems confirmed by both references to what appears to be his edict on the vineyards, and to Domitia's child, divinized on his death (A.D. 83) and pictured on coins.

At the opening of the third seal the third rider appears on a black horse with a balance in his hand. A voice is then heard:

> A quart of wheat for a denarius, and three quarts of barley for a denarius; but do not harm oil and wine.[32]

Death by famine was to come with the fourth rider, 'whose name was Death, and Hades followed him', along with death by the sword, pestilence and wild beasts. The third rider therefore brings a lesser but real crisis. Domitian was to address such a crisis.

Suetonius informs us that there had been a problem of a scarcity of grain caused by the overplanting of vineyards that had led to a glut of wine at the expense of wheat crops. His edict forbade planting any more vines in Italy, and ordered similarly for the provinces, where only up to one half was to be allowed to remain standing.[33] A denarius for a quart of wheat was a day's wages, indicating that the third rider was bringing about famine.[34] Furthermore, in thwarting Domitian's solution – and indeed the edict never was fully implemented – the third horseman was therefore behaving destructively and exacerbating the famine in Asia Minor.

In addition to the clear influence of the edict on the composition of John's vision, we have also Domitia's dead child, originally born in A.D. 83.[35] Domitian himself claimed divinity during his lifetime, and in official letters used the title '*dominus et deus* (lord and god)'.[36] Domitia was, in his words, after their reconciliation in A.D. 92, described as being recalled 'to the divine couch'.[37]

---

31. Irenaeus, *Adv. Haer.*, V.30.3 (95–97).
32. Rev. 6:6.
33. Suetonius, *Dom.*, 7.2.
34. J. Sweet, *Revelation* (SCM Pelican Commentaries; London: SCM, 1979), p. 140.
35. Suetonius, *Dom.*, 3.1.
36. Suetonius, *Dom.*, 13.2.
37. Suetonius, *Dom.*, 13.1.

So too, following his birth, the child could be described on the reverse of a gold coin (A.D. 83) bearing on its obverse side the image of Domitia, as 'divine Caesar son of the emperor Domitian'. Here we observe the naked form of 'divine Caesar', depicted as baby Jupiter seated on a globe with seven stars around him. After this event we have coins associating Domitia with Ceres, Demeter and Cybele.[38]

The production of such divine imagery surrounding members of the imperial household, Domitian's own changes to the ritual celebrating the Capitoline games which, as we shall see, involved the incorporation of his own image into priestly crowns of gilded laurel leaves along with the Capitoline Triad, and his assumption of divine titles while still alive, all represented a program of innovation into the imperial cult practices that we shall argue were to be reflected within Asia Minor. These changes were felt deeply in Roman society, and resented by the senatorial elite, a resentment that Pliny was to express on Trajan's accession (A.D. 108) where of the new emperor, in contrast to Domitian, he says:

> On no occasion should we flatter him as a god, nowhere as a divine presence (*numen*),
> for we are speaking not of a tyrant but of a citizen, not of a despot but of a father.[39]

John the Seer, from the standpoint of Asia Minor, also felt grave forebodings regarding the new innovative program to extend and emphasize the imagery of sacred imperial power. There has been much discussion about the veracity of claims by early Christian writers, such as Melito and Tertullian, that Domitian initiated a persecution, and that it was to this persecution that John was responding in his apocalyptic vision.[40] Eusebius claimed such a persecution on the grounds that Flavius Clemens and Flavia Domitilla were Christians, and that these were two well-known figures mentioned by pagan writers as punished under Domitian. Clemens was executed and Flavia exiled. Dio Cassius does indeed mention these two figures, but as those who had 'turned away to Jewish customs'.[41] I have discussed the issue of a Domitianic persecution in detail elsewhere.[42] Suffice it to say here that, whether or not there was an actual persecution, the imagery of Domitian's innovations in emperor worship was to

---

38. *BMC* 2, p. 311, no. 62 and plate 61.6, cf. 63–65, plates 61.7–9. See also A. Brent, *The Imperial Cult and the Development of Church Order: Concepts and Images of Authority in Paganism and Early Christianity before the Age of Cyprian (VCSup,* 45; Leiden: E. J. Brill, 1999), p. 167 and plates 21–22.

39. Pliny, *Paneg.*, 2.3.

40. Tertullian, *Apol.*, 5(1–35); Melito of Sardis apud Eusebius, *H.E.*, IV.26.

41. Dio Cassius, LXVII.14.1–3.

42. Brent, *Imperial Cult*, pp. 141–44 for full bibliography, but see also L. W. Barnard, 'St. Clement of Rome and the Persecution of Domitian', in *Studies in the Apostolic Fathers and their Background* (Oxford: Blackwell, 1966), pp. 5–15, cf. D. L. Jones, 'Christianity and the Roman Imperial Cult', in *ANRW*, II.23.2, pp. 1023–54 (1032–35).

produce a strong Christian reaction, and the belief that such a persecution was in inevitable prospect.

The imagery of Domitia, and her divine child surrounded by the seven stars, was not the only haunting image of imperial divine power. The spin-doctors had produced other divine depictions, such as the image of a divinized *Aeternitas Augusti*, of the eternal character of the Augustan empire, where the goddess stands holding the heads of the sun and moon in her hand. Statius writes in his verse of Domitian as 'rising with the new sun and the lofty stars, himself shining more brightly, and with a light greater than the morning star'.[43]

In the face of such haunting imagery, John the Seer writes under the inspiration of a different divine being to the emperor, namely to Jesus Christ, who is to come as the morning star whose gift is promised by the angel of the church of Thyateira to those who resist such worship.[44] In place of the goddess *Aeternitas*, with the sun and moon in her hands, John describes voices proclaiming after the seventh trumpet blast: 'The kingdom of this world has become the kingdom of our God and of his Christ, and he shall reign forever.' This is his riposte to the 'eternity (*aeternitas*)' of the Roman Empire. Following the declaration of the 24 elders that 'the Almighty' reigns, and the portents are to follow, John continues:

> Now a great sign appeared in heaven: a woman robed with the sun, standing on the moon, and on her head a crown of twelve stars. She was pregnant and in labour, crying aloud in the pangs of childbirth. Then a second sign appeared in the sky: there was a huge red dragon with seven heads and ten horns, and each of the seven heads crowned with a garland crown. Its tail swept a third of the stars from the sky and hurled them to the ground, and the dragon stopped in front of the woman as she was on the point of giving birth, so that he could eat the child as soon as he was born. The woman was delivered of a boy, the son who was to rule all the nations with an iron sceptre, and the child was taken straight up to God and to his throne, while the woman escaped into the desert where God had prepared a place for her to be looked after . . . Then the dragon was enraged with the woman and went away to make war on the rest of her children, who obey God's commandments and have in themselves the witness of Jesus.[45]

The woman like *Aeternitas* is associated with the sun and the moon, but like Domitia's child surrounded in this case by twelve rather than by seven stars. Domitia's child was dead and deified, and thus in the heavenly realm like the child of the woman caught up to heaven, who is clearly to return as Jesus Christ and rule over the nations. The dragon who goes to war on the rest of the woman's children is clearly an image of the force of paganism seeking to crush the Church, but promising, not the *pax deorum* that the Roman emperors

---

43. Statius, *Silv.*, IV.1.3–4.
44. Rev. 2:28 and 22:16.
45. Rev. 12:1-6 and 17.

claimed, but indeed threatening the portents of a *natura discors* as it sweeps away and hurls down one third of the stars.

Domitian's spin-doctors, Statius and Martial, continue the theme of his divinity. The former claims Domitian as Jupiter's vice-gerent on earth, and the latter equates Domitian with Jupiter himself. Martial speaks of Domitian as Rome's Jupiter, of whom he is a loyal servant, but otherwise acknowledges him as 'lord and god (*dominus et deus*)' in issuing an edict.[46] Statius affirms: 'See! He is a god, him whom Jupiter orders to rule over the glad earth on his behalf.'[47] On coins Domitian now appears as Jupiter holding a thunderbolt and crowned by Victory.[48] Thus we find such conceptual shifts regarding the emperor's present divinity represented in the ritual of the imperial cult at the celebration of the Capitoline games (A.D. 86), which were repeated every 5 years.

These games were celebrated in connection with the restoration of the temple of Jupiter on the Capitol. Domitian presided wearing 'a purple toga in the Greek fashion' and, like the *agonothete* of a Greek procession as we shall see, wore a *stephanos* or *corona* of laurel leaf gilded with gold leaf, in which was set small medallions as images (*imagines* or τύποι) of the appropriate tutelary deities, in this case those of Jupiter, Juno and Minerva. As leader of the procession, he was accompanied nevertheless by the appropriate priestly college of the *Flaviales*, and thus by members of the Flavian imperial cult set up on the model of the *Augustales* of Augustus' cult.

But those who witnessed this scene in the stadium on this occasion saw another innovation in the ceremony of the cult, in which veneration for the Capitoline Triad, in particular Jupiter, was being assimilated with the worship of the emperor. Each of the *Flaviales* was also wearing στέφανοι with the customary three *imagines* (or τύποι) of the Triad, but in their case a fourth image had been added, that of Domitian himself. What new message was being conveyed by this innovation? Clearly the emperor's image ranks with the other gods, but also he assimilates their divinity to his own person: he is their living image or representative so that he needs no image of himself on his *corona*. When the people look upon him, they worship him with the worship that they would also apply to the Triad.

This theology of images was an innovative theology in terms of the imperial cult, whose ritual extended throughout Asia Minor in a state of dynamic development. This is not to say that the imperial cult was centrally organized, nor to deny a continuing degree of local initiative. But such ideas and innovations from the centre rapidly caught on.

Thus it was in Asia Minor, as witnessed by the archaeological and literary remains of some of the very cities to which the letters to the churches of the opening three chapters of Revelation are addressed. Laodicea boasted a temple

---

46. Martial, *Epig.*, V.8.1, cf. IX.28.10; see also VI.10.3–4; VIII.15; XIV.1.2.
47. Statius, *Silv.*, IV.3.128–129.
48. *BMC* 2 pp. 77, no. 381, see also Brent, *Imperial Cult*, pp. 172–74.

of the imperial cult from Domitian's time, to which coins bear witness that celebrate Domitian's fictitious victories with the picture of a temple. We have furthermore the remains of a triple gate and towers dedicated to: 'Jupiter, great saviour, and the Emperor Domitian, Caesar Augustus, *Pontifex Maximus.*'[49] We should remember that a high priest of a cult could represent the divinity of the cult present in their person through the image that they bore in the *stephanos* that they wore or elsewhere such as on breastplates.[50]

In a similar assimilative fashion, Domitian associated his cult with that of Artemis at Ephesus, whose cult had originally grown out of a tree-shrine to which John, in the letter to the church of Ephesus, juxtaposes the promise of the 'tree of life in the paradise of God'.[51] It was in the sacred grove (or τέμενος) that Domitian was to locate his own temple that thus became associated with Artemis as the tutelary deity of the city of Ephesus. Domitian's cult statue was of huge proportions.[52] Pergamon had an imperial temple dedicated to Tiberius and Livia, and from their time, and they had assimilated their cult to that of Asklepius, the tutelary deity, whose claim to be 'god of Pergamon and saviour' John negates in his letter to the church of Pergamon with his image of 'the old serpent who is the devil'.[53]

As the ritual of a developing emperor worship insinuated itself into more traditional pagan cults, John the Seer thus envisaged the outcome in a universal decree that all the emperor's subjects worship in the cult of the state religion that was never to materialize until Decius (A.D. 251): persecutions of Christians were to remain more or less local until that time. John sees all these currents of pagan emperor worship coming to their climax in the aftermath of the divine child, destined to rule the nations, but snatched away to heaven for a time:

> Then I saw a beast emerge from the sea: it had seven heads and ten horns, with a *stephanos* on each of its ten horns, and its heads were marked with blasphemous titles. I saw that the beast was like a leopard, with paws like a bear and a mouth like a lion; the dragon had handed over its power and his throne and his immense authority. I saw that one of its heads appeared to have a fatal wound but that this deadly injury had been healed and the whole world had marvelled and followed the beast. They prostrated themselves in front of the dragon because he had given the beast his authority; and they prostrated themselves in front of the beast, saying, 'Who can compare with the beast? Who can fight against him?' The beast was allowed to mouth its boasts and blasphemies for forty-two months; and it mouthed its blasphemies against God and his heavenly Tabernacle and all those who are sheltered there. It was allowed to make war against

---

49.   Brent, *Imperial Cult*, p. 189.

50.   A. Brent, *Ignatius of Antioch and the Second Sophistic* (STAC 36; Tübingen: Mohr Siebeck, 2006), pp. 146–64.

51.   Rev. 2:6 and Brent, *Imperial Cult*, pp. 178–79.

52.   Price, S. R. F., *Rituals and Power: The Roman Imperial Cult in Asia Minor* (Cambridge: University Press, 1984), p. 187.

53.   Rev. 20:2 and Brent, *Imperial Cult*, p. 180.

the saints and to conquer them, and given power over every race, people, language and nation; and all the people of the world will worship it, that is everyone whose name has not been written down from the foundation of the world in the book of life of the Lamb sacrificed.[54]

Like the Markan Apocalypse, the antecedents of John here are to be found in Daniel and related literature, as we have seen. The last beast that arose from the sea in Daniel's vision had ten horns, and finally one further that symbolized Antiochus Epiphanes and his Hellenistic kingdom. This image reappears in John's vision here in application to the Roman Empire, as the agent of the dragon identified with Satan.[55] Already he had associated the temple of the imperial cult in Pergamon, dating from Tiberius' reign, with what he calls 'the throne of Satan'.[56]

It would be wrong to see the writing of names in 'the Lamb's book of life' as a reference to a citizen roll from a census against which names could be checked in order to ensure a universal act of sacrifice. Such citizen rolls, that may have been used to enforce Decius' Edict (A.D. 251) for a universal sacrifice by all subjects of the Roman Empire were to await for their possibility the Edict of Caracalla that entailed census lists to include all newly enfranchised citizens throughout the Empire (A.D. 212). Rather John may be referring to lists kept by Jewish synagogues of their members that had excluded Jewish Christians from around A.D. 95 onwards, the date of the putative Synod at Jamnia that had issued curses on the 'excommunicated (*ha-minim*)'.

Following the destruction of the temple at Jerusalem (A.D. 70), the tax paid by the Jews of the Diaspora for its support now became, at Vespasian's command, the *fiscus Judaicus* to be paid annually to the temple of Juppiter Capitolinus at Rome by all Jews, irrespective of their place of residence. By paying the tax it was conceded that they could continue 'to observe their ancestral customs', which clearly exempted them from participating in the State religion.[57] With the spreading of the imperial cult and its dynamically developing ritual, what appeared to be becoming more probable was the exposure of Jewish Christians no longer on the synagogue roll to pressure to conform to the state religion, particularly on the occasion of public festivals when non-participation would be obvious, and raise the usual suspicion of practising occult and illegal magical rites in place of those approved by the state.

John the Seer bears witness to the division of Church and Synagogue, and the very real bitterness felt by the former about that division in such circumstances as these. He writes to the angel of the church at Smyrna of 'the blasphemy of those who call themselves Jews but are not, and are nothing more than a

---

54. Rev. 13:1-8.
55. Dan. 7:7 ff. and Rev. 20:2.
56. Rev. 2:13.
57. Josephus, *BJ*, 7.218; Dio Cassius, LXV.7.2.

synagogue of Satan'. The Jews are regarded as in league with Satan or the dragon, which personifies the Roman Empire arising as the last great kingdom from the sea. As a counterpart to those whose names are no longer on the synagogue list of those who are exempt from participation in imperial worship, their 'names are written in the sacrificed Lamb's book of life'. In bearing his sacrificial sufferings they are members of his community, and are so inscribed in his book.

Thus we find the effect of Domitian's changes in the ritual of the imperial cult upon Jewish Christian relations. But what of the clash between the Church and the imperial cult in Asia Minor, as John the Seer envisages it?

We find that John will go on to focus the universal worship of the beast upon his 'image (εἰκών)'. Each inhabitant of the world is to 'worship the beast and its image and receives on his forehead or on his hand the mark . . . of his name'.[58] We must now endeavour to answer this question with reference to pagan imagery in processions in Asia Minor, and to what we know of mystery cults specifically devoted to the imperial cult, and their reflections in the language of John's text.

2. *The Image of the Beast and Pagan Processional Imagery*

We have seen already one explanation of worshipping the image of the beast in Domitian's insertion of a medallion bearing his image into the *coronae* of the priests of Jupiter at the festival of the Capitoline games. Indeed, some Jews might, on the other hand, infer that the casting of two drachma coins into the treasury of the temple of Juppiter Capitolinus was an act of pagan worship. We have very many examples from Asia Minor of garland crowns or *stephanoi*, with medallion images of tutelary gods of the various cities, or indeed of members of the dead and deified imperial family or indeed mixtures of both.

We have the decree of the People and Council of Sardis honouring Menogenes son of Isidore, who was to be appointed priest of the temple of Roma and Augustus. He was authorized as an ambassador to lead an embassy to Augustus that was to seek the emperor's approval for the consecration of a day commemorating his grandson Gaius' assumption of the *toga praetextata* (5 B.C.). We find here a description of the ritual creating a cult statue to a member of the imperial family.

> . . . all dressed in resplendent clothes shall wear crowns, and the *strategoi* each year shall present sacrifices to the gods and make prayers through the sacred heralds for his safety, and they shall set up and consecrate his statue in the shrine of his father . . . and an embassy be sent on these matters to go to Rome and to congratulate him and Augustus . . . and there were chosen as ambassadors Iollas son of Metrodorus and Menogenes son of Isidore . . .[59]

---

58. Rev. 14:9 and 11; 15:2; 16:2; 19:20; 20:24.
59. *IGRR*, IV.1756 I.10–23.

We note here the character of the imperial cult as something for which there has to be a request through a formal embassy of a Menogenes, who is rising up the social ladder and using what is probably his new wealth to buy social status as an imperial priest. 'Emperor Caesar son of God, Augustus, high priest . . .'. replies subsequently in approval, and Gaius receives cult and a statue.[60] Reverence to the statue involved a procession, with participants suitably vested wearing garland crowns of gilded laurel, with vestments or *coronae* impressed with images if they were worn by priests.

When John the Seer describes the whole world prostrating themselves before the dragon and the beast, and marvelling at the might of their dominion, in what kind of act were they engaged?[61] Were they imagined simply as prostrating themselves before an image like that of Gaius and/or of Augustus at the direction of high-priest Menogenes in the imperial temple at Sardis? Or was John indicating that he had in mind a more complex ritual involving the manipulation of images? John was to continue:

> I saw another beast coming from the earth and having two horns like a lamb and he was speaking like the dragon. And he acted with the whole authority of the first beast in his presence and caused the earth and its inhabitants to worship the first beast whose fatal wound had been healed. And he performed great signs so that fire descended from heaven upon the earth when men were present. He led astray the world's inhabitants through the signs granted him to perform in the presence of the beast, whilst he commanded those inhabitants to construct an image in the beast's honour, who had received the blow from the sword and who had lived. He was allowed to give life to the image of the beast so that the image of the beast could speak to the effect that as many as would not worship the image of the beast should be slain.[62]

It would appear that the 'beast coming from the earth' as opposed to the first beast from the sea refers to the Greek city-states of Asia Minor, who had found a rapprochement with the Roman imperial power in the imperial cult. Indeed there was rivalry between Smyrna, Ephesus and Pergamon over who had the status of Neokoros or 'temple keeper' of the imperial cult the longest, and how often for how many different emperors. John the Seer envisages the city-states of Asia, formed into a Hellenic confederation or *Koinon*, with its centre at Ephesus and huge statue of Domitian, as a beast of supernatural appearance symbolizing, as in Daniel and other Jewish apocalypses, a pagan empire.[63] But this second empire/beast has forced not only its inhabitants, but also those of the whole world, to worship the first beast by setting up an image of it. Ruler worship was, as we have seen, originally a Hellenistic and eastern concept introduced as a response to Augustus' victory after the near fatal wound of the civil war.

60. *IGRR*, IV.1756 II and Price, *Rituals and Power*, p. 66 and p. 259, cat. no. 56.
61. See above, footnote 54 and associated text.
62. Rev. 13:11-14.
63. Price, *Rituals and Power*, pp. 196–99.

In John's garbled vision of the cult, the augurs and *haruspices* who deal with signs and portents are regarded as being the source of them, unless he is referring more definitely to magical acts. These were certainly visible on the procession of the *Ara Pacis*. Fire descending from heaven fairly describes several prodigies such as when at Rome (91 B.C.), during the Italian war, 'about sunrise, a ball of fire flashed forth from the northern heavens with a great noise in the sky'.[64] We find the other signs that the Beast performed paralleled later in the second century in a decree from the city of Stratonica in Asia Minor that records miracles performed by their divinities Zeus and Hecate against the enemies of the Romans, namely the Parthians, and also earlier during the Mithridatic war. The decree initiated a great festival associated with 'the goddess Roma benefactor' under the name of 'Hecate, Saviour made Manifest:'

> Statues are set up in the council chamber of Augustus of the aforementioned gods (Zeus and Hera) that produce most splendid deeds of divine power because of which also the whole population sacrifices and offers prayers with incense and thanksgiving always to those gods who are thus so made so manifest, and it is fitting to reverence them with a solemn procession accompanied by hymns and with divine worship . . .[65]

On the image of the beast, specifically speaking, we might, as a parallel, cite Agrippina, in her quest to marry Claudius, supplicating the speaking image of the Clarian Apollo in his temple at Rome.[66] Furthermore, Lucian describes a visit to the temple of Juno-Atargatis in Syria where he saw

> . . . rich works and ancient dedications and many marvels and statues provoking divine awe. And gods frequently make their appearances to them. For amongst them images sweat and move and voice oracles, and a voice arises often in the shrine when the temple has been closed and many hear it . . . There are many oracles amongst the Greeks and Egyptians, and some in Lydia and many in Asia. But they do not speak apart from priests and prophets, but this statue of Apollo moves of itself and he accomplishes what he prophesies.[67]

John the Seer introduces, therefore, the second beast as a personification of the *Koinon* of Asia, whose Asiarch also could claim to be a sacral representation of the imperial divinity performing wonders in the presence of a talking image of the emperor. But can we document more closely the kind of image that the city-states of Asia Minor, the second beast, would have set up in honour of the

---

64.   Julius Obsequens, 54.

65.   L. Robert, *Études Anatoliennes*, (Paris: Boccard, 1937), p. 522 and F. Sokolwski, *Lois sacrées de l'Asie Mineure* (École Français d Athènes 9: Paris: Boccard, 1955), p. 162, no. 69.

66.   Tacitus, *Annal.*, XII.22. See also F. Poulsen, 'Talking, Weeping, and Bleeding Sculptures: A Chapter in the History of Religious Fraud', *Acta Archaeologica*, 16 (1945), pp. 178–95 (187).

67.   Lucian, *De Dea Syriae*, 10.

first beast. Was it, for example, a standing image in a temple with an oracular statue? Or was it a portable image that could be moved around, as indeed Lucian described his Syrian Apollo being moved around, by his priests?[68] And if so, what was the liturgical and ritual context. Was it the ritual of an oracular shrine or a mystery procession with a mystery play?

There is of course Domitian's huge, standing image at Ephesus in the magnificent temple built in his honour and set on the western side of the upper square, whose northern 'royal' portico housed statues of Augustus and Livia, and a temple of Roma and Julius Caesar. At the centre of the square stood a temple to Augustus.[69] This was the scene that marked Ephesus as the home of the provincial assembly of Asia, the *Koinon*, where the high-priest of the imperial cult had the title of Asiarch or 'ruler of Asia'.[70] But these images were not considered to have oracular powers and to speak.

Furthermore, in this passage we have particular reference not simply to an image or statue that spoke as in an oracular shrine, but to an image which the spirit of the first beast, the Roman Empire and emperor, moved to speak. We have an image, but also a definite figure associated with the image as representative of Asia Minor. The city-states sent delegates to the *Koinon*, which the imperial cult made a religious as well as a political body, the status of whose city was marked by the place in the religious procession to the altar of sacrifice to the dead and deified emperors.[71] We have, therefore, a priest performing signs and wonders associated with an image of the Roman Empire as the embodiment of Rome, as suggested by the title of various temples dedicated at Ephesus to Domitian, to Roma and Julius Caesar, and to Augustus.

It is to be emphasized that it would be wrong to translate the closing line of this quotation as 'he was allowed to give *his* spirit to the image', as opposed to 'give *spirit* to the image'.[72] 'Spirit' here refers to the giving of the power of life, and can be translated 'breath'. We have in the literature only one reference to an image, which both moves and speaks, and that is in the Lucian passage that we have just quoted. Moving images are generally portable images, as in the temple at Hierapolis, but which move as part of a procession in which they are carried with an accompanying ritual and liturgy.

The use of images in rituals of the imperial cult can be further documented from the reign of Hadrian in the benefaction of C. Julius Demosthenes whose

---

68. Lucian, *De Dea Syriae*, 36.
69. Price, *Rituals and Power*, p. 139, fig. 3.
70. R. A. Kearsley, 'The Asiarchs', in *The Book of Acts in its Graeco-Roman Setting*, edited by W. J. Gill and C. Gempf, in *The Book of Acts in its First Century Setting* (Michigan and Carlisle: Eerdmans/Paternoster Press, 1994), II, pp. 263–376.
71. Price, *Rituals and Power*, pp. 128–129.
72. Rev. 13:15: καὶ ἐδόθη αὐτῷ δοῦναι πνεῦμα τῇ εἰκόνι ...

terms are set out in an epigraph recording the decree of the city council of Oinoanda in Lycia (5th July A.D. 125). Demosthenes was to dedicate:

> . . . to the city both a golden crown carrying relief portraits of the emperor Nerva Trajan Hadrian Caesar Augustus and our Leader, the ancestral god Apollo, which the *agonothete* will wear, and an altar decorated with silver, which has an inscription of the dedicator.[73]

The golden garland crown with its 'relief portraits' was to be worn by the leader of the procession, the *agonothete*, playing therefore a sacerdotal role similar to that of Domitian at the Capitoline ceremonies. At the beginning of each New Year, he is to make a ceremonial entrance wearing in addition a purple robe, and for the emperor's birthday (1st January) he is to perform, in procession, 'pious rituals for the emperor and for the gods of the homeland', such as offering wine and incense.[74]

Demosthenes' epigraph gives some indication of in what such 'pious rituals' might consist. We find references to 'ten *sebastophoroi* (σεβαστοφόροι)', as well as '*theophoroi* (θεοφόροι)' or 'image bearers'. The *sebastophoroi* are clearly bearers of the images of the deceased and deified imperial house. The agonothete is instructed:

> . . . ten *sebastophoroi* should also be chosen by him, who, wearing white robes and crowns of celery will carry and lead forward, and escort, the images of the emperors, the image of our ancestral god Apollo and the previously mentioned holy altar . . .[75]

Here we clearly do not have simply images 'borne' in the sense of 'worn' as medallions in a gilded laurel or bay garland crown. These are portable images, moving images, carried like the portable altar, in a procession. In what further way would the processional ritual now proceed?

3. *The Imperial Mysteries and the Emperor's Image*

We have other references, both literary and epigraphic, to the particular ritual and liturgical context in which such portable images were used. Such images, whether portable and carried in a procession, or as medallions on headdresses, were employed as part of the enacted drama of a mystery play. One such epigraphic example was found in 1926 on a three-sided marble pillar that was unearthed on the Via Tusculana between the Via Labicana and the Via Latina. Here we have a list of names of a Dionysiac cult association, a *synodos* or

---

73. *SEG*, XXXVIII.1462.C. For an alternative English translation, see S. Mitchell, 'Festivals, Games, and Civic Life in Roman Asia Minor', *JRS*, 80 (1990), pp. 183–87.

74. *SEG*, XXXVIII.1462.C.56–58.

75. *SEG*, XXXVIII.1462.C.62–63.

thiasos, in columns, stating the names of the priests and priestesses and other named officials, and the roles assigned them in the mystery play often indicated by the particular sacred object or image that they bore in the procession.[76] Agrippinilla's name appears first on the list as priestess and head of the association. But in the list we find the names of Gallicanus and Dionysius, who are called 'bearer of the gods (θεοφόροι)'.[77] In Julius Demosthenes' inscription, the 'bearer of the god (θεοφόρος)' has been renamed 'bearer of the divine emperor (σεβαστοφόρος)', as in the Ephebic inscription from Athens.[78] We see therefore transference of the bearing of a divine image of Dionysus in a mystery rite over into a procession in which the emperor's image is to be borne.

A literary example of such image bearing in the context of a mystery rite may be found in Apuleius, where he describes the procession that is part of initiation into the Isis mysteries before the final secret rites that he cannot disclose. He informs us:

> The foremost high priests . . . carried before them the distinctive attributes of the most powerful gods . . . the second . . . carried with both hands an altar, that is, 'a source of help', whose special name was derived from the helping providence of the supreme goddess.[79]

Here clearly in the Isis mysteries we have *theophoroi* bearing images that will be used as part of the mystery drama, in which participating the worshipper will attain union with the divine. The images in those who bear them and play their roles in the mysteries are thus images that move.

What the significance of the image of Augustus may be in a mystery procession is difficult to divine, since we have no account of specifically imperial mystery rites. And yet a further inscription shows us that such rites must have existed.

We have a four-sided altar from Pergamon in Hadrian's time, with inscriptions on each side, whose original location was the temple of Roma and Augustus. It was dedicated to 'Hadrian saviour and founder' by a choir of the imperial cult, who are 'the hymn-singers of divine Augustus and of the goddess

76. *IGUR*, 160.IA.5–15 and Brent, *Ignatius and the Second Sophistic*, pp. 147–53. See also F. Cumont, 'La grande inscription bachique du Metropolitan Muséum, II. Commentaire religieux de l'inscription', *AJA*, 37 (1933), pp. 215–63.

77. M. P. Nilsson, 'The Dionysiac Mysteries of the Hellenistic and Roman Age', *Acta Instituti Atheniensis Regni Sueciae*, 8, 5 (Lund: Gleerup, 1957), p. 46 and pp. 56–57.

78. L. Robert, 'Hellenica II, Inscription Éphébique', *R.Phil.*, 13 (1939), pp. 122–28 (123–25), reprinted in *Opera Minora Epigraphie et antiquités grecques* (Amsterdam: A. M. Hakkert, 1969), II, pp. 1275–81. See also Price, *Rituals and Power*, p. 189.

79. Apuleius, *Metam.*, 11, 10, see also Brent, *Imperial Cult*, pp. 236–37, and *Ignatius and the Second Sophistic*, p. 146.

Roma'.[80] One of the few still legible names is Capito, one of the family of 'A. Castricius Paulus, who dedicated the altar from their private means'. Capito's role in the cult is given as θεολόγος, which is of course the name that was given in later Christian tradition to John the Seer.[81]

But originally it referred to the person who composed the eulogy of the emperor to be sung in the cult's liturgy, or perhaps who also wrote the lines for the actors in the mystery drama around the emperor's person and his divine accomplishments. We know that at Ankyra the imperial cult under Hadrian was assimilated with the Dionysiac mysteries there. Our evidence is found in 'a decree of the international association of the craftsmen of Dionysus' where Hadrian's name is added to the cult's new title as the 'new Dionysus'. The decree honours one Ulpius Aelius Pompeianus, who had been instructed by the Senate to 'exhibit the mystery spectacle granted by the emperor'.[82] The decree indicates what was involved in this task:

> . . . shrinking back at no expense, and with speed of concern, he summoned the players already on their journey, and he provided for every part of the mystery, contributing to the association the prizes, and controlling the mystery play only because he had been chosen to benefit the city We decree, therefore, because of his observation of honours for the Emperor and for Dionysus, and in order to spread his fame forever to the city, the man is to be honoured with a statue . . .[83]

Thus we have an example of a mystery play, with roles assigned specifically in relation to emperor worship, that was being assimilated to the Dionysiac mysteries. Capito at Pergamon as θεολόγος was therefore the person responsible for scripting, and therefore as acting as producer for such a drama.

We have already seen how the bearing of images would relate to such a drama. Agrippinilla's inscription at Rome involved a specification of the roles that members of the cult would play in a Dionysiac mystery drama. Here we found some of the actors in that drama were called θεοφόροι because they bore or wore (the Greek word is the same) images of Dionysus, whether as portable statues, medallions in their *coronae*, or indeed as actors' masks. In the case of Aelius Pompeianus, although the term is not used specifically in his inscription, nevertheless the play for which he was assigning roles we may reasonably infer, on the Dionysiac model, had θεοφόροι. Only in their case they would not have been called by this term but by an adaptation of it, namely σεβαστοφόροι. These were the image bearers or image wearers with whom

80. *IGRR*, IV.353.A.4–5.
81. *IGRR*, IV.353.A.30–32, cf. A.17–18. For John as theologos, see Brent, *Imperial Cult*, pp. 193–96.
82. *SEG*, VI.59.1–5 (= *IGRR*, III, 209).
83. *SEG*, VI.59.8–28 (= *IGRR*, III.209).

we met in the case of Julius Demosthenes, where the celebration was clearly in honour of the divine emperor in association with Apollo, the traditional deity of the city. We can therefore reasonably safely conclude that here too the bearing or wearing of images was part of an imperial mystery play or some ceremony very like it.

Though the title of θεοφόρος had been transformed into σεβαστοφόρος in the case of Julius Demosthenes, in the case of the imperial mysteries at Pergamon the former title remained, even though the mysteries were clearly imperial. So too the title θεολόγος was not yet transformed into σεβαστόλογος as it was in Caligula's time. In the temple of Apollo in Didyma, we find a pillar of an imperial shrine to this emperor. One of the dedicators is named as Protomachus, with the title of 'chief temple-keeper (ἀρχινεωκορος) and priest of Augustus' shrine (σεβαστονεῦς), and σεβαστόλογος'.[84]

We therefore can see a pagan cultic background in the city-states of Asia Minor for the Seer's description of the image of the first beast made by the second, and the compulsion to worship that image, surrounded by the performance of signs and wonders, as the second beast breathed life into a image that spoke. Here was not a static image, but one that moved as part of a procession and spoke as part of a drama, in which the actor who bore or wore the image spoke in the person of the god and as his sacral representative.

Our Pergamon inscription specifies the celebration of Augustus' birthday on 1st August, and Livia's on 21st September. But it also makes it clear that the hymn singers are involved not simply in a celebration with eulogies of the birthdays of the dead and deified imperial family. These rites are called specifically 'mysteries (μυστηρία)':

> The conductor is to provide both for Augustus' birthday and for the rest of the birthdays
> of the dead and deified emperors and they shall crown with garlands the hymn-singers
> and the mysteries in the choir hall . . .[85]

We read of bread and wine that are to be provided for these mysteries, along with lamps, sacrificial cake and incense. We hear of 'lamps for Augustus', which are clearly to illuminate his image, but there is also a blanket with which to veil 'the images of the *Augusti*'.[86] Here we have rites relevant to the illuminating, veiling and unveiling of imperial images in connection with what are clearly specified as μυστήρια, and which involve souls of departed members.[87]

---

84. See Th. Weigand, 'Siebenter vorläufiger Bericht über Ausgrabungen in Milet und Didyma', in *APAW*, (1911), I, (pp. 1–71), p. 65, III, inv. Nr 156.9–10.

85. *IGRR*, 4.353.B.12–19.

86. *IGRR*, 4.353.C.4–7; 10–11.

87. See further Brent, *Ignatius and the Second Sophistic*, pp. 155–56.

Pleket has related the veiling and unveiling of the imperial images to the term σεβαστοφάντης with which we meet frequently in the epigraphy of Asia Minor.[88] The lamps and unveiling enabled the images to be illuminated in a glaring light to those who were being initiated, as in the case of the Eleusinian mysteries. When Proclus was to reinstate into Neoplatonism a sacramental element, he describes the 'completion' of the rites of initiation as one that made the cult image 'alive (ἔμψυχον)' and 'irradiated from the divine being'.[89]

Once again we are within the cultural context and discourse which gives meaning to the image of the beast given life (ἔμψυχον = δοῦναι πνεῦμα (to give life)), and functioning as a part of an act of worship.[90] Furthermore, in the contrast between earth and heaven in the Seer's vision, reflections of the imperial mysteries are to be given a more positive shape. He who was to be later and, I believe, with some accuracy, described as the θεολόγος, did indeed act in a way analogous to his pagan counterpart as he described his initial vision like such an illumination through a mystery rite. At the very beginning, when instructed to write the letters to the seven churches, he 'turned to look at the voice which was speaking to me', and 'I saw seven lamps of gold and in the midst of the lamps one like a human being.'

The Seer here refrains, in this scene, from naming what he sees as an image (εἰκών) of Christ like the images of the imperial family illuminated by the lamp light at the completion of the imperial mystery play. Although εἰκών is used elsewhere in the New Testament for Christ as the image of God, John refrains from so using it in view of his loathing of the image of the imperial beast. The figure for him, like Daniel's Son of Man, is human, unlike the beasts that rise from the sea. The figure that appears to the Seer 'holds in his right hand the seven stars', like the figure of Domitia's dead child divinized and surrounded by the constellations, and present in the imperial mysteries.[91]

John the Seer clearly regarded his vision as being a counterpart to the pagan experience of 'completion' at the conclusion of a mystery rite:

> The mystery (μυστήριον) of the seven stars, which you have seen on my right hand and the seven golden lamps: the seven stars are the angels of the seven churches, and the seven lamps are the seven churches.[92]

The apocalypse which follows, beginning with the letters to the seven churches, may thus be regarded as the work of a Christian θεολόγος or θεοφάντης,

---

88. *IGRR*, IV.522 (= *OGIS*, 479), see H. W. Pleket, 'An Aspect of the Imperial Cult: Imperial Mysteries', *HTR*, 58, 4 (1965), pp. 331–47 (337–38).

89. Pleket , 'Aspect', pp. 343–44.

90. Rev. 13:15 and above, footnotes 62 and 68 and associated text.

91. See above, footnote 84 and associated text.

92. Rev. 1:20.

who reveals the true mystery of neither the emperor nor of Dionysus but of Jesus Christ, and the mystery play that celebrates his triumph over chaos and evil personified in the empire of the beast, Roman Babylon on her seven hills.

The contrast throughout his apocalyptic vision is between the pagan mysteries and their ritual drama of the beast, who comes alive and speaks in the enactment of the pagan imperial mystery drama, and the mystery of the churches with their seven lamps burning before the throne of God, whose heavenly elders chant their victory songs around the throne of God and of the Lamb. We see this contrast now brought into focus in the contrast between the mark of the beast and Christian baptism.

4. *The Mark of the Beast and Pagan Initiation*

Immediately following his description of the image of the beast given life and a human voice, the pagan signs and wonders performed, and the worship demanded, we read:

> He forced them all, the small and the great, and the rich and the poor, and the free and the slaves to be given by him a mark (χάραγμα) upon their right hand and on their foreheads so that no-one could buy or sell without having the mark of the name of the beast or the number of his name.[93]

The number of his mysterious name was '666'.[94]

The Seer now proceeds to make this mark the distinction between the suffering, downtrodden church and the Roman Empire. Regarding death in martyrdom as victory, in a heavenly scene:

> I saw another sign in heaven great and wonderful, angels having the seven last plagues, a wonder in the sense that in these plagues the wrath of God was to be completed.[95]

With these are now joined in heaven those slain for not worshipping the beast and his image, and who had not received his mark: these will preside over a sea of fire that comes rolling in:

> And I saw like a sea of crystal mixed with fire even those who had conquered in the face of the beast and his image, and the number of his name, who were standing upon the crystal sea holding the harps of God . . .[96]

The harps that they play, and the 'song of Moses' that they sing, are not those of the garlanded 'hymn singers and mysteries' in the choir hall at the Pergamon

93. Rev. 13:16-17.
94. Rev. 13:18.
95. Rev. 15:1.
96. Rev. 15:2.

temple to Roma and Augustus, celebrating in the mystery rite the birthdays of the deified imperial family, and the power and might of their empire.[97] It is not in the presence of their images, come to life as performed under the direction of the pagan θεολόγος. Rather their song is:

> Great and wonderful are your works,
> Lord God the Almighty;
> Just and true are your ways,
> the emperor of the nations;
> who shall not fear, O Lord,
> and glorify your name?
> Because you alone are holy,
> Because all the nations shall come
> and they shall worship in your presence,
> because your just acts have been revealed . . .[98]

In a final scene, Christ appears as a horseman on a white horse, with many *coronae* upon his head, and with blood-soaked robes, 'having a name which no-one knows', and thus as mysterious as the mark of the beast, only the Seer reveals that it is 'the word (λογός) of God'. 'Upon his garment and upon his thigh a name is written "king of kings and Lord of Lords".' He is none other than the child snatched up into heaven to escape from the dragon, who now, as promised, is to 'shepherd the nations with a rod of iron'.[99] The fate of Rome's empire now follows:

> The beast was struck down, and with him the false prophet who performed the signs in his presence and by which he had deceived those who had received the mark of the beast, and those who worshipped his image were cast alive, both of them, into the lake of fire . . .

But what, then, was this 'mark' of the beast, and with what is it to be contrasted in the case of the servants of God?

Earlier, the 'servants of God' are 'sealed' by in order to give them protection from the four avenging angels:

> I saw another angel ascending from the rising of the sun, having in his hand the seal (σφραγίς) of the living God, and he cried with a loud voice: 'Do not harm the land and the sea nor the trees until we have sealed the servants of God upon their foreheads'.

Clearly the 'mark (χάραγμα) of the beast' on the foreheads of his worshippers contrasts with the 'seal (σφραγίς)' on the foreheads of the servants of God.

---

97. See above, footnote 84 and associated text.
98. Rev. 15:3-4.
99. Rev. 19:11-12 and 15-16. With 'he shall shepherd the nations with a rod of iron', cf. Rev. 12:5 and above, footnote 45 and associated text.

Paul speaks of 'God who has anointed us, and who has sealed us, and given us the foretaste of his spirit in our hearts', in a verse in which it is reasonable to infer that both anointing and sealing are images of Christian baptism.[100] Abraham's circumcision is described as a 'seal' in the New Testament, where also circumcision is considered replaced by baptism.[101] Both Hermas and the anonymous author of 2 Clement specifically use this term of baptism, the latter specifically in terms of preserving one against hell-fire.[102]

There is of course no historical basis for every inhabitant of the Roman Empire ever needing to receive a mark (χάραγμα) that determined, like a food-rationing book, what they could buy or sell. We need to ask what particular social and religious practice could have blossomed in the Seer's fervid imagination to result in such a scene as this? The answer once more would appear to be in the mystery cults in general that gave their features to the imperial mysteries, whose existence, following Pleket, we have hypothesized.

Kraybill has pointed out how guilds such as the *Augustales* both promoted the imperial cult, and spread to many cities throughout the empire. Such cults provided status for their members, particularly in terms of trade and commerce, and particularly at Ostia in terms of mercantile trade. We have an inscription from there honouring 'M. Junius Faustus . . . priest of divine Titus', who is clearly both priest (*flamen*) of the imperial cult, and also a grain merchant and quaestor of the public treasury.[103] Religious devotion and commercial networking clearly went hand in hand.

We have a second-century bas-relief from Ostia, in which a merchant ship prefigures unloading its cargo, alongside which Neptune, with his trident, arises from the sea. The ship's captain with his wife is performing on board a sacrifice. Behind the ship there is a lighthouse with its flame, on which stands a statue of the emperor being crowned by Victories. Thus is celebrated the nexus between religion, social networks and commerce.[104] Such a scene, magnified and universalized in the Seer's vision, could be seen as portending the exclusion of Christians from access to the wherewithal to life if excluded from the guilds.

But what of the meaning of the 'mark (χάραγμα)' of the beast? The term refers to a mark that is engraved, printed or branded. Somewhere at the end of the second and the beginning of the first century B.C. an anonymous tract was compiled describing three episodes in the life of Ptolemy IV Philopator, and his relations with the Jews, beginning with the battle of Raphia (217 B.C.). In the third episode Ptolemy persecutes the Jews in Alexandria.

---

100. 2 Cor. 1: 21-22, cf. Pseudo Paul, Eph. 1:12-13 and 4:30.
101. Rom. 4:11 cf. 1 Pet. 3:21.
102. Pseudo Clement, 2 Cor. 7.6; 8.6; Hermas, *Sim.*, 72 (VIII.6.3); 93 (IX.16.3–4).
103. J. N. Kraybill, *Imperial Cult and Commerce in John's Apocalypse* (*JSNTSup*, 132; Sheffield: Academic Press, 1996), p. 133, fig. 6.
104. Kraybill, *Imperial Cult*, pp. 128–30 and fig. 5.

> Having erected a pillar on the tower in the courtyard, he carved an inscription that
> no-one who had failed to sacrifice should enter their holy courts, and that all the Jews
> should be subjected to being enrolled in a census and to servile status, and that some
> who voiced opposition were brought by force to their execution, but others were to be
> tattooed (ἀπογραφομένους) and branded (χαράσσεσθαι), by means of fire applied
> to the body, with the mark of Dionysos with his ivy leaf. These are also to be relegated
> to their former restricted status. But in order that he should not appear antagonistic to
> everyone, he added to the inscription: If any of the Jews should choose to join those
> who had been initiated into the mysteries, these would enjoy equal rights with the
> Alexandrians.[105]

χάραγμα is derived from χαράσσεσθαι and therefore can be used as the
mark or tattoo of a member of a mystery cult such as that of Dionysus, or
indeed of the imperial mysteries with which we have argued that such a cult
had become assimilated.[106]

A cognate term for χάραγμα, for the mark that makes one a member of a
mystery cult, is στίγμα. In Herodotus, for example, we read that in Egypt, on
the coast at the Canopic mouth of the Nile, there is a temple of Heracles 'where,
if a household slave of anyone having fled for refuge receives sacred brandings
(στίγματα ἱρά) indicating that he delivers himself to the god, it is unlawful
to touch him'.[107] It is clear therefore why John the Seer should focus on the
branding of a sign of membership of a cult as what he expects of a persecuting
empire that battles against the servants of God sealed with the seal of their
baptism.

Thus we see that, for John the Seer, the relationship between Church and
Empire is a war to the end: imperial society is not redeemable but rather is to
be replaced. 'The kingdoms of this world' are destined to become 'the kingdom of our God and of his Christ', and until they do so, there is little point in
the Christian engaging with them.

Let us now see how John's apocalyptic approach can be read in the context
of a political history of early Christianity.

5. Revelation and the Political Position of Early Christianity

We have seen that John's apocalypse presented a serious political challenge to
the imperial power. This work must not be understood in the manner of those
modern cults that use the document to produce an otherworldly religion, in
which people try to escape from the present into a dream world to which their
contemporaries outside their group have no comprehension. Wittgenstein once
said that it would be impossible to refute someone who believed that the

---

105. 3 Macc. 2:27-30, cf. N. Clayton Croy, *3 Maccabees* (Septuagint Commentary Series;
Leiden: Brill, 2006), pp. ix–xii and pp. 8–9.

106. See above, footnote 77 and associated text.

107. Herodotus, 2.113.

universe was only 150 years old, and confronted by such groups, we seem to be in a similar position regarding their particular beliefs.[108]

The reason was that there would be no community of judgement and belief that we shared with such a person by means of which we could possibly understand the claim that he was making, and even judge the difference between what we meant by such a claim, and what he meant. It is not simply that we have available 'facts' that that person does not know, or that he knows 'facts' that we do not. The problem is that we have no shared agreement on what would count as the evidence for such 'facts', and how it should be applied.

John the Seer and his community shared sufficient agreement in perspective with his contemporaries for them to understand the character of the claim that he was making, and to consider this a danger. On what was that danger and the fear of it based?

Clearly both the community of John the Seer and their pagan contemporaries believed in portents and prodigies, or signs and wonders. Both believed that adverse portents indicated breakdown in both the natural and the social order, as sympathetic reflections of each other. Both believed in a supernatural, divine power able to end the chaos and create 'a new heaven and a new earth'.[109] Both believed in a predetermined fate controlling both human destiny and the operation of nature.

One substantive difference was that the community of the Seer believed that history had as its final goal the transformation of the natural and social order in the reign of God and his servants. The pagan community, as we have seen, subscribed, despite some scepticism by some opinion formers, to a belief in the historical cycles of decline and renewal advocated by a Stoic eschatology, and justified in terms of its metaphysics. And the latter, it must be said, served well the political rhetoric – and, I would suggest, more than rhetoric, since it involved the ruler's personal conviction – that legitimated imperial rule.

Any period such as that which preceded the century before Augustus' accession, could be represented as a period of chaos and decline. The onset of a new order could then be represented as the returning golden age, in the bringing about of which the new ruler was the agent of destiny. But if history were cyclic, if there was to be another decline of the golden age into one of brass and iron, then the peace and prosperity of the new order was to have a fragile quality: it could easily be lost. We saw that the millennial and even messianic iconography of the *Ara Pacis* admitted such a warning note: there were lizards and scorpions in the foliage threatening its luxuriance and fecundity with destruction. Threats of instability and chaos are the stock in trade of dictatorial regimes. John's community offered the final reign of God, reached through the tribulation that would precede it, according to the Dominical words of

---

108. L. Wittgenstein, *On Certainty*, edited by G. E. M. Anscombe and G. H. von Wright, translated by Denis Paul and G. E. M. Anscombe (Oxford: Blackwell, 1974), p. 190, para. 185.
109. Rev. 21:1-3.

Mark's Gospel. But there was to be, on the one hand, neither a violent uprising, nor, on the other, any compromise with the pagan present.

But if John's community were non-violent, why could they not simply be left in peace by the Roman imperial power and simply be dismissed as otherworldly cranks doing not real harm, as we would be inclined to do with such groups?

The answer is that for the pagan Romans the case was not parallel with our own, post-Enlightenment response. Here it was not a clash with a model of the physical universe that has undergone what Weber described as 'disen-chantment'.[110] When we hear such claims of apocalyptic groups, we rest secure on a model of the universe that is a clockwork world of material cause produc-ing material effect so that nature is controllable through scientific technology. In the light of that technology, we are able to predict eclipses of the sun, the falling of meteors, tidal waves and hurricanes, etc.

It is a picture of the world that owes much – even if we cannot follow an extreme relativist and say 'everything'– to the way in which social groups in community construct a shared view of a reality that they suppose to be 'beyond' such communities. Probability theory in post-Einsteinian physics has severely dented the ultimate metaphysical foundations of a clockwork universe of cause and effect. Hume, to whom Einstein expressed his indebtedness, had famously remarked: 'Tis by no means impossible that the sun might not rise tomorrow.'[111] But we console ourselves with statistical probability that such an event is remote. And thus politically and socially we can cope with those who announce that the end of the word is nigh: they do not disturb our confidence in our present political arrangements. Thus within the socially constructed security of our clockwork world, our political demands of governments are that they keep the 'machinery of government' in order so that with the right technological advice the outbreak of foot and mouth disease, for example, can be controlled and eliminated. If such natural disasters occur, it is because governments have been incompetent in understanding and operating the machinery of the clockwork universe with which we are confronted.

In such a post-Enlightenment world, religion poses no threat to our social construction of reality so as to produce fear and alienation. We must try to understand the Islamic (and Irish Catholic) community, if we can, and if they are anxious themselves to assure us that 'true' Islam or 'true' Catholicism wishes to live at peace with non-adherents, and will have no truck with 'terror-ism'. Indeed, we are anxious not to offend particular food and dress customs that do not terribly inconvenience us. But we can remain secure and unassail-able within our clockwork universe of cause and effect, whose foundations are not thus challenged. And the reason that they are unchallengeable, given their

110.   M. Weber, *The Protestant Ethic and the Spirit of Capitalism* (New York: Scribner, 1958), pp. 104–105.

111.   P. Schilpp (ed.), *Albert Einstein: Philosopher-Scientist* (La Salle, Illinois: Open Court, 1969), p. 13.

ultimately socially constructed, metaphysical assumptions is because the groups that would challenge it are in the position of Wittgenstein's man who asserted that the universe was 7 days old: there is no shared community of judgement by which we could refute him or he us: our social constructions of reality completely diverge.

But in the world of John the Seer, there was sufficient convergence between his socially constructed world and that of paganism to make such a challenge threatening. Those whom he confronted believed in the possibility of future metaphysical events in the terms in which they had interpreted their immediate historical past. They believed in the adverse signs and portents, the prodigies and wonders, that they believed the Augustan golden-age returned had banished with its promise of a fruitful earth, of a peace between the realms of sea and land reflected in peace between nations at land and at sea. They believed that the *augurium pacis* had secured, in the main, the banishment of such adverse omens and the continued office of augur and *Pontifex Maximus*, occupied by the Augustus who held also supreme political power, would ensure that the golden age continued, and that such adverse omens would not return. It was precisely this that the Seer's apocalyptic vision was to challenge.

John the Seer claimed that such prodigies and portents, such signs and wonders, were about to return. The very apparatus of the cult that controlled such portents, the imperial mysteries in which what was for him the 'image of the beast' spoke and performed positive omens, was destined to be overthrown. The security of a pagan social construction of reality was thus undermined. It was as if someone challenged our post-Enlightenment clockwork world in the way that, say, a radical proponent of alternative medicine might present his or her challenge. Our reaction will be hostile and interventionist, particularly if children are involved.

The security of imperial rule was celebrated and experienced at the *aduentus* of an emperor, and the ceremony of his reception in a city-state. The citizen body at Cyzicus (*c.* A.D. 37) was instructed, in a civic reception, to greet the kings restored by Caligula after their deposition by Tiberius in a ceremony that testifies to the divinity of the emperor, by whose will they have been restored. The kings were met and conducted by priests and priestesses around the shrines of the deified imperial family, in 'religious veneration (εὐσεβεία) of the divine emperor (Σεβαστός)'. Caligula is the 'new Sun', who 'has wished to illuminate with his rays' these kings. The decree speaks of the 'greatness of his immortality', and of his 'immortal favour'. Games were celebrated in honour of Drusilla as the 'new Aphrodite'. Their images were to be adorned in their shrines. Both archons and wearers of sacred *coronae* are to be present. Prayers are offered 'for the eternal continuance of the rule of Gaius Caesar, and for the safety (σωτηρία) of these persons'.[112]

---

112. *IGRR*, IV.145.

Thus we capture the feeling of such an official welcome, whether for kings as in this case, or for the emperor himself, who though here absent is in a sense present in the ceremony of welcome. The celebration is of social order restored after chaos, of the hope for stability and 'continuance', of indeed 'safety' or 'salvation (σωτηρία)'. We have, moreover, some details, although incomplete, of the imperial *aduentus*. Aune, in his seminal study of this issue, pointed to the kind of chanting hymnody characteristic of what crowned priests and choirs would sing in welcoming procession.[113] Dio tells us of how the senate in Caligula's reign 'went up to the Capitol in a body and offered sacrifices and bowed worshipfully to the chair of Gaius set up in the shrine'.[114] Tacitus adds that under Nero:

> It was then that Roman knights were first enrolled under the title of *Augustiani*, men in their prime and remarkable for their strength, some from a natural frivolity, others from the hope of promotion. Day and night they kept up a thunder of applause, and applied to the emperor's person the voice and epithets of deities.[115]

Aune quotes, furthermore, the albeit late document *Gesta Senatus Urbis Romae* as recording time hallowed and traditional material from earlier centuries. Here we have the assembly of senators chanting repeatedly, anything between eight and twenty six times such acclamations as 'Our hope is in you, you are our salvation,' and 'For the good of the human race, for the good of the Senate, for the good of the State, for the good of all.'

John the Seer, as we have shown, directly assails that sentiment of peace and divine order by calling the images carried in such processions, and sometimes in imperial mystery procession, the 'image of the beast', and claiming the recurrence of the very portents and prodigies that the Augustan religious revolution that accompanied his political one had claimed to have banished. John now proceeds to set before his audience such scenes of victory and peace, with the accoutrements of chanting hymns, crowned officials and sacrifice, but applied, not to the empire of the beast and his worshippers, but to the heavenly hosts bringing about 'the kingdom our God and of his Christ'.

The 'elders' surrounding the 'throne of God and of the Lamb' are present at the sacrifice of the 'Lamb, slain as it were from the foundation of the world'.[116] Several hymns, both of the elders and the general crowds, as in an imperial procession, chant with such expressions as 'salvation (σωτηρία)', 'glory (δόξα)', 'thanksgiving (εὐχαριστία)', 'might (κράτος)' and 'wealth (πλοῦτος)', exemplified as themes of imperial honour in literary works,

---

113. D. G. Aune, 'The Influence of the Roman Imperial Court Ceremonial on the Apocalypse of John', in *Papers of the Chicago Society for Biblical Research*, 28 (1983), pp. 5–26.
114. Dio Cassius, LIX.13.4.
115. Tacitus, *Annal.*, XIV.15 quoted in Aune, 'Influence', p. 16.
116. Rev. 4:2 and10; 5:5 and 8; 11:16, etc.

epigraphs and coins.[117] But these are not in honour of the Roman Emperor as he comes in the flesh, or is held to be spiritually present in a vacant chair, nor is a 'worshipful bow (προσκύνησις)'[118] offered to him, but to the unseen God who will overthrow the kingdom of the beast, accompanied by horrendous portents that belie his claimed achievement of having brought about the *pax deorum* in nature and in society.

The Greek words for 'ambassador (πρεσβυτης)' and 'embassy (πρεσβεία)' are both related to the word for 'elder (πρεσβύτερος)'. The scenes involving elders in the book of Revelation are evocative of scenes in which ambassadors and other leading officials of the city-states greet in procession the *aduentus* of the emperor. Such processions or 'embassies (πρεσβείαι)' met the emperor Maximinus (A.D. 235), with the leading citizens dressed in white and wearing laurel wreaths. They carried also in procession statues of their gods and golden crowns.[119] Ambassadors (*c.* 27 B.C.) from Mytilene presented a golden crown or στέφανος on behalf of the city to Augustus and Octavia.[120] Imperial priests, as we have seen, wore *coronae* in processions, bearing the divine images of the imperial house along with traditional deities such as Apollo, Artemis and the Capitoline Triad.

John the Seer once again produces an alternative version to this taken for granted picture of the theatre of imperial power and prestige, with its guarantee of a divine order and stability through the rites (*auspicia*) by which the emperors claimed to have achieved the *pax deorum*. His picture is of the imperial order collapsing in ruins, with portents and prodigies. Over against that picture, he presents, a heavenly order entering the present age, and marked by processions of elders who also chant and wear *coronae*, or gilded, wreathed crowns. Here we find, as it were, reversed images of the imperial power that the Seer is confronting in his oracle.

John describes his God who is coming to reign as 'seated on a throne', from which issue the real divine portents – 'lightning, voices, and thunders'. The throne is illuminated by 'seven burning lamps that are the seven spirits of God', and before the throne stands 'a sea of glass like crystal'. In the throne itself are the images of four living creatures. But there are twenty-four thrones, set in a circle around God's throne, on which 'sit twenty four elders, clothed in white garments, and upon their heads golden *coronae*'.

Here we may have an image of the church in heaven reflected in the church on earth in a period before Ignatius of Antioch, and before what we shall see to be the emergence of single, and in some sense monarchical, bishops. There is evidence in the early Church that he who presided at the Eucharist sat in the

---

117. Rev. 4:10 and 7:10. For full details and references see Brent, *Imperial Cult*, pp. 205–208.

118. Aune, 'Influence', p. 13.

119. Herodian, VIII.7.2 and Aune, 'Influence', p. 12.

120. *IGRR*, IV, 39 b.30–31: πεμφθῆναι δὲ καὶ στέφανον ἀπὸ χρυσῶν δισχιλίων ὃν καὶ ἀναδοθῆναι ὑπὸ τῶν πρεσβέων.

centre of a broken, horseshoe, circle of presbyters or, we should say, 'presbyter bishops' in a time when both offices, as we shall see to be the case of Clement of Rome, were not yet clearly distinct.

But in the Seer's fantastic vision, the presbyter-bishops at the Christian Eucharist have become assimilated to the pagan priests in imperial and ambassadorial processions, wearing the *coronae* of their office. The church triumphant mirrors the imperial power that it is to replace, as God's providence is worked out in the historical flux of events. Like imperial sacrifices and ambassadorial processions, the elders wear white, and then they reverence the throne of God, like those Senators who performed their act of 'worship προσκύνησις)' before the throne of the emperor Maximinus.[121] Did they place their *coronae* at the feet of the throne, as the heavenly elders now do?:

> The twenty four elders were falling before him who sits upon the throne, and they offer προσκύνησις to him who lives forever and ever. And they were casting their crowns before the throne, saying:
>
>> Worthy art thou,
>> our Lord and God,
>> to receive glory,
>> and honour,
>> and power,
>> because it is you who have created all things,
>> and by your will they have existed and been created.[122]

It would certainly be difficult to kneel or prostrate oneself in obeisance as a pagan priest when one was wearing the kind of ornate, laurel-wreathed and gilded *corona*, complete with medallions depicting pagan deities. It is likely, rather than have them fall off and ruin the atmosphere of the ceremony before the emperor's throne, they would have removed them and placed them on the ground and at his feet. The Senators, at the conclusion of their procession to the temple of Jupiter Capitolinus, presented the divine ruler, Gaius, with a *corona* as they did obeisance to his empty chair.[123] Thus the elders of the heavenly church mirror their pagan counterparts, as they cast their crowns of gold before God's throne, chanting, as I have suggested in my breakdown of lines in the previous quote, like those who chanted in ambassadorial processions.

Thus emerges a developing, apocalyptic response to the Roman Empire that continues in many ways that of the Markan apocalypse. By the time of

---

121. See above, footnote 116 and associated text.
122. Rev. 4:10-11.
123. Dio Cassius, LIX.24.3–4, cf. Aune, 'Influence', pp. 13–14, who cites also XLV.6.5; LIII.30.61. See also L. Ross Taylor, *The Divinity of the Roman Emperor* (American Philological Association, Monographs, 1; Connecticut, 1931), p. 87, note 15 and D. J. Weinstock, *Divus Julius* (Oxford: Clarendon Press, 1971), p. 283[526:9.11] NWG. [779.1]

Vespasian, or perhaps better Domitian, it is not the destruction of Jerusalem that is to mirror the tribulation woes immediately preceding Christ's second advent as Son of Man. Rather John, under the cryptogram of 'Babylon', sees Rome itself as the centre of the beast and his worship, in the universal context of the general collapse of nature and society, marked by terrifying *prodigia* and portents, or 'signs and wonders'.

But John's vision does not confront his contemporary pagan society in the way that it does ours, like the man's claim in Wittgenstein's example who considered the universe is only 150 years old, a claim that is so alien and contrary to our taken for granted world that we regard it as unintelligible and quite innocuous. His vision contains images of imperial power and authority, and the cultic means for their celebration, but reversed so that they apply to the 'kingdom of our God and of his Christ'. Furthermore, the favourable omens that indicate the predestined rule of Augustus and his heirs are equally reversed: the image of the beast and the mystery processions with which it is involved produce metaphysical collapse, and not the claimed, new and eternal, metaphysical order. This was why the vision of the Seer was so politically challenging: it threatened a whole set of political assumptions and their metaphysical basis. In terms of the social psychology of those who dwelt within a pagan and imperial symbolic universe of meaning, the group reaction that it elicited to the affective disturbance that it caused was quite violent.

The equivalent today would be the kind of group-reaction and emotions caused by someone who claimed that there were such things as human races, and one or another were inferior to others, or that men and women were intellectually different, or that there is a gene pool of talent so that universal education is quite pointless. Such claims would not be unintelligible – there would be sufficient overlap between the discourses of those making such claims to make discussion about them possible. But these issues, and the reaction to them, cannot simply be held to be items of academic discussion – a case of reasoning about the facts and finally reaching a consensual conclusion. Their mere assertion so fundamentally challenges our whole egalitarian perspective with its assumptions, no doubt justifiable, in terms of human rights, etc. that they provoke social-psychological unease that results in a repugnance which sometimes expresses itself in quite violent forms. Such was the effect of the vision of John the Seer upon his contemporaries.

The vision of John the Seer did not represent a physical threat of armed uprising such as Jewish apocalyptic that had been provoked in A.D. 70 and was to provoke in the case of Bar Cochbah in A.D. 135. The coming of the reign of God was supernatural and providential, with the saints suffering at the hands of the imperial power before reigning in glory. But Augustus's reign had been providential as well, and delivered by Fate or Destiny that was the divine logos immanent in the cyclical process of a history of decline and renewal. Such a metaphysical view was real to John's pagan contemporaries, so that, however non-violent was the historical process that he was predicting, it was nevertheless a felt, political threat for the pagan world in which he and his group existed.

John the Seer had produced, in Aune's words, an antithesis to the pretensions of pagan imperial power. But the nature of a politics that produces such antitheses is that there is no compromise with the present political arrangements: they are to be replaced rather than to undergo painstakingly piecemeal transformation. In this respect the political stance bears some similarity with a later Hegelian and Marxist theoretical political stance, with the immanent Stoic λόγος and world spirit transformed specifically into a dynamic of nature and of history.

If the nature of the world spirit was rational, then it followed, according to Hegel, that both natural and social events could be understood, interpreted, and even predicted in terms of a human argument, of a divine mind in dialogue with itself and hence in terms of a 'dialectic'. Thus for historical development we looked first at the thesis stated at the introduction to a human discussion. Feudal society was such a thesis, in which there were warm and personal associations between human beings, if you like 'love', but no freedom. The ties that bound master and servant, feudal lord and serf were those of mutual protection and benefit that went beyond the cold clauses of any contract limiting obligations on both sides. But the serf was tied to his liege lord's lands that he farmed – there was no freedom to go elsewhere. The servant was obliged to serve his protecting and loving master for life.

But to any such thesis an antithesis will arise in the process of a rational argument that will contradict the initial thesis. So, in the process of historical development, bourgeois society arises in which there is freedom but no love and belongingness: the social bond between human beings is purely contractual. Thus we may be contractually obliged in order to earn a livelihood to serve our employer but we feel no love or belongingness: with a better offer we resign, serve our notice, and depart for greener pastures!

But to the thesis and its antithesis or contradiction, according to Hegel's transformation of Stoic pantheism, a historically inevitable and determined synthesis will arise, as in the progress of a human argument, in which neither the thesis nor its contradiction will finally prevail. Rather both thesis and antithesis will be reconciled or synthesized resulting in a synthesis. In the case of our crude Hegelian example, a society will arise in which there is both freedom and love. We see this in the emerging political culture of nineteenth century Prussia, in which there is the love and belongingness of the family in which our obligations, parents to children, wives to husband are fulfilled with no curtailment of our freedom. Hegel saw in the Prussian family the 'service in which there is perfect freedom'. The Prussian state and its political institutions became the family writ large under 'our father the Kaiser!'

Marx of course in some of his phases took over Hegelian dialectic but denied any personal, supernatural or spiritual dynamic to the dialectic. The driving forces of the determined course of history were economic and material. Thus we call his view of history, and the development of political institutions, as 'dialectical materialism'. Capitalism represented the thesis, to which its contradiction was emerging, namely the dictatorship of the few on the basis of the dictatorship of the proletarian majority. In building socialism, the antithesis of democratic movements will still rely on the coercive power of the state, only one that is exercised on behalf of the many and not the few. Coercive elitist institutions will be replaced by coercive, democratic ones, namely trade unions, which will be as intolerant of opposition as the autocratic institutions that they are replacing. But in the resultant end of history, neither the few of the thesis nor the many of the antithesis will rule. The subsequent synthesis will see neither the many nor the few ruling but the withering away of the state in a Marxist, communist Utopia.

Such an approach is an all-or-nothing approach. There can be no compromise with existing institutions that are to be replaced not reformed or transformed. In this respect, Marxism resembled the apocalypticism represented by the Markan and Johannine apocalypses. Marxist ideology, for its success, fed upon an Enlightenment view of the world that made its claims plausible. Nature and society were conceived in terms of a materialism that saw the universe as a machine of cause and effect, driven by a nature that was blind and otherwise purposeless. Capitalism was fundamentally exploitative: if one's boss made one million out of one's labour this year, he would have to make two next. He would not be able to waive such an increase: if his company, listed on the stock exchange, did not make a substantial profit then the share value would go down, it would be taken over, and he would lose his position to someone who would have to do what he had failed to do.

The blind forces of a material nature would brook no opposition. But equally, though a worker might be willing, having produced a million pound profit for his boss this year, to see himself doubling it for him the next, nevertheless, progressing to a third year or more, the spring of economic oppression would be wound tighter and tighter so that eventually and inevitably the workers would recoil and readjust the equilibrium of a capitalism machine that would become increasingly dysfunctional: there would be a classless society whose equilibrium would be seen the equality enjoyed by all its citizens. The 'false consciousness' produced by the ideologies of parliament, church and the law courts would finally fail to hold back the final recoil of the spring wound down so tightly in the exploitation of the workers.

John the Seer has a different worldview, not clearly that of the Enlightenment but of the late Roman Republic and early Empire. His claims were not intelligible in terms of a the depersonalized, clockwork, materialist worldview, but in terms of a popular Stoicism that justified, as we have seen, political institutions, however much individual members of the elite may have expressed various degrees of scepticism about it. The justification in political theory of the Principate was of a universe moved, not by blind, materialist forces, but by a divine purpose, by a pantheistic world-spirit whose nature was reason or λόγος. Providence rescued periodically and cyclically nature and society from chaos and produced a new golden age, whose progress or decline could be observed in portents and prodigies, in signs and in wonders. This was the world that John the Seer addressed, sharing many of its formal assumptions, but challenging and reversing the claims made from them about the permanence and goodness of continuing Roman imperial power.

But, like Marxist materialists, it was an all-or-nothing challenge. If the future emerged as predicted, then forces beyond human control would assure the victory to what they saw as their progressive political movement. So too with John the Seer. Neither the Marxists, originally, nor the Seer's community, sought armed insurrection. Some Marxists were subsequently to do so but early Christianity, as far as we know, did not go down that route. John's community was a persecuted, downtrodden community without force of arms, and without the spread of a technology sufficiently cheap and spread widely without central control that would enable small and otherwise insignificant groups to produce them. As with the apocalypse of Daniel, and indeed, we believe, the claims of the Jesus of history, the coming of the kingdom of God was a wholly supernatural event: the 'temple made with hands' would be replaced by a 'new temple not made with hands'. As John reports, 'he who sat upon the throne said: "Behold, I make all things new".'

But playing an all-or-nothing political game, what happens if the 'all' does not transpire and one is left with the 'nothing'? Marxism in Russia and Europe, even when it had triumphed by force of arms, nevertheless collapsed during the nineties of the last century. Some Marxists who survived the failure of the future to conform to the expectations of the political theory were destined to survive, but as smaller groups becoming increasingly ineffective. Part of that failure is undoubtedly due to such claims becoming increasingly implausible, as the general plausibility structures of the social groups to which they address themselves undergo change: physicists, upon whose initial discourse materialist views of nature and society were originally founded become themselves disenchanted with a clockwork world producing any determinate 'end' of nature or of history.

Similarly with the apocalyptic visionaries of early Christianity when Middle and Neo Platonism will provide its justification for imperial order rather than Stoicism, how can traditionalist pagan eschatology be addressed by the apocalyptic of portents and prodigies in a way that is plausible, and can either disturb or positively convince?

Mainstream Marxism or mainstream Christianity was not content to continue, increasingly as a minority group, whose claims were increasingly unintelligible in addressing the political order of a society that it originally expected to replace 'root and branch'. But how were both to change? Only by a fundamental shift from the all-or-nothing strategy, and the metaphysics on which it was based.

The present social and political order need not be so much replaced as transformed. Capitalism could be changed so as to become benign by general and formal 'socialist values' being applied in the context of free market economies: 'productivity' was the answer to claims that capitalism meant necessarily exploiting the worker and increasing his toil. A considerable part of the Marxist Left in Old Labour was to appropriate the New Labour agenda, and in doing so abandoned the metaphysics of dialectical materialism as accounting for social and historical change and development. Thus the Blair-Mandelson 'Project' was born.

We shall now see from Clement of Rome, Luke-Acts in the New Testament, and Ignatius of Antioch how early Christianity was to produce its own version of the 'Project'. These writers, in their different ways, were to open up the possibility of the transformation of pagan, imperial political order by the requirements of a Christian monotheism, and the possibility of a Christian political society as preparatory for the Second Coming, but not dependent upon its imminent arrival.

Chapter 5

EARLY CHRISTIAN COSMIC REORDERING:
ST LUKE, CLEMENT AND IGNATIUS

In the late eighties or nineties of the first century, three writers were to
articulate in embryo the political ideas and strategies that were to lead eventually, over two more centuries, to the toleration of Christianity, and then its
final emergence as the dominant religion of the Roman empire, in the one form
that would make it politically effective. The late eighties were in fact around
the time in which the Seer of the book of Revelation was publishing what we
have seen to be his deeply subversive oracle. But three writers were to address
the inhabitants of a pagan and imperial construction of social reality in quite
different terms, and thus develop an alternative political project to that which
simply awaited apocalyptic intervention.

Both the writer of Luke-Acts and Clement of Rome were to express a
Christian engagement with pagan and imperial culture in quite different terms
to an apocalyptic approach that sought no rapprochement with that culture.
An apocalyptic approach, however much it may reflect the power structures of
the contemporary society to which it wishes to respond, seeks a root and
branch replacement of those structures with which it cannot compromise:
Great Babylon was to fall in a disaster of annihilation. In the early twentieth
century Tsarist Russia experienced a Marxist revolution in which the old secret
police became the new Chekha and Lenin the new Tsar: the revolutionaries had
held up an alternative that was a mirror image of the society that they opposed,
and with that image they sought to reconstruct it. The Seer and his community
represent a similar reaction of a community regarding itself as downtrodden,
but in this case appealing to spiritual and transcendental forces that would
create 'the kingdom of our God and of his Christ'.

But the early Christian community that has left us the record found in the
New Testament of the *Gospel of Luke* and of the Acts of the Apostles was
prepared to countenance a far closer engagement with contemporary, Graeco-
Roman imperial culture than was his near contemporary on the isle of Patmos.
The Seer of Revelation, as we saw, challenged the political legitimation of
the Augustan revolution. That revolution had been ideologically founded
on the claim that a *pax deorum* in nature and in society had been achieved by
Augustus' augural act, in which the signs and portents of a *natura discors* had

been banished in a new, millennial reign of peace. The Seer had claimed that these signs and portents were reappearing, that nature was collapsing once again in disorder, that there was 'war in heaven' corresponding to war, pestilence and famine upon earth. Only when 'the kingdoms of this world have become the kingdom of our God and of his Christ', with Babylon (Rome) overthrown, could the true peace of God come about.

From such a view the author of Luke-Acts was to dissent. He was, as we shall now see, to claim that the end of history was 'not yet', and that there was an indefinite period of secular history in which the Church would exist. Christians were not, therefore, as Tacitus had described them, 'haters of the human race'. The author thus was the first Christian writer to espouse what was to await almost one and one half centuries, and appear as the Eusebian ideology according to which only a Christian Emperor of an imperial church could secure the true peace in nature and in society. Contemporary society was to be embraced, engaged with, and transformed so as to produce eventually the assumption of power by what had previously been a persecuted and minority movement.

Let us see in what terms, specifically, the author of Luke-Acts was to make the claim that we have just sketched.

1. *Luke-Acts:* Pax Augusta *and the Peace of Jesus Christ*

The Markan Apocalypse, as we saw, had predicted the signs and portents presaging Christ's return as Son of Man as the outcome of the siege of Jerusalem in A.D. 69. Matthew was convinced that the events would still take place in some indeterminate 'holy place', Jerusalem having been destroyed. But Luke securely detaches the destruction of Jerusalem from the time of the end, and so relegate the apocalyptic events to an indefinite and distant future:

> When you shall see Jerusalem encircled by armed camps, then know that its desolation (ἡ ἐρήμωσις αὐτῆς) has drawn nigh . . . and Jerusalem shall be trodden down by the pagans until the times of the pagans (καιροὶ ἐθνῶν) are fulfilled.[1]

The destruction of Jerusalem is indeed its 'desolation'. But it is not caused by the mysterious apocalyptic cause that was Daniel's 'desolating sacrilege (βδέ λυγμα τῆς ἐρημώσεως)'. The apocalyptic pageant will still occur,[2] but only after the indefinite 'times of the pagans' have run their course. The 'desolation' of Jerusalem is just one more event in secular history.

The risen Jesus, furthermore, is not imminently to appear in Galilee as in Mark, nor to be with the disciples 'to the end of time' as in Matthew. He appears for 40 days, and then ascends into heaven, promising to return in an unspecified

---

1. Lk. 21:20-24.
2. Lk. 21:25-27.

future,[3] with a promise of the supernatural power of the Spirit that will come for the long interim required for them to preach the gospel 'in Judea and Samaria and to the uttermost parts of the earth'.[4] The apostles are not to 'stand gazing up into heaven' as if expecting the immediate return of a Jesus who had been quite impervious for requests for an answer to the question: 'Will you at this time restore the kingdom to Israel?' They are informed about the Spirit to be given for a protracted mission in the present age.[5]

But in using what imagery is the continuing present rather than future eschatology now described? The present social order of the Christian community is made to reflect the metaphysical claims for the Augustan Principate in securing the peace of the gods upon nature and society. After the Spirit has been given, the early Christian community is a community of unity and peace. The poor of the community are cared for according to need, in fulfilment of Mary's joyful exultation in the God 'who has lifted up the humble and meek':

> They continued daily of one accord (ὁμοθυμαδόν) in the temple, but breaking bread
> at home, receiving nourishment with the joy of exultation and in simplicity of heart,
> praising God and enjoying favour with all the people.[6]

Acts will later continue what had been true of the apostles and others earlier in the Upper Room:

> The multitude of believers had one heart and mind, and neither was there one who said
> that any of his possessions were his own, but everything was shared by them.[7]

The angel song at Bethlehem had been of 'glory to God in the highest, and peace to his people on earth', and the 'crowd of disciples' had hailed Jesus as 'the emperor (βασιλεύς) who comes in the name of the Lord'.[8] The 'year of the Lord's favour' begins with Jesus' ministry, not in the transformed future world of the apocalyptists' vision, when the blind are to see, captives be released and Jesus is 'to preach the gospel (εὐαγγελίσασθαι) to the poor'.

Luke's Gospel, like Acts, begins with an idyllic scene of harmony and peace, characterized by the angels' song at Bethlehem. The birth of John the Baptist is introduced as the forerunner of Jesus, but with all apocalyptic imagery expunged from his portrait. Luke well knew and reproduced John's prophecy from Mark that the coming one would 'baptise you in the Holy Spirit and

---

3. Acts 1:9.
4. Acts 1:6-8.
5. Acts 1:9-11 and 1:6.
6. Acts 2:46-47.
7. Acts 1:13-14; 4:32.
8. Lk. 2:14 and 19:38. See also Brent Kinman, *Jesus' Entry into Jerusalem in the Context of Lukan Theology and the Politics of His Day* (AGJU, 27; Leiden: E. J. Brill, 1995).

in fire'.[9] He adds from Q his words of coming judgement.[10] But even here Luke highly modifies the traditional picture of the apocalyptic preaching of John with his own addition that makes John a teacher of a conventional morality for this world: tax gatherers are to be honest and soldiers satisfied with their pay and not revolt. Clearly for this 'John', despite some future expectation, the established order is, for the present, to be maintained.

In Luke's own material, in the first two chapters, the birth of John is foretold and described, and the traditional image of Elijah is invoked in the description. But there are significant omissions from that description. The Old Testament text on which Luke relies reads:

> And behold I will send Elijah the Tishbite before the great and terrible day of the Lord comes and shall appear, who shall restore the heart of father towards son and the heart of a man towards his neighbour lest I come and strike the earth angrily.[11]

Regarding the messenger, identified by all three Gospels as John who dresses as Elijah, this text has previously read:

> Behold I send my messenger and he shall prepare a way before my face . . . and who shall endure the day of his coming; or who shall stand upright in his sight; because he shall come as the fire of a furnace . . . and he will purify the sons of Levi and he shall pour them forth as silver and as gold . . . [12]

This then is the John as forerunner of Luke's tradition, coming with the dress and diet of Elijah and promising the fire of God's judgement and preaching repentance so as to flee the 'wrath to come'.[13] But in Luke's first portrait of John we read:

> For he shall be great before the Lord . . . and shall go before him in the spirit and power of Elijah, to turn the hearts of the fathers towards their children and the disobedient to the good sense of the righteous, to make ready a people for the Lord.[14]

All references to the eschatological 'refinement' with fire and to the judgement of the Lord's coming are therefore edited out in Luke's text.

When John was born, his father Zacharias recovered from his dumbness and proclaims:

> You child shall be called prophet of the most high,
> For you will go before the Lord to prepare his ways,

9. Lk. 3:6 cf. Mk 1:8 and Mt. 3:12.
10. Mt. 3:7-10 (= Lk. 3:7-9).
11. Mal. 3:23 (LXX).
12. Mal. 3:1-3.
13. Mt. 3:7 (= Lk. 3:7).
14. Lk. 1:15-17.

> To give knowledge of salvation (σωτηρία) to his people,
> In the forgiveness of their sins,
> Through the sure mercy of our God,
> In which the dawn from on high has visited us
> To appear to those in darkness and the shadow of death,
> And to guide our feet into the way of peace (εἰρήνη).[15]

Thus the picture of John emerges as a figure preparing the way for the *pax dei*, the peace of God upon earth, with no reference to 'refining the sons of Levi', no coming of the fire of judgement, etc.

At the centre of the scene of 'peace' thus described stands Israel's messiah or 'Christ', who is additionally described as σωτήρ or 'saviour', uniquely in Luke in the synoptic gospels.[16] He is also 'son of God' as the result of a divine birth, though the 'Spirit of the Lord', who 'overshadows' Mary's womb, is described in studiously non-physical terms, unlike the union of Anchises with Venus that gave birth to the *gens Julia*. And we have here all the features of Augustus' claims that, by the peace of the gods and his divinity, he has secured peace on nature and on society cleansed from all destructive signs and portents. The σωτηρία that was for the Seer of Revelation an apocalyptic deliverance through the coming kingdom of God is here realized in the ministry of a peaceful John, the peace of the babe of Bethlehem, and of Zechariah's prophecy.

The Lukan themes mirror both those of the *Ara Pacis Augustae* that we have seen, and a commentary on them as expressed in an inscription of 9 B.C. from the letter of the governor of the Province of Asia. He announces the beginnings of the *saeculum aureum* with a new calendar in the following words:

> . . . from previous gods we have received favour . . . whether the birthday of the most divine Caesar is more pleasant or more beneficial which we would justly consider to be a day equal to the beginning of all things . . . If not [the beginning of all things] in nature, at least in the order of the useful, for even if there is nothing in a fallen condition and changed into an unfortunate condition he had not set right, he has given to the whole world a different appearance, which would [as a world] have gladly welcomed its destruction had not for the common good fortune Caesar been born . . .[17]

In this inscription there follows the decree of the *Koinon* of Asia that informs us:

> The Providence that has divinely ordered our life, has brought us regard and honour, and arranged our life with perfect goodness when it brought to us Augustus, whom

---

15. Lk. 1:76-79.
16. Lk. 1:47; 2:1; Acts 5:31; 13:23, cf. Jn 4:42.
17. V. Ehrenberg and A. H. M. Jones (eds), *Documents Illustrating the Reigns of Augustus and Tiberius* (Oxford: Clarendon Press, 1976), no. 98a.5-9; R. K. Sherk, *Rome and the Greek East to the Death of Augustus* (Translated Documents of Greece and Rome, 4, edited by E. Badian and R. Sherk; Cambridge: University Press, 1984), no. 101, pp. 124-27.

Providence has filled with virtue for the benefit of mankind, and granted both to us
and to those after us as our saviour (σωτῆρ), who has made war to cease and ordered
the world with peace (εἰρήνη).[18]

Here then we have declared the aims of the Augustan metaphysical program as
indicated in the imagery of the *Ara Pacis Augustae*. A world that would have
'gladly welcomed its destruction', whether in nature or in society, has been 'set
right' because divine Caesar has been born as a 'saviour (σωτῆρ)' bringing
'peace (εἰρήνη)'. Luke therefore offers as the alternative the birth of Jesus
Christ as σωτῆρ who brings the εἰρήνη.

The celebration of Augustus' divine birthday is 'equal to the beginning of
things' in a world restored and at peace. So also will in parallel Luke introduces the birth of Jesus Christ. Luke does not yet begin writing history with the
birth of Christ at year 1, as the province of Asia's calendar now did with that of
Augustus. This was to be the later achievement of the Chronographer of 354.
But he does introduce chronographic notes from secular history, such as the
dating of the census that 'first took place when Cyrenius was pro-consul of
Syria', or of the beginning of Jesus' ministry: 'In the fifteenth year of the reign
of Tiberius Caesar, when Pontius Pilate was procurator of Judaea, and Herod
the tetrarch of Galilee . . .', etc.[19]

Part of Augustus' metaphysical program was the conduct of a census which,
at first sight, may seem simply the act of a revolutionary purging the Senate of
those who had opposed him. But there was a religious dimension to a census,
which is also called a *lustrum*. The latter term refers to the religious acts that
accompany a census, cleansing by means of sacrifices the city boundary
(*pomerium*), making pure those who dwelt within them duly recorded on the
census rolls. The taking of the census with these accompaniments made the
ritual, like the inauguration of the *Ara Pacis*, part of the initiation of the *saeculum aureum*. Thus in contrast Luke's census of Augustus begins the true peace
of God with the birth at Bethlehem. The angel message and song had announced
to the shepherds 'peace (εἰρήνη) to his people on earth', and with it a 'saviour
(σωτῆρ) who is Christ the Lord'.[20] Paralleling the claim that Augustus has
been 'filled with virtue' by Providence, Jesus is 'filled with the Spirit' at his
baptism rather than simply 'led' or 'impelled' as in Matthew and Mark.[21]

Thus in parallel Luke begins his story of the birth of Christ with a decree of
Caesar Augustus that the whole world should be enrolled in a census.[22] The
historical basis for such a census has always proved extremely elusive since, as
an historical event, it is frankly incredible. Admittedly the birth at Bethlehem

18.   Ehrenberg and Jones, *Documents*, no. 98b.32–37.
19.   Lk. 2:2; 3:1-2.
20.   Lk. 2: 11 and 14.
21.   Mt. 4:1 and Mk 1:12, cf. Lk. 4:1.
22.   Lk. 2:1.

was required by prophecy,[23] and Jesus had always been known as Jesus of Nazareth, suggesting that he had been born there. Both Matthew and Luke needed, therefore, an account of how he could have been born in Bethlehem. But the invention of a census was not the only way in which such a difficulty could be overcome, as Matthew shows by claiming instead that the holy Family had always lived at Bethlehem, but were forced to flee by Herod to Galilee and the city of Nazareth.

The historical difficulty with Luke's world census is that it was impossible to administer at that time. Decius (A.D. 249), for example, organized, or tried to organize, a universal, certificated act of sacrifice on all citizens throughout the empire, but this did not involve a wholesale dislocation in which everyone had to travel to their place of birth, with the social and economic chaos that this would produce. Furthermore, such a universal act of sacrifice was dependent upon universal citizenship that was only granted under Caracalla's citizenship law (A.D. 212), and taxation registers. Such a requirement was, therefore, impossible at any time, let alone Augustus' time.

Luke's universal census is not therefore to be regarded as a fiction designed to explain the birth at Bethlehem as Messianic fulfilment. Rather it is an ideological device that parallels Augustus' census at Rome founding his pagan *saeculum aureum*, whose themes are reflected in the idyllic scenes in the temple and elsewhere with which his gospel commences, with its shepherds, priests and prophetesses, with Anna as a prophetess in the temple like the Sibyl who prophesied the golden age.[24] The true age of joy and blessedness, the *pax* of the one true God in nature and in society, is achieved, not in Augustus but in Christ whose birthday is rather 'the beginning of things'.

To whom did this idyllic picture of the nature and purpose of Christianity appeal?

Luke's constituency was clearly different from that of the Seer of Revelation, and the terms of engagement with contemporary society were quite different. Perhaps the clue for answering this question is the addressee of the two volumed work whose name is Theophilus. The latter has a title, namely 'your excellency (κράτιστος)', implying an official of some rank. Furthermore, the author's purpose in writing to him is one of reassurance: he writes 'in order that you may know the certainty of the things in which you have been instructed'.[25] Since the provenance of Luke-Acts would appear to be the Asia Minor that we read so much of in Acts itself, it is reasonable to suppose that the Christian group to which Theophilus belongs is situated there. The ideology of the imperial cult that we have seen reflected in Luke's reversed, Christological images was characteristic of pagan Asia Minor. Here the cult itself had began, with those city-states petitioning Augustus to be allowed to offer religious cult to the

23. Mic. 5:2; Mt. 2:5-6; Lk. 2:4-5.
24. Lk. 2:36-38.
25. Lk. 1:3-4; Acts 1:1.

deified Augustus, and sacrifices and other forms of devotion offered to members of the imperial house.

Such cities enjoyed public celebrations after their ambassadors returned with the 'good news (εὐαγγελια)' relating to the imperial family. εὐαγγέλιον is of course the word for 'gospel' in the New Testament. We have a restored inscription from the Peloponnese referring to a priest 'sacrificing' in view of 'good news (εὐαγγέ[λια])', 'concerning the whole household of the divine *Augusti*', and another from Samos in the time of Augustus referring to a festival (ἡμέραν εὐα[νγέλιον]) celebrating good news from Rome.²⁶ Sardis decreed a sacred festival in celebration of the assumption of the *toga virilis* by Gaius Caesar, Augustus' nephew. When the ambassadors brought back the good news of the ratification of the decree, the city is described as 'evangelised', and 'prayers for salvation (or "safety" (σωτηρία))' are offered 'by sacred heralds'. As a result, 'the city has the good news announced (or is "evangelised": εὐανγελίσθη ἡ πόλις)'.²⁷

Luke associates the common New Testament word 'gospel (εὐαγγέλιον)' with the word 'to preach the gospel (εὐαγγελίζομαι)'. But he associates the term characteristically with, not suffering and the cross, but with joy, as when the angel at Bethlehem brings 'good tidings of great joy' like the ambassadors returning to Sardis, or like Jesus beginning his ministry with the promise that he is to bring 'glad tidings to the poor'.²⁸ Luke thus recreates Augustan political messianism in the image of Christ.

Theophilus and his group were part of a social movement in which, as we saw, low status Equites were excluded from the patrician centres of former Republican power. It was this group of wealthy landless, who were to benefit from the Augustan revolution. Such men could celebrate and advertise their newly achieved status by endowing temples to the imperial cult with their wealth, gaining prestige for their cities as well as themselves. They would parade their grand gesture by holding priesthoods of the Imperial Cult. Moreover, in public games with public banquets celebrating such cults, such a rising individual would acquire a προεδρία or presidential seat at such events in the theatres and amphitheatres.²⁹

Luke, in addressing his gospel and its catechesis to those from the background of a Theophilus, was therefore well 'on message' to their former, positive commitment to pagan, imperial society. They had joined in the rejoicing of the cities of Asia Minor at imperial events, and the possibilities of rising

---

26. Both are cited in Horsley, *New Documents*, III, p. 13. The Peloponnese inscription is reconstructed in L. Moretti, 'Un nuovo proconsole d'Acaia', *ArcCl*, 5 (1953), pp. 255–59, the Samian, in *IGRR*, IV.996.
27. Ehrenberg and Jones, *Documents*, no. 99 = *I. Sardis*, VII.1.8.12–14 = *IGRR*, IV.1756.14.
28. Lk. 2:10; 4:18.
29. P. Zanker, *The Power of Images in the Age of Augustus*, translated by A. Shapiro (Ann Arbor: University of Michigan Press, 1990), pp. 129–31; pp. 319–28.

socially in the new order that this had brought. Luke reflects their mood when he speaks of God 'throwing down the mighty from their seats' in their prominent position in the decks of spectators in amphitheatres or at banquets, and 'exalting the humble and meek'. They may be assured that their new religion grants them the same experience, though they must exchange the pagan virtue of 'ambition', which as φιλοτίμια was a virtue ('love of honour'), with the Christian one of meekness and humility.

But above all, Luke's reformulation of the Christian message in terms of εἰρήνη in nature and society as the result of a σωτηρία achieved under a divine son had great resonance with Theophilus and his group, who had been part of a political movement whose metaphysical aim had been to achieve the *pax deorum*. They had witnessed, as we saw in Chapter 2, a century of civil war in which the old Republic had crumbled, and Octavian had finally emerged, after bloodshed on a massive scale, to set up a military autocracy. They as pagans in the Greek city-states of Asia Minor had suffered from the clash of conflicting armies on their soil. The battles between the Triumvirs had been at such places as Philippi, and in the wider Greek East, Pharsalus and Actium.

Our explanation of such disastrous civil conflicts might be in terms of a governmental machine that was malfunctioning, taking our model from a view of the cosmos in terms of Newtonian mechanics. But their interpretation of such events, witnessed in the historiography of Cassius Dio and Suetonius, and in the epic of Lucan, was the metaphysical need to secure, not the anger of the gods manifested in such events, and the signs and portents that went with them, but rather instead the peace of the gods. More philosophically, in terms of Lucan's Stoicism, a 'nature at variance with itself (*natura discors*)' needed to be set right with a *pax* that required an emperor (*princeps*). The Augustan ideology, expressed iconographically in the *Ara Pacis*, had expressed well this ideology as we have seen, as had the decree of the province of Asia in its language of a collapsed natural and social order needing restoration.

Converts such as Theophilus and his group were confronted therefore by a dilemma. They had, with their fellow citizens, welcomed Augustus' succession to power with all the joyful hope of the advent of the returning *saeculum aureum*. Theirs was the joy expressed in the Pro-consul's letter of 9 B.C. creating the new calendar, and welcoming Augustus as the saviour of their world from chaos and destruction. But were they not, in their conversion to their new faith, threatening the *augurium pacis* that Augustus had performed and all that it meant regarding the banishment of portents and prodigies and securing *pax*?

The author of Luke-Acts is therefore assuaging such fears and such guilt at abandoning Augustus' remedy. He assures them that their newfound faith gives them a saviour who produces the peace of God in nature and society in a mirror image of Augustus' millenarian ideology. The fulfilment of their political hope is to be in Christ, who will preserve their empire and their well-being.

The Christians of Mark's community, just as had those of the Seer of Revelation, saw the solution to their situation in the future apocalyptic events, and not in the present order of things that they rejected. Graeco-Roman paganism may have misinterpreted that response as concealing an insidious design to produce by magical means the very signs and portents of the end that they had predicted. But as Tacitus well understood, the difference between Jewish signs and portents, and those experienced by Romans, was that the latter had the cultic and ritualistic means of controlling them whereas the former did not. But both communities awaited deliverance in the future kingdom of Christ, the Son of Man and had little wish to engage with the present.

We have seen that matters were different for the Theophilus and his circle, for whom Luke wrote his two volumed work. These had been engaged with Graeco-Roman society as pagans, and found it quite repugnant to abandon the metaphysical achievements of that society. Luke gave to them a reconstruction of Christian theology that enabled that engagement to continue for them as Christians, and indeed to confirm its metaphysical achievement of a present *pax dei* on nature and on society. But in doing so, the theological engagement and reconstruction became a proposal for the political reconstruction of pagan society itself, as it existed in this order of space and of time. The question that needed to be posed, and that Luke did not pose, was now how the political order of Christian society would be reflected in the political order of civil society?

Emperors ruled pagan society, and were, with their lesser collaborators, priests as well as kings. Nature and society were one, and the natural and social order were but expressions of the metaphysical order. Were leaders of the Christian community priests? Did the Christian community even have priests as opposed to the plurality of elders, also called 'bishops', and appointed by the Holy Spirit, such as those whom Paul addresses in Acts as his last will and testament to the churches of Asia Minor?[30] These were to be the later questions that Luke does not answer, and to which we shall be returning as our account further unfolds.

But let us turn for now to Clement of Rome, Luke's near contemporary.

2. *Clement of Rome: Church Order and Imperial Order*

Probably around A.D. 95, in the reign of Domitian, an anonymous letter was written in the name of 'the church of God that resides at Rome' to 'the church of God that resides at Corinth'.[31] We know that the author was a man named Clement because some near contemporaries inform us of that fact. We have a letter written by Dionysius of Corinth, partially preserved by Eusebius, in which he mentions Clement as the author of a letter from the Church of Rome.[32]

---

30. Acts 20:17, cf. 20:28.
31. Clement, *Cor.*, praef.
32. Dionysius of Corinth, apud Eusebius, *H.E.*, IV.23.11.

Furthermore Irenaeus mentions his name in a succession list for the Church of Rome, and a letter that he wrote to Corinth.[33]

Clement appears on later episcopal succession lists as either third or first bishop after St Peter at Rome. But the anonymous writer whom others name claims no office as Paul had done when he wrote to various churches as 'Paul, servant of Jesus Christ, called apostle',[34] or, as we shall see, Ignatius of Antioch was to do when he claimed also the title *Theophorus*, let alone the designation of later popes such as 'Clement, bishop, servant of the servants of God, with the Holy Fathers, for everlasting memory'. Furthermore, he does not claim the title of a single bishop of Rome for himself or for others. His words presuppose that there are a plurality of presbyter-bishops in the Church of Rome as there are at Corinth, since he uses the word 'presbyter' and 'bishop' interchangeably.

When he speaks of the apostles knowing that there would be 'strife over the bishop's office', he goes on to make it clear that he is referring to the office of a number of presbyters whom the Corinthians had expelled.[35] Clement uses the term ἐπισκοπή in relation to the presbyterate as an apostolic institution, just like the pseudepigraphic *Teaching of the Twelve Apostles* will refer to their commandment to 'elect (or "ordain") bishops and deacons' in place of charismatic 'apostles' or itinerant missionaries.[36] But outside of references to alleged apostolic origins, he prefers the term 'presbyters': 'Let Christ's flock be at peace with the presbyters who have been appointed (μετὰ τῶν καθεσταμέ νων πρεσβυτέρων).'[37]

That there was no one and only bishop was true not only of Corinth, but of Rome from where he writes the letter, as indicated by the Letters of Ignatius of Antioch. Here the writer is demanding a single bishop, together with a number of presbyters and deacons, as the invariant and valid church order of any Christian church in each major city of Asia Minor. As I have argued elsewhere, the emergence of single bishops was new at this time.[38] Although, however, he can identify various named persons as bishop such as Onesimus of Ephesus, Damas of Magnesia, Polybius of Tralles, Polycarp of Smyrna, etc. he is unable to name any bishop in Rome.[39] The strong implication must be that there was no single bishop that he could thus address in Rome at this time.

But it should not be assumed that there was a single congregation, whether in Rome or in Corinth at this time, with a collection of presbyter-bishops

---

33. Irenaeus, *Adv. Haer.*, III.3.3 (34–44).

34. Rom. 1:1; 1 Cor. 1:1; Gal. 1:1, etc.

35. Clement, *Cor.*, 44.1, cf. 4–5.

36. *Did.*, 15:1.

37. Clement, *Cor.*, 54.2, see also B. E. Bowe, *A Church in Crisis: Ecclesiology and Paranaesis in Clement of Rome* (Harvard Dissertations in Religion 23; Minneapolis: Fortress Press, 1988), pp. 149–50.

38. A. Brent, *Ignatius of Antioch and the Second Sophistic* (Studien und Texte zu Antike und Christentum 36; Tübingen: Mohr Siebeck, 2006).

39. Ignatius, *Ephes.*, 1.3; *Magnes.*, 2.1 ; *Trall.*, 1.1; *Pol.*, praef.

conducting worship together over that single congregation alone. Though it may have been possible to hire a large lecture hall on some occasions, it would seem to have been the case that as the church, particularly in an urban context, grew numerically, then the original church in a house had no space for expanded numbers with the result that the church became, in Lampe's words, 'fractionalized' rather than 'factionalized' into several house churches.[40]

We hear about 'church in a house' not about lecture theatres. Paul will greet Prisca and Aquila 'and the church which is in their house'. The Church in Laodicea gathers as the 'church that is in the house' of Nymphas. In his salutation to Philemon he includes Aphia and Archippus and 'the church which is in their house'.[41] In the generation after Clement we meet with Justin Martyr's group, modelled on a philosophical school, that met 'above the baths of Martin'.[42] But given the development of such networks of house churches, each with its own presiding presbyter bishop, the tendency for one group to cease to be, as it were, a 'fraction' of the whole, and to become instead a discrete 'faction' was unavoidable. Such a tendency led sometimes to an absolute breach with 'the whole church', and was an endemic feature of such a house-church organization. In Corinth, for example, we have examples of groups claiming 'I am of Paul, and I of Apollos, and I of Cephas, and I of Christ.'[43]

However, it would appear that it was possible sometimes for the different house churches to meet together as 'the whole church', perhaps by hiring a lecture room. Paul speaks of 'when the whole church comes together', and also considers Gaius as 'a guest of the whole church'.[44] Clearly in the former case the 'whole church' was concerned in a case of incest, since this affected the continuing bond of intercommunion between the house groups.

One aid to unity by Clement's time was that it would seem that the office of presbyter-bishop could not be granted to someone on the decision of one group alone. Ordination, in whatever form, seems to have been the decision of the 'whole church'. Clement's presbyter-bishops had been appointed as successors to the apostles 'with the whole church consenting', and therefore they could not simply be deposed when blamelessly exercising their ministry over their particular congregations.[45]

We have a document which, I believe, emanates from the Roman community about a century after Clement's time, but which might support a situation that

40. P. Lampe, *Die stadtrömischen Christen in den ersten beiden Jahrhunderten* (WUNT, 2.18; Tübingen: Mohr Siebeck, 1989).

41. Rom. 15:5; 1 Cor. 16:19; Col. 4:15; Phlm. 2. See also Bowe, *Clement of Rome*, pp. 12–16.

42. Acta Justini, III.3, see also Lampe, *Stadtrömischen Christen*, pp. 238–41 and Brent, *Hippolytus and the Roman Church in the Third Century: Communities in Tension before the Emergence of a Monarch-Bishop* (VCSup, 31; Leiden: E. J. Brill, 1995), p. 400.

43. I Cor. 1:11.

44. Rom. 16:23.

45. Clement, *Cor.*, 44.3.

existed in his day. The so-called *Apostolic Tradition* of the Hippolytan community at Rome records, in the present state of its text, that bishops from neighbouring dioceses should gather according to a custom that arose arguably only from Cyprian's time onwards. The text of that document, now also found incorporated into the *Apostolic Constitutions* and in the so-called *Canons of Hippolytus* and the *Testamentum Domini*, has undergone considerable modification.

But among these modifications sticks out a strange rubric in the rite for ordaining a bishop. The rubric expressly states that while the bishops lay hands on the episcopal ordinand, the presbyters shall stand by in silence.[46] As Ratcliff pointed out, rubrics normally give instructions what to do, not what not to do.[47] It would seem that this rubrical prohibition conceals an earlier practice in which the presbyter-bishops from all the Roman congregations in their house-churches came together to say the prayer of ordination, and to lay hands on the new bishop for a particular congregation. We see here a graphic example of what Clement had meant a century earlier when he had spoken of '. . . the whole church'.

We also have parallel with the Hippolytan *Apostolic Tradition*, at least in some form that is clearly only fragmentarily recoverable, the anonymous *Refutation of All Heresies*, attributed to Hippolytus of Rome. The author has a dispute with Callistus, the precise character of which we shall need to explore in greater detail in our next chapter. But for now, let us examine one particular passage in which the relationship between his group and that of Callistus becomes explicit. Rather than being the antipope that many accounts wrongly describe, the following scene presents the very antithesis to a situation in which there are two rival contestants to a single chair over the whole Roman community:

> He was the first to plan to forgive men their sins for their pleasures, declaring to all men
> that sins would be absolved by him. For if someone assembled with some different
> person (παρ' ἑτέρῳ τινὶ συναγόμενος) and is called a Christian (καὶ λεγόμενος
> Χριστιανός), if he should commit any sin, he declares, the sin is not reckoned on his
> account if he should take refuge in the school (σχολῇ) of Callistus.[48]

Clearly in the situation between the author and Callistus, his opponent there were other groups, gathering under different persons, who could nevertheless

---

46. *Ap. Trad.*, 2.
47. E. C. Ratcliff, '"Apostolic Tradition": Questions Concerning the Appointment of the Bishop', in *Liturgical Studies*, edited by A. H. Couratin and D. H. Tripp (London: SPCK, 1976), pp. 156–60. See also Bradshaw et al., *The Apostolic Tradition, Translation and Commentary* (Hermeneia; Minneapolis: Fortress Press, 2002), pp. 1–17 and Stewart-Sykes, *Hippolytus, on the Apostolic Tradition, an English Translation with Introduction and Commentary* (Crestwood, NY: St. Vladimir's Seminary Press, 2001), p. 50.
48. Hippolytus (Pseudo), *Ref.*, IX.12.20–21.

be regarded as Christians, and therefore members of the whole church at Rome. The 'chair of the bishop's office' that Callistus had desired was not the chair over the whole community, however much he might have desired that it should be. The Greek word here for 'gather (συναγόμενος)' is cognate with such words for gathering together for Jewish worship (συναγωγή), and is also used by Ignatius for gathering together for the Eucharist under a bishop. Clement himself exhorted 'so we should gather together, (ἐπὶ τὸ αὐτὸ συνα χθέντες) in concord'.[49] Callistus' offence was to welcome into his group those whom other presbyter-bishops, like the anonymous author, had expelled from theirs.

Thus we can now see that Clement cannot be the bishop of the whole Church of Rome in the later sense. We may reasonably conclude that he was a presby-ter-bishop of one congregation, but with a role that Brown and Meier characterized as secretarial regarding the presbytery and the whole church that could meet on special occasions.[50] We can see, furthermore, details of such a role in a mid-second century document, Hermas, who mentions a Clement at Rome as one who is to receive a record of his vision. The Lady Elder addresses him in the following terms:

> You will then write two books, and you will send one to Clement, and one to Grapte. Clement will then send one to the cities outside, for this has been committed to him (ἐκείνῳ γὰρ ἐπιτέτραπται); and Grapte shall advise the widows and orphans. But you shall read them to this city accompanied by the presbyters who preside over the church .[51]

Here Clement has the entrusted ministry (ἐπιτέτραπται) of writing to exter-nal churches on behalf of the Roman community. But we observe that the visionary Hermas is to read them to Rome itself in the company of 'the pres-byters who preside over the church'. We see here the presbyter-bishops from the various congregations assembling with Hermas. We see also that there is one recognized as the letter writer to external churches, as, in Lampe's words, a kind of 'foreign secretary'.[52]

Clement therefore is a figure with an entrusted ministry, and no 'mere' sec-retary. But he exists as such among a collection of presbyters, each with their particular congregation meeting in various houses throughout the Roman com-munity. This too was the situation witnessed by Paul in his day, and by implication continuing at the time when Clement addressed this same church. Clement we observe writes on behalf of the Roman community to a Corinthian

49. Clement, *Cor.*, 34.7.
50. R. E. Brown and J.-P. Meier, *Antioch and Rome: New Testament Cradles of Catholic Christianity* (New York: Paulist Press, 1982), p. 164.
51. Hermas, *Vis.,* 8 (II, 4, 2–3).
52. Lampe, *Stadtrömischen Christen*, p. 339.

church that is divided by warring factions. A symptom of their divisions is their deposition of some of the presbyter-bishops by some of the house groups who have ignored the fact that they were ordained by 'the whole church', and who were further successors of the apostles and a fulfilment of an Old Testament prophecy. The text of the prophecy that he quotes we cannot however verify, namely 'I will appoint their bishops in righteousness and their deacons in faith.'[53] Clement writes to address the situation and to call for unity.

But why, we must ask, did he do so? What were the concerns of the Roman presbytery that he was called upon to articulate and express in his letter on their behalf? Clement, as we have seen, is not a monarch bishop making Petrine claims of supremacy over all other bishops in the Roman world. We cannot therefore read this document as evidence for the early development of the Papacy, and the acknowledgement of Rome's overall authority, in some embryonic form, from almost the beginnings of Christian history. The rhetorical style of the letter exhorts, encourages, and persuades, rather than commands: the characteristic verb used is a first person plural exhortatory subjunctive, 'let us consider noble examples . . . let us set before our eyes . . . we write these things, beloved, not only admonishing you but also to remind ourselves . . .', etc.[54] Why should therefore the presbyters of the Roman congregations have decided that Clement should be instructed to go to such literary lengths to secure peace in a distant Eastern city across the Adriatic from Rome?

The reason, I believe, was to make an assertion, both to themselves and to those outside the Church, of the kind of organization that it was, and with the kind of political aims that it had. Just as in the case of the Jews at Alexandria, the Christian church, Clement assumes, is a πολίτευμα, and should seek to exist as such within the framework of the Roman Empire, whose concepts of power and authority Clement will seek to appropriate. Clement was thus rejecting the approach of John the Seer, and of other forms of Christian apocalypticism, or indeed of the tradition that was to emerge in the Jewish *Sibylline Oracles*. Like Luke, he was seeking to understand not simply the Christian community but, more definitely, its internal authority structures, in terms of the objective of Roman and Graeco-Roman ideas of polity within an imperial ideology. It is to a consideration of this case that I now turn.

2.1 *Jewish Communities and the Idea of a* πολίτευμα

The word πολίτευμα refers to both a corporate body of citizens, particularly an ethnic body living in a foreign city, and also to the exercise of citizenship and to a constitution. The Jews at Alexandria were such an association, and Josephus, when telling the legend of Aristeas on the translation of the Septuagint, refers to 'the chief officers of the corporate body (τοῦ πολιτεύματος οἱ

---

53. Clement, *Cor.*, 42.5 (Isa. 60:17) and 44.1–3.
54. Clement, *Cor.*, 5.1 and 3; 7.1.

προεστηκότες)'.[55] As such an association, they were allowed to follow their ethnic customs and some of their ethnic laws, while remaining part of the constitutional structure of the wider city-state.

As we saw in a previous chapter, a constitution of a city-state was not viewed in terms of Graeco-Roman culture as a machine, as the state would be viewed after the European Enlightenment. Nature and society were one, and the order of society was reflected in nature and vice versa. Such was the metaphysical basis of the political ideology of the *Ara Pacis Augustae*. It should not surprise us therefore that πολίτευμα should mean both a body of citizens within a constitution and their exercise of citizenship in leading a good life in conformity with the laws both of their human nature and of society. Josephus applied such Hellenistic concepts to the Law of Moses, when he promises his readers that 'I have undertaken this present work with the intention of revealing to the Greeks its worthiness of attention; for it will embrace our whole ancient history and our constitutional arrangement (τὴν διάταξιν τοῦ πολιτεύματος).'[56]

Philo before him had applied Stoic natural law concepts to such a discussion. Of Adam before the fall he could write:

> Since every well ordered city has a constitution, the citizen of the world necessarily operated with the same constitution as that by which the whole world operated. This constitution is right reason (ὀρθὸς λόγος) . . . which is divine law, according to which what befits them and falls to them is assigned to each one of them. There had to be citizens of this city and constitution before man, who might be fairly named 'citizens of the great city', being allotted as the place of their dwelling the greatest precinct of all, and having been enrolled in the greatest and most perfect citizen body. And who should these citizens be but rational and divine natures, some incorporeal and mental, and others with the kind of bodies as those possessed by the stars.[57]

There was, before society, therefore, no Hobbesian nature 'red in tooth and claw', in which life was 'nasty, brutish and short'. The book of Genesis on which Philo was here commenting was the first book of the law of Moses, describing, not the legislation of Mount Sinai, but God as giver of the natural law establishing a common order for both nature and for society.

Thus Philo could engage with pagan society politically, and establish a place within the constitution for his own group with their own customs and laws in which they would be able to live at peace. That end was further served by the fact that the metaphysical assumptions of both pagan Stoic and Jewish political philosophy had become highly similar in his recasting of their political situation in such terms. But Philo's Jewish group was not alone in such an enterprise;

---

55. Josephus, *Antiqu.*, 12.108. See also (Sidon) *OGIS*, 592; (Egypt) *CIG*, 5361.21.
56. Josephus, *Antiqu.*, 1.5.
57. Philo, *Opif.*, 50.143.

it was also shared by the city-states of Asia Minor in what is known as the Second Sophistic, as we shall now see.

2.2 *Integration of Separate City-States within an Imperial Whole*

It is interesting to observe that the survival and propagation of social groups with their own group identities, with their claim to political control over their own affairs, was not confined to the Hellenistic Judaeism of Josephus and of that of Philo and the Alexandrian community. It also applied to the Hellenistic world of mainland Greece such as Corinth, and also to the city-states of Asia Minor, as well as the Egypt of the heirs of the Ptolemies. The heirs of the empire of Alexander the Great had left behind such continuing monuments as such city-states.

It is significant for our discussion that, from around Domitian's time, the movement known as the Second Sophistic began. The movement attempted to revive the political ideal of the Greek city-state as it had developed in Athens before the conquests of Alexander the Great. Aristides was to set the tone in his orations that continually invoked examples drawn from fourth century Athens. When he exhorts the Rhodians to concord he says:

> There is the benefit to be enjoyed from the past addressing well-known examples to contemporary events. And these examples . . . are not without their relevance applied to you who are pure Greek, and have been raised from childhood in these traditions.[58]

Aristides then continues with examples from Sparta, under Lycurgus, and from Athens during the Persian Wars.[59]

As Aristotle had argued, the city-state was the final goal of human existence to which the nuclear and extended family had tended. There was no natural political organization beyond the city-state in the government of which all citizens could participate, with slaves playing their natural part as fulfilling the role that their nature desired to fulfil. That city-states should be subsumed into a wider imperial whole, and made subject to it, was anathema to Hellenic principles. A wider collection of city-states would not be a natural, functioning whole, but something like a herd of wild animals with no defined organized structure in which component parts had become integrated into the whole.

The state was natural and could be understood, therefore, by analogy with a human organism. Clearly this was the particular conclusion to which Aristotle was led by the general Hellenistic principle that we have frequently noted,

---

58. Aelius Aristides, *Or.*, 24.2.3.

59. Aelius Aristides, *Or.*, 24.23–24. See also for further examples, G. Anderson, *The Second Sophistic: A Cultural Phenomenon in the Roman Empire* (London: Routledge, 1993), chapter 5. See also M. W. Gleason, *Making Men: Sophists and Self-Representation in Ancient Rome* (Princeton, New Jersey: Princeton University Press, 1995).

namely that nature and society are a metaphysical unity. As different organs of the body co-operate together when the body is well, but are at strife with each other when it is sick, so different parts of the constitution of the city-state must co-operate in harmony if the state is well. It is in the belief in a natural mean that is harmonious between extremes that Aristotle, like Polybius after him, was to see the virtue of a 'mixed constitution' that was neither democratic, aristocratic, or monarchical but a natural balance between all three.[60]

Natural order must therefore be reflected in social order so that 'concord' or ὁμόνοια became a natural quality. Aristides (A.D. 149), addressing the city of Rhodes on the internal strife between social groups over debts, speaks of the 'natural good of concord (ὁμόνοια)'.[61] *Homonoia* or Concord was to become the watchword of the Second Sophistic. It marked the internal relations that must exist within a 'natural' society that fulfilled the good goal of human nature, offering to human nature the perfect realization of its potentialities. Concord was both natural and divine, and the precondition of the ideal of the city-state as autonomous, as self-governing.

The principle of *Homonoia* in nature was that parts of an organism freely and naturally co-operate for the health of the whole: one organ does not coerce or repress the other, but each allows the other to perform its natural function to secure the rational order of the whole. So also the well-ordered society in which no individual institution of the constitution coerces or intimidates the other behaves naturally and healthily. Social life is like a group of individuals forming a choir or orchestra, and agreeing to join together to give a symphony concert: no one is compelled but each sings or plays their respective notes and parts according to the musical score, willingly and with a view to producing something beautiful that they desire. As Dio says in his speech to the Council at Prusa in A.D. 101:

> . . . when the rulers and presidents are prudent and wise, and the rest of the community are administered, lawfully and moderately, according to their judgment, one should call such a city-state a real city, moderate, and wise, and under law's rule, because of their administrators; just we might possibly call a choir musical, when its conducting head is, and its remaining members follow him together, and utter no sound contrary to the melody, whether too small or sung indistinctly.[62]

Dio considered citizens in a state of faction (στασιάζοντες) as like a chorus singing out of tune.

Philo had said 'the citizen of the world necessarily operated with the same constitution as that by which the whole world operated', and thus Adam had

---

60. Polybius, VI.4.5–10; 57.9, and A. Brent, *Imperial Cult and the Development of Church Order* (Vigiliae Christianae Supplement. 45; Leiden: E. J. Brill, 1999), p. 55.

61. Aelius Aristides, *Or.*, 24.9.

62. Dio Chrysostom, *Or.*, 36.21.

been a citizen of a cosmos inhabited by 'rational and divine natures, some incorporeal and mental'. Dio Chrysostom similarly believed that the constitution of an ideal city should reflect:

> the city of the blessed gods in the heavenly sky, without strife and defeat, they perform their functions without let or hindrance and with unvarying friendship of all toward all in common, the most conspicuous amongst them each pursuing an independent course – I do not mean wandering in mindless error, but rather dancing a dance of happiness, coupled with wisdom and supreme intelligence – whilst the rest of the celestial hosts are swept along by the general movement, the entire heaven having one single purpose and impulse.[63]

Human society should therefore reflect the divine order of nature reflected in the life of the gods.

Dio Chrysostom had said to the Nicaeans:

> But it is fitting that those whose city was founded by gods should enjoy peace (εἰρήνη), and concord (ὁμόνοια), and friendship with each other . . . For is it not clear that not only those who are the rulers, but also the gods, pay attention to those who live in concord, but those who live in a state of faction do not even hear each other? For no one easily hears what choirs say that sing out of tune, nor cities that are at variance.

Homonoia was therefore the mark of a community whose individuals and constitutional parts were in harmony with themselves, and in which neither 'rebellion (στάσις)' nor 'strife (ἔρις)' was to be found. Only under such natural conditions could the ideal of human autonomy be realized, in which human laws were accepted as rationally binding but upon free agents, without any external force subjugating the individual or group.

If however *homonoia* applied to relations between individuals and parts of political constitutions within a city-state, it applied equally to external relations between city-states. If the city-state is the final end of a fulfilled human life, in which all human excellences can be realized and flourish, then there is no further imperial whole to which individual cities can be organically related. The proper relation between city-states sharing a common Hellenic culture was not the relationship between the subject and the ruler based upon the exercise of coercive power. Rather it was a unity freely entered into by equals, in a relationship of *homonoia*. Like the 'natural' and 'rational' harmony or *homonoia* of different parts of the ideal constitution, so too the interrelationship of self-governing city-states was to be a *homonoia* between equals. And here the concept of *homonoia* can be seen as an ideological assertion against the Roman conception of εἰρήνη or peace achieved through the imposition of imperial order by force, and celebrated by Vergil. Indeed it might be thought that the

---

63. Dio Chrysostom, *Or.*, 36.22.

Second Sophistic was little more than a cry of the oppressed Greek city-states under Rome's domination, and as such a nostalgic longing for their lost and very past autonomy: their governments had little more power than town councils. But it was more than that.

The Second Sophistic was an attempt to create an inner psychological space in which autonomy could still be celebrated and enjoyed. Price has seen the phenomenon of the spread of emperor worship as a kind of social-psychological process, in which external imperial power could be accepted without upsetting the internal constitutional arrangement of those city-states. Significantly Dio had reminded the Nicaeans that their internal strife was not a purely internal matter, but involved not only the gods but the 'rulers' who will 'pay attention to those who live in concord'. The 'rulers' are presumably the Roman rulers, and the only hope of influencing the imperial power clearly lies in exhibiting εἰρήνη and ὁμόνοια. By externalizing the emperor's power as divine, they did not need to regard it as upsetting their internal constitutional autonomy. Furthermore, we should remember that ideal of the city-state presupposed a frugality in economic activity: enough for self-sufficiency but not for ostentatious consumption. The imperial economic exploitation and, indeed, outright appropriation was the source of grievance, as clearly shown by Rome's condemnation on such grounds both in the book of Revelation and in the Jewish *Sibylline Oracle*. But that economic exploitation failed to appear in the rhetoric of the Second Sophistic as it would have done had that movement been of the kind that Marxist materialism would warrant.

The ideological characterization of political relations between and within city-states was not lost upon the Emperor Domitian, in whose reign probably Revelation and Clement *Corinthians* were both written.[64] Here we find in the coinage the legend '*Homonoia*' used instead of '*Pax*'. The imperial peace of Augustus was imposed by force: it did not involve what the Greek city-states meant by *homonoia* as a rational agreement reached by autonomous equals. But in Domitian's coinage we find the ideology of *homonoia* appropriated by the imperial power: the suggestion is that the Greek city-states are part of an imperial whole, whose parts hold together rationally and in unison, without needing imposition by force and the infringement of anyone's autonomy.

We find then Rome's imperial ideology entering the inner social-psychological space of the city-states of the Second Sophistic, and converting the apprehension of subjection by force into the *homonoia* of nature and of the stars in their rational and musical harmony. Indeed, this was to lead to the somewhat paradoxical political narrative of *homonoia* treaties celebrated in the coinage between city-states at rivalry with one another. Such treaties clearly presupposed the discourse of autonomy: rivalry and disagreement could only

---

64. C. J. Hemer, *The Letters to the Seven Churches in Their Local Setting* (JSNTSup., 11; Sheffield: Acadmic Press, 1986), pp. 158–59 and 175; Brent, *Imperial Cult*, chapter 5.

be concluded by a treaty freely concluded as the result of the persuasive argument, and not by the imposition by force of the will of one city upon another. But the subject of this rivalry only to be ended by such an exercise of autonomy by both sides was over who had pre-eminence in terms of how many times they had been designated as *Neokoros* or temple-keeper of the imperial cult. This was in essence the source of rivalry between Pergamon, Ephesus, Smyrna in the course of the second century. Thus the discourse of autonomy is part of the discourse of subjection within an imperial whole. But emperor worship, as Price indicated, was itself a social-psychological mechanism for creating a space for the subjective experience of autonomy in a situation in which objectively quite the reverse held. Finally both the discourse of *homonoia* and the discourse of imperial cult have the same social psychological function.

It was against such an ideological backcloth that both Clement and Ignatius of Antioch were to redefine the character of the Christian community, as we shall now see.

2.3 *Clement of Rome: The Christian Community as a Politeuma*

We saw in our first section how Clement wrote to Corinth as the secretary of the Roman presbyterate in order to exhort unity to a community divided by strife:

> Because of the sudden and repeated misfortunes and reverses that have happened to us, brothers, we acknowledge that we have been somewhat slow in giving attention to the matters of dispute amongst you, dear friends, especially the detestable and unholy schism, so alien and strange to those chosen by God, which a few reckless and arrogant persons have kindled to such a pitch of insanity that your good name, once so renowned and loved by all, has been so greatly reviled.[65]

It has been doubted whether 'repeated misfortunes and reverses' refers to an actual and full-blown persecution, the existence of which, in Domitian's time, is controversial.[66] John the Seer also wrote his apocalypse in Domitian's time, as we argued in defence of Irenaeus' dating, and his work at least anticipates such a general persecution, but one which may never have been actualized. But the fact that he could have produced his work with such an expectation indicates some kind of tension between the Christian, Roman community and the Roman state.

It may be asked, however, why 'the Church that abides at Rome' wrote on such an issue to 'the Church that abides at Corinth', using Clement, the official

---

65. Clement, *Cor.*, 1.1.

66. B. W. Jones, *The Emperor Domitian* (London: Routledge, 1992), p. 16; L. W. Barnard, 'St. Clement of Rome and the Persecution of Domitian', in *Studies in the Apostolic Fathers and Their Background* (Oxford: Blackwell, 1966), pp. 5–15.

secretary of the presbyterate in such matters, to present the issue on their behalf? If his position at this time were secretarial, it was not like a later pope writing to command another diocese that he claimed the right to control, as Stephen was to do in the rebaptism controversy. Why then should strife and discord in the Christian Corinthian community, organized in house groups, have required the Roman Christian community to produce such a letter? Clearly there is more in the situation than meets the eye.

Clement records:

> It is disgraceful, beloved, utterly disgraceful, and unworthy of conduct in Christ, that it should be reported that the ancient church of the Corinthians, of such a firm foundation, should be in a state of faction against the presbyters. This report has not only reached us, but also those who turn aside from us so that blasphemy rains down on the name of the Lord on account of your folly and you create a danger for yourselves.[67]

Clearly 'those who turn aside from us (ἑτεροκλινεῖς)' are pagans, as were the inhabitants of Sodom who were the subject of God's 'punishment and torment', and so described by this exact term.[68] Thus the Church at Rome is experiencing difficulties with the pagan authorities because of reports current at Rome of the situation within the Corinthian Church. The danger is of pagan intervention in such internal disputes in the light of such stringent criticism ('blasphemy') that has thus accrued to any society bearing the Christian 'name'.

Clement is not simply, therefore, writing for the benefit of those within the Corinthian community: his words are intended to have a reassuring effect to those without. His message well conforms to Roman political discourse in the context of which he plans to be persuasive both to Pagan and to Christian alike. Far from describing Rome, as his contemporary, John the Seer had done, as 'the Harlot of Babylon', whose downfall was imminently predicted, instead he proclaims a devotion to Roman imperial order that is almost unqualified:

> Let us march as an army, men and brothers, with all zeal under his blameless commandments. Let us focus our attention upon those who march under their pro consuls, how in good order, how obediently, how submissively they execute their orders. Not all are prefects or tribunes, or centurions or captains of fifty and so on, but each in his own rank executes the orders laid down by the emperor or pro consul.[69]

As if to emphasize his commitment to the imperial ideal, he now goes on to give Paul's image of the head and the body, recast in the form of the fable of Menenius Agrippa, well used in Roman political theory.

67. Clement, *Cor.*, 47.6–7.
68. Clement, *Cor.*, 11.1.
69. Clement, *Cor.*, 37.1–4.

Thus, as the legend goes, when the plebeians departed from the patricians in a kind of general strike leaving the city of Rome defenceless (494 B.C.), Menenius had made a speech exhorting their return. In the manner of Aesop, he had spoken of how the state was like a human body, where the various members of the body were at variance with one another, each assuming a voice of its own, forming a conspiracy in which the hands did not convey food to the mouth, the mouth would not accept food, the teeth would not masticate the food, and sought thereby to starve the belly into submission.[70] As Dionysius of Halicarnassus records the speech:

> A city-state is like a human body. For each city is composed of many parts. Each part does not have the same power as the other parts within them, nor does it provide for exactly the same needs.[71]

Clement therefore continues:

> The great cannot exist without the small, nor the small without the great. There is a certain blending of everything and a function in them. Let us take as an example the body. The head without the feet is nothing and thus neither the feet without the head. But the very least members of our body are necessary and beneficial to the whole body. All conspire together, and operate through mutual subjection for the preservation of the whole body.[72]

His words in this passage might sound like those of Paul to the Corinthians, who proclaims his doctrine of the Church as corporate body of Christ against earlier divisions at Corinth.[73] But his argument was an internal one, and was not set as is Clement's securely within the context of the political discourse of pagan imperial order.

As we saw in Chapter 4, the concept of imperial order was set in the context of a metaphysical peace that united nature and society into one cosmic whole. So also Clement shares this perspective when he speaks of the divisions at Corinth as violating the principles of natural order. But Clement will prefer *homonoia* to εἰρήνη as his exhortation progresses, for reasons concerned, we shall argue, with his claim that a Christian community in relationship with the Roman power is a kind of πολίτευμα of the sort enjoyed by the Jews of Alexandria. It is a combination that fits well with a Domitianic date for Clement's letter, since it was from that time that the imperial ideology sought to appropriate the *homonoia* discourse that had been founded on the principle of political autonomy.

---

70. Livy, II.32.9–11.
71. Dionysus of Halicarnassus, VI.86.1.
72. Clement, *Cor.*, 37.4–5.
73. 1 Cor. 12:4–26, cf. Clement, *Cor.*, 37.5.

That ecclesial order is part of cosmic order Clement makes plain when he says:

> Let us run towards the goal of peace that has been handed down to us from the beginning, and let us gaze at the father and creator of the whole cosmic order, and let us cleave to his magnificent and abounding free gifts and benefits of peace . . . The heavens are moved by his organizing power and are subject to him in peace (εἰρήνη). Day and night complete the course in the order laid down by him, one not impeding the other. Sun and moon and the choruses of stars circle in concord (ἐν ὁμονοίᾳ), without any deviation according to his direction, the courses laid down by him . . . The seasons, spring and summer and autumn and winter, give way in succession to one another, in peace (εἰρήνη) . . . Even the smallest living things come together in concord and in peace (ἐν ὁμονοίᾳ καὶ ἐν εἰρήνῃ).[74]

The *homonoia* and *eirene* that are at the centre of the cosmic order must also be reflected in the Christian community:

> Beware, beloved, lest his many benefits may turn into a judgment upon all of us if when we conduct ourselves civically (πολιτευόμενοι) in an unworthy manner, we fail to do with *homonoia* (μεθ᾽ ὁμονοίας) what is good and well pleasing in his sight.[75]

Dio Chrysostom had emphasized, as we have seen, the city-state should in its perfect form reflect 'the city of the gods in the heavenly sky'. Here too in Clement we find *homonoia* and *eirene* characterizing both natural, and social and political order. But we find here an additional concept, derived likewise from the political discourse of the Hellenistic city-state. Although Clement does not use the term πολίτευμα in reference to the proper constitution of a Christian community, he does as in this passage use the cognate verb (πολιτευόμενοι).[76]

We saw that the Jews in Egypt were considered to be a πολίτευμα, and were accepted as such by the Roman imperial power. It is as such that Clement wishes the Christian community to be regarded at Rome, and other Christian communities with which it is associated. At all events, in pagan Egypt too, pagan cults required recognition by the civic authorities in order to practice. Schubart published a papyrus fragment from the reign of Ptolemy Philopator IV (244–204 B.C.):

> By the commandment of the king, those who throughout the land celebrate rites to Dionysus . . . are to be enrolled with Aristobulus at the record office . . . and also they are forthwith to declare from whom they have been handed down the rites up to the

---

74. Clement, *Cor.*, 19.2; 20.1–3, 9–10.
75. Clement, *Cor.*, 21.1.
76. Clement, *Cor.*, 3.4; 6.1; 44.6; 51.2; 54.4.

previous three generations, and they are to state their sacred story in a document authenticated with a seal, with each name . . .[77]

The religion of Dionysus had, as we have seen, been viewed as a disorderly religion likely to upset the peace of the gods, in nature as in society, through the introduction of strange and magical rites. Here clearly the rites are to be brought under public control by several means.

Firstly practitioners of the Dionysiac rite must be duly registered in the official registry. Then, secondly, they must reveal what is the myth of the cult, the 'sacred story (ἱερὸς λόγος)' enacted in the rite. But thirdly, and important for our discussion, three names must be given for the living priest, and at least two of his forebears, stretching back for three generations. Thus the cult, though Dionysiac, may be shown to be one of order and of concord: it would not involve, as the Dionysiac riot at Rome was later to involve, groups of people in riotous delirium, with the suspicion of cannibalism and incest in their rituals engaged in with gay abandon.[78]

Ernst Bammel pointed to the significance of this papyrus decree for understanding what Clement says about the Christian cult and the order of the Christian community.[79] It is important to appreciate, in this connection, the liturgical role that is at the centre of the ministry of the presbyter-bishops. Although there is a tendency to translate λειτουργία generally as 'ministry' or even, in its 'minister of state' meaning of 'administration', 'liturgy' in this case is a better translation as indicative of a role in a cult of someone with the right to perform a particular 'liturgy'. We should therefore understand that Clement's charge is that presbyter-bishops 'have been expelled from their liturgy' in the same sense in which he speaks of the parallel between the Christian ministry and the Old Testament hierarchy in the words:

> For to the high priest his appropriate liturgies have been assigned, and to the priests their own place has been assigned, and to the Levites their own ministries have been imposed. The layman is bound by the layman's rules. Let each of you, brothers, celebrate the eucharist (εὐχαριστείτω) in his own proper rank (ἐν τῷ ἰδίῳ τάγματι), in essence with a good conscience, not overstepping the defined rule of his liturgy, with reverence.[80]

Bammel's contention is that Clement is reflecting provisions such as existed in Egypt for any cult requiring official toleration, and therefore reflected the

77. W. Schubart, Ägyptische Abteilung (Papyrussammlung): Ptolemaeus Philopator und Dionysos, in *Amtliche Berichte aus den preussischen königlichen Kunstsammlungen* (= *Beiblatt zum Jahrbuch der preussischen königlichen Kunstsammlungen*), 38 (1916/1917), p. 190.

78. Livy, XXXIX.8.1–19. See also Brent, *Imperial Cult*, p. 7 and above, chapter 2, section A.

79. E. Bammel, 'Sukzessionsprinzip im Urchristentum', *StEphAug*, 31 (1990), pp. 63–65.

80. Clement, *Cor.*, 40.5–41.1.

general philosophy of the πολιτεύμα whose special status the Jewish community of Alexandria enjoyed.

Clement is therefore warning the Corinthians that unless they can show their cult to be one of order and concord, then they risk intervention by the Roman state. In Roman eyes there would be little difference between a Christian charismatic community and a Dionysiac community: both could lapse into abandoned rites in which both bounds of sexuality and self-control were crossed, and both represented a depraved religion with magical powers producing both civil and cosmic disorder and even, in the Christian case, prophesying and welcoming such a disorder. It was this political and external dimension to the disorder at Corinth that was the backcloth to Clement writing his official letter in the name of the Roman community.

The specific requirement for the legal permission for such cults, whether Christian or Dionysiac, was, as we saw, that they show that 'they have been handed down the rites up to the previous three generations, and they are to state their sacred story'. Clement will claim that likewise:

> Our apostles likewise knew, through our Lord Jesus Christ, that there would be strife over the bishop's office. For this reason, therefore, having received complete foreknowledge, they appointed the previous mentioned and subsequently they confirmed their continuity so that, should they fall asleep, other approved men should succeed to their liturgical role. Those therefore who were appointed by them or, later on, by other approved men, with the consent of the whole church, and who have performed their liturgy to the flock of Christ blamelessly, with humility, quietly and unselfishly, having testimonials from all over a long time, these we consider to have been unjustly expelled from their liturgy.[81]

Clement, unlike the compilers of the later succession lists to whose activities we must later return, can mention no names to prove three previous generations of the orderly conduct of the Christian cult. But we do have in his text the construction of an impression of three generations in that we have 'our apostles', then 'other approved men' succeeding them after their death, and then those appointed 'later on by other approved men'. Thus order and continuity is guaranteed.

There is a second piece of epigraphic evidence connected with the Egyptian cult of Serapis as it was celebrated at Delos. The cult was initially celebrated without its own temple. A *Serapion*, could only be erected after at least two generations, when the cult could show an orderly priestly succession of three priests, grandfather, father and son.[82] In the face of suspicion of disorder, the existence of an ordered, continuous succession had to be established. Clement refers to the authors of the 'rebellion' as those who: 'bring judgement against

81. Clement, *Cor.*, 44.1–3.
82. *IG* XI, 4, 1299.

themselves rather than against the harmony that has been well and justly handed down to us',[83] just as the Egyptian Dionysiac priest had 'to declare from whom they have been handed down the rites'.

Though Clement mentions no names representing the 'three generations', those who compiled the later succession lists were to do so. Irenaeus records, perhaps from a list whose origins come from Hegesippus:

> The blessed apostles, laying the foundations and building the church, handed on the liturgy of the episcopal office to Linus: of this same Linus Paul makes mention in the letters to Timothy. And Anecletus succeeded him. After this man, in third place from the apostles, Clement inherited the bishop's office . . .[84]

Bammel saw fulfilment of Clement's condition, derived from his apologetic purpose, in the origins of the episcopal list.[85]

That Clement is seeking a place for Christianity within the structure of Roman imperial society is shown at the conclusion of his letter in two ways. The first is the doxology to the Roman rulers at the end of his letter that clearly belies the notion that his appeal is a purely internal one within the Christian community:

> Grant concord (ὁμόνοια) and peace (εἰρήνη) to all who dwell on earth . . . while we subject ourselves to your almighty and well-beloved name, and to our rulers and governors on earth. Your master have granted them the authority of imperial rule . . . so that we, recognising the glory and honour granted them by you, we may be subject to them, not opposing your will. Grant them O Lord health, peace (εἰρήνη), concord (ὁμόνοια), and stability to the end that they may administer the government that you have granted them without blemish.[86]

It is interesting to compare and contrast these words with those of John the Seer, his contemporary. In the latter's work, the heavenly presbyters had sung 'blessings and honour and glory' to God who is alone worthy on his throne and to the lamb, in anticipation of the near coming of 'the kingdom of our God and of his Christ'.[87] Here Rome, as Babylon or the Beast, was not given 'glory', 'honour', or 'power' nor had God given these to earthly rulers. But Clement is clearly at ease with Roman, pagan power as by divine sanction, and with the necessity of the Church to conform, within limits, to Roman imperial order. This is why the Church of Rome needed to respond to the situation at Corinth that suggested that its purpose was inimical to imperial order.

---

83. Clement, *Cor.*, 51.2.
84. Irenaeus, *Adv. Haer.*, III.3.3 (30–35), referring to 2 Tim. 4:21.
85. Bammel, 'Sukzessionsprinzip', p. 70.
86. Clement, *Cor.*, 60.4–61.1.
87. Rev. 4:11; 5:12–13, etc., cf. Rev. 11:15.

Clement does not share in the complaints of Asia Minor and the Eastern provinces that Rome has stripped them of all their wealth and resources. As we have seen, in a Domitianic pattern, he combined the concept of imperial peace as subjection by force to an imperial political order, and the concept of *homonoia* as the natural and rational order freely accepted by the citizen of the autonomous city-state. There is, however, a reflection of the discourse of autonomy of the city-states of Asia Minor regarding the principle of *homonoia* in Clement's letter.

It is here we come to the second way in which Clement's desire to construct the Christian community as a πολίτευμα can be evidenced. We saw that a feature of the discourse of autonomy was the notion that disagreement between Hellenistic city-states could not be settled simply by the imposition by force of the will of one city upon another. *Homonoia* and not peace was the desired state in which the rivalry between one city and another would be overcome.

There was the famous dispute between Ephesus, Pergamon and Smyrna over which city was to claim the title 'first city of Asia' on the grounds of how many times and how early had one of them been granted the title of *Neokoros* or 'temple keeper' of the imperial cult. We have examples of coins intended to commemorate the conclusion of a *homonoia* treaty.[88]

It is in the context of such a pagan Hellenistic backcloth of political assumptions and ideas that Clement now proposes to end the discord at Corinth. We have seen how the principle of natural and rational order, of *homonoia*, should operate both between cities at variance with one another, and within cities the various parts of whose constitutions, elders, aristocrats, tradesmen, farmers are in conflict with each other. Clement finally concludes that both is the case. The Church of Rome is in conflict with the Church at Corinth, since the disorder of the latter is critically affecting its own relations with the imperial government at Rome itself. Hence the letter is to be carried by men who are to act like negotiators of a *homonoia* treaty.

They are in consequence of the letter to be 'living in concord (ὁμονοοῦντες) without nursing hatred, in love and peace'. They are 'to cease from this vain rebellion . . . and to root out the unlawful anger in accordance with the appeal we have made for peace and concord (περὶ εἰρήνης καὶ ὁμονοίας) in this

---

88. P. R. Franke and M. K Nollé, *Die Homonoia-Münzen Kleinasiens und der thrakischen Randgebiete* (Saarbrücker Studien zur Archäologie und alten Geschichte, 10, Hrsg Furtwängler A., Franke P. R. and Reinsberg C.; Saarbrücke: Druckerei und Verlag, 1997). See also D. Kienast, Die Homonoia Verträge in der romischen Kaiserzeit, *Jb Num*, 14 (1964), pp. 51–64; S. Goldhill (ed.), *Being Greek under Rome: Cultural Identity, the Second Sophistic, and the Development of Empire* (Cambridge: Cambridge University Press, 2001); M. K. and J. Nollé, Vom feinen Spiel städtischer Diplomatie zu Zeremoniell und Sinn kaiserlicher Homonoiafeste, *ZPE*, 102 (1994), pp. 241–61 (241). See also Brent, *Ignatius and the Second Sophistic*, pp. 276–96.

letter'.[89] But the letter is to initiate a kind of negotiation on the part of those who bear it:

> We have also sent faithful and sober men, who have conducted themselves blamelessly amongst us from youth unto old age, who will be witnesses between you and us. This we have done in order that you may know that our entire concern has been that you should find peace with the utmost urgency . . . Now send back urgently those commissioned by us, Claudius Ephebus and Valerius Bito, with also Fortunatus, in peace and with joy, so that they may proclaim the good order and peace for which we have yearned, so that we may as quickly as possible have cause to rejoice concerning your right order.[90]

'Rejoicing' and 'proclaiming' represent examples the stereotyped vocabulary of what ambassadors do, as we shall see also in Ignatius' letters written in a different, early Christian context.

Clement is therefore suggesting that a Christian community is like a πολιτεύμα in Alexandria, or like a city-state in Asia Minor, but one that is able to conduct treaties that produce ὁμόνοια and thus integrate within an imperial whole. He has assumed, in so constructing social and political reality in such terms, that what 'ought to be' in fact 'is'. Clearly he does not find formal pagan political structures alien in his doxology (which reads like a panegyric) to the imperial power. And so he is prepared to use the rhetoric of the Second Sophistic and its ideology as a powerful persuasive tool to order or reorder the structure of Christian communities, in a form conducive to a continuing symbiosis with pagan society. In this respect his project is far more radical than either that of the Seer of Revelation, or of the author of Luke-Acts.

A political movement that is to succeed in coming to power needs more than an ideology that appeals to broad, non-committed groups of outsiders such as Theophilus of Luke-Acts, becoming a Christian but needing reassurance that his new faith served the political ends of contemporary society in providing the true means for the peace of God on human society rather than the *pax deorum* of Roman pagan rites and ceremonies. It needs more than Clement's definition of a self understanding, which appeals also to others, that it is not alien to the present political structures with which it co-exists, however much it may actually transform them. It requires an effective organization in order to maintain its self-identity by the exercise of a relevant discipline, but an organization that will also appear as legitimate to those outside with whom it is seeking to engage.

We may see in such a formal perspective the world in which Christianity was born, flourished, sought recognition and finally came to power. As Clement, the author of Luke-Acts, and the Hellenistic city-states of the East well knew,

---

89. Clement, *Cor.*, 62.2 and 63.2.
90. Clement, *Cor.*, 63.3–4 and 65.1.

though the Seer of Revelation did not, the Roman empire was at least for the foreseeable future, indestructible. The majority throughout the Empire had no wish to see its destruction, nor to experience again the carnage of civil war in which, with 'a nature at variance with itself (*natura discors*)', they had experienced 'not peace but the anger of the gods', in famine, pestilence, invasion, piracy and civil disorder. It is on such a basic premise that the self-understanding of the Greek city-states constructed a social psychological space for the feeling and celebration of autonomy that it expressed and reinforced by the *homonoia* discourse. An early Christianity that was both to survive, flourish and triumph was a movement that proceeded also from such premises, and promised a *pax dei* mediated by Christ the λόγος of God permeating both the natural and social order, and giving both creative order and stability. But to move beyond acceptance to the challenge of political influence and then power, it needed a clear organization that seemed legitimate in terms of pagan society, while being ably thus legitimately to confront and transform it.

And so we come to Ignatius of Antioch.

3. *Ignatius of Antioch: Bishops as Cult Leaders of Mystery Associations*

In Ignatius of Antioch we find, for the first time, what was later to become the historic Church order of Christendom. In order to be a community that was, securely and completely, a Church, the ministry had to be in the threefold form of a single bishop, with priests (presbyters) and deacons in co-operation with him. Unlike in the case of his contemporary, Clement, these clerics were not appointed by the apostles, nor by other men of whom they approved. Furthermore, they were not regarded, as Irenaeus was to regard them, in a teaching succession, like that of a Hellenistic philosophical school, receiving from their immediate predecessor the office that they exercised. Nor was there as yet the fully fledged, Cyprianic doctrine that to be within the true Church you needed to be in communion with a bishop who was in communion with every other bishop throughout the world, forming one communion as each bishop mutually recognized the other and met in councils to determine definitively issues of doctrine and discipline. But, nevertheless, Ignatius' embryonic view is that any valid church order in any truly Christian community needed to be shaped in terms of the threefold order of bishop, presbyters and deacons.

Viewed in one way, Ignatius' theology of church order was political theology. Paul had declared to his communities that 'we are the body of Christ, and members one of another'. But Paul had in mind Spirit-filled communities, whose unity lay in the transcendent realm of the Spirit. Since full salvation comes only at the eschaton, he can still assure the Spirit-filled community that 'now is your salvation nearer than when you believed', and that they would, as Christ's saints, 'judge angels'. There was no church order other than an unstructured, charismatic church order in Paul's communities, though they were under his apostleship, with its tradition handed down by the Lord and received directly by him in revelation.[91]

The author of Luke-Acts, as we have seen, in his argument that Christianity could fulfil the Principate's metaphysical aims of 'peace' in nature and society, had pushed the apocalyptic events far into an indefinite future, and made room for the age of the Church continuing in secular history. But his sources came from an earlier generation in which the twelve apostles, commanded not to depart from Jerusalem but to wait for the promise of the Father, were commanded to wait for the apocalypse in which all would be transformed, and the twelve apostles would sit on their twelve thrones judging the twelve tribes of Israel. Luke-Acts will reinterpret that command as the command to wait for the coming of the Spirit at Pentecost. But initially the community needed no political structure other than the office of the twelve apostles, anticipative of the judgement of the twelve tribes of Israel.

Luke-Acts will make the apostles founders of the Church in this age, and guarantors of the authenticity of the traditions of Jesus, but can give no account of their ever leaving Jerusalem nor transmitting their office to their successors, other than having to make up the number to twelve following Judas' suicide. Indeed at Antioch in Syria, later to be Ignatius' own church, we find ministers called 'prophets' and 'teachers', who also later in the first century to be found in a document called the *Didache*. In both Acts and in the *Didache* 'apostle' covers more than a member of the Twelve, but refers to a missionary sent out by one Christian community to another. 'Apostle' in Paul's writings refers to a wider group than that designated 'the twelve', marked out by the charismatic 'sign' of an apostle in the ability to perform miracles.[92]

The government of the Church at Jerusalem is by a group of presbyters, like Jewish elders centred on James, not the apostle whose martyrdom is early, but the 'Lord's Brother'. The claim of the 'Lord's Brothers' in the blood line of the Messiah to rule the church at Jerusalem was to continue well into the late first century. Josephus had recorded James' death by stoning in A.D. 62, on the orders of a Sadduceean high priest named Ananus and during an interregnum between successive Roman governors. Eusebius preserves a fragment of the early historian Hegesippus that, after this event, James' brother Symeon succeeded him, even though Cleobutis had been the unsuccessful candidate in what Eusebius regarded as an episcopal election. Domitian, according to another Hegesippan fragment in Eusebius, had brought before him the

---

91. H. von Campenhausen, *Ecclesiastical Authority and Spiritual Power in the Church of the First Three Centuries*, translated by J. A. Baker (London: Adam and Charles Black, 1969), chapter 3.
92. W. Schmithals, *The Office of Apostle in the Early Church*, translated by J. E. Steely (London: SPCK, 1971), pp. 32–38.

surviving *Desposyni* or 'Lord's brethren' on charge of seeking to restore the Davidic kingdom. But when he saw their work soiled hands, he dismissed them with contempt.[93]

Sometimes presbyters were also called 'bishops', as we have seen, both in the New Testament as in Clement's work. But, as we have seen, in addition to government by a collection of elders, there appears to have been in the early Church a plurality of forms of Church government, charismatic apostles as wandering missionaries, prophets and teachers, the Twelve as representatives of the New Israel to emerge at Christ's second coming, etc. Ignatius' claim that the Church could only validly be governed by a single bishop, with a council of presbyters and a number of deacons, was thus a novel one. Yet it was, as we shall see, the production of a form of government that addressed the political concerns, of both the imperial power, and the pagan societies of Hellenistic Asia Minor in which it took place, in a way that its predecessors had not. Ignatius' Church order was to confront directly the cultic concerns of imperial rulers in a way that even Clement had not.

Ignatius' question that we can understand from within our twenty-first century discourse is, given Paul's assertion that 'we are the body of Christ', how can that corporate body exist in space and time and history? Given that we exist as both flesh and spirit, what concrete historical and political form must the Christian community assume in time and space? His answer, inevitably, will be in the form of the political discourse of the second, and not the twenty-first century, but let us see what precisely that answer is.

Ignatius claims that when a Christian community gathers, it will display its common life in the form of human icons in whom are represented the saving events. The church gathered for the Eucharist will perform a drama of replay, in which the bishop will sit as an image of God the Father, sending to the people the deacons to receive their gifts as a replay of the ministry of Jesus Christ who 'came forth from the one Father and remained with the One and returned to the One'. As Ignatius has said just before these words:

> Be eager to do everything in God's concord (ὁμόνοια), with the bishop projecting an image of God, and the presbyters the council of the apostles, and the deacons, who are specially dear to me, entrusted with the ministry of Jesus Christ . . . Let there be nothing among you that is capable of dividing you, but be united with the bishop and with those who lead, as an image (τύπος) that teaches incorruptibility.[94]

We note the role of the presbyters as representing the apostles, but not in any teaching succession as Irenaeus will later claim. Rather he has in mind the

---

93. Josephus, *Antiqu.*, 20.200; Hegesippus apud Eusebius, *H.E.*, III.19 and IV.22.
94. Ignatius, *Magnes.*, 6.1–2, cf. 7.2.

Johannine Pentecost, set in the Upper Room on the very evening of the resurrection. Here the seated disciples (apostles) become Spirit-filled when:

> Jesus said then to them again: 'Peace to you. Even as the Father has sent me, so I am sending you.' And having said this, he breathed into them and said to them 'Receive the Holy Spirit. If you forgive the sins of anyone, they will be forgiven them. If you retain any, they will be retained'.[95]

Note that according to this passage the Spirit, as Jesus' other-self that can only come when Jesus is no longer with them, is 'breathed in (ἐνεφύσησεν)' directly from his risen body into them. Thus Ignatius will allude to this scene, and the incorruptibility given thus to the Church: 'For this cause the Lord received anointing on his head that he might breathe incorruption upon the Church.'[96]

It is this scene that Ignatius has in mind as one that continues in the present church whenever it assembles for the Eucharist, and which began on the evening of the resurrection. The presbyters sit in a horseshoe around the bishop's chair, as the standing deacons proceed to and from the bishop, bringing him the people's gifts to consecrate. He thus exhorts them: 'Be eager to be confirmed in the teachings of the Lord and of the apostles . . . together with your worthily esteemed bishop, and the worthily woven, spiritual garland-crown of your presbyterate, and of the deacons according to God.'[97] The liturgy, therefore, celebrates the acts of redemption, of the Father-bishop sending the diaconal Son in the presence of the apostles inbreathed with the Spirit at the resurrection, but continuing in the timeless liturgical moment. But the three-fold order is sacramental for Ignatius because, it consists of concrete images of Father, Son and Spirit-filled apostles, effecting what they symbolize and symbolizing what they effect. It is as such sacramental images (τύποι) that realize afresh the saving acts that they are to be reverenced:

> Likewise let all revere the deacons as Jesus Christ, even as they do the bishop who is the image (τύπος) of the Father, and the presbyters as God's council and as a band of apostles: without these a church cannot be summoned.[98]

The church can only thus be constituted as a church, with persons in such liturgical roles coming together for the performance of the 'drama of replay'. It is only through these roles that the laity can 'be united with the bishop and

---

95.   Jn 20:21-23.

96.   Ignatius, *Ephes.*, 17.1, cf. Jn 20:22. Schoedel, *Ignatius of Antioch: A Commentary on the Letters of Ignatius of Antioch* (Philadelphia: Fortress Press, 1985), p. 81 detects, in addition, parallels in *Odes of Solomon*, 11.15, and in the *Gospel of Truth* [NHC 1], 33.39–34.34, and the *Gospel of Philip*, [NHC 2], 77.35–78.12.

97.   Ignatius, *Magnes.*, 13.1.

98.   Ignatius, *Trall.*, 3.1. See also *Philad.*, 5.1.

with those who lead, as an image (τύπος) that teaches incorruptibility'.[99] The unity with the bishop and one another is compared to that of 'Jesus Christ in the flesh . . . to the Father, and as the apostles were to Christ and the Father.' The object of that unity and subjection is 'that there may be a unity, both physical and spiritual'.[100] Thus what had begun with 'Peter and those with him' at the resurrection, when 'immediately they touched him and believed, being closely united with his flesh and blood',[101] now continues in the timeless liturgical moment through the iconic representation of those saving acts by bishop, presbyters and deacons.

Ignatius' purpose is not simply to assert the process by which the individual is saved by participating in incorruption. Already we have seen that his purpose is to exhort to concord (ὁμόνοια), using the political watchword of the Greek city-states in their relationship with the imperial power. For him, as we have argued to be the case with his pagan contemporaries, political order reflects metaphysical order: the unity with the bishop in the threefold hierarchy not only leads to 'incorruptibility' in uniting the timeless spiritual realm with the temporal carnal one, but it also leads to such heavenly concord reflected in an undivided church. Certainly this seemed to be how Ignatius, who described himself as a man 'constrained to unity', regarded his mission to his own church at Antioch in Syria.[102]

Ignatius appears to have left his church as a condemned prisoner, but as a result of internal discord within the Christian community that had spilled over into the general pagan community. Ignatius was apparently the centre of that discord. It was in the wake of his departure as a martyr that peace came about within the Church at Antioch. Indeed, he seems to connect his martyrdom with such a peace, using such terms as 'scapegoat sacrifice' in order to describe his role.

Ignatius choreographs his situation as a condemned prisoner taken under armed escort by guards that he calls 'ten leopards (that is a company of soldiers), who only get worse when they are well treated'. He is accompanied by various clerics, who come and go from this entourage, taking news back to churches that have sent clerical representatives to visit him and to 'refresh' him with food, and his guards with bribes. They proceed from Antioch across Asia Minor along the *cursus publicus*, the official highway reserved for the legions and public officials.[103] Some clerics go ahead to announce beforehand to the churches that Ignatius' procession is passing through so that they can send representatives to visit him in his imprisonment.

---

99. Ignatius, *Magnes.*, 6.2.
100. Ignatius, *Magnes.*, 13.2.
101. Ignatius, *Smyrn.*, 3.2–3.
102. Ignatius, *Philad.*, 8.1.
103. Brent, *Imperial Cult*, pp. 246–48.

Ignatius now represents his entourage as a triumphal procession, spreading peace and concord as it progresses towards its goal that is the city of Rome itself:

> Grant me nothing more than to be poured out as an offering to God while there is an altar ready, so that in love you may form a chorus and sing to the Father in Jesus Christ, because God had judged the bishop of Syria worthy to be found in the west having summoned him from the east. It is good to be setting from the world in order that I may rise to him.[104]

In joining his entourage, whether on the way or at its destination, they are forming a 'chorus' or 'choir' praising the Father that the bishop from the east is confronting, in the arena, the emperor of the west. Yet his martyrdom confronts the imperial power in order to reject its values:

> Neither the ends of the earth nor the kingdoms of this age are of any use to me. It is better for me that I die for Jesus Christ than to reign over the ends of the earth.[105]

The political culture within which he operates is nevertheless that of the Second Sophistic. It is by means of the sophistic rhetoric of *homonoia* that Ignatius will seek to secure peace both within and between early Christian communities.

Dio Chrysostom, as we saw, had seen the city-state naturally at peace within itself by analogy with a choir singing in unison, or like the earthly reflection of the heavenly city of the gods. So too Ignatius will exhort:

> It is fitting for you to run in harmony with the resolution of your bishop, even as you do. For your council of presbyters, worthy of God, is so attuned to the bishop as cords to a lyre. Therefore in the concord (ὁμόνοια) and in the harmony of love Jesus Christ is sung. So each one of you join the chorus in order that, singing harmoniously in concord, taking your pitch from God, you may sing in unity with one voice through Jesus Christ to the Father, in order that he may hear you and recognise because of what you do well through being members of his Son . . .[106]

Thus for Ignatius the Eucharist is understood, analogously, to a pagan festival, with choral music, as an expression of the unity and identity of the life of a Greek city-state. We saw that, in asserting their Hellenistic identity over against Roman imperialism, the Greek city-states were asserting concord both internally, and externally between cities sharing in a common Hellenic culture and civilization. Likewise those Christian communities whose internal structure is the threefold order of bishop, presbyters and deacons, will acknowledge a common unity with other communities who share such a structure productive

---

104. Ignatius, *Rom.*, 2.2.
105. Ignatius, *Rom.*, 6.
106. Ignatius, *Ephes.*, 4.

of *homonoia*, and that, to use a word used for the first time by him, share a common 'Christianity (χριστιανισμός)' over against a 'Judaeism' (Ιουδαισ μός)' or a 'Hellenism (τὸ Ἑλληνικόν)'.[107]

The term 'common (κοινός)' in Greek has multiple connotations. One meaning, as a neuter noun, means 'council (τὸ Κοινόν)', as the council of the association of city-states of Asia Minor based in Ephesus. Thus Ignatius refers to the different churches to which he addresses letters as possessing Christ's 'common name', or the 'name that we share', for which he has been made prisoner. The unnamed bishop of Philadelphia possesses 'a ministry pertaining to the association'.[108] At another point he proclaims: 'Wherever the bishop appears, there let there be a gathered church, even as where Jesus Christ is, there is the catholic church'.[109] Polycarp, bishop of Smyrna, too, has therefore a 'ministry pertaining to the association', since the presence of the threefold order in a church in one place secures its concordant relations with the church in all others: it constitutes the Christian association, namely the catholic church.

The sophists of the Second Sophistic were often appointed, as ambassadors, to negotiate what we have seen were the *homonoia* treaties between city-states in order to end rivalry between them. The *homonoia* coinage celebrating such treaties depict, on occasions, the joint sacrifice or συνθυσία ending the rivalry and cementing the treaty. Ignatius describes himself as a 'sacrifice (θυσία)'.[110] He also uses specifically a word for 'expiatory sacrifice or ransom (ἀντί ψυχον)' in order to explain the nature of his martyrdom in the arena that has begun as a transit prisoner: he is a ransom 'for those subject to the bishop, presbyters, and deacons'.[111] He also sanctifies himself as 'your scapegoat sacrifice (περίψημα)'. Such language is suggestive of a social-psychological explanation, in which his arrest and martyrdom, in consequence of divisions within the church at Antioch, actually have the effect of cooling the situation down and chastening his former opponents to end their factionalism under his preferred ecclesiastical solution, namely to be 'subject to the bishop, presbyters, and deacons'.[112] The θυσία of his martyrdom is thereby evocative of images of a pagan συνθυσία that effects unity at the conclusion of a *homonoia* treaty re-uniting divided communities.

It was over the process of treaty negotiation, and its ceremonial and sacrificial conclusion, that such sophists as Dio and others presided as ambassadors and representatives of their cities, as they exhorted to, and then proclaimed, *homonoia*. Scopelian, for example, in Domitian's time, 'went on many embassies

107. Ignatius, *Magnes.*, 10.1 and 3; *Rom.*, 3.3; *Philad.*, 6.1.
108. Ignatius, *Philad.*, 11.2.
109. Ignatius, *Smyrn.*, 8.2.
110. Ignatius, *Rom.*, 4.2.
111. Ignatius, *Pol.*, 6.1, cf. also *Ephes.*, 21.1, *Smyrn.*, 10.2; *Pol.*, 2.3.
112. Brent, *Ignatius and the Second Sophistic*, pp. 222–29.

to the emperor'.[113] Such embassies played an important role both in obtaining concord within city-states, but also between city-states themselves, and the imperial power. Ignatius regards those who represent their communities, and who visit his entourage likewise as clerical ambassadors. To the Philadelphians he says:

> Since it has been reported to me that in answer to your prayer and the compassion that you have in Christ Jesus the church in Antioch in Syria has found peace, it is proper for you, because you are a church of God, to elect a deacon to go there as an ambassador on God's embassy, to express our shared joy with them when gathering as the church and to glorify the Name.[114]

Like ambassadors who proclaim *homonoia*, the deacon will take back their resolution expressing joy to Antioch. Clearly the internal strife there that led originally to Ignatius' arrest by the civil power, and despatch to the arena at Rome, has now ceased, and as a result of Ignatian rhetoric in the form of letters and official communication from such 'ambassadors'. We note here, as earlier with Clement's view of the community as a πολίτευμα, that Ignatius was regarding the Christian church (ἐκκλησία) like the identically named, pagan assembly of the city-state in Asia Minor. As the latter appropriately and cus-tomarily elected ambassadors to conclude and celebrate such a *homonoia* treaty, so it was appropriate for the former so to act, thus electing a diaconal ambassador for the purpose 'because you are a church (assembly = ἐκκλησία) of God'.

In a similar vein, he exhorts the Smyrnaeans:

> Your prayer went forth to the church at Antioch in Syria from where, coming as a prisoner, I greet you all, not being worthy to come from there, being the very least of them. But I was deemed worthy by the divine will, not moved by my own conscience, but from the grace of God, which I pray may be perfectly given to me to the end of my attaining God through your prayer. In order that your work may be fully completed, both upon earth and in heaven, it is fitting for the honour of God that the church elect an ambassador of God who, going as far as Syria, will share the rejoicing together with them that they are at peace, and have regained their proper stature, and that their very own corporate life has been restored to them. It appears to me, therefore, a deed worthy of God, to send one of your own with a letter in order that he might join with them in glorifying the tranquillity that by God's will has come to them . . .[115]

In these passages Ignatius clearly interprets interrelations between different churches by analogy with relations between city-states, in which the institution of electing and sending ambassadors played a major role. The stereotyped

113. Philostratus, *Lives*, 1.520.
114. Ignatius, *Philad.*, 10.1.
115. Ignatius, *Smyrn.*, 11.2.

language, witnessed in much of the epigraphy,[116] is once again ambassadorial: the ambassadors' role in achieving *homonoia* was to be marked by their ability to produce 'rejoicing (συγχαρῆναι)' and 'glorifying (συνδοξάζειν)' that will be common, 'together' or 'joint', as shown by verbal forms in which the Greek word σύν has been incorporated. Like an ambassador, this person is to be elected, and to take with him a letter recording the resolution of the whole church, as much in this regard clearly an ἐκκλησία as a Greek city-state. Indeed, Ignatius is very conscious of the defined role of an ambassador, so much so that he has to qualify language that might appear too equivalent with the term altered as '*God's* ambassador'.

But the imagery of this passage is also sacrificial in that the participants are to pray as though they were conducting a pagan sacrifice in which Ignatius will be their victim, their 'scapegoat' or 'propitiatory sacrifice'. He has already explained in other letters how 'to attain to God' is for him to become a 'sacrifice on an altar now ready' in the amphitheatre at Rome.[117] The 'completion' of their 'work' was therefore sustaining and supporting his martyr entourage going through Asia Minor like a sacrificial procession. In thus 'joining in' the procession they were like city-states celebrating together a 'joint sacrifice (συνθυσία)' that has brought peace and *homonoia* to communities in disarray, either between or within themselves.

Ambassadors bore images of gods, and we have seen that Ignatius likens his threefold order of bishops, presbyters and deacons to image bearers or wearers. Sometimes those images were on coins, celebrating *homonoia* treaties between states on which the tutelary deities of the two city-states are seen hailing each other in *homonoia*, as in the treaty between Ephesus, Smyrna and Pergamon. Here Artemis of Ephesus, Nemesis of Smyrna and Asclepius of Pergamon are depicted in imagery indicative of harmony.[118] The priest of the deity whose image he is carrying is believed to stand in the place of that deity. Thus the deities of the pagan ambassadors to Alexandria are considered to lead their embassy because the ambassadors carry their images in the coins in their hands. In the emperor Caracalla's letter to Ephesus, furthermore, he regards the ambassadors who greeted him as divine representatives, when he says by virtue of the image that they bear that 'your ancestral goddess Artemis heads your embassy'.[119]

We see a further use of imagery in ritual as a sacrament of political unity in the decree of the citizens of Oinoanda recording the bequest of Julius Demosthenes of a music festival. The *agonothete* or leader of the procession

---

116. Brent, *Ignatius and the Second Sophistic*, pp. 272–74.
117. Ignatius, *Ephes.*, 1.2; *Rom.*, 2.1-2; 5.3; *Pol.* 1.7, cf. *Smyrn.*, 10.2; *Pol.*2.3; *Ephes.*, 8.1; *Rom.*, 4.2.
118. Franke and Nollé (1997), 1, pp. 38–39, nos 305–316, and Tafel 18, especially 1 (309). and 2 (312), see also Brent, *Ignatius and the Second Sophistic*, pp. 245–49.
119. Brent, *Ignatius and the Second Sophistic*, pp. 262–63.

of the festival is to wear a garland crown, a *stephanos*, in which there are embossed images (τύποι). Thus we may conclude that not he, but the deities that he represents, head or lead the festival, standing out prominently from his headdress. But who are these deities? They are 'our Leader and ancestral god Apollo', but two further added, those of the emperor Hadrian himself, and of the dead and deified emperor Augustus. But there are other, portable images carried by chosen officials called 'sebastophoroi' or 'bearers of images of divine emperors', who also bear images of the ancestral gods. In other epigraphy, such images bearers are called 'theophoroi' or simply 'bearers of divine images'. But in Demosthenes' case, we find a high degree of assimilation between cult offered to the traditional deities of the city, and those of the imperial cult.

In terms of political theology, we have here what we may describe as a 'sacrament' of imperial unity. Emperor worship is not replacing the worship of traditional and ancestral deities, but simply becoming associated with it. Imperial power and the life of the autonomous city-state are experiencing through such a ritual of image bearing and image wearing an assimilation into a single political cosmos in which divine order and political order are in complete peace and concord.

It is directly on such a pagan political theology of ritual that Ignatius draws, as a 'man constrained to unity', when he describes the bishop, presbyters and deacons as 'projecting an image' of, respectively, Father, Spirit-filled apostolic council and Jesus Christ. Those who join his procession, and those who elect ambassadors to proclaim peace, are not only participating in a joint sacrifice or proclaiming its significance as they accompany the martyr bishop wearing the τύπος of the suffering Father-God. They are specifically acting in the Christian liturgy by analogy with those who bear or wear divine imagery appropriate to the ritual to secure such *homonoia* or to celebrate such a συνθυσία. The bearing and wearing of images had of course a role in the dramatic re-enactment of the sacred story of a cult, such as that of Dionysus. In his case, as we have argued, we have the sacred story of the Father-God represented by the bishop sending his diaconal Son in the Johannine scene in the Upper Room, with its Spirit-filled circle of the apostles looking on.

That Ignatius is modelling his Christian cult with its bishop as cult leader like an *agonothete*, he cannot make more clear. In the heading of each letter he describes himself as 'Ignatius, who is also Theophorus'. This word has invariably been translated as if it were a Roman cognomen, even though there are no prosopographic citations. The term has a clear meaning in the epigraphy, however, as a priest who is an 'image bearer (or wearer)' in a pagan cult such as that of Dionysus. We saw too *theophorus* used as a term equivalent to *sebastophorus*, but applied generally but not exclusively to the bearer of images of the dead and deified imperial family. But there are other clear allusions to pagan cults and their plays and processions.

His entourage had the appearance to all the world as that of a condemned prisoner under escort and in chains, proceeding on the northern route taken by the *cursus publicus*, Groups of representatives of the church at Ephesus journeyed forth to meet him and greet him on the way. The idea of his entourage as a procession of some sort had clearly caught on, since other churches behaved in such a way too, and there was no absence of persons going on ahead to advise the churches of his progression.[120] But Ignatius declares to those who thus had come that they are joining a cultic procession:

> Being imitators of God, and being enflamed in the blood of God, you completed perfectly the task so suited to your nature. For when you heard, you hastened to see one who was in chains from Syria on behalf of the name that we share and its hope, and one who hoped by your prayers to reach the goal of combating wild beasts at Rome in order that I might reach the goal of being a disciple.[121]

Ignatius thus regards them when he so describes them as members of a mystery cult 'imitating' their god in the rite that they were performing involving a sacrifice that he as the cult leader was representing. They came in ecstasy and awe as they became what they were imitating. They were 'enflamed with the blood of God', of which Ignatius as *theophorus* was an image bearer. They saw in the martyr bishop the suffering Father-God, whose image he was wearing or bearing, like a priest of Attis bearing the entrails of his god, with an axe in his hand.[122]

Furthermore, Ignatius calls those who join his entourage as 'cult associations (σύνοδοι)', whose members carry in their ritual processions various kinds of images:

> You are members of cult associations, God bearers, temple bearers, Christ-bearers, bearers of holy things, adorned in every respect with the commandments of Jesus Christ.

Thus his entourage are compared with the kind of procession of priests holding sacred objects that Apuleius describes in connection with the Isis mysteries, or that of the Agrippinilla inscription in the parts assigned to participants in a Dionysiac association in Rome.[123]

In a celebrated passage from Philostratus' *Life of Apollonius of Tyanna*, Apollonius, when informed by a ship owner that he is carrying statues of gods to Ionia, asks whether this is because they are to be used to found a cult. The same author, however, also mentions people carrying images of Demeter

---

120. Ignatius, *Rom.*, 9.3.
121. Ignatius, *Ephes.*, 1.1–2.
122. Brent, *Ignatius and the Second Sophistic*, pp. 121–23; pp. 135–37 and plates 13–17.
123. Apuleius, *Metam.*, 11.10; *IGUR*, 160, cf. Brent, *Ignatius and the Second Sophistic*, pp. 145–52.

and Dionysus, and claiming to be nourished by these divinities. We must remember too the kind of pagan theology regarding bearing images that regards them as apotropaeic, or as capable of averting the wrath of the gods when carried or displayed.[124] Plutarch, for example, describes Sulla as carrying a small portable image against his warring enemies.

We noted in an earlier chapter that, although both Jews and Romans witnessed portents and prodigies that formed part of their expectations for the future, Tacitus claims that the later had the appropriate ritual to control them whereas the former did not. The ideology of the Principate itself had been founded on the notion that only Augustus and his successors could perform the *augurium pacis* that produced the peace of the gods in nature and in society. Ignatius, in his view of the Christian cult founded on bishop, presbyters and deacons as wearers or bearers of the divine, now claims that through its cult with its distinct office holders Christianity has the appropriate ritual to produce peace in heaven and on earth.

We have argued that Ignatius views a church as validly gathered at the Eucharist as having a liturgy celebrated by those who play the roles of bishop, priests and deacons who 'stand out pre-eminently as an image (τύπος)' of Father, Spirit-filled apostolic council, and Jesus Christ. They are thus, by being regarded as bearing, in a spiritual sense, an image, understood as producing a mystery drama, in which the laity join, imitating divine persons and becoming absorbed into them as a result of such imitation. But to whom is such a drama with its images displayed?

Not to the unconverted outside the Church, but rather to the cosmic powers. As he says to the Ephesians:

> Be anxious, therefore, to come together for God's Eucharist and for his glory. For whenever they meet frequently as a church, the powers of Satan are overthrown and his destruction is dissolved in the concord (ὁμόνοια) of your faith. There is nothing better than peace, by which all warfare amongst those in heaven and on earth is abolished.[125]

Clerics of all three orders wave, as it were, the images that they bear at the cosmic powers, ending their destruction and producing both peace and *homonoia*.

Ignatius has performed, therefore, something of a tour de force. Luke had argued that the metaphysical objectives of the political ideology of the Principate in securing the peace of the gods is really achieved by the peace of Bethlehem and of the triumphal Entry. Clement has sought to ground his community as a πολίτευμα in which concord is established within communities and between them by an orderly succession of ministry. Eschatology is

124. Philostratus, *Vit. Apol.*, 5.20, cf. Brent, *Ignatius and the Second Sophistic*, pp. 207–210.
125. Ignatius, *Ephes.*, 13.1–2.

realized in the age of the church. But Ignatius, for whom eschatology is also realized, now goes a stage further. He argues that it is a specific structure of church order, that of bishop, presbyters and deacons, that realizes the eternal events in time. The Christian mysteries, Mary's virginity, giving birth, Christ's death were mysteries 'concealed from the ruler of this age'. When revealed in the life of the church and in the incorruption granted by the Eucharist as the 'medicine of immortality', then the eternal order is realized now and not in future time. When the star of Bethlehem proclaimed the incarnation:

> Consequently all magic, and every kind of spell were dissolved, the ignorance so characteristic of wickedness vanished, and the ancient kingdom was abolished when God appeared in human form to bring the newness of eternal life, and what had been prepared by God began to take effect. As a result, all things were thrown into ferment, because the abolition of death was being carried out.[126]

The celebration of the Christian mysteries, with its image bearers waving, as it were, their human images at the cosmic powers, defeat Satan and the cosmic chaos that he has wrought. This is why the Eucharist has such a potent force: when they 'meet frequently as a church the powers of Satan are overthrown and his destruction is dissolved in the concord (ὁμόνοια) of your faith'.[127]

Thus the 'bishop sent from the sun's rising' now found in the west 'at the sun's setting', and rejecting the values of the imperial power through his suffering in the arena ('I do not desire to reign over the ends of the earth') issues his own unique riposte to imperial claims. Christianity, and not the Roman pantheon with its imperial cult duly incorporated, produces the true *homonoia* and *pax* both on earth and in heaven for which Luke and Clement sought. But, for Ignatius, this *homonoia* is realized specifically through the ministry of a church structured by analogy with a pagan cult such as a mystery cult, with rites involving image bearing that was also apotropaeic. Tacitus had been wrong to claim that Roman cultic ritual could reorder a disordered world of portents in a way that Judaeism could not. Augustus' *augurium pacis* had not produced 'peace in earth and in heaven', but rather the Christian community with its threefold order of bishop, presbyters and deacons.

Ignatius' view of church order, by a tortuous route and in an amended form, was to become the historic church order of later Christendom. Given the force of its political ideology, it could work as the order of a society in conflict with the Roman state. But when that state, under Constantine and his successors, was to acknowledge its claims, then another kind of problem was to arise. It was the religious function of emperor as augur and *Pontifex Maximus*, to secure the peace of the gods in nature and in society. Should not therefore the Christian emperor function instead like the pagan emperor and become

---

126. Ignatius, *Ephes.*, 19.2–3.
127. Ignatius, *Ephes.*, 13.1.

Pontifex Maximus of the Church, with the appropriate ritual, by analogy with the *augurium pacis*, to secure the Christian God's millennial peace in nature and in society. We shall need to examine later why this did not happen. But for the moment, let us pursue the beginnings of the process that was to lead in that direction in the work of the Christian Apologists of the second century.

Chapter 6

THE APOLOGISTS AND THE POLITICS OF THE TRINITY: LOGOS AND COSMOLOGY

So far we have examined the implications of theological developments within early Christian communities for their relations with the pagan, imperial power. We have witnessed a desire on the part of two mainstream writers, Luke-Acts and Clement of Rome, to develop a form of Christianity within which its adherents could live at peace with the imperial power and participate in secular society. We have witnessed on the part of two earlier writers, the author of the Markan Apocalypse and the Seer of Revelation, efforts to confront the imperial power with the promise of its eschatological overthrow. We have seen in Ignatius of Antioch a writer that will confront the imperial power aggressively and apparently uncompromisingly, but offer the means to achieve its metaphysical objectives by way of a different religious cult to its own. But such theological developments were incidental and not consciously programmatic.

There was no self-conscious attempt by Luke-Acts, Clement, or Ignatius to address directly the imperial power with an argument for recognition and legal status. Rather their reconceptualization of the nature of their religion and its claims was executed under pressure of internal exigencies. Luke was concerned with converts such as Theophilus, whose desire to be a Christian yet participate in the metaphysical concept of imperial peace was to be satisfied, while maintaining intact a Christian identity. Clement was concerned with the implications of internal divisions within the Church at Corinth for general relations of the Roman Christian community with the Roman state. Ignatius, while through his experience of martyrdom felt the confrontation of Christianity with imperial ideals, nevertheless addressed the internal divisions of Christian communities in Syria and in Asia Minor in terms in which the Hellenistic and pagan political discourse of the Second Sophistic had sought to live at peace within an imperial structure.

In the course of the second century, a number of Christian writers were to address defences of Christianity or 'apologies' to Roman governors or emperors. Whether they were actually delivered and considered, or whether they were a rhetorical and literary device for a literary public is a moot point. Essentially they appear to begin with the situation created by Trajan's rescript in reply to Pliny, with which we dealt in detail in a previous chapter. But in defending

Christianity in terms of versions of Stoicism and Platonism, they were to proceed to refashion pagan metaphysical and cosmological order in terms of a
new, Christian order, in which Christ as Logos proceeded from the Father in a
universe of rational order. As we have constantly been reminded, in a world
in which there was no distinction made between natural and cosmological
order and social order, the one reflecting the other, such a claim to a Christian
cosmos fashioned in Stoic and Platonic terms would inevitably give rise to
questions about how such divine order could be reflected in human society.

Thus we consider the process of the transformation of pagan cosmology in
the Apologists in our first section (1), and the corresponding question of to
what kind of political order such a transformation was to look forward (2). We
shall find too that pagan political theology and cosmology was itself experiencing with the Severans considerable development towards a new, metaphysical
justification of imperial order.

1. *The Apologists and the Cosmic Christ as Logos*

Both Athenagoras and Tertullian, who also wrote a work in this genre, deploy
the argument that it is unjust to condemn Christians simply for the name that
they bear without there being any charges attaching to the name.[1] Athenagoras
mentions the accusations of Oedipodean banquets and Thyestien feasts.[2] The
former referred of course to Oedipus who, unknown to himself, killed his own
father and made love to his mother. Hence the charges made of incest, particular at 'love feasts' or agape meals. Thyestes had sexual relations with his own
daughter in response to an oracle.[3]

In reply to the accusation of sexual immorality, Athenagoras replies:

> But we are so far from promiscuity that it is unlawful for us to look with desire. For, he
> says, 'he who looks at a woman because he desires her has already committed adultery
> with her in his heart'. It is unlawful for them to look at anything other than that for
> which God has created eyes, namely to give light to us, and for them it is adultery to
> look with pleasure upon things other than those for which the eyes were created. They
> will be judged for their thought. How can these men not be believed to be chaste? . . .
> To remain a virgin and abstain from sexual intercourse brings us nearer to God . . .[4]

Likewise Athenagoras makes short shrift of the charge of infant cannibalism:

> Who can accuse those of manslaughter or cannibalism, when they do not allow them-
> selves to remain looking at someone executed by process of law? Who among you does
> not with enthusiasm attend the contests that are conducted under your patronage either

1.   Athenagoras, *Leg.*, 2.1–2; Tertullian, *Apol.*, I.11–13 (57–71).
2.   Athenagoras, *Leg.*, 3.1.
3.   Athenagoras, *Leg.*, 32.1.
4.   Athenagoras, *Leg.*, 32.2, cf. Mt. 5:28.

with gladiators or with wild beasts? But it is we who believe that looking at a man being murdered is almost to kill him: we have renounced such spectacles . . . We insist that women who indulge in practices of abortion are both murderers and will give account to God for the abortion . . .[5]

Theophilus of Antioch, similarly, wrote an apology to one Autolycus. He begins principally with a discussion on the nature of the Christian God, which he defends, characteristically as an apologist, with Greek philosophy. But he does eventually address these charges by which Autolycus has apparently been convinced:

For 'being wise you yielded gladly to the foolish', else you would not have come under the influence of mindless men so as to be led astray by their baseless accounts and believed a prejudiced rumour when godless mouths falsely made their accusations against we who are called the godly as well as Christians. Their assertions are that our women are the common property of us all, and spend their lives in indiscriminate sexual relations, and, still more, we have sexual intercourse with our own sisters. The most ungodly and savage charge of all is that we partake of the flesh of humans.[6]

Theophilus' reply takes the form of a 'pot-calling-kettle-black' argument. He points to examples of pagan philosophers and writers whom he claims to be supporters of cannibalism. He then refers to Plato's Republic as advocating holding wives as common property. On the positive side, he can produce a version of the Mosaic Ten Commandments, forbidding murder and adultery.[7] Like Athenagoras, he cites coveting another's wife as forbidden, along with attendance at gladiatorial shows and other spectacles where the devouring of Thyestes' children is enacted.[8]

Justin Martyr similarly begins with a refutation of the charges of cannibalism and incest, refuting them with the same proof texts as Athenagoras and Theophilus.[9] Justin also mentions Christ's injunction to 'render to Caesar the things that are Caesar's'.[10] So far their defence of Christianity may seem obvious and inconsequential: a mere dispelling of prejudice that had led at some points to quite savage consequences. But the third charge levelled along with incest and cannibalism had been atheism. None of the apologists address directly the accusations made for example in the *senatusconsultum* of A.D. 14 against the Magi and Chaldeans, under which the practice of magic or of divination of the future was made illegal. They dealt directly instead with the charge of atheism.

---

5. Athenagoras, *Leg.*, 36.4–6.
6. Theophilus, *Ad Autol.*, 3.4, quoting 2 Cor. 11:19.
7. Theophilus, *Ad Autol.*, 3.6 and 9.
8. Theophilus, *Ad Autol.*, 3.15.
9. Justin, *1 Apol.*, 15.
10. Justin, *1 Apol.*, 17, cf. Mt. 22:15-21; Mk 12:13-17; Lk. 20:20-25.

It is at this point that their doctrine of the *logos* becomes critical.

Let us recall the Classical and pagan roots of this concept. According to Plato's heirs, at least those who followed Alkinous rather than Speusippus, the *logos* was the mind or reasoning of God, and the transcendental Platonic forms or essences of things were ideas in that mind. Philo, the Jewish writer at Alexandria, was heir to that tradition when he regarded the creation of Genesis 1 as the blueprint for the actual creation in Genesis 2. According to Philo, the world created in Genesis 1 was Plato's transcendental or noumenal world created in the mind of God, only later to be embodied in the phenomenal world in Genesis 2.

According to the Stoics, on the other hand, there was no ultimate distinction between matter and form: the *logos* was God's mind and the ground plan of the universe that permeated all things. Though the *logos* was Spirit, there was no final distinction between spirit and matter: their view is described as 'hylomorphism'. This world-Spirit or *logos* was ultimately material, as was God with whom it was identified. This was the divine essence that pervaded all things in the form of a refined breath whose substance was spiritual. As this essence was *logos*, it was rational, and comprehensible by human reason (*logos*) of which it was a part. But not simply nature, therefore, but also human society was governed by a rational order that a 'holy *logos* leads and controls'. The 'right reason' in nature was continuous with and reflected in the 'right reason' governing the moral life.

Athenagoras had concluded that Christian lives could not be involved in the cannibalism and immorality of the pagan theatre because their lives were governed by reason:

> Far be it from the Christian to think of doing such a thing with whom sobriety dwells, self-control is exercised, single marriage is observed, purity guarded, injustice driven out, sin is uprooted, righteousness is cultivated with concern, law is the principle of civil life, reverence for God is practiced, God is confessed, truth judges, grace preserves, peace protects, holy Logos is our guide, Wisdom teaches, Life controls, God reigns.[11]

But if the Christ within the human heart was *logos* and wisdom, and if these were also part of the structure of the natural order of creation, then Christ was the divine reason permeating the world. The 'peace' of Christ in the human heart was also the divine 'peace' in the natural order. The apologists shared Athenagoras' theme. And here was to emerge another, Christian, reflection of the themes of Augustus' *Ara Pacis* that had expressed the political and metaphysical claims of the Principate.

Justin Martyr insists that if the Christ as *logos*, whether in a Platonic or in a Stoic sense (and he works with both conceptions), was eternal, therefore he

---

11. Theophilus, *Ad Autol.*, 3.15.

existed at creation as its oldest first principle. Christianity was therefore not to be dismissed as a new, charismatic or Dionysiac religion that had recently broken out with a manifestation of irrational frenzy, but was as old as time, in fact the most ancient religion. Because Christ as *logos* was pre-existent, then there had been Christians before the birth at Bethlehem, in fact all true philosophers who had followed right reason in their conduct and in their teaching were in some sense witnessing to the truth of Christ.

The Stoics had spoken of σπέρματικοι λόγοι, or 'seeds of the *logos*' in terms of the immanent reason in each individual human being. To this notion Justin Martyr was to appeal:

> We have been taught that the Christ is the first begotten of God and we have previously intimated that he is the Logos in which the whole human race shares. And those who have lived their lives in the company of the Logos were Christians, even if they were thought to be atheists, for example Socrates and Heracleitus amongst the Greeks and those like them, and among the barbarians Abraham, and Ananias, and Asarias, and Misael and Elias . . . so that those who came before and had lived without the Logos lived without purpose and were enemies of, and murders of, those whose lives were conducted with the Logos. But those who had lived and those who now live with the Logos remained without fear and undisturbed.[12]

Justin, however, explains parallels between pagan myths and Christian truths as due to a perversion of the indwelling *logos* by pagans.[13] Zeus was called 'father of the gods and men', and Hermes was one of his sons, who is also called 'the angelic *logos* from God's presence'.[14] Perseus was 'born of a virgin', Asclepius healed the sick, and Zeus' children suffered.[15] These examples show pagans with access to the *logos*, but only comprehending darkly and perversely what the logos reveals about himself.

With mention of Heracleitus, from whom the Stoics derived their hylomorphism where the *logos* was of the nature of fire, we find Justin's debt to Stoicism in his *logos* Christology, despite his avowal of the role of Plato's philosophy in his conversion.[16] Justin's *logos* theology sees Christ pre-existing, but as he says, 'taking shape' at the incarnation:

> For not only amongst the Greeks were these truths established through argument by the Logos through Socrates, but also amongst the barbarians by the same Logos when he changed his form and became man (ὑπ' αὐτοῦ τοῦ Λόγου μορφωθέντος καὶ ἀνθρώ που γενομένου) and was named Jesus Christ . . .[17]

---

12. Justin, 1 *Apol.*, 46.2–4.
13. Justin, 1 *Apol.*, 20.
14. Justin, 1 *Apol.*, 22.1–2.
15. Justin, 1 *Apol.*, 22.3 and 5–6.
16. Justin, *Dial.* 2.2–6.2.
17. Justin, *Apol.*, 5.4.

Justin's words here regarding the *logos* before the incarnation can only have the conclusion that he wishes them to have because he is dependent upon a Stoic metaphysics. The λόγος ἐνδιάθετος that when spoken becomes προφορικός is inseparable from matter as a fiery breath or spirit, permeating all things and giving them their shape and order. Thus the 'word (*logos*) of the Lord' that comes to the prophets is not simply a sign or symbol pointing to a mental image that is a prevision of the Christ who is to come. Rather the *logos* or fiery breath that is uttered by the prophet is an already existent entity, a configuration of the λόγος ἐνδιάθετος that pervades all things.

The equation of Christ as the Stoic λόγος ἐνδιάθετος meant that the 'word of the Lord' that came to the prophets was no mere 'word' according to our Enlightenment view of language and reality. The Stoic hylomorphism of the *logos* as a fiery breath or spirit permeating all things and giving them their shape and order meant that the λόγος coming to the prophets existed in a quasi personal form, albeit without a bodily form (ἀσώματος). Since there was no final distinction between matter and spirit, the words uttered by the prophets represented a kind of pre-incarnational incarnation. Under a similar, hylomorphic influence, Clement of Alexandria had at one point claimed that John's claim 'the *logos* became flesh' did not apply only to the incarnation at Bethlehem:

> 'And the Logos became flesh', not only at his presence when he became a human man but also 'in the beginning', when the Logos in his constant identity, became the Son by his being delimited (κατὰ περιγραφὴν) as such and not in his essence (κατ᾿ οὐσίαν).

> And again he became flesh coming into actuality through the prophets (διὰ προφητῶν ἐνεργήσας).[18]

In a Stoic, hylomorphic universe the λόγός προφορικος could be no empty word, no *afflatus vocis*, no empty breath emitted by the vocal cords, as the medieval philosophical theologian Roscelin would claim.[19] Rather the λόγος was already in a sense enfleshed, since its nature was of a refined yet corporal fire.

It is such an account of Justin's *logos* theology that now helps us to understand a curious feature of his use of Gospel material in his dialogue with Trypho. We clearly have sayings of Jesus cited that come from Matthew and Luke, and some allusions to both the birth stories and the passion narrative.[20]

---

18. Clement of Alexandria, *Excerpt. Theod.*, 19.1–2.

19. As reported by Anselm, *De Fide Trinitatis*, chapter 2 and John of Salisbury, *Metalogicus*, Lib. II, Cap. 13.

20. Justin, *Dial.*, 77.4 (Mt. 2.1-2); 78.1–5 (Mt. 2:2; 2:11-12; Lk. 2:1-5); 78.7–8 (Mt. 2: 12-18); 81.4 (Lk. 20:35-36); 84.4 (Lk. 1:57); 85.7 (Mt. 5.44); 88.3 (Mk 1:9-10; Lk. 3:21-22); 88.7–8 (Mt. 3:1-11; 13:55; Mk 1:4 and 6; Lk. 3:3 and 23); 93.2 (Mt. 22:37-39); 96.3 (Mt. 5.45; Lk. 6.36).

But he seems to prefer the λόγος to speak with the words that he used through the prophets, actualizing the events of which they had prophesied.[21] The words of the suffering servant in Isaiah, or of the righteous sufferer of the Psalms, occurring before Christ came at Bethlehem, are, quite apart from being more evidential, full expressions of who and what the *logos* is.

Thus Moses in the burning bush was confronted by a real and personal entity: Christ was seen in the configuration of the fire:

> In the form of fire (ἐν ἰδέᾳ πυρός) from the bush our Christ conversed with him . . . and he received mighty power from the Christ who spoke with him in the form of the fire (ἐν ἰδέᾳ πυρός), and he went down and led out the people, having performed great and marvellous deeds . . .[22]

Thus he speaks of the pre-incarnate Christ as assuming a pre-incarnate form or ἰδέα, thus using a cognate term to that which he had used of the incarnation when the '*logos* changed his form (τοῦ Λόγου μορφωθέντος)'. As Justin continues:

> . . . the Logos, the first begotten of God, exists also as God. And previously he appeared to Moses through the form of the fire (διὰ τῆς τοῦ πυρὸς μορφῆς) and through an image without a body (καὶ εἰκόνος ἀσωμάτου).[23]

Thus Justin clearly uses ἰδέα, μορφή, and εἰκών as synonyms, as we see also in his concept of change in the Eucharistic elements:

> This food is called amongst us 'Eucharist', in which no one is allowed lawfully to participate other than one who believes our teachings to be true . . . For we do not receive the bread and the wine as though they were ordinary. But in the manner in which Jesus Christ our saviour became flesh through God's *logos* and possessed flesh and blood for our salvation, in the same way the food eucharistized through the word (*logos*) of the prayer that comes from him from which our blood and flesh is nourished by being transformed (κατὰ μεταβολὴν) we teach to be both the flesh and the blood of that Jesus who was made flesh.[24]

Although it is controversial, it would appear to me quite clear that Justin has produced a kind of doctrine of transubstantiation that draws on a Stoic hylomorphism rather than a later, Aristotelian system of accidents and essences used by Aquinas. The λόγος ἐνδιάθετος, in 'changing his form and becoming man', did at the same time 'become flesh', having previously appeared

---

21. Justin, *Dial.*, 97–99.2 (Ps. 21 (22) 17–19) with the barest summary of information found in Mt. 27:35 = Mk 15:24 = Lk. 23:34 and in Mt. 26:37-39.
22. Justin, 1 *Apol.*, 63.3.
23. Justin, 1 *Apol.*, 63.15–16.
24. Justin, 1 *Apol.*, 66.1.

'through an image without a body'. It is the power of the *logos*, thus permeating all things, to configure and reconfigure himself in this way. The same *logos*, spoken now by the 'president' of the Eucharist, though no longer by the prophet, has the same hylomorphic reality as before: the *logos* comes forth from his mouth as a personal existence and configures or transforms (κατὰ μεταβολήν) bread and wine in a new kind of incarnation.

Justin had sought, in giving his account of the Eucharist in an *apologia*, no doubt to repeat the case that Pliny, at all events, had previously conceded. He gives perhaps our earliest account of what happens at a Christian Eucharist, while preserving the *disciplina arcani*, the requirement that the baptized do not reveal to pagans the details of the Christian mysteries. His account ends with mention of the 'memoirs of the apostles', being read with their account of the Last Supper but with no reference of any actual words and acts that the 'president' may have performed, though the Western rite words of institution are obviously implied. Justin, moreover, in describing the character of Eucharistic blessing of the material elements, and in explaining what Christians clearly meant by 'the body and blood of Christ', could show that there would be no question about something like the entrails of Attis being consumed, let alone the flesh of a newborn infant. But the introduction of the *logos* doctrine into his discussion is now clearly taking him beyond a mere *apologia*. He is reformulating in Christian terms a Stoic worldview whose metaphysics lay at the heart of pagan political theology, as we have shown.

We saw in our third chapter that the compendium of Pythagorean authors, compiled by Stobaeus, had seen the ruler mediating the divine order of nature to civil society. The king bore the same relation to the state as God or the divine *logos* did to the world, and thus became the guarantor of a harmonious political order. In one sense Justin's *logos* was therefore part of his *apologia* in that it made the point that Christianity was not a Dionysiac cult seeking to upset by magical means the peace of the gods in nature and in society. In this respect early Christian reflection on the Trinity reflected a desire for cosmic, and, therefore, social peace and order that paralleled the Roman quest also for social order in which the peace and harmony of nature and that of society were one.

We may pursue this point by looking at the forms of Christianity to which nascent Trinitarian and incarnational theology was opposed. As Irenaeus was to show, there were other forms of Christianity that did not regard creation as the work of God the Father and his *logos*, proceeding as a rational, cosmic order. Sethian Gnosticism, associated by Irenaeus with Valentinus, had taught that the present cosmos was a chaos produced by a catastrophe, in which one of 30 divine emanations or 'aeons', Sophia, had been thus cast out of a godhead of 32 persons, and who had produced the world as an abortion. Such a form of Christianity was highly individualist, requiring personal meditation in order to effect the escape of the imprisoned soul and its reuniting with the pleroma or godhead whence it had with Sophia fallen. The material world was alienated from God and was not redeemable: redemption was a question of escape.

We considered with approval in chapter 1 Valantasis' account of the *Gospel of Thomas*, in which this gospel represented such a group, pursuing together meditation that was designed to produce personal enlightenment by a kind of *via negativa*: separate sayings or *logia* of Jesus were juxtaposed so as to represent antitheses producing 'disturbance' or perplexity that would be resolved only through a mystical experience that uncovered a deep truth hidden in their apparent contradiction. Such an individualistic view of religion in terms of personal salvation admitted only at least minimal political engagement. The world that was the product, not of a benign act of creation, but of the chaos that remained from a cosmic catastrophe, was a world from which the soul must escape rather than engage with it.

But Justin and the apologists rejected such a worldview that they associated directly with Marcion and other heretics. Marcion, a radical interpreter of St Paul's writings, had taught that there were two gods, an evil or perhaps better 'imperfect' god who had made the world, and a good or 'perfect' God who had sent Jesus Christ. But such a view of the divine order represented a metaphysical picture of disorder, of a 'nature at variance with itself' that Lucan, as we have seen, saw as the religious function of the Principate to set right, just as the *Ara Pacis* had claimed that Augustus had set nature as well as civil society right, and that the epigraphy had proclaimed. In proclaiming the work of the *logos* in creation as well as redemption, Justin and the apologists were presenting a cosmos rationally and harmoniously ordered.

Instead of 33 aeons within the Valentinian godhead, Justin assures us that there are but 3, who proceed from one in due order, without any conflict or disturbance among them. After 'the creator of this universe':

> Having learned that he is really the Son of God, and holding him in the second place (ἐν δευτέρᾳ χώρᾳ) and the prophetic Spirit in the third rank (ἐν τρίτῃ τάξει), we have demonstrated that we honour him with the *logos*. In consequence they accuse us of being delirious (μανίαν), claiming that we give second place to a crucified human being after him who is the unchangeable and always existing God and procreator of the universe . . .[25]

Here Father and Son are assigned due place and rank (τάξις), just as ministers and laymen were to keep to their appointed rank in an ordered community according to Clement, as we have seen.

Christians follow this *logos* that orders both creation and human society, and determines the course of human history, declaring what is to come before it takes place. Thus clearly Christians do not practise magic arts that produce a 'nature at variance with itself' in which the peace of the gods has been upset.

25. Justin, 1 *Apol.*, 13.3–4.

The daemons are hostile to those who follow the *logos* that orders a harmonious cosmos:

> They strive to have you as their slaves and underlings, sometimes through manifestations in dreams and sometimes through magical spells . . . This is the way in which we have put them away following our conversion to the *logos*, and in which we are following the only Unbegotten One through the Son. Those who formally rejoiced in fornication now welcome only chastity. Those who employed previously magic arts now have dedicated themselves to the good and unbegotten God . . .[26]

Thus following the *logos* is to conform to a rationally ordered cosmos: magical spells upsetting the metaphysical order of both nature and society are clearly alien to such a Christian commitment.

Thus far Justin and the Apologists had pursued an account of Christianity consistent with a *logos* Christology that could assure pagan Rome that the cult of Christ believed in the rational and orderly cosmic order that imperial religion sought to sustain in both nature and society. But regarding matters in such terms required a considerable shifting in the tectonic plates at the foundation of how political and natural order were to be conceived, and of which Justin and the Apologists were only dimly aware. Let us now pursue this point in more detail.

The very language in which the Apologists expressed the nascent doctrine of the Trinity reflected a developing pagan ideology of political unity. In one respect political concepts derived from metaphysical concepts made this inevitable, since metaphysical order and political order were generally in human cultures before the European Enlightenment believed to be one. The word for 'origin' or 'beginning' in Greek is ἀρχή, that is to say identical with the word for 'rule' or 'empire'. The unity of an empire was therefore its derivation from a single first principle or beginning, a μοναρχία as was also the unity of the cosmos.

Justin claimed, in speaking with Trypho, that philosophical disputations were 'about God . . . and about his position as single first principle (μοναρχία)'. It was in defence of that *monarchia* that he was prepared to speak of the Logos as 'in the second place'.[27] Nevertheless he struggled to find the words to express anything like the later distinction between persons in the Trinity. The generation of the Logos from the Father is like giving 'birth to a reasoning entity, not projecting it by cutting it off (κατὰ ἀποτομήν) from the reason that is in us so as to reduce it'.[28] Yet the Logos is 'different (ἕτερος) from the God who made the universe, in number but not in purpose'.[29]

26. Justin, 1 *Apol.*, 14.1–2.
27. Justin, 1 *Apol.*, 13.3.
28. Justin, *Dial.*, 61.2.
29. Justin, *Dial.*, 56.11.

Athenagoras addressed his *Apology* to the emperors Marcus Aurelius and Commodus (A.D. 176–180).[30] But one apologetic move that he makes is to employ an analogy between their constitutional relations, and those of Father and of Son in the godhead:

> May you find it possible to examine, by your own efforts, also the heavenly kingdom; for as all things have been subjected to you, a father and a son, who have received your kingdom from above, for 'the king's life is in God's hands', as the prophetic spirit says, so all things are subordinated to the one God and the Logos that issues from him, whom we consider his inseparable Son.[31]

But elsewhere the *logos* must be made subordinate to God the Father in order to preserve the notion of a single first principle (μοναρχία) from which all other things are derived. But certainly Christian theology now, both Theophilus and Tatian claim, in its insistence on the cosmic *monarchia*, will be antithetical to the pagan claim of a plurality of gods in a universe thus without strict order.[32] Christian Monotheism therefore becomes more politically correct than paganism, and, by implication, more supportive of imperial order.

Theophilus accuses Plato of failing to establish the *monarchia* required by any cosmological order. If matter can co-exist eternally alongside an uncreated God, then there must be two first principles (or empires, ἀρχαί) and not the required one as the source and origin of a single cosmic order. The Platonists have failed: 'the unique sovereignty of God' or 'his status as the underived first principle' from which all else is derived, 'is not demonstrated'.[33] Christian monotheism, and its justification in a philosophical theology of the *logos*, was therefore far more satisfactory and, indeed, 'rational'.

Tatian, Justin's disciple, also insists that the quest of the Christian apologist is for a Trinity that can explain better than paganism a cosmic *monarchia*. Indeed, he records his conversion from paganism to Christianity as the result of being convinced that the latter had a better explanation of cosmic order. Dissatisfied with the immorality of the mystery religions, he sought to discover the truth:

> I chanced to read certain writings in an uncultured language both more ancient in comparison with the teachings of the Greeks, and more divine in comparison with the error of the latter. And I believed in them because of . . . their clear grasp of the creation of the universe and of their foreknowledge of the future, and the doctrine of the cosmic monarchy.[34]

---

30. Athenagoras, *Leg.*, praef.
31. Athenagoras, *Leg.*, 18.2.
32. See e.g. Athenagoras, *Leg.*, 18–19.
33. Theophilus, *Ad Autol.*, 2.4–6.
34. Tatian, *Orat.*, 29.1–2.

In consequence, he addresses the Greek world in general when he says: 'You exercise the rule of the many rather than of one (μοναρχία)' in a world of gods who are really warring daemons.[35]

We do not know how many were convinced by the claim of the Apologists to produce by means of a Christian monotheism a better account of cosmic order, or who they were. But that a cosmic order in which there was a single first principle was critical for the political ideology of pagan, imperial order was not lost on the pagan establishment's spin-doctors of the time.

Apuleius, when asking how the universe could be directed 'from one first principle (ἐκ μιᾶς ἀρχῆς)', used the analogy of the Persian emperor sending instructions by means of light signals.[36] It is the same image of the burning torch that Tatian used, just like Justin before him, to explain how the Logos could be separate from the Father yet at one with him:

> Just as many fires may be kindled from one torch, but the light of the first torch is not diminished because of the kindling of the many, so also the Logos, coming forth from the power of the Father, does not make thereby the begetter of the Logos deprived of reason.[37]

But for Apuleius it was a quest for a pagan and not a Christian monotheism in which imperial order could be shown to reflect cosmic order.

Furthermore, we have the epigraphy that preserves the hymnody of the goddess Isis in which we witness the currents that were leading to a pagan monotheism. We have an inscription, as early as 103 B.C., from the Iseum at Cyrene, in which the goddess Isis is declared 'only ruler of this age . . . the greatest of the gods in heaven'. Around A.D. 100, in another inscription she is hailed as 'queen of the gods', and 'mistress of the world'.[38] She is the source of all life and of all law, and the names of other gods and goddesses, far from naming separate divine beings, are but other names for her. And the philosophical theology that underpins such pagan worship is that of the principle of *monarchia*: there is an Isis hymn from Andros that speaks of 'the sign of your monarchy, O Queen (σᾶμα τεᾶς, δέσποινα, μοναρχείας)'.[39]

We find a clear association of such an Isiac universalism with images of imperial power following its earlier repression under Tiberius. Yet in a similar religious motivation to that which led the Greek East to offer cult to Augustus, we find, nonetheless, an inscription from Egypt (A.D. 23) in which Julia

---

35. Tatian, *Orat.*, 14.1.

36. Apuleius [Pseudo Aristotle], *Mundo*, 6.398a, 31–35.

37. Tatian, *Orat.*, 5.11–15, cf. Justin, *Dial.*, 61.2.

38. *SEG*, IX.1.192 and VIII.1.548, cf. A. Brent, *The Imperial Cult and the Development of Church Order: Concepts and Images of Authority in Paganism and Early Christianity before the Age of Cyprian* (VCSup, 45; Leiden: E. J. Brill, 1999), pp. 256–57.

39. W. Peek, *Der Isishymnus von Andros und verwandte Texte* (Berlin: Weidmann, 1930), p. 15.6, cf. Brent, *Imperial Cult*, p. 302.

Sebaste is described as 'a new Isis'.[40] Thus the suggestiveness of the *Ara Pacis* was assuming a new form on Egyptian soil: she who, as queen of the gods represented the universal order of nature, was present in the person of the empress as the guarantee of political order. The ideological possibilities were not lost on Tiberius' successor, Caligula. In his reign a temple of Isis at Rome was either built from new or repaired. Isis' consort was Osiris, and their child was Horus, with whom his imperial family were identified.

The Vespasian myth recorded the healing of a blind and lame man sent by Osiris to Vespasian as the incarnation of Horus, to whom Isis had given birth.[41] Vespasian was clearly open to the integration of Isis into the metaphysical aim of the Principate, namely the *pax deorum* IN nature and in society.[42] Domitian was depicted being crowned by Isis on the Obelisk in the Piazza Navona. Hadrian, and his empress Sabina were associated in Alexandrian coinage with Sarapis and Isis (A.D. 132–134).[43] The empress of Marcus Aurelius, Faustina II, is also associated with Isis on coinage.[44] The cult of Cybele or Mater Magna also underwent such associations with imperial power.[45]

We find a pagan political theology of Isis that regards her power over the natural order channelled through the ruler further expressed and developed in a fragment found in the *corpus Hermeticum* called 'Maiden of the World'. Here the earth prays to her to maintain order by means, if not of herself, by 'a certain sacred effluence (ἀπόρροια)' of herself. Isis declares that the terrestrial sphere is to receive its order from 'the one who becomes emperor from time to time . . . the gods give birth to emperors . . . and rulers are emanations of the emperor'.[46] Thus we find the divine order of what is elsewhere described as Isis' *monarchia* pervading through all existence to divine monarchy in the earthly, political sphere. *Aporroia* is the concept used also for the procession of the Logos from the Father in the Trinitarian reflections of the Apologists.

As Athenagoras says:

> For as we say, God, the Son his Logos and Holy Spirit are united in power but distinguished in rank as the Father, the Son, and the Spirit, since the Son of the Father is mind, Logos, wisdom, and the Spirit is effluence (ἀπόρροία) of God, as light from fire . . . [47]

40. *IGRR*, I.1150.

41. Tacitus, *Hist.*, 4.81; Suetonius, *Titus*, 5.3. For a thorough discussion of these actions and their precise historical location, with an analysis of the sources, see S. A. Takács, *Isis and Sarapis in the Roman World* (EPRO, 124; Leiden: E. J. Brill, 1995), pp. 96–98.

42. Takács, *Isis and Sarapis*, p. 107, and Brent, *Imperial Cult*, p. 259.

43. *BMC*, 3.339 and 489, cf. p. 485 for Isis alone.

44. *BMC*, 4, p. 545 n. (= H. Cohen, *Description Historique des Monnaies* (Paris: Rollin and Feuardent, 1884), nos C.298, C.299 and C.304).

45. Brent, *Imperial Cult*, pp. 261–64.

46. Corpus Hermeticum, *Fragments*, 24.1–2.

47. Athenagoras, *Leg.*, 24.2.

At another point, the Spirit 'is the effluence of God which flows forth from him, and returns like the rays of the sun'.[48] It is at this point that we can see that the *logos* theology of the Apologists, with its emphasis on Christian metaphysics, teaching a cosmology of order, must have possessed for the pagans who first read it a highly political edge. Such metaphysics of order, unlike those of Gnosticism, were not in spiritual isolation, with no implication for the present political order other than the need to escape from it. If Christ as *logos* was the firstborn of an orderly progression of creation that proceeded in terms of a doctrine of *monarchia*, then who was the earthly representative in the case of the Christian symbolic universe of meaning? Could it be the emperor?

No Christian theologian of the early centuries had ever suggested the kind of parallel between Church and State that Cranmer was to do in the sixteenth century. Since religion was so essential to political order, Cranmer was to answer the question 'who was the head of the Church in the time of Peter and Paul' with the reply 'the emperor Nero'.[49] We shall see that Eusebius was however to attempt to find a place for a Christian emperor such as Constantine within such a duly modified concept of divine rulership. He was to fail because the developing logic of Trinitarian theology made such a monarchical view of divine order heretical.

As we have emphasized, in the cultural and historical, Graeco-Roman environment in which early Christianity evolved, political order reflected cosmic order. What political implications were there for the Christian claim that Christ as *logos* was the firstborn of all creation, through whom the divine order was mediated both to nature and to human life? It was to be historically a long path, but logically, if that is not too much of a pun, a straight one from the *logos* doctrine of the apologists to the mosaics of Ravenna. Here the emperor Justinian and his imperial court would prefigure in an iconographical pattern in which both nature and Christian imperial power flowed from a cosmos permeated by Christ as *logos*. Or, we could take as another example, the mosaics decorating the domed roof of Santa Constanza, in which the empress is depicted at the centre of vine leaves and nature scenes, or the golden mosaics of the Upper Church of San Clemente. In the latter we find nature scenes of twirling acanthus in the tradition of those of the *Ara Pacis* above which we have observed the procession commemorating Augustan imperial order arising out of a nature at peace. But at the centre of that scene stands the cross as the tree of life, from which the nature scenes depicted arise. It was to take a Eusebius, as we shall see, to connect a Christian empire and emperor with a Christian construction of cosmic order in terms of the *logos* Christology.

---

48.   Athenagoras, *Leg.*, 10.4–5.
49.   J. E. Cox (ed.), *Miscellaneous Writings of Thomas Cranmer* (London: Parker Society, 1844), vol. II, p. 219; O. P. Rafferty, 'Thomas Cranmer and the Royal Supremacy', *Heythrop Journal*, 31 (1990), pp. 129–49 (134).

But what now followed for Christianity, from the second half of the second century onwards, was the issue of how the developing *logos* theology would be reflected, not in pagan order but in Christian political order. If political order reflects metaphysical order, how internally would the Christian community be constructed or reconstructed in order to reflect it?

2. *Church Order and Cosmic Reconstruction from Ignatius to Callistus*

At Rome we have argued the form of church government was in one sense presbyteral, with a group of presbyters forming a kind of central board, but drawn from the different house-churches over which they presided. Clement of Rome, as Ignatius' near contemporary, represents the Church of Rome as governed by a plurality of presbyter-bishops, but he draws no connection between them as such and figures in a divine cosmology. He argues that the role of leadership is to produce a divine state of affairs in society, an ordered πολίτευμα, which reflects the order of nature infused with the power of the Stoic *logos*-spirit: *homonoia* is the divine principle by which the city of this world will reflect the city of the gods, which Clement sought in a Christianized form. But as yet there is no identity of the political structure with the transcendent order of things, with the Trinity in unity.

It was only with the Apologists, as we have seen, that such parallels were drawn, if only half-consciously, of Christ as *logos* identified with the order of creation in order to show the inherent authority structures of Christian assemblies, without drawing the consequences for where concretely in ecclesial structure such representation can be found. But Justin did not consider himself as the mediator of the *logos* in creation and in redemption to the laity under his authority, like a Hellenistic ruler reflecting the divine order of nature flowing as *logos* into human society. He regarded his group, meeting 'above the baths of Martin', by analogy with an Hellenistic school of philosophers over which he presided, wearing no doubt his philosopher's gown.

Ignatius of Antioch, whose traditional date we accept, had developed a form of Church order in which the threefold order of bishop, presbyters and deacons reflected the metaphysics of the saving events. The three orders were part of a drama in which they, as τύποι or images, realized in time the activity of timeless divine personages through union with whom 'incorruption' was to be obtained. As such, church order, we might say, reflected metaphysical order: Father, Son, as 'the λόγος proceeding from silence', and the Holy Spirit found their reflections in bishop, deacons and the presbyteral council, sitting in its liturgical circle around the bishop. But in its day such a view was highly idiosyncratic: it certainly was never to survive in its original form since it is the presbyter, and not the deacon, who at the altar was later to be considered to be *in persona Christi*.

Ignatius' message was the prophetic message of an individual martyr seeking a unity and union that was both physical and spiritual within and between Christian communities. It was an individual and highly original message, proclaimed by one who had all the authority granted by his status as martyr. Polycarp found his entourage, and the interpretation that Ignatius placed upon it, very strange and enigmatic. Notwithstanding, Ignatius had claimed as martyr to represent the suffering God, 'Jesus Christ who really suffered'. In consequence, Polycarp welcomed nervously the group at Smyrna, and sent them on their way, even entering into the spirit of the drama by getting the *ekklesia* (church) of God at Smyrna to 'elect' deacon 'ambassadors' and 'speed runners', as though they were the *ekklesia* (assembly) of a Greek city-state gathered as a self-governing community. But Polycarp barely understood such an Hellenized and secular view of Church order.

Polycarp described to the Philippians how he had seen Ignatius' entourage at Smyrna, and how he imagined them too sending them on their way to Rome.

> I greatly rejoice with you in our Lord Jesus Christ, since you made welcome the imitations of true love, and conducted forward, as opportunity fell to you, those bound with bonds that befit their sanctity, which are the diadems of those truly chosen by God and our Lord.[50]

Polycarp's language reflects a desire to come to terms with Ignatius' novel vocabulary that parallels Ignatius' Christian procession with that of a pagan mystery one. Ignatius along with his companions are 'imitations of true love', but he cannot bring himself to suggest that as bishop and as martyr he is an image or *typos* of the suffering god, able to 'enflame' those who see it 'with the blood of God'. For similar reasons he describes Ignatius' bond as 'befitting in sanctity (ἁγιοπρεπής)', but he cannot comprehend how, in Ignatius' typological sense, they can be 'befitting divinity (θεοπρεπής)'.[51] Polycarp therefore retreats into abstractions.

Polycarp also found Ignatius' conceptualization of ecclesial order rather hard to manage. He does not use the word 'bishop' of his or anyone else's office, though he can bring himself to insist that the laity 'be subject to the presbyters and deacons as to God and Christ'.[52] He cannot quite get his head around being subject to these ministers because they 'create an image (εἰς τύπον)' of God or Christ. Ignatius addresses him as the bishop, but clearly he sees his role as a presbyter among presbyters, as in the way that his letter begins: 'Polycarp and his fellow presbyters'. Here is a de facto pre-eminence that has not yet become *de iure*. Otherwise, Polycarp's church order seems at home in that

---

50.   Polycarp, *Philip.*, 1.1.
51.   Ignatius, *Smyrn.*, 12.2; 11.1; *Pol.* 7.2. See also, Brent, *Ignatius and the Second Sophistic*, pp. 127–131.
52.   Polycarp, *Philip.*, 5.3.

of the Pastoral Epistles, with orders of presbyters who in the latter are called 'bishops' too, and with also an order of deacons and of widows.[53]

Indeed, the only person really to understand the purport of Ignatius' message was the pagan satirist, Lucian of Samosata, who constructed many features for his mainly fictional portrayal of two wandering charlatans, Peregrinus Proteus and Alexander from his genuine contact with Ignatius' entourage, or at least the effects that this had on Ignatius' contemporaries. In his portrait of Peregrinus, he recorded the impression that Ignatius had created of a Christian martyr bishop as his entourage had advanced across Asia Minor along the imperial highroad, the *cursus publicus*, towards Rome. Lucian's caricature shows how 'on message' Ignatius was with the pagan background of the Hellenistic city-states in that province. Lucian describes Ignatius' function as a Christian leader as 'their sole prophet and cult-leader (θιασάρχης)', and Christianity as 'a new mystery cult (καινή τελετή)'.[54] In consequence 'they conducted him in procession as though he were a god', thus parodying Ignatius' claim as Image Bearer (θεοφόρος) to bear in his flesh the 'image of the Father', as 'an imitator of the suffering of my God'. His sarcastic description, placed in the mouth of Theagenes, is that 'his holy image will depart from men to the gods', but not yet as in him 'the divine image (ἄγαλμα) was not yet completely fashioned'.[55] Here there is an allusion to Ignatius' radical reconceptualization of church order as celebration of cult, though Ignatius would have preferred a less physical term for 'image', namely τύπος rather than ἄγαλμα.

Like Ignatius, Peregrinus 'dispatched to almost all the glorious cities letters . . . and laws', just as Ignatius did with his reconceptualization of church order that was in effect a new constitution of which he was the 'lawgiver (νομοθετής)', as when he commands the Philadelphians to obey bishop, presbyters and deacons.[56] In order to spread the new constitution, advocated with the authority of the martyr imitating the 'sufferings of my God', Lucian has heard that Ignatius himself (rather than the churches of Smyrna and Philadelphia) 'ordained (ἐχειροτόνησεν)', certain ambassadors (πρεσβευτάς) for this purpose from among his comrades, giving them their titles as 'messengers from the dead (νεκραγγέλους)' and 'underworld couriers (νερτεροδρόμους)'.[57] Thus Ignatius' description of such ambassadors as '*God's* ambassadors' by means of a specially invented term 'θεοπρεσβύται' is parodied by means of equally invented terms that reflect their message of the martyr's scapegoat sacrifice producing peace within and between communities.[58]

53. Polycarp, *Philip.*, praef.; 4.3; 5.2–3; 6.1, cf. 1 Tim. 3:7-8 and 12; 5:3-17; 19; Tit. 1:5, Phil. 1:1, cf. Brent, *Ignatius and the Second Sophistic*, pp. 24–25.
54. Lucian, *Pereg.*, 11. See also Brent, *Ignatius and the Second Sophistic*, pp. 185–212.
55. Lucian, *Pereg.*, 6.
56. Ignatius, *Philad.*, 9.1.
57. Lucian, *Pereg.*, 41, cf. Ignatius, *Philad.*, 10.1–2; *Smyrn.*, 11.2; *Pol.*, 7.2.
58. Brent, *Ignatius and the Second Sophistic*, pp. 222–29.

Though Lucian may have thus grasped the subtleties of Ignatius' message, it was to be lost on the Christian community for another 80 years. Polycarp had clearly not grasped the intricacies of Ignatius' account, paralleling ecclesial ministerial order with divine, nascent Trinitarian order that such order in a sense incarnated. Irenaeus, moreover, though acknowledging Ignatius somewhat circumspectly and anonymously as 'one of our martyrs', accepted him because he accepted Polycarp. Irenaeus needed the person of Polycarp in a previous generation in order to make his case for the antiquity of orthodox teaching. But if Polycarp is orthodox, so must his associate Ignatius also be in Irenaeus' eyes, despite any doubts that he might otherwise have had.

Irenaeus did not connect his Trinitarianism with ministerial order in the church. For him the order of the church was not to be a reflection of divine order, as the political ruler as *logos* was the mediator of cosmic order. Rather for him, unlike even Clement before him, the church was not to be regarded by analogy with civil society, with a *politeuma*, but was rather to be modelled upon an Hellenistic philosophical school. Like Justin, each congregation had a figure who was a 'president', presiding like the successors of Plato (the Academy), Aristotle (the Peripatetics), Panaetius, Poseidonius, etc. (the Stoics), or the followers of Epicurus, with the right to superintend the continuance of teaching within these schools in rightful succession (διαδοχή). It was on these grounds that Irenaeus was able to distinguish congregations of whom he approved from those of the 'heretics' (Marcion, Valentinus, Basilides, etc.) of whom he disapproved. Thus he attempted to construct succession lists showing how that the antecedents of the heretics went back in a kind of genealogical tree to Simon Magus, the opponent of the Apostles, whereas those of 'orthodox' or 'catholic' congregations went back to the apostles.[59]

Irenaeus was indebted to a predecessor, Hegesippus, fragments of whose works are preserved in Eusebius. In the relevant fragment, Hegesippus asserts that 'until the time when Primus exercised the office of Bishop, the church of the Corinthians remained steadfast in orthodox doctrine'.[60] Eusebius does not otherwise mention Primus, so that we cannot fix any date for him.

At the time when Eusebius wrote, church order in terms of single monarch bishops in every See had been firmly established, with the clear dates of their accessions to their See and the duration of their 'reigns' clearly fixed. Furthermore, notoriously, Eusebius had no concept of the development of ecclesial institutions: therefore, if there were bishops as successors to the apostles over geographical territories meeting in council and advising Christian emperors in the fourth century, so there must have been bishops as such in the first, and named succession lists for every See back to the apostles must in principle be possible.

---

59. Irenaeus, *Adv. Haer.*, I.27.4 (67–68).
60. Eusebius, *H.E.*, VI.22.2.

But Hegesippus did not here claim to have a named succession list for Corinth up until the time of Primus. Eusebius wrote with the preconception that there must have been one, and with Clement's letter to Corinth by his side. Hegesippus' fragment itself makes no mention of Clement. Eusebius knows of the letter, sees the words 'up until the time when Primus was bishop', and concludes that Hegesippus is looking at a list of names. But we have seen from our examination of Clement's text that there was no single bishop at Corinth: the presbyter-bishops that he records being deposed as successors to the apostles are a plurality.

All that Hegesippus claimed was that among the Corinthians he had 'spent a certain number of days in the course of sailing to Rome during which we were refreshed by their orthodox doctrine'. Here his claim is simply that what is taught is in accordance with a historical tradition that goes back to the apostles and not the heretics. It was only when he came to Rome that he claimed either that 'I established a succession of teaching' or that 'I established a succession list of teachers, until the time of Anicetus, whose deacon was Eleutherus, and after Anticetus, Soter was successor, after whom came Eleutherus. In each succession and in each city it is accordingly the case that the law is preached along with the prophets and the Lord.'[61] We note that in this passage Hegesippus gives no names of Roman bishops other than the three that were his contemporaries. For him the congruence of doctrine from one generation to another was what was important and not the specific names of the teachers.

Irenaeus thus took over from Hegesippus this concept of διαδοχή as the means of establishing the difference between heretical and orthodox groups. He did not claim that there was one bishop alone who could claim the teaching authority of the διαδοχός or 'successor'. When he begins his famous list of names for Rome, he refers to a plurality of successors with the words: 'those who have been appointed by apostles bishops in the churches and their successors', and whom 'they left as their successors, handing on to them their very own teaching position'.[62] But before we assume that his primary focus is necessarily upon one person over a territory circumscribed geographically, we should note that for him 'presbyters' as well as 'bishops' share in the διαδοχή:

> Again, whenever we make our appeal to the tradition from the apostles that is preserved through the successions of presbyters in the churches, they oppose the tradition, claiming that they are not only wiser than the presbyters but also than the apostles . . .[63]

61. Eusebius, *H.E.*, VI.22.3. For the discussion of the precise translation of διαδοχὴν ἐποιησάμην, see See also N. Hyldahl, 'Hegesipps Hypomnemata', *Studia Theologica*, 14 (1960), pp. 70–113, and Brent, *Hippolytus and the Roman Church in the Third Century: Communities in Tension before the Emergence of a Monarch-Bishop* (*VCSup*, 31; Leiden: E. J. Brill, 1995), pp. 448–49.
62. Irenaeus, *Adv. Haer.*, III.3.1 (4–6; 12–13).
63. Irenaeus, *Adv. Haer.*, III.2.2 (17–22).

Nevertheless what Hegesippus had suggested did not go far enough for Irenaeus' purpose.

Irenaeus not only wished to interpret διαδοχή strictly in terms of a succession of teachers within a philosophic school, although he regarded the latter as strictly true only of the heretics: the catholic succession was parallel, but not on the same level. If he could tie congruence of doctrine with an actual list of names in succession to one another, then he could make his point more strongly: he would not need to rest his case upon revered names associated with the apostles from the past like Polycarp, in contrast with opponents of the apostles like Simon Magus, claiming that the orthodox were like the former and the heretics like the latter. He could claim instead a definite inheritance of the presidency of the school of the apostles from one clear figure to another. But it was at this point that matters became confused, and was to produce a political maelstrom at Rome.

Irenaeus had no lists for any other Christian congregations at the great centres such as Corinth, Athens, Alexandria, or even Jerusalem, even though far later a Eusebius was to provide one. What he had was the correspondence of the kind of official that we have argued Clement of Rome to have been, a secretarial figure writing on behalf of and in the name of the Roman congregations of house churches to external churches, and receiving the incoming mail. If there were no such lists already, he could follow Hegesippus' list of three presbyter-bishops (who like Clement exercised this 'entrusted' ministry of secretary and letter writer), and extend this backwards to Peter and Paul.[64] He would not fail to incorporate some historical details about revered figures, like Polycarp or Clement himself.

Irenaeus makes the list in desperation, knowing that he has no means of constructing succession lists for other churches, but with the bravest of faces when he says:

> The tradition of the apostles is clear throughout the whole world, and can be examined in every church by all those who are willing to see what is true, and we are able to enumerate those who have been ordained bishops in the churches and their successors up until our time.[65]

To these, as we have already said, Irenaeus claims that the apostles left, as their 'successors', their 'teaching position'.[66] But of a single name he gives not one example. But then, nervously, he exclaims:

> Since it would take too long in such a book as this to set out the successions of all the churches, we point to both the tradition and the faith that has come down to us, through

64. Irenaeus, *Adv. Haer.*, III.1.1 (17–18); 3.3 (30–31).
65. Irenaeus, *Adv. Haer.*, III.3.1 (1–5).
66. Irenaeus, *Adv. Haer.*, III.3.1 (11–13),

the successions of the bishops proclaimed to the human race, of the greatest and most ancient church in Rome, whose foundations were laid and established by the two most glorious apostles, Peter and Paul, as is recognised by all . . .[67]

In reality the only list at his disposal, or one that he had documents from which to construct one, was the list of figures like that which we have shown Clement to have been, a secretarial figure over a loose confederation of house churches at Rome, each with its own presiding presbyter-episcopus. Justin Martyr had been such, as 'president' of his congregation 'above the baths of Myrtinus', though he appeared on no episcopal succession list.

Irenaeus, in mentioning that presbyters as well as bishops are teaching successors of the apostles, clearly does not wish to attribute sole authority to the list of secretarial figures. They are simply an example of the handing down of the διαδοχή, an infallible proof, if you will forgive the pun, of the fact of a continuity of teaching through orthodox teachers. But his strategy in defeating Gnosticism by regarding ecclesial teaching authority by analogy with the passing down of teaching within Hellenistic philosophical schools was to have unexpected consequences in the next generation. The unresolved question that it was to raise was: if teaching authority was possessed by those in a succession traced in the secretarial list, was it the sole teaching authority to which all other teachers and teaching must be subordinate? Or, alternatively, could it be said that every presbyter-bishop, over every group, organized in a loose confederation of house churches, 'shared' or 'participated' in the διαδοχή: when the presidents of the other congregations considered that one of them had ceased to do so, then they ceased communion and as a sign no longer exchanged the *fermentum* or particle of consecrated Eucharistic bread. Natalius had been one such as had probably Valentinus.[68] The issue of one sole possessor of teaching authority by a monarch-bishop, who was no longer simply the secretary of the presbytery, was to be the issue in the next generation, as we shall now see.

The principal figures in what was now to transpire, from around A.D. 217 onwards, was the Callistus who became 'pope Callistus 1st' in the kind of succession list that was now to be in process of construction, and his anonymous opponent, often confused with Hippolytus his successor, and otherwise named by various writers Josippe or Gaius. We know of the disputes between these two opponents from the account of this anonymous writer, who clearly gives his own biased account of what transpired.

In the middle of the 19th century a work was rediscovered in the Mount Athos Library, the *Refutatio Omnium Haeresium*, attributed initially to Origen, but now identified questionably as the work of a Roman controversialist, some would

---

67. Irenaeus, *Adv. Haer.*, III.2 (16–23).

68. Brent, *Hippolytus*, pp. 414–15, 420–21, 430–34 and P. Lampe, *Die stadtrömischen Christen in den ersten beiden Jahrhunderten* (WUNT, 2.18; Tübingen: Mohr Siebeck, 1989), pp. 326–27.

say Hippolytus. The author, in the tradition of Irenaeus, claims to be able to produce a genealogical tree of all heretics showing that they go back, not to Simon Magus as Irenaeus had claimed, but to Greek philosophy, which in turn came from those who worshipped the snake, the Naassenes. By the time he reaches book IX, he comes to the last and greatest of the heretics, Callistus, whom he accuses, as we shall see, of error regarding the Trinity, denying distinct persons, and espousing a form of Monarchianism in which Father, Son and Holy Spirit are but modes of each other: on Calvary the Father suffered, he said, not as the Son, but, equally reprehensibly, in the Son.[69] Before, however, we examine Callistus' version of the Christian cosmos and the implications for ecclesial order to be drawn from them, let us examine how the conflict proceeded in terms of the organization of the Roman community that this document in fact implies.

This conflict has been interpreted grossly anachronistically in the light of the kind of church order that was to emerge with Cyprian and subsequently in the time of Eusebius and Constantine. Neither Hippolytus nor his anonymous predecessor appear on the later succession lists, but only Callistus, in succession to Victor and Zephyrinus. In consequence it has been concluded that the writer of the *Refutatio*, whether Hippolytus or his predecessor, reveals himself to be the first anti-pope, setting himself up against the rightful and canonical bishop of Rome.

But let us reflect on what that would imply, and whether this text actually supports drawing such an implication. If the author of the *Refutatio* had been an antipope in the later sense, it would imply that he had arisen within a single community and challenged the orthodoxy of the presiding bishop. Charges would be laid on both sides, and having lost his case, he and his supporters would set up a rival church claiming to be the only true church, and finding at least three bishops to consecrate him in his rival's place. A council of bishops from other dioceses, at least throughout Italy or even beyond, would have been summoned, and the issue over who was the rightful bishop discussed and resolved. If one side did not accept the verdict, then they and their supporting bishops would have founded, like Novatian was to do a generation later, a rival church consisting of a network of dioceses in communion with each other, but having broken off communion with their rivals.

Such a process has left not a single trace upon surviving records, and here the silence of Eusebius is truly deafening. Eusebius, who believes that the later, Cyprianic view of church order that existed in his fourth century had existed since the time of the apostles, certainly reinterpreted the events at Rome in which Victor excommunicated from his own group an Eastern (Quartodeciman) congregation celebrating Easter at a different date than that on the Western calendar. For Eusebius this meant that it had been Eastern dioceses in Asia

---

69. Brent, *Hippolytus*, pp. 427–29.

Minor across the Adriatic, and not within Rome itself, as if Victor had been able to act like Stephen began to act in A.D. 257 on the issue of rebaptizing heretics, or indeed like fourth-century popes acted. But Eusebius not even tries to impose upon his narrative a 'schism' in this later sense: rather he ignores the conflict with Callistus entirely.

Let us begin with the actual words of the anonymous author's summary of how he stands in terms of ecclesial authority with Callistus:

> The wizard behaved so rashly and founded a school, having thus taught against the Catholic Church; and he was the first to plan to allow people to yield to their pleasures, claiming that they could all have their sins forgiven by him. For he who gathered with a different person (συναγόμενος) and was called a Christian, if he sinned, asserted Callistus, the sin would not be reckoned to him if he would flee to the school of Callistus. This rule pleased many, whose conscience had become hardened and, at the same time, many who became excommunicated under the influence of many heresies, and some who had been expelled from the church by us at an examination, attached themselves to him and swelled into his school . . . and in their vanity they attempted to call themselves the Catholic Church.[70]

These words imply, not the deposition of a bishop by an episcopal council of his peers and his replacement, with his followers exhorted to communicate only with that successor, but two existing groups among several within the city of Rome that acknowledge the Christianity of each other. Callistus is presbyter-bishop of one group and the author the presbyter-bishop of another. It is quite clear that it is possible to gather with a different group as a church (συναγόμενος) and nevertheless still be 'called a Christian'. That there were more than two communities within Rome under their own presbyter-bishops was not the problem, nor did this of itself raise the spectre of what later would be called 'schism'. This was not clearly what the dispute was about.

What was at issue here was that Callistus as presbyter-bishop of one group was prepared to absolve mortal sins of those excommunicated by other groups: 'some' were expelled directly by the author from his group after examination so that Callistus was expanding his group by a deliberate policy of leniency. But in doing so he was threatening the bonds of intercommunion between the loose confederation of Roman congregations, and the exchange of the *fermentum* as the sign of their being part of the one Church.

When, therefore, the anonymous writer claims that Callistus 'found a school having taught against the catholic church', he is not referring to a single congregation breaking up, with one group leaving and setting up in premises elsewhere. Simply by changing the doctrine he has ceased to be part of the διαδοχή of the apostles, and has refounded his group as a degenerate school

---

70. Hippolytus (Pseudo), *Ref.*, IX.12.20–21 and 25.

of Hellenistic, pagan philosophy. There was inevitably Trinitarian doctrine involved as well as practice, as we shall shortly see.

The further charges that the anonymous author makes against Callistus shows that there was a plurality of presbyter-bishops over a plurality of congregations at Rome at this time. He refers to bishops, presbyters, deacons married twice or three times without being deposed. Once again these words have been read anachronistically as if Callistus was monarch bishop of Rome allowing universal laxity in clerical discipline, through an acknowledged jurisdiction over all dioceses throughout the Roman Empire. But this situation clearly did not prevail at this time. What the anonymous author is protesting about is that once one of the congregations relaxed the pseudo Pauline, apostolic tradition that clerics were allowed one wife, and if widowed could not remarry, then it was impossible to hold the line with the rest of such congregations unless communion be broken off on grounds of failure to maintain the διαδοχή.

It is reasonable to suppose that Callistus owed his place on the succession list as Zephyrinus and Victor before him not because he was a single monarch bishop over every congregation at Rome, but because, like Victor and Zephyrinus before him, they had appeared as continuations of Irenaeus' list of secretarial figures like Clement had been. It was Victor who had granted Callistus a pension after, according to the anonymous writer, a very questionable career as the slave of a banker named Carpophorus, leading to his imprisonment in the salt mines of Sardinia only to be questionably included on a role of Christian martyrs released under an amnesty of Commodus' mistress, Marcia. Victor is simply described by the anonymous author as one who was a 'bishop of the church at this time'[71] in a Rome that, as we have argued, had a plurality of presbyter-bishops.

Yet according to Eusebius, as we have seen, Victor did see Irenaeus' use of a succession list to make concrete the existence of the διαδοχή of the apostles at Rome as capable of implying that it was the figures on the secretarial list who were in fact the sole guarantors of that διαδοχή. He, after all, sought the excommunication of the Quartodeciman congregation from the loose Roman confederation by not exchanging the *fermentum* with them himself, and no doubt encouraging other presbyter-bishops to do the same. Thus he behaved in an unprecedented fashion towards them, and earned Irenaeus' rebuke for such an interpretation of his succession list:

> Never before were people excommunicated for this cause, but the presbyters before you who did not observe the practice used to send the Eucharist to those from other dioceses (or 'local congregations').[72]

---

71. Hippolytus (Pseudo), *Ref.*, IX.2.10.
72. Irenaeus, apud Eusebius, *H.E.*, V.24.15.

We glimpse here the process by which Victor established their exclusion and it was not simply by a universal decree which all other bishops and clergy were obliged to follow.

We know that his successors, Zephyrinus and Callistus, faced charges from presumably the council of presbyters of all congregations in intercommunion at a formal meeting, and were simply prepared to brazen things out. Callistus, for example, after the death of Zephyrinus, had sought 'to subvert the charge against him before the church'.[73] If we are correct that Victor, Zephyrinus and Callistus, on Irenaeus' succession list, held the same secretarial office as Clement, one of the earliest on that list, we are witnessing a clear push on behalf of those entrusted with writing and receiving the correspondence to assume greater authority. But such an authority was disputed by the anonymous writer. Callistus was persuading Zephyrinus to 'continually to stir up acts of civil disorder in the midst of the brotherhood'.[74]

Clearly Callistus was desiring and claiming to be more than the secretarial figure that Clement had been. The *Elenchos* describes him as 'yearning after the throne of episcopal oversight'.[75] But its author neither acknowledges that Callistus had achieved this, nor that he himself rightfully possessed it instead: he simply records that

> He, after Zephyrinus' decease, thinking that he had achieved what he desired, excluded Sabellius for his unorthodox opinions because he had come to fear me, and thinking thus he would be able to subvert the charge against him before the church on the grounds that his opinion was not alien.[76]

The anonymous author does not therefore claim that the 'throne of episcopal oversight' is his own, but rather that it existed purely as a twinkle in Callistus' eye: he was only 'thinking that he had achieved what he had desired'.

We have here then a Callistus who is claiming sole authority as successor or διαδοχός to interpret the teaching of the apostles: his place on Irenaeus' succession list is not just as one such example of a congregation preserving traditional teaching. He is being opposed by the author on the grounds that Callistus feared him, and as a political move before the presbyterial committee of the Roman congregations had excluded Sabellius, who was simply a more extreme proponent of heretical doctrines that Callistus' himself had held. The *Elenchos* resolves Irenaeus ambiguity firmly on one side, and Callistus on another, as to whether the secretary who writes in the name of the whole church is the sole διαδοχός, or whether he shares in the διαδοχή held by others,

73. Hippolytus (Pseudo), *Ref.*, IX.12.15.
74. Hippolytus (Pseudo), *Ref.*, IX.11.1.
75. Hippolytus (Pseudo), *Ref.*, IX.11.1.
76. Hippolytus (Pseudo), *Ref.* IX.12.15.

by presbyters as well as bishops or by presbyter-bishops. As the anonymous
author says:

> These doctrines no different person will refute other than the Holy Spirit, handed down
> in the church, which previously the apostles received and handed over to orthodox
> believers. We happen to be their successors, and share in the same grace as well as
> high priesthood (ἀρχιερετεία) and teaching office, and since we are also reckoned
> as guardians of the church, we do not allow our eye to dose nor do we keep silent
> regarding the true discourse . . .[77]

The office is a shared teaching office. As Irenaeus had previously said, those
whom he calls presbyters as well as bishops are in the succession of the apostles. The anonymous writer thus represents the protest of the presbyter-bishops
of other congregations at the assumption of sole teaching authority by Callistus
over all other congregations: he is not claiming that sole authority for himself.

We have already seen how Callistus proposed to increase the numbers of his
congregation, and at the expense of the others, by deliberately relaxing by a
policy of leniency the traditional boundaries, the 'ancient canons', determining
church life and practice regarding clerical remarriage and mortal sin after
baptism. The political gamble that was to pay off was that the consequence of
breaking off communion would be too awful to contemplate so that the other
congregations would simply fall in line, and recognize both the new doctrine,
and he who claimed the sole right to define what it was. It is a situation not
unlike that in the episcopally governed, Anglican communion as of this day.
One large, Western group claims that it is an imperative both of their individual
consciences, and indeed of the gospel, that women should be ordained and
same sex unions be consecrated. The effects on the bond of intercommunion,
and indeed the integrity and self identity of the communion as a whole, are
disregarded. What one side claims as the imperative of conscience is seen by
the other as in fact a cynical power play: the bond of intercommunion is forcing
them to assent to that which they do not wish to assent. Yet the alternative of
breaking off communion is too awful to contemplate.

We find a strikingly similar situation in what the *Elenchos* further tells us
about the relations between Callistus and its anonymous author. Before he succeeded Zephyrinus to whatever office it was that they both had had, both had
cultivated a group led by one Kleomenes, whom, he claims, was a disciple of
Noetus of Smyrna who denied that there were persons in the Trinity. Like
Callistus his successor, 'Zephyrinus thought that he was managing the Church'.

> Zephyrinus was persuaded by the pecuniary incentive offered him, and communicated
> with those joining Kleomenes as his disciples, and he himself, being in course of time
> dragged down, he was moved in the same direction since he had Callistus as counsellor

---

77. Hippolytus (Pseudo), *Ref.*, I, praef., 6.6.

and fellow protagonist in these evils . . . The school of these men continued to be adopted and to increase due to the assistance of Zephyrinus and Callistus, even though we never communicated with them, but we often opposed them and refuted them, compelling them reluctantly to confess the truth. They for a time showed shame, and drawn to conclusions by the truth, confessed it, but not long afterwards they were rolling themselves again in the same mire.[78]

The situation here clearly is not one in which the anonymous author has got himself set up by sympathetic bishops outside Rome so as to create a parallel church. The author does not claim here that he and his group broke off communion with Zephyrinus and Callistus. Rather the charge is that the latter agreed to accept those under the presidency of Kleomenes as those who 'gathered with a different person (συναγόμενος)', but nevertheless could be called Christians.[79] But the anonymous author denied that they should be in communion with them and exchange the *fermentum*. He then endeavoured to publicly examine them, and sometimes they vacillated so as to avoid any final breakdown in the intercommunion that they had established. Zephyrinus and Callistus behaved in this fashion too, sometimes agreeing with the author and then reneging, in a tortuous series of events aimed at craftily getting their way and increasing their authority.[80]

Thus the writer of the *Elenchos* has exposed for us the situation of the Roman Christian community around A.D. 217. It was a community in tension in which one group, by a policy of leniency in granting absolution for mortal sins, was seeking to swell its numbers and increase the authority of its leader above those of the presbyter-bishops of other groups. A revolution in church order was in process, though not yet complete. A figure like Clement had had a secretarial role in representing the presbyter-bishops as a whole in letters to external churches, and receiving the incoming mail. But Irenaeus had needed to use a list with Clement's name, and those of his successors and predecessors (if he had not indeed composed this himself), in order to exemplify graphically the coherence of Christian doctrine that had come down from the past, on the model of the succession of teachers in a philosophical school. But Victor had behaved towards the Quartodecimans, and Callistus apparently claimed the right to so behave, as the only διάδοχός with the right to pronounce on doctrine and practice.

But the model of a philosophical school was to prove not sufficiently absolutist as the model by which the Christian Roman community was to be governed for those who were now emerging and continuing Irenaeus' succession list, not as exemplifying the shared διαδοχή with any presbyter-bishop, but to those alone on the originally secretarial list. A monarchical model would be far

78. Hippolytus (Pseudo), *Ref.*, IX.7.1–3.
79. See above, footnote 70 and associated text.
80. Hippolytus (Pseudo), *Ref.* IX.11.1–2.

more satisfactory in legitimating such absolutist ends. And in this respect the development of the theology of the Trinity and of the church order of Callistus and his group was to be assisted by parallel developments in the pagan theology legitimating pagan imperial order.

3. *Callistus and the Rise of Pagan Monotheism in the Period of the Severan Dynasty*

Some 5 years before the putative date of the controversy between Callistus and the author of the *Elenchos*, the Severan emperor Caracalla had produced the legislation known as the *Constitutio Antoniana* (A.D. 212). Here was found embodied the Severan imperial policy of uniting all nations and cultures into one empire, with one common purpose. Consequently, with some minor exceptions, he granted citizenship to all freemen throughout the Roman Empire. The historian Cassius Dio regarded his actions somewhat cynically as an attempt to raise taxation revenue.[81] But we have a surviving papyrus fragment of this Edict that makes quite clear Caracalla's motive: in thanksgiving 'to the immortal gods' he granted citizenship so that all nations and cultures will supplicate to them for imperial peace after a recent disaster.[82] His aim was for a universal pagan religious consensus.

Elagabalus, as his successor, was to continue such a policy, but by more radical means. He sought to set up a universal, pagan monotheism based upon the sacred black stone of his native city, Emesa in Syria, where he was priest of Elagab. From the time of Hadrian this eastern divinity had been associated with the cult of *Sol* or the sun god, and the title *Sol Invictus Deus* ('the Unconquered Sun God'), but Hadrian had deliberately abstained from associating himself and his consort with this deity, in the way in which he had clearly done in the case of Sarapis, Isis and Cybele.[83] But Septimius Severus, and Julia Domna his wife, are represented (in A.D. 203) as Sarapis and Isis on the arch of Leptis Magna in North Africa. But in the coinage Septimius is equated with Sarapis only in so far as the latter is himself associated with the Unconquered Sun (*Sol Invictus*).[84]

Geta, Caracalla's murdered brother, is associated with Sol Invictus, both in words inscribed on coins, and in his image wearing the sun's crown.[85] We have here a development in which the cult of the sun god is absorbing other deities

81. Dio Cassius, LXXVIII.9.5–6.

82. *P. Giss.*, 40, I.3–7 reproduced in P. A. Kuhlmann, *Die Giessener literarischen Papyri und die Caracalla-Erlasse-Edition, Übersetzung und Kommentar* (Berichte und Arbeiten aus der Universitätsbibliothek und dem Universitätsarchiv Giessen, 46; Giessen: Universitätsbibliothek, 1994).

83. G. Halsberghe, *The Cult of Sol Invictus*, (EPRO; Leiden: Brill, 1972), pp. 45–49.

84. Brent, *Imperial Cult*, pp. 267–69.

85. Brent, *Imperial Cult*, pp. 292–93.

such as Serapis, Isis, Zeus, etc. who are ceasing to be separate deities, but have come to be regarded as images of the one God, the Sun, as source of life and well-being. The one God is furthermore being associated with the divinity of the Roman Empire: once again political order is reflecting cosmic order, and the development of the one affects the development of the other. But it was Elagabalus who was to make the attempt to organize a specific universal cult.

Following Caracalla's murder in a plot instigated by Macrinus (8th April 217), the latter had seized power. However, he had failed to hold on to that power due to his unpopularity with the legions. These accordingly turned to Elagabalus, who claimed to be the illegitimate son of Caracalla by Julia Maesa, who had been exiled by Macrinus to return to her native Emesa. He had been dedicated to the sun god, Elagab, who was worshipped, not in any human or animal representation, but in the form of a huge black stone, 'rounded at the base and coming to a point on the top, conical in shape' with 'some small projecting pieces and markings . . . which . . . are a rough picture of the sun'.[86]

Following his accession, Elagabalus transported the black stone to Rome, where a temple was built to house it on the Palatine alongside the imperial residence. Juppiter was to be replaced by Elagab as head of the Roman pantheon. Public ceremonies took place in honour of Elagab, now *Sol Invictus*, in one of which, in midsummer A.D. 219, the black stone itself was conveyed to a new temple on the outskirts of the city in a chariot led by Elagabalus himself. Minerva was associated with Elagab as his consort, now identified with the Punic earth goddess Tanit.[87]

As we have seen in connection with the pagan background to Ignatius, the priest of the divinity, bearing or wearing his image of the god, becomes identified in word and act with the god of whom he is the sacred representative. The sacred marriage of sun and moon, of Elagab with Minerva-Tanit, was now given sacramental form in a sacred marriage between Elagabalus, who had divorced his wife for the occasion, and the Vestal Virgin Aquilia Severa. Public and private festivities were to be held to celebrate this ceremony (A.D. 220).[88]

Elagabalus has been subjected by Roman historians to a great deal of vilification for his Syrian style of dress, and for various sexual practices. Whatever the truth in these reports, they must not allow us to conceal his true intentions. He gave as his reason for the 'sacred marriage':

> I did this to make godlike children to be begotten from my office as high priest, and from this same woman's office as high priestess.[89]

---

86. Dio Cassius, LXXIX.31.1; Herodian, V.3.5.
87. Cassius Dio, LXXX.12.3; Herodian, V.6.2.
88. Herodian, V.6.3–6.
89. Dio Cassius, LXXX.9.3. See the discussion of these passages in connection with Severan universalism, Brent, *Imperial Cult*, pp. 227–28; 255–71; pp. 311–13.

He saw from their union, the sacral representation of the union of Elagab and Minerva-Tanit, the emergence of a universal monotheism, in which the sun's light expressed the divine essence of the one god flowing into all lesser divinities, and making them but expressions, aspects or modalities of his own. Thus there would be one political, imperial order that would embrace and subject to itself all other peoples, cultures and religions within its syncretistic embrace. Thus this imperial order would reflect a reordered cosmic order. His mistake was no doubt to have been to emphasize too blatantly oriental practices and rituals associated with his sun god. But that such a pagan universalism was increasingly developing as the means of legitimating imperial unity was to be made clear by its far more successful implementation in the later reign of Aurelian (A.D. 270–275).

We may ask what effects such an abortive revolution may have had upon Christian communities throughout the empire at this time. We have the famous Avercius inscription, whose author, Dieterich believed, had been a spectator at the ceremony of midsummer A.D. 219 at which the sacred marriage had taken place.

> . . . a disciple of the Chaste Shepherd
> who grazes his flocks on hills and in plains
> who has great eyes which look everywhere
> For he taught me faithful writings
> and sent me to Rome to gaze upon a kingdom
> and to see the Queen with golden robes and golden sandals
> and I saw there the stone marked by the shining seal
> . . . I had in all places brothers
> since I had Paul as my companion
> And Faith preceded me everywhere,
> and provided as nourishment everywhere the fish from the Fountain
> a great pure fish which the Holy Virgin caught,
> and this she gave to her friends to eat continually
> and she had excellent wine which she gave mixed with bread . . .
> Let the whole company who grasps these words pray on Avercius' behalf . . .[90]

Although Avercius is regarded as a bishop of Hierapolis in Egypt in later centuries, debate continues as to whether this epigraph is Christian at all. The mention of 'Paul' and 'Faith' seem to clinch the argument so that the reference to 'the Shepherd' is to Christ as the 'Good Shepherd', so that the 'Holy Virgin' or 'the Queen' refers either to the Blessed Virgin Mary or to the Church personified, the 'fountain' to baptism, the 'wine . . . mixed with bread' to the Eucharist.

---

90. A. Dieterich, *Die Grabschrift des Aberkios* (Leipzig: Teubner, 1896), pp. 28–34, cf. M. Guarducci, *Epigrafia Greca* IV: *Epigrafi sacre pagane e cristiane* (Rome: Istituto poligrafico dello stato, 1978), pp. 380–81.

Moreover, the received version of the text refers, not to 'the stone (λαᾶς)' but to 'the people (λαός) marked by the shining seal', which would have been a further reference to baptism, though I have produced here Dieterich's amendment and Elagabalan interpretation. But granted that the epitaph was Christian, it clearly reflects a popular Christianity that felt at home in accommodation with the surrounding, pagan religious culture, and a desire to assimilate its vibrant and expressive imagery. The form of the monumental grave thus inscribed is of a pagan altar (βωμός), with curses pronounced on whoever dares to violate the body buried there.[91]

Furthermore, Avercius refers to a member of a Christian church (ἐκκλησία) by such expressions as 'he who grasps (ὁ νοῶν) these (mysterious) words' and 'the whole company (πᾶς ὁ συνῳδός)' that would be more usual in application to a pagan, cult association. Christ as the Good Shepherd here is associated with an image of a god like Attis, with 'eyes gazing in all directions', as in a mystery hymn to Attis recorded by the author of the *Refutatio*.[92] Avercius might be thinking of the Church or the Blessed Virgin Mary but 'the Queen with golden robes and golden sandals' shows a high degree of assimilation in his mind with Isis: his experience reads not unlike that of Apuleius when he reaches the final stage of initiation into the Isis mysteries.[93] But the context is that of the movement towards a universal monotheism based upon a universal syncretism that very much reflected the mood of Elagabalus' attempted revolution.

While such an abortive revolution was taking place within the wider, pagan world, we have seen a revolution attempted in Rome itself within the Christian community. The political turmoil witnessed at Rome within the pagan community we might see paralleled within the Christian community. It was Callistus, like Elagabalus, who 'stirred up endless uprising among the people' on account of his teaching on the Trinity.[94]

Elagabalus had perished, at the hands of the Praetorian guard, on the orders of Julia Mamaea and Severus Alexander, her son. According to Cassius Dio his body was thrown into the Tiber after he had made an unsuccessful attempt previously to escape in a chest.[95] According to Herodian, after Soaemias and her son were mutilated, 'he was thrown into the sewers that run down into the river Tiber'.[96] According to a later source, Elagabalus' body was mutilated and dragged around the circus, and through the streets with the intention of throwing it into Rome's sewer, the Cloaca Maxima. But that failing, a weight was attached and the body thrown into the Tiber.[97]

91. Lines 20–22.
92. Lines 3–5, cf. Hippolytus (Pseudo), *Ref.*, V.9.60.
93. Lines 7–8, cf. Apuleius, *Metam.*, 11. 3–4.
94. Hippolytus (Pseudo), *Ref.*, IX.11.3.
95. Dio Cassius, LXXX.20.2.
96. Herodian, V.8.9.
97. SHA, *Elagab.*, 17.1–3.

We have a late account of Callistus' martyrdom, the details of which are thus historically unreliable. It is nevertheless interesting how Callistus is considered to have been martyred in a riot, in which he was 'thrown through the window of a house and, with a stone tied to his neck, submerged in a well and rubbish piled upon him'.[98] But though the details may be unreliable, the parallel development of a legend shows an association in the popular imagination between the two historical characters: the end of Callistus is assimilated to the end of Elagabalus because their roles within their respective communities had left the impression of being so similar.

Callistus caught the mood of contemporary pagan political events moving towards centralization on the basis of a centralized organization of the pagan cosmos. Political unity was to reflect cosmic unity. Thus his model of political power was to go beyond the authority of the teaching successor in a Hellenistic philosophical school to that of a political monarchy. On this basis, like Elagabalus, the office of high-priest was important to him as the monarch's right to define the religiously based rules of the community's life, even though Callistus did not claim this title himself. However, his behaviour was to suggest that this was the kind of figure that he appeared to Tertullian, following Callistus' move to aggrandize his own community at the expense of others in the loose confederation of house churches.

The reference of Tertullian's words to Callistus has been much discussed, but I remain of the opinion that the former had the latter in mind when he said:

> I hear that there has been published an edict, and that a final edict. The Pontifex (mark you!) Maximus that is the bishop of bishops, ordains: 'I absolve both the sins of adultery and fornication when penance has been performed'. O edict to which there cannot be a note added: 'A good well done!' And where is that generosity published? In the same place, I conjecture, [as] on at the entrances of [houses of] lust, under the very arch that bears the title of those houses. Forgiveness ought to have been declared where the offence was committed. There you shall read of your pardon where you enter in customary expectation of it. But this edict is read in the church, and in the church it is proclaimed, and she is a virgin.[99]

Note that the unnamed bishop is described as *Pontifex Maximus* in this passage, which, though it was to become a later Papal title, referred to a pagan high priest and not to a Christian bishop. Furthermore, following Augustus, this office was held by Roman emperors as head of the state cult and was particularly used by Elagabalus, as the coinage makes clear.[100] The title was particularly pertinent in Elagabalus' case since he held the hereditary high

98. *Acta Callisti*, 8, in Migne, *P.L.*, 10, col. 120.
99. Tertullian, *Pudic.*, 1.6–8 (26–37). For a full discussion and bibliography, see Brent, *Imperial Cult*, pp. 319–22, and Brent, *Hippolytus*, pp. 504–35.
100. Brent, *Imperial Cult*, pp. 320–21.

priesthood of the sun god of Emesa. As we have mentioned, he saw a new, universal cult that he established being administered from the divine progeny of priests that issued from their sacred marriage.

We see that the image of *Pontifex Maximus* applied sarcastically to the bishop in this passage is also associated with a figure that, like a Roman emperor, pronounces an Edict that destroys the customary disciplinary organization of the empire over which he rules. Such an image was not unlike that projected, however maliciously, of Elagabalus in Cassio Dio, Herodian, and the *Scriptores Historiae Augustae*. These writers had perhaps gone overboard in their descriptions of Elagabalus' self-mutilation, his cross dressing, his desire for sex change operations, and his practice of child sacrifice at his rites.

Tertullian shares the puritanism of the author of the *Refutatio*, who accused Callistus of supporting both fornication and child murder in his practice of allowing the unions of patrician Roman ladies with their freed slaves, and the subsequent abortion producing drugs that they were using as a result of pregnancies from these unions. Such a union involved a capital offence under Roman law for the lady in question for degrading her rank.[101] It was not surprising therefore that they might have sought such desperate remedies. But the total impression created by the anonymous writer is one of gratuitous self-indulgence, though not quite to the extremes of pagan historiography in connection with Elagabalus:

> For he even allowed women, if they should be without husbands and they burned due to their youthful age for a man, they [being] of noble rank, if they were unwilling to degrade their rank in a legal marriage to take someone whom they should choose as a bed partner, whether household slave or free, to treat this person as in place of a husband even though she was not married by law. In consequence women who were so called believers began to try even to bind themselves round with medicines against conception in order to abort what they had conceived because they were unwilling either to have a child from a slave or from one of lower class, because of their noble and superior birth. You see to what enormous impiety the lawless fellow has descended, teaching at the same time adultery and murder.[102]

Callistus, if not a pope in the later sense, was nevertheless hardly in favour of abortion. The anonymous writer does not here accuse him of this directly, but of rather creating the general, lax moral environment in which such developments took place. Such was the consequence of allowing 'people to yield to their pleasures', by freely absolving those excommunicated by other

101. K. von Preysing, 'Der Leserkreis der Philosophoumena Hippolyts', in *ZKT*, 38 (1914), pp. 421–45 (425–29) who gives an illuminating reconstruction of the social class of the circle of the author of *El.* based upon the patrician sympathies of his criticism of 'adultery' and 'murder'. See also Justinian (Modestinus), *Dig.*, 1.9.8; 23.2.42. See also Brent, *Hippolytus*, pp. 428–29.

102. Hippolytus (Pseudo), *Ref.* IX.12.24–25.

presbyter-bishops in their congregations, and thus aggrandizing his own. A reorganization of the Roman church into a monarchical hierarchy was in process that suggested parallels with that of Elagabalus.[103] Callistus may not have married a Vestal Virgin contrary to Roman law as had Elagabalus, but he certainly had contravened pagan, matrimonial law. Furthermore, in allowing clergy, who might also include himself, to be married more than once, he was being equally sexually indulgent!

Callistus had not literally issued an Edict, formally in writing, like a later pope, to be nailed upon the archways at the entrances of other house-churches in the Roman confederation. Tertullian has engaged in rhetoric. But the rhetoric of declamation only works in a context in which readers or hearers are aware of features of the actual person and his situation that give the rhetorical hyperbole point. Callistus appeared, like Elagabalus, to be reforming the Christian cult as an emperor issuing an Edict and acting as Pontifex Maximus.

Callistus appeared to be claiming to be, as in fact he was, not simply one presbyter-bishop among others, with the duty of secretary of the Roman presbytery writing in their name, as Clement had, to external churches. Rather he was now 'bishop of bishops (*episcopus episcoporum*)', and creating virtually an episcopal monarchy. It should be remembered that it was not only Tertullian who made reference to the 'high priesthood', but also the anonymous writer of the *Refutatio*. As we have seen, he was to protest that, of the apostles:

> We happen to be their successors, and share in the same grace as well as high priesthood and teaching office, and . . . we are also reckoned as guardians of the church.[104]

For the anonymous writer there was not simply a 'succession (διαδοχή)' in which he and his fellow presbyter-bishops were to 'share', but also a 'high priesthood (ἀρχιερετεία)'. He had clearly understood the implications of what Callistus was doing as an implicit claim to both, and he was firmly resisting such a claim.

Callistus had initiated a revolution whose model was not that of a philosophical school, but of a monarchy subjecting all independent congregations within an imperial whole. We may furthermore see indications of that plan and its fulfilment a generation later in the archaeology of the catacomb of Callistus that occurred under Fabian's developments. We can also see the beginnings of the concept of an episcopal monarchy in features of the evolution of the succession list of the Roman community now recording the succession of the sole bishop, and not of a succession of secretarial figures, as a political monarch and not as the president of a philosophical school.

Before his appointment to the deaconate, and subsequent succession to Zephyrinus' particular seat, Callistus had suffered what for the *Elenchos* was a

---

103. Hippolytus (Pseudo), *Ref.*, IX, 12.20–21 and 25.
104. Hippolytus (Pseudo), *Ref.*, I *praef.*, 6.6.

quite spurious martyrdom. As a freed slave Callistus had served a Christian banker named Carpophorus, whose clients he had swindled, and staged a riot in a Jewish synagogue, subsequent to which he had attempted suicide. He had been arrested and tried by Fuscianus, and sent to the salt mines of Sardinia. But while there, when Marcia, mistress of the emperor Commodus provided the presbyter Hyacinthus with a letter for an amnesty for Christian martyrs, Callistus managed to get himself included on the list.[105]

Zephyrinus recalled Callistus to Rome only after Victor's death:

> After his death, Zephyrinus, wishing to have him as his co-operator by ordination to the clergy, he honoured him to his own harm, and to this end he brought him from Antheium to the cemetery and placed him in charge of it.[106]

Lampe has established that these words cannot mean that Callistus was in charge of the sole Christian cemetery in Rome: there were a variety of sites in different areas of the city, and in his time it was in no way the central site. Such sites also along the Via Appia Antica would be that of Ss Peter and Paul, Ad Catacombas, renamed in the course of the fourth century in commemoration of an obscure martyr in Diocletian's reign, St Sebastian. Another appears to have been the catacomb of Domitilla, with the latter in the vicinity of that bearing Callistus' name, but never joined with it into a single cemetery. We might also mention the Priscilla catacomb on the opposite side of the city to those on the Via Appia Antica. But most significantly there was the Lucina region of the Callistus Catacomb, separate from it as a distinct cemeterial complex before the insertion of the connecting route for pilgrims during the middle ages.

Furthermore, to clinch matters, Callistus was not buried in the catacomb that now bears his name. The *Liber Pontificalis* is the ancient record formed from Irenaeus' episcopal list and its continuation in the early middle ages and embellished with other information from a variety of sources. Here we have the record, confirmed by archaeological excavation, of the interment of the remains of Callistus in the cemetery of Calepodius on the Via Aurelia. The character of the cemetery of which Callistus had charge was not therefore that of the property of the whole Roman Church at this time.

Indeed, the discussion remains open as to the manner in which the Roman community, or any individual congregation within it, could have held property at this time as a corporation given that the Church was an illegal institution. Lampe's solution, with which I agree, is that Zephyrinus, being a wealthy man though not necessarily the greedy money grabber described by the *Elenchos*, was the private owner of the land. He constructed an aboveground cemetery for himself, but went underground to provide for the burial of members of his Christian community, some of who would be moderately poor. These were

105.   Hippolytus (Pseudo), *Ref.*, IX.12.11–13.
106.   Hippolytus (Pseudo), *Ref.*, IX.12.14.

responsible for the first Christian art to be found in the so-called 'cubicula of the sacraments'.[107] As far as Zephyrinus was concerned, internally the administration was by a deacon such as presumably Callistus was, and his successor as bishop, but as far as the external pagan authorities were concerned, they were simply personal heirs to his will and fortune.

After that of Zephyrinus comes the name of Callistus, after him that of Urban, after Urban, that of Pontian (A.D. 231–235), Anteros (A.D. 235–236), and then Fabian (A.D. 236–250). The *Liber Pontificalis* attributes to Fabian extensive building works throughout the cemeteries, and archaeological excavations have traced a new development in the catacomb of Callistus from around this time. At the entrance to the corridor off which the original graves and their iconography are found, the so-called 'cubicula of the sacraments' named after the frescoes that adorned the plastered over spaces (*loculi*) cut to contain bodies, a large cubiculum was constructed. Here the epitaphs whose remains have been discovered reveal it to have been the tomb of the first papal mausoleum.

But Callistus, as we have said, was not buried there nor was Urban, interred nearby in the cemetery of Praetextatus. Anteros becomes the first pope to be buried there in A.D. 236, by Fabian, clearly. Fabian additionally now brings back the remains of Pontian from Sardinia where he has been martyred along with Hippolytus, who has been identified with the anonymous author of the *Elenchos*, but whom I have identified with his successor in the Hippolytan school.[108] We have, in the document that Irenaeus' succession list was to grow into, the Chronographer of A.D. 354, a biographical addition to Pontian's entry which reads:

> Pontian [reigned as] bishop five years two months and seven days. It was during the time of [Emperor Severus] Alexander, from the time when Pompeian and Pelignian were consuls. At that time bishop Pontian and presbyter Hippolytus were deported as exiles to Sardinia, an unhealthy island, when Severus and Quintianus were consuls. On the same island he died on 25th September and in his place Anteros was ordained on 18th November.[109]

Whether Callistus' original opponent or his successor, we note that only one of them has the title 'bishop' and the other 'presbyter' according to the Chronographer who represents the time when there was only one, monarch bishop in Rome.

107. P. C. Finney, *The Invisible God: The Earliest Christians on Art* (Oxford: University Press, 1994), pp. 154–57.

108. Brent, *Hippolytus*, pp. 525–35, 377–79.

109. 'Chronographer of 354', in T. Mommsen, *Chronica Minora, Saec. IV. V. VI. VII*, (Monumenta Germaniae Historica IX; Berlin: Weidmann, 1892), vol. 1.13, pp. 73–76.

The Chronographer of 354 has however included another document in his text, namely a *Depositio* briefly setting out, in a tabular form, where the remains of the martyrs are laid to rest. Among these there are only three popes, namely:

> viii Idus Aug. Xysti in Calisti
> Idus Aug. Ypoliti in Tiburtina et Pontiani in Calisti
> Pri. Idus Octob. Calisti in via Aurelia, miliario iii.

But with Pontian, on the 13th September, a single presbyter is commemorated, on the same date, and indeed the date of the pagan festival of Diana that commemorated the entry of the Italian allied states into the Roman Empire.

Was Hippolytus the only presbyter to be martyred at this time? If he was not, then he must have been a very special presbyter to have been singled out and commemorated with the bishop of his community. If he was, then he was one of the leaders of the Roman church, since it was in the persecution of Maximus that Eusebius informs us was directed only against 'leaders of the church'.[110] Cornelius, writing about Novatian later in A.D. 254, was to speak of the latter's ignorance that

> . . . there should be one bishop in a catholic church; yet he was not ignorant (for how could he be?) that in it there were forty-six presbyters, seven deacons, seven sub-deacons and over fifteen hundred widows and persons in distress . . .[111]

It is a plausible conjecture that presbyter Hippolytus and his group are here acknowledged as being reconciled to that of his opponent's, with the acknowledgement of Pontian as the one bishop of Rome. Cornelius had clearly learned from Cyprian the theology of the new ecclesial order that he was to further develop, which may not have been understood or accepted by Novatian as secretary to the Roman presbytery.

Certainly the dignity awarded to Pontian by Fabian was a new dignity, for both he and his successor were to be the first bishops of the Roman community listed on the secretarial list to be buried in a cubiculum in the catacomb of Callistus exclusively reserved for popes. There Fabian himself, no doubt at his own request, was to be laid to rest. And there were to join him the majority of the popes after him, some thirteen, until Leo Ist, who was the first to be buried next to the putative tomb of St Peter on the Vatican hillside (A.D. 461). The distinction awarded to bishop Pontian rather than presbyter Hippolytus was a novel one.

110. Eusebius, *H.E.*, VI.28.
111. Eusebius, *H.E.*, VI.43.11.

As Borgolte has pointed out, the concept of a burial place exclusively reserved for leaders of a community marks a critical ideological shift to a model of monarchical power.[112] Such a concept is difficult to parallel in pagan, Roman society. In this case, as for example, the Vatican excavations have made clear in the pagan cubicula there unearthed, senatorial, patrician, and other wealthy families were buried in family graves, where their extended families included their domestic and freed slaves. The Roman, Jewish community, may provide us with an example of a council of elders drawn from individual synagogues that parallels our reconstruction of the loose organization of presbyter-bishops who presided over groups that formed the Christian community. But Jewish cemeteries yield no instance of an area specifically and exclusively reserved for the burial of community leaders: 'rulers of synagogues (ἀρχισυναγ ωγαί)' were buried indiscriminately alongside their people. The true parallel is with the tomb of Augustus, erected for himself and his heirs and successors: Callistus' centralized episcopate was to be now monarchical in form.

The nature of Fabian's concept was so breathtaking that, even after Cyprian, bishop of Carthage (died 258), was to define against Novatian all episcopates throughout the Roman world in such terms, it was only gradually conformed to in burial practice. Cornelius (A.D. 251–253), Fabian's immediate successor, even though protesting that Novatian had not understood that there could only be a single bishop in Rome to which all other presbyter-bishops (like Hippolytus) must now be subject, did not follow Fabian's example: the community interred him in the Lucina area that was at that time quite separate from the Callistus complex. His epitaph was written in Latin, as befitted one who, whether as citizen or freed slave or descendant of such, bore the distinguished name of the *gens Cornelia*, and presumably had been laid to rest in a family grave. But Lucius 1st and Stephen 1st saw the point, and were interred with their fellow episcopal monarchs, as was Sixtus II who contributed to the further development of the papal mausoleum as a monument.

Novatian, now in the eyes of the catholic church of Cyprian and Cornelius an antipope, desisted, as did his followers, from making a similar point. His tomb, where his remains were finally brought to rest after death in exile (*c.* A.D. 266), found on the via Tiburtina opposite San Lorenzo fuori i muri, was monumentalized in the second half of the fourth century. There are however, in the surrounding cemeterial complex, no epitaphs honouring and marking the burial place of the succession of 24 Novatianist bishops, corresponding to that number of catholic bishops of Rome from Cornelius to Celestine Ist.[113] But this was no

---

112. M. Borgolte, *Petrusnachfolge und Kaiserimitation. Die Grablegen der Päpste, ihre Genese und Traditionsbildung* (Veröffentlichungen des Max-Planck-Instituts für Geschichte 95; Göttingen: Vandenhoeck & Ruprecht, 1989), pp. 33–36.

113. R. Giordani, 'Novatiano beatissimo martyri Gaudentius diaconus fecit. Contributo all' identificazione del martire Novaziano della catacomba anonima sulla via Tiburtina', *RivArchCr*, 68 (1992), pp. 233–58 (239).

doubt because they did not wish to play Fabian's particular game of giving a new expression to the implications of Callistus' revolution.

For a second corroboration of the ideology of an episcopal monarchy that was receiving embodiment in Fabian's construction of the tomb of the popes we must now turn once more to the development of Irenaeus' episcopal succession list. We have argued that he either discovered this for himself, or found it in one that Hegesippus had managed to compose from the one piece of material evidence of a list of individual and concrete successors in authority in the Roman community, namely the secretary, like Clement, of the presbytery. But originally, as is clear from Irenaeus, the list was an undated succession list: it simply recorded the name of who succeeded whom.

We have, in the work of the Chronographer of A.D. 354, a continuation of that list as it resulted in that year, ending with the pontificate of Liberius. Here each bishop of Rome, commencing with St Peter, are assigned dates. But as we read this list, we are met now with an oddity. Bishops before Pontian manage to die when consuls leave office, and are succeeded when their successors enter their office. Only from Pontian are bishops assigned dates quite independent of when the consuls enter or leave office, and only then is the specific date given, for example, Pontian dies, iiii Kl. Octobr. A.D. 235, and Anteros succeeds him on xi Kl. Dec. A.D. 235. No longer is the reference to a succession of teachers, in which no dates are necessary, but simply the bare record that there was a named successor as president of the philosophical school. Now dates are given, because bishops are considered monarchs, and it was necessary to state specifically the beginning and the ends of their reigns: if Callistus could be regarded, albeit sarcastically and metaphorically, as issuing 'edicts' as 'bishop of bishops', then the heirs to his monarchical revolution needed to have years, months and days of their reigns.

The author of the continued list after Urban was operating within a new chronographic tradition, witnessed by the contemporary Chronography of Julius Africanus, and, partly by two writers within the Hippolytan community who composed a table of dates of Jewish Passovers and a brief note of associated, Old Testament events that were to be inscribed on the right side of the chair of the so-called Statue of Hippolytus in the Vatican Library. On the left side was a table for calculating the dates of Easter from the first year of Severus Alexander (A.D. 222).[114]

As the Chronographer of 354 exemplifies, chronography was a case of endeavouring to produce the materials for a world history, in which first lists of Jewish, Persian, Greek and Roman consuls were constructed in parallel columns along with columns for Olympic Festivals, Jewish Passovers, etc. Equivalence of dates between them could thus be drawn, and a quite artificial

---

114. Actually, it was originally the Statue of Themista of Lampsacus, a lady philosopher in the school of Epicurus, reused by the Hippolytan community with an allegorical meaning, see Brent, *Hippolytus*, chapter 1.

chronology was thus established. Between the columns a space could then be created, a so-called 'historical space (*spatium historicum*)', that would be filled with famous events and persons, with the latter recorded simply as 'flourishing' at the approximate time of consuls (who were also for the most part emperors) or kings on either side. When therefore the author of the continuation of what was originally Irenaeus' undated list gave bishops dates, he was assigning to them a regnal list comparable to those who were consuls (emperors) and kings.

It was therefore no accident that Urban was the last to have implausible dates assigned by a later Chronographer on an original list with no dates, and he was also the last not to be generally buried in the Callistus catacomb, and in Fabian's tomb of the popes. Pontian and Anteros were the first to be so buried, and the first to whom the regnal system of dating was supplied, with the need to supply artificial dates for those on the existing undated list to which these new entries were being added. The ideology that required regnal dates, and the construction of a papal mausoleum, was the same, and it was new and quite revolutionary.

We have stressed the relationship between metaphysical order and social order in Graeco-Roman, pagan political theory. Political order reflected cosmic order. Thus a revolution in political structure needed to be accompanied by a reformulation of one's picture of the cosmic order. Elagabalus as *Pontifex Maximus* had proclaimed a universal, pagan monotheism, in which there was the μοναρχία of *Sol Invictus*, the veneration of the sun as supreme deity from whose essence were derived all other deities. As we have said, the political concept of 'a single rule', and the metaphysical concept of a single first principle from which all other being is derived, is expressed by the same term, μοναρχία.

But we have seen how, from Justin Martyr onwards, and even from Ignatius before him, Christian accounts of creation and Christ's redemption are increasingly discussed and understood in terms of a Platonic and Stoic cosmology. For Luke-Acts, the political rapprochement between Christian and Roman society may have been in terms of Augustan eschatology of the returning golden age and the peace of the gods, with little attention to the correspondence between power and authority in Christian social order and the cosmos as such: there is no human figure as ruler set over against Augustus other than Christ. For Clement the church as a πολίτευμα reflected generally the concord of the natural with the political order, without tying authority figures directly with the gods in the heavenly realm. But Ignatius had seen the bishop as an image of the suffering God, with the deacons representing the ministry of Christ, and the presbyteral, apostolic council the continuing imparting of the Spirit of the Johannine Pentecost.

For Justin, his authority figure, the president, was simply the teaching successor in the church as a philosophical school, but he had associated the Christ of Christianity, God's Son, with the Logos in creation and redemption.

But he had ignored the logic of the metaphysical discourse that he was thus employing, where the Logos that pervaded the cosmos had as a particular representative and mediator between earthly and heavenly society, namely the divine, Hellenistic ruler. St John may have been content with the Logos made flesh in the incarnation as that mediator, but he also believed that the Church is the extension of the incarnation.[115] Although he may have not derived any conclusion from this regarding the authority structure of the community, Ignatius of Antioch certainly did so: the incarnation continued in the timeless moment of the liturgy, in which through the action of the three ministerial image-bearers redemption continued and 'incorruption' was attained.

We do not know how Callistus himself saw the character of his ministry. But others inferred from the behaviour of 'the bishop of bishops' in seeking an episcopal monarchy over all the Roman congregations that he was behaving like a pagan emperor, like Elagabalus whose political authority was based upon his holding the office of Pontifex Maximus as the earthly representative and mediator of *Sol Invictus* as the μοναρχία. Certainly Callistus' reconstruction of the cosmology of the Christian God and Logos involved the monarchian notion that a divine being must be simply a mode or phase of the divine first principle. As his critic expressly says:

> Thus he thinks that he has established the *monarchia* (μοναρχία), asserting that Father and Son subsist as one and the same being, becoming not different the one from the other, but the same from himself.[116]

In such a metaphysical reconstruction of the cosmos, there was no room for a godhead of two or three persons, consubstantial and co-eternal, co-equal in power and divinity. The presbyter-bishop of one community, co-existing with others as such in a διαδοχή in which all equally shared, and exchanging the *fermentum* in an act of mutual recognition could well protest:

> But having the poison residing in his heart, and simply thinking nothing whilst he was ashamed to tell the truth because in public he had insulted us and said: 'You are ditheists', and other things as well because of Sabellius' constant accusation that he had transgressed the primitive faith, he devised the following heresy. He said that the Logos himself was the Son and himself the Father, being called by name Son and Father, but being one, the indivisible Spirit.[117]

---

115. Jn 20: 22-23; A. Brent, *Cultural Episcopacy and Ecumenism: Representative ministry in church history from the Age of Ignatius of Antioch to the Reformation, with special reference to contemporary ecumenism* (Studies in Christian Mission 6; Leiden: E. J. Brill, 1992), pp. 73–80, 97–98; 'Ecumenical Reconciliation and Cultural Episcopates', *ATR*, 72.3 (1990), pp. 255–79 (258–66).

116. Hippolytus (Pseudo), *Ref.*, IX.10.11.

117. Hippolytus (Pseudo), *Ref.*, IX.12.15–16.

Callistus does not allow any divisions in the cosmic μοναρχία than, as 'bishop of bishops', he allows within the political structure of the community that he leads, and which must reflect that cosmic order.

We have seen how, from Hadrians time, the Isis cosmology had entered the iconography of imperial power, where the order of the world was 'a certain sacred effluence (ἀπόρροια)' of herself, mediated through 'emperors', of whom all other rulers are 'emanations'.[118] Athenagoras had spoken of 'God, the Son his Logos, and the Holy Spirit united in power but distinguished in rank', with the Spirit, who might be equivalent to the Logos, as his 'effluence (ἀπορροία), like rays of the sun'.[119] Tatian had spoken of the cosmic μοναρ χία.[120] In developing a doctrine of the Trinity, the Apologists were reflecting against a background of pagan political theology, as we have seen. And the implications for the doctrine of the Trinity were monarchical, as Callistus well knew, with distinctions 'of rank', and of no persons but modes of being characterized as 'effluence (ἀπορροία)'. The Logos was 'called by name Son and Father, but being one, the indivisible Spirit'.

Thus Callistus' ecclesial centralization paralleled Elagabalus' imperial μοναρχία: political currents outside the Christian community were being mirrored in similar currents within it. His ἀρχιερετεία must be, like Elagabalus' office as the Pontifex Maximus of *Sol Invictus*, one and indivisible, in which no other presbyter-bishop could share any more than a pagan priest of any other cult. Callistus had thus suggested an answer to the question posed by the incorporation of Stoic and Platonic logos cosmology into Christian theology of the role of the earthly ruler in mediating divine and cosmic order into human political order.

The scene was thus set for the last piece in the metaphysical jigsaw, in which a claim could be made for a political ruler and a political empire reflecting, not a pagan cosmic order but a Christian one. We shall see how this was to become possible with Constantine, but how that possibility was never finally to be realized and for what reason. For the moment, let us observe how, under Cyprian and the emperor Decius, both pagan and Christian ideology were to resume those apocalyptic concerns with which the early Church originally found itself in conflict with the Augustan metaphysics of power.

118.　See above, footnote 46 and associated text.
119.　Athenagoras, *Leg.*, 24.2; 10.4–5. See also footnotes 47 and 48, and associated text.
120.　Tatian, *Orat.*, 29.1–2. See also above, footnote 34.

Chapter 7

CYPRIAN AGAINST DECIUS: OPPOSING ESCHATOLOGIES AND THE CREATION OF A STATE WITHIN THE STATE

The reign of Maximinus (A.D. 235–238), following the death of Alexander Severus and his mother, Julia Mamaea during the war with the Persians, had witnessed the martyrdom of both 'bishop' Pontian and 'presbyter' Hippolytus. Successful in war, he provoked a revolt that was to lead to his downfall as a result of his expropriation of private wealth to fund such successes. Thus was initiated a period of considerable instability that was to last until the reigns of Valerian and Aurelian, if not until that of Diocletian.

Gordian Ist, his son, together with his grandson, attempted to constitute an imperial dynasty in a revolt against Maximinus. Recognized by the Senate, they were nevertheless opposed by Capellianus, a general loyal to Maximinus, against whom Gordian and his son were to fall in battle and by suicide. Maximinus, nonetheless, was to be murdered by his own troops. After the murder in turn by their own troops of those whom the Senate had now appointed, namely Pupienus and Balbinus, the surviving grandson Gordian III became emperor at the age of 13 (A.D. 238), with a large section of Rome burned down in flames. Gordian III was murdered by his own soldiers following his defeat by the Persians (A.D. 244).

Thus Philip the Arab entered Rome as emperor on 23rd July 244. In A.D. 248 Pacatianus, an officer in the army, was now to lead a revolt against him. At this point, with an empire weakened by civil war the Goths, could now invade, along with several Vandal tribes. Instead of such an international threat reuniting the empire, Jotapianus began a revolt from the Syrian East. He was joined separately by Uranius Antoninus as the third contender, who alone among them managed to continue for a further 4 years (until A.D. 253–254). Decius' election by his legions (A.D. 249) was quickly followed by the end of Jotapianus and Pacatianus.[1] The Sassanian conquest of Persia created an enduring threat to the Eastern frontiers, with raids that went deeper and deeper into Roman territory.[2]

---

1. J. Drinkwater, 'Maximinus to Diocletian and the "crisis"', in *CAH²*, XII.1.2, pp. 38–41.
2. M. Corbier, 'Coinage, Society and Economy', in *CAH²*, XII.4.11, pp. 393–94.

The collapse of the empire at its frontiers, and the further revolts within, were exacerbated by the economic strain of continual war, with the debasement of the silver coinage. Thus 'continual warfare not only increased the main structural weaknesses of the empire, but also spread or created new agonies such as disease, social and economic disruption and a decline in morale'.[3] Though there has been considerable discussion, in terms of post-Enlightenment economic 'objectivity', of how 'real' the crisis in fact was,[4] our quest, in a political history, is not so much how things might have been in terms of 'our', twenty-first century definition of reality, but how they appear in the perspective of the third-century inhabitants of their social construction of reality. It should be remembered that many governments have lost elections even though an 'objective' economic analysis might be held to have established that they were 'good' governments, delivering the economic success which appears to be the sole measurement of contemporary democracies.

Our evidence for the perspective of the inhabitants of the Roman empire of the third century comes from some small general, historiographical notices, some sparse pagan literary sources not always accepted as reliable, non-literary evidence mainly from the imperial coinage, and the correspondence and other surviving writings of St. Cyprian. They reveal in essence, whether on the Pagan or the Christian side, a revival of the eschatological claims witnessed, as we have argued, in the iconography of the *Ara Pacis* and associated literature, and in the Christian response, whether in terms of Lukan accommodation or those of the hostility found in the book of Revelation.

We shall argue in this chapter that the Decius Trajan, whom the church faced in persecution in the persons of Cyprian bishop of Carthage and Cornelius bishop of Rome, shared in the eschatological project of pagan political ideology that experienced a fresh revival in the general imperial chaos of the mid-third century. In our first section (1), we shall trace that renewed ideology in the claims and counter claims of those with whom Decius waged civil war for the prize of becoming emperor. In our second section (2), we shall see how Decius, in his brief reign, made a novel contribution to that imperial ideology, while sharing its fundamental assumptions. We shall trace how (section 3), though his persecution did not identify Christianity as such as its object, it was to create, in Cyprian's response, the blueprint, rapidly realized, of a universal church throughout the Roman empire under an episcopal structure that produced a state within a state confronting the state itself: Valerian was to recognize as such the creature both of Decius and of Cyprian in his direct attack on the hierarchy of the church itself. Thus will emerge a decisive change in the relationship of church and state, and of a new politics that was to emerge with the accession of Constantine.

---

3. B. Campbell, 'The Severan Dynasty', in *CAH²*, XII.1.1, p. 61.
4. See, for example, footnotes 1–3 above.

1. *The Revival of Eschatological Claims in the Legitimation of Imperial Power*

One view of apocalyptic is that it is a form of social-psychological experience generated within an oppressed community in which elements from its mytho-logical conception of the past are projected onto an imminent historical future. Indeed we find in the circumstances of a pagan Roman Empire, and in those of a persecuted church the recreation of the phenomena of the apocalyptic imagination. There arose a general feeling of decline and collapse, of being overwhelmed by forces outside of human control, and the expectation of a new and eternal order arising from the ashes. After the disastrous civil wars that for a century had made the Republican constitution inoperable, and which had brought finally an Augustus from out of the chaos, the dream of the golden age, returning after all things had collapsed into the ages of bronze and of iron, needed to be realized, and seemed to be being realized. This eschatological notion of decline and renewal now reappears in the historiography of Cassius Dio and of Herodian.

Cassius Dio claimed the death of Commodus (A.D. 192) as the point at which 'history now declines from a kingdom of gold to one of iron and rust'.[5] For Herodian it was Maximinus, who marked the moment in which kingly rule had experienced a 'transformation (μεταβολή)' into tyranny:

Maximinus, in taking over the empire, executed the greatest transformation (μεταβολή), adopting the harshest authority and based on fear, and he tried to make a complete transformation from a mild and gentle kingship to the most savage tyranny.

Dionysius of Alexandria was also to use the same expression, μεταβολή to describe the change from the good rule of Philip, to the evil one of Decius, asserting its eschatological significance in terms of Matthew's version of the Synoptic Apocalypse.[6] The notion of different forms of government, good and bad, each changing into its opposite and then yielding to its successor in a his-torical cycle of decline and renewal, had characterized Roman historiography from Polybius onwards.[7] The myth of the returning golden age, justified philo-sophically in terms of a Stoic metaphysic of ἐκπύρωσις, was being reborn in the political ideology of the third century.

Certainly each of the contenders for the imperial purple regarded the nature of the conflict between themselves and their rivals in terms of who could claim to be the agent of Fate bringing back the golden age to replace their world now degenerated into the age of iron. This is the message of each contender, recorded

---

5. Dio Cassius, LII.36.4, cf. G. Alföldy, 'The Crisis of the Third Century as seen by Contem-poraries', *GRBS*, 15 (1974), pp. 89–111 (92) (= Alföldy, *Ausgewählte Beiträge*, pp. 273–94 (322)).
6. Eusebius, *H.E.*, VI.41.9 quoting Mt. 24:24.
7. Polybius, *Hist.*, VI.4.2; 6.12; 7.1.

from artefacts and remains, and particularly through coins that the rivals minted as they did battle with each other in a propaganda war.

Augustus had set great store on the fact proclaimed by the iconography of the *Aurae* on the *Ara Pacis* that peace had been secured by land and by sea as the foundation for the inauguration of the golden age. Augustus had refounded Rome by an act of augury, and the 'augury securing peace (*augurium salutis*)' had been successfully performed by him.[8] In consequence, the gates of the temple of Janus could be closed.[9] With the accession of Gordian III, one writer informs us:

> He opened the twin door of Janus, which was a sign of war being declared, and set out against the Persians with a considerable army and so much gold that either with its help, or due to the soldiers, he easily overcame the Persians.[10]

Thus those who idealized the Gordians portrayed an Augustan reign of peace otherwise disturbed by an easily overcome Persian threat.

Gordian III has left us with an epigraph that proclaimed that he as 'restorer of the world (*restitutor orbis*)', and as such is inaugurating a 'new age (*saeculum nouum*)'.[11] Valerian later seeks to appropriate Gordian's title for himself, when he remints one of his coins that also bears the legend RESTITVTOR ORBIS.[12] We find him also honoured with the Augustan title of 'saviour of the wide world'.[13] Augustus was 'saviour' precisely because: 'there is nothing in a fallen condition and changed into an unfortunate condition that he has not set right'.[14] Clearly both Gordian III and Philip are claiming this imperial and divine role that Augustus had claimed in the first, in a third century in chaos. We have a dedicatory inscription in which Gordian is, furthermore, described as 'great unconquered (*magnus inuictus*)' on one epigraph, and on another as 'the greatest unconquered one (*inuictissimus*)', epithets that were found also in the cult of the divinity *Sol Inuictus*.[15] Philip was to appropriate this title for his son, Philip II.[16]

---

8.   Suetonius, *Aug.*, 7, Dio Cassius (Xiphilinus), LI.20.4, cf. Brent, *Imperial Cult*, pp. 38–41.

9.   Augustus, *Res Gest.*, 13.

10.   SHA., *Gordiani Tres*, XX.26.3.

11.   *CIL*, VIII.20487.1–3; XIII. 9119: VI.1092.

12.   *RIC*, IV.3, p. 41, no. 246.

13.   E. De Ruggiero, *Dizionario Epigrafico di Antichità Romane* (Rome: 'L'Erma' di Bretschneider, 1962), III, p. 557.

14.   Ehrenberg and Jones, *Documents*, no. 98.6–9.

15.   *CIL*, VIII.10079 and 11160. See also L. Cerfaux and J. Tondriau, *Le Culte des Souverains dans la Civilisation Gréco-Romaine* (Bibl. de Théol., Sér. 3, 5; Paris-Tournai, 1956), p. 374 to whom I am indebted for these references.

16.   For Gordian III, see *SEG*, IV.523.1, and Philip II, *IGRR*, I.1480.

As 'the providence that governs the universe'[17] had directed Augustus, so too does the anonymous panegyrist declare in the case of Philip.[18] The panegyrist describes the shaking of the fabric of empire in terms of storm and earthquake. But the new emperor is to be a remedy for this decline, and willed to be such by providence:

> . . . the providence (πρόνοια) that administers the universe and orders it has also caused this man to sit on the royal throne as the most righteous and holy of kings.[19]

Thus under his rule there was the enjoyment 'of good fortune (τύχη) from him and from providence (πρόνοια)', as had been the case with Augustus. Appropriately, therefore, Philip's coins now display the announcement of the SAECVLVM NOVVM, the new returning golden age that transforms the third century world of bronze and of iron.[20]

In A.D. 248, Philip staged lavish games marking his new celebration of the returning golden age with the celebration of the 1,000 years of Rome's founding, the MILIARIVM SAECVLVM.[21] He was to associate his family with him in this project, when he issued coins with this inscription for his wife, Otacilia Severa,[22] and his son, Philip II.[23] He also challenged Gordian III's claimed title by honouring Philip II as 'the new Sun'.[24]

Philip's celebration of the millennium of Rome's founding was commemorated with lavish games marked by his coinage and inscribed with the legend of SAECVLARES AVGG.[25] Scenes from the games themselves, nevertheless, have, in addition, the she wolf nursing the twins Romulus and Remus, and thus we see his games as replicating the first founding of Rome.[26] Pacatianus, who led a revolt against Philip, made his own claim to being Fate's true agent of the millenarian project: he issued a coin with the legend 'to Rome eternal, year 1001 (ROMAE AETER. AN. MILL. ET PRIMO)'.[27] In our own time, there was some dispute over when the third millennium should begin: was A.D. 2000 not really the final year of the old millennium that should really

17. Ehrenberg and Jones, *Documents*, no. 98.8–10.
18. E. Croag, 'Die Kaisarrede des Pseudo-Aristides', *Wiener Studien*, 40 (1918), pp. 20–45; L. J. Swift, 'The Anonymous Encomium of Philip the Arab', *GRBS*, 7 (1966), pp. 267–89.
19. Pseudo Aristides, Εἰς Βασιλέα, 35.14.
20. *RIC*, IV.3, p. 71, nos 25 (a) and (b).
21. *RIC*, IV.3, p. 88, no. 157.
22. *RIC*, IV.3, p. 93, no. 199.
23. *RIC*, IV.3, p. 103, no. 271*.
24. *IGRR*, I.1480. See *IL*, VIII.8809.
25. *RIC*, IV.3, pp. 70–71, nos 12–24; p. 81 no. 107 and no. 111 (with a reverse of Otacilia Severa).
26. *RIC*, IV.3, p. 70, nos 15–16 and Plate 6.9.
27. *RIC*, IV, p. 105, no. 6.

begin with A.D. 2001? Pacatianus insists that it is he who initiates the second thousand years of Rome's foundation, and who begins the new golden age with the correct date that differs from that of his rivals.

Decius was to put paid to Pacatian's revolt, as he was to that of Jotapianus. We must consider Decius, contribution to the ideological project of pagan politics in a moment in further detail. But let us mention first the role of Uranius Antoninus, the third contender who was to be put down by Valerian some 2 years after Decius' death. (A.D. 253–254). He too was to lay claim to the SAECVLARES AVGG, and to initiating the new age that these began.[28] His coinage also continues the solar iconography that we have seen Gordian III had also employed, but he specifically, from his Syrian headquarters, attempted to revive the cult of *Sol Invictus* in the form that Elagabalus had established it, the emperor from whom Uranius claimed descent.[29] The kingdom of the sun was to replace in his imperial ideology that of Vergil's fourth eclogue, where 'the age of iron shall cease, and a golden race arise throughout the world, through the child of the Virgin and the returning kingdom of Saturn'.[30]

In his definitive study, Potter has established that the first edition of *Sibylline Oracle*, 13, hostile to Decius, ended with the rise of Uranius (A.D. 253), who is the figure there of eschatological significance:

> Again with the world becoming disordered with its men destroyed in plague and war, the Persians will again rush to the toil of Ares raging against the Ausonians. Then there will also be a rout of the Romans . . .[31]

But then we are assured:

> . . . but immediately thereafter a priest will come, the last of all sent from the sun, appearing from Syria, and he will do everything by craft; the city of the sun will arise, and around her the Persians will endure the terrible threats of the Phoenicians.[32]

Thus we find the ideological context in which Decius was to argue his claim to imperial power, and to advance his unique solution to the metaphysical decline and collapse, in nature as well as society, which, as we have argued, it was the sacral political function of the emperor to address.

---

28.   *RIC*, IV.3 p. 205, no. 7 and Pl. 15,18.

29.   *RIC*, IV.3, p. 206, no. 8, see also H. R. Baldus, *Uranius Antoninus: Münzprägung und Geschichte* (Antiquitas 3.11; Bonn: Habelt, 1971), p. 144, St. 6–7 and taf. VI.53–54 cf. taf. V.43.44. For the entire series and discussion, see R. Delbrück, 'Uranius of Emesa', *Numismatic Chronicle*, 8 (1948) pp. 11–29, see H. R. Baldus, 'Die 'reformerten' Tetradrachmen des Uranius Antoninus', *Chiron*, 5 (1975), pp. 452–55.

30.   Vergil, *Ec.*, 4.5–10, cf. *Aeneid*, 6.792–794.

31.   *Orac. Sibyl.*, 13.147–50.

32.   *Orac. Sibyl..*, 13.150–54.

2. *Decius' Specific Contribution to the*
Project of Metaphysical Renewal

Decius entered Rome as emperor late in A.D. 249. His coinage, in contrast with the claims of Gordian III, Philip and Uranius, seem remarkably conservative and traditional, making no claims for identification with *Sol Invictus*, and a Hellenistic ruler ideology in which the emperor was the divine source through which cosmic order entered human society.

Decius' reign was a brief one, ending within 2 years with his death at the hands of the Goths at Abrittus in June 251. Nevertheless, despite his conservatism, his spin-doctors did not fail to associate him with the historiography of decline and renewal, and the divinity of imperial power. On his accession, he took the name of 'Trajan' thus identifying him with the past golden age before Commodus and decline. On one coin we find continued the theme of SAECV-LVM NOVVM.[33] There is also Philip II's reminted coin, with the name of his own elder son and heir on the obverse side, Herennius Etruscus, who died with him in battle in 251. Accompanying Philip's image we have SECULARES AVGG.[34] Thus Decius' spin-doctors were clearly to continue the millenarian project.

As a guarantee of Decius' role as the agent of the gods in bringing into existence the 'new age', his spin-doctors were to issue a series of coins dedicated to the divine emperors or *diui* of Rome's glorious past. Emperors considered bad are omitted such as Tiberius, Nero, Domitian and Elagabalus. The latter, of course was associated with his Syrian rival, still alive and active, Uranius Antoninus. On each coin, against the emperor's name is depicted an eagle rising from the funeral bier of the dead emperor, as the traditional depiction of the image of his soul departing to heaven and divinized, to which the legend CONSECRATIO bears testimony. Significantly, Severus Alexander ends the series: it was at the end of his reign that Herodian had considered that the empire had changed from gold to iron.[35] Furthermore Decius considered himself the 'restorer of sacred rites (*restitutor sacrorum*)'.[36] How he proposed such a restoration we must now see.

Decius now produced an Edict, decreeing that all citizens throughout the Empire should take part in a universal sacrifice. The nature of the sacrifice was a *supplicatio* or rite of thanksgiving, but also an apotropaeic rite that averted the 'anger' and obtained 'the peace of the gods'. When a plague broke out in Rome in 181 B.C. accompanied by such portents as showers of blood, in the precinct of the temple of Vulcan and Concord, the Senate decreed such a

---

33. *RIC*, IV.3, p. 128, no. 67; p. 148, no. 205*.

34. *RIC*, IV.3, p. 141, no. 162.

35. *RIC*, IV.3, pp. 130–32, nos 77–99. D. S. Potter, *The Roman Empire at Bay, A.D. 180–395* (London: Routledge, 2004), p. 244.

36. C. L. Babcock, 'An Inscription of Trajan Decius from Cosa', *AJP*, 83 (1962), pp. 147–58.

supplicatio.[37] Decius was now organizing, not simply such a rite in Rome, but universally, throughout the Roman Empire, in order to remedy the extraordinary situation in which a flawed cosmos could be set right.

A later writer claimed anachronistically for Gordian III that before he opened the gates of Janus in order to go to war, there had been an earthquake that indicated the 'sickness of the universe (*mundanum malum*)'. This metaphysical instability was to be corrected, through a *supplicatio* called for by the Sibylline oracles, not only in Rome itself, but 'throughout the whole wide world'.[38]

In fact it was Decius who was the first to organize such a universal *supplicatio*. His act constituted a major change in itself in a rite that was organized and administered centrally. Previously such cults were the result of local initiative, for example like those of the imperial cult in Asia Minor: the Greek city-states themselves took the initiative in seeking permission for such a rites.[39] In order to avail himself of the means of securing the universality of such a sacrifice, his edict ordered the setting up of commissions in each city. Every citizen was to offer sacrifice to the gods of the Roman state, and to secure from the commissioners a certificate or *libellus* duly signed, witnessing that they had so complied.

For such arrangements Decius already had both a model, and the bureaucratic means for it to function. Caracalla, earlier in the century, had passed his law granting almost universal citizenship throughout the Empire. According to Cassius Dio's cynical reflections, it was a ruse to raise taxes.[40] This is an explanation that had appealed too readily to contemporary historians. We have a papyrus fragment of Caracalla's edict that reads as follows:

> I grant to all throughout the wide world citizenship of the Romans with the just entitlements of their own constitutions preserved . . . To the immortal gods I give thanks that, when so great a disaster occurred, they preserved me. Therefore, thinking that I should be able to make the return that would correspond to their majesty, if I were to gather to the sanctuaries of our gods the alien non-citizens if only they could enter the ranks of my people.[41]

The 'disaster' to which he refers may have been the failed conspiracy of his brother Geta.

---

37.   Livy, XL.19.4–5.

38.   SHA, *Gordiani Tres*, XX.26.1–2.

39.   J. B. Rives, 'The Decree of Decius and the Religion of the Empire', *JRS*, 89 (1999), pp. 135–54.

40.   Dio Cassius, LXXVIII.9.5–6.

41.   *P. Giss.*, 40 I.3–9 reproduced in P. A. Kuhlmann, 'Die Giessener literarischen Papyri und die Caracalla-Erlasse-Edition, Übersetzung und Kommentar', in *Berichte und Arbeiten aus der Universitätsbibliothek und dem Universitätsarchiv Giessen*, 46 (Giessen: Universitäts-bibliothek, 1994), p. 222. I have supplied gaps in consultation with Kuhlmann, 'Caracalla-Erlasse', pp. 226–27 and Oliver, *Greek Constitutions*, pp. 498–99. See also Gaius, *Institutiones*, 1.14. For a discussion and bibliography, see Kuhlmann, 'Caracalla-Erlasse', pp. 235–237.

Frend was to claim, contrary to Clarke, that it was in fact the legislation of Caracalla that made possible Decius' general edict because it established taxation registers on which names could be ticked off.[42] We have 44 such *libelli* from Egypt, dated between 12ᵗʰ June and 14ᵗʰ July 250.[43] A typical example reads as follows:

> To those appointed commissioners superintending the sacrifices, from Aurelia Ammo-narion of the village of Theadelphia, and always as one who customarily offers sacrifice and shows reverence to the gods as well as my children, who are surnamed Aurelii Didymus and Nouphius and Taas, we have completed the declaration even now in your presence, in accordance with the Decree we have poured libations and sacrificed, and of the sacred victims we have tasted, and I request of you to issue a certificate to this effect on my behalf. With kind regards. We Serenus and Hermas Aurelius have seen you offering the sacrifices. I Hermas certify it.[44]

The *libellus* resembles very much the form of a tax return.[45] Here the ritual conditions appear very stringent in that

1. The sacrificer has to swear that he or she has 'always' and 'customarily' offered sacrifice to the gods of the state;
2. All members of a household individually perform the act; and
3. Animal sacrifices as well as libations of wine and incense are both offered.

There is, however, evidence from some *libelli* that sometimes heads of households were allowed to offer on behalf of other members.[46] Cyprian's evidence, moreover, is that many were allowed to simply offer incense (the *thurificati*), which was the concession originally granted to (former) Christians by Pliny.[47]

---

42.   W. H. C. Frend, *The Rise of Christianity* (London: Darton, Longman and Todd, 1986), p. 408. See also J. R. Knipfing, 'The Libelli of the Decian Persecution', *HTR*, 16 (1923), pp. 354–55, cf. G. W. Clarke, 'Some Observations on the Persecution of Decius', *Antichthon*, 3 (1969), pp. 68–73 and G. Clarke, *The Letters of St. Cyprian*, vols I–IV, translation and commentary by G. W. Clarke (Ancient Christian Writers, 43, 44, 46 and 47; New York: Newman Press, 1984–1989), I, pp. 26–28.

43.   For texts of forty-one see Knipfing, 'Libelli', pp. 345–90; H. Leclercq, 'Les certificats de sacrifice païen sous Dèce en 250', *Bulletin d'ancienne littérature et d'archéologie chrétienne*, 4 (1914), pp. 52–60; 188–201; P. Roasenda, 'Decio e i libellatici', *Didaskaleion*, 5.1 (1927), pp. 31–68. For the last to be discovered see J. Schwartz, 'Une déclaration de sacrifice du temps de Dèce', *RB*, 54 (1947), pp. 1–11, and *P. Oxyr.*, 41.2990.

44.   Knipfing, 'Libelli', p. 368; Roasenda, 'Libellatici', no. 4.

45.   For Commodus' reign (A.D. 180–192) we have such a taxation certificate in *P. Oxyr.*, 58.3918.4.

46.   Knifing, 'Libelli', pp. 381–82, no. 30.8–12. For a discussion of this and other texts, see A. Brent, *Cyprian and Roman Carthage in the Third Century* (Cambridge: University Press, 2009), chapter 5, A.2.2.

47.   See above, Chapter 2, Section 1.

Despite the continuing objections of Keresztes,[48] it would appear that Decius' edict was not directed against Christians alone, particularly in view of the fact that one *libellus* is completed and certified for Aurelia Ammonous, a priestess of the crocodile-god, Petesouchos.[49] Decius, therefore, was not directly confronting Christianity by his edict. His objective rather was a more positive one, to secure, by a centrally organized universal *supplicatio*, the peace of the gods as a remedy for the disunity whose cause was metaphysical, and needed addressing as such. And so the Church was inevitably brought into conflict with the Roman state, for the very reason that it had always been persecuted: its refusal to participate in rites held to be critical for the maintenance of social as part of cosmic order.

Thus Dionysius, bishop of Alexandria, described the arrival of the edict in his city:

> And so of course the edict arrived . . . and so all stood frozen . . . Of the many *personae insignes* some immediately came forward in their fear, while others in public service were induced by the nature of their duties, and others still were dragged by their companions. Summoned by name, they approached the profane and unholy sacrifices.[50]

But the effect upon the Church, and upon its view of its role and mission in the world and the nature of its hierarchy, was to be witnessed in the writings of St Cyprian, as our surviving primary documentary evidence bears witness. It is to this aspect that we must now turn.

3. *The Response of the Church of Cyprian*

The arrival of the edict in Carthage did not initially lead to scenes of reluctant compliance, as they had done at Alexandria. Cyprian describes the scene there as one of ready and enthusiastic compliance, in the following words:

> They did not wait to be interrogated and to ascend the Capitol under arrest in order to deny Christ. They did not allow themselves only unwillingly to be seen sacrificing to idols. Of their own accord they rushed into the Forum, hastening of their own accord to their death, as if they had ever desired this, as if they were embracing an opportunity being granted for which they had joyfully prayed. How many had to be held there overnight by the magistrates because evening was pressing on, how many even begged that their destruction should not be thus postponed? [51]

48. P. Keresztes, 'Rome and the Christian Church I', in *ANRW*, II.23.1, pp. 247–315; P. Keresztes, The Decian *libelli* and Contemporary Literature, *Latomus*, 34.3 (1975), pp. 761–81. See also Brent, *Cyprian and Roman Carthage*, chapter 5.
49. P. Foucart, 'Les certificates de sacrifice pendant la persécution de Décius (250)', *Journal des Savants*, 6 (1908), p. 172, quoted in Knipfing, 'Libelli', p. 362.
50. Dionysius of Alexandria, *Ad Fabianum*, (= Eusebius, *H.E.*, VI.41.10–11).
51. Cyprian, *Laps.*, 8.148–55.

Cyprian's picture is therefore of a large number of previously faithful Christians eagerly wishing to offer a pagan sacrifice – an event that he finds mysterious.

Cyprian's view of their action is uncompromising. They have succumbed 'to a dreadful crime'.[52] They had reversed their baptismal confession and had lost the eternal life granted at the font: 'Could the servant of God stand there and speak and renounce Christ who had already renounced the Devil and the present age (*saeculo*)? Was not that altar his funeral pyre . . . ?'[53] Furthermore, many had been anxious to give also to their young children the sacrificial food and drink:

> But for many their own destruction was not enough. The crowd drove themselves to their fatal end with words of mutual encouragement. They hurried on to their eventual dying by drinking a poisoned cup that they shared with each other. And in order that nothing might be lacking to cap the crime, even infants (*infantes*), placed in their parents' hands or led that way, lost now as small children what they had acquired in baptism right at the first moment after their birth.[54]

That was how Cyprian saw matters. But what of those who so eagerly complied, with no threat of torture or indeed torture itself such as that to which others would later succumb? How did these see matters?

On their own later admission, they had felt 'impelled by an overwhelming urge'.[55] But what was the character of this 'urge'? Cyprian had been trained in at least some aspects of Roman Law. In legal and in philosophical argument, one derives conclusions from the application of logic to first principles. Such systematic reasoning, like systematic theology, distinguishes clearly between different conceptions of reality, ruling out one in the light of the other. But lay members of Christian congregations, worshipping mainly on Sundays, though perhaps gathering, if particularly devoted on other days such as Saints days for commemorative meals at their cemeteries, almost invariably, have neither the time nor the inclination to engage in systematic theology or philosophy.

Such ordinary worshippers inhabited the same world of social reality as did their pagan contemporaries, and felt the imperatives of sociological forces, which might be experienced within the individual psyche as 'an overwhelming urge'. Like Theophilus and his group, whom Luke addressed before them, they lived their lives in dependence on imperial structures, both social and economic, that were in a high state of collapse. Thus they felt a high state of relief and enthusiasm for a universal *supplicatio* that would bring divine peace and order into a disordered world at war with itself. Furthermore, unlike the

---

52. Cyprian, *Laps.*, 8.158.
53. Cyprian, *Laps.*, 8.161–63.
54. Cyprian, *Laps.*, 9.170–75.
55. Cyprian, *Laps.*, 8.155–57.

children of the European Enlightenment, they could not explain this in terms of
nature or society behaving like a malfunctioning machine that needed setting
right by purely human ingenuity.

Christians in the third century did not live in such a social world in which
nature and society had been thus separated and de-divinized in a phenomenon
that Weber described as the 'disenchantment' of the world. Early Christian art
represents an ambiguity, which is unexpressed in such systematic, verbal pres-
entations as those of Irenaeus and the author of the *Elenchos*. Jonah, sleeping
under the gourd, is portrayed in a fashion highly reminiscent of Endymion
awaking from sleep for his nightly trysts with the moon goddess. The image
of Christ riding the chariot of the sun, and radiate with the Chi Rho, is very
reminiscent of Apollo and *Sol Invictus* in Aurelian's contemporary political
theology.[56]

It may well have been that those Christians who rushed to sacrifice felt
the same need as their Pagan contemporaries, whether subjects or rulers, to
remedy the metaphysical collapse of nature and of society that were at the
transcendental root of the woes of the third century. Perhaps in their imagination there was a certain ambivalence about participating both in pagan sacrifices,
and in the Eucharist, for which their lack of leisure or inclination to engage in
systematic theology had deprived of the means of clarification. At all events,
Cyprian shows that he fully agreed with his pagan contemporaries, formally
least in terms of their popular Stoicism, on the metaphysical roots of the crisis
in government and imperial disunity.

In two works, one addressed to the pagan magistrate Demetrian, and another
to those within his church who needed consolation on the death of loved ones
in the plague, Cyprian's eschatological language shows a high degree of convergence with the worldview of Decius, though not his solution for instituting
the *nouum saeculum*:

> On this subject, though you are ignorant of what God knows, and a stranger to the truth,
> you ought to have grasped in the first place that the world has at this point of time
> grown old. It no longer consists of those vital powers of which it had previously con-
> sisted, nor is it endowed with the superior force and vitality with which it was endowed
> in the past. Even if we hold our peace, and do not put forward any evidences from the
> Holy Scriptures and God's formal pronouncements, the world even now is telling its
> own story and bearing witness by producing the evidence for its decline in the form of
> its own universal defects.[57]

Thus Cyprian feels what his pagan contemporaries feel regarding nature's
universal defects, reflected in 'the world's old age', with harvests no longer

---

56. Brent, *Cyprian and Roman Carthage*, chapter 5, section B.1.1.
57. Cyprian, *Demet.*, 3.39–46.

bearing abundant fruit, the mines worked out, labourers disappearing from the fields, and babies born old and with white hair:

> So, at its very dawn, birth at the present time hastens to its premature end, so whatever now comes to birth declines due to the old age of the world itself. Consequently, no one ought to be amazed that individual and particular elements in the world have begun to run out, when already the world itself as a whole is in eclipse and at its final end.[58]

The 'world is tottering and collapsing', with the 'house of the world' in a state of collapse.[59] Christ, in the Gospel apocalypses, had prophesied 'wars and famines and earthquakes and pestilences' before the End.[60] There had been a golden age, like the pagans believed, from which the present world has lapsed. But it is not Decius' *supplicatio* nor the millenial games of Philip or Pacatianus that restored this, but Christ's Second Advent:

> The kingdom of God, most beloved brothers, has begun to be imminent. The reward of life and the joy of eternal salvation, and everlasting gladness, and the gaining possession of a paradise once lost, are now coming with the passing of the world . . . Only someone who does not believe that he is beginning to reign with Christ will be unwilling to go to him.[61]

Cyprian clearly places these events within a Christian apocalyptic alternative to that of Decius and his contemporary pagans. With the persecution, particularly that of Valerian later in A.D. 257, the time of the Antichrist was approaching.[62]

Christians, however, were members of the body of Christ, and thus should exhibit a unity free from the flaws and defects that mark the fabric of the world tottering in the weakness of its old age towards its final sunset. They share a 'common condition of the body' with pagans, with whom they must dwell together for the moment 'within the one house'. Only 'when the present age is fulfilled' will 'members of humanity split into two opposing parts . . . separated one from another for the dwellings of either eternal death or those of immortality'.[63] But the Church as the vehicle of salvation must exhibit unity as well as purity, as a mark of its true and enduring transcendental character, uncontaminated by the world's corruption that is a sign of its metaphysical disorder awaiting renewal.

And here was the problem. Cyprian's church was a divided church in consequence of Decius' persecution and its aftermath. The comparatively short

---

58. Cyprian, *Demet.*, 4.76–80.
59. Cyprian, *Mort.*, 25.416–23; 426–7.
60. Cyprian, *Mort.*, 2.15–22.
61. Cyprian, *Mort.*, 2.29–37.
62. Cyprian, *Ep.*, LVIII.1.2 (13–15), 2.1(30–31), and 7.1 (161–2).
63. Cyprian, *Demet.*, 19.368–74; 21.405–7.

persecution came to an end, perhaps terminated by Decius' death at Abrittus (A.D. 251), or perhaps because he believed that his *supplicatio* had been successfully completed. It was at this point that Cyprian returned to Carthage following his much criticized retreat into hiding that he characterized as the pains of a martyr's exile.[64] But the church to which he returned was one that was divided on how to treat the lapsed who had fallen in persecution and offered animal sacrifice (*sacrificati*), or had compromised by simply offering incense (*thurificati*), or who had, in true Roman fashion, simply bribed the magistrate to give them a certificate saying that they had performed a sacrifice when they had not (*libellatici*).

Cyprian's church was thus to split three ways on this issue. The laxist party around Felicissimus claimed that those who had apostatized should simply, on confession, be absolved and readmitted to communion. The rigorist party around Novatus and Novatian claimed that there could be no readmission to communion in this life, or perhaps only on one's death bed, and that the final judgement should be left to God alone. Cyprian was to assume a mediating position, claiming no readmission to communion for the lapsed while the persecution was on, but once ended, a council of bishops from North Africa would assemble. Then, like magistrates presiding over a court, they should specify the appropriate punishment for each degree of offence, holding out the promise of a pentitential period at the conclusion of which readmission to communion should take place.

But how, in such a divided church, was unity to be established? The problem was for Cyprian, well educated as a Pagan in Roman jurisprudence, a problem of social order and control. One problem was that there was at Carthage an alternative form of ministry to that of the one bishop such as we have seen to have been the creation of Callistus at Rome, and its ideological expression in Fabian's almost contemporary construction of a papal mausoleum as a tribute to the new, monarchical concept of episcopal authority. It was a form of ministry that was also found elsewhere, such as at Lyons and Vienne in Gaul, namely a sacramental ministry that could be performed by the martyrs.

The *Apostolic Tradition*, arguably the Church Order of the Hippolytan community at Rome, makes the following significant statement: [65]

A Confessor, however, if he has been in chains on account of the Lord's name, hands shall no be laid on him for the diaconate or presbyterate. For he has the honour of the

---

64. Brent, *Cyprian and Roman Carthage*, chapter 6.
65. Brent, *Hippolytus*, pp. 287–89, cf. J. A. Cerrato, 'The Association of the name Hippolytus with a Church Order now known as *The Apostolic Tradition*', *St. Vladimir's Theological Quarterly*, 48.2–3 (2004), pp. 179–94 and A. Brent, 'St. Hippolytus, Biblical Exegete, Roman Bishop, and Martyr', ibid. pp. 207–31.

presbyterate through his confession. If however he is to be ordained bishop, hands shall be laid on him.[66]

A confessor must, however, be brought before a magistrate, and not simply be verbally abused or simply given a beating like a schoolboy or a disobedient slave. There had to be real, physical suffering. A martyr needed no baptism in water, since his suffering witnessed his baptism in blood. So too a confessor who had so suffered like a martyr, but had managed to survive, needed no formal ordination through the bishop's hands, but was ordained deacon or presbyter, by virtue of his suffering alone.

In the Church of North Africa, as Cyprian makes plain, presbyters could offer the Eucharistic sacrifice. It is quite clear from a Syrian document that confessors did come into Christian congregations and claim, without ordination, the right to offer the Eucharist:

> If a confessor, not having received the imposition of hands, shall forcibly steal for himself some such honour as this on the grounds that it is his by virtue of his confession, he shall be thrust aside and cast out. For he is not, since he has denied Christ's ordinance and 'is worse than an unbeliever'.[67]

Clearly here was a challenge to the authority of the one bishop, particularly in Cyprian's Carthage, and in the following way.

The normal expectation of martyrdom had been death, and to have survived one's confession and thus been a 'confessor' and not a 'martyr' must have hitherto been rare. But Decius' persecution was not aimed primarily at punishment and execution, but in forcing compliance with the universal *supplicatio* aimed at securing the *pax deorum*. In consequence, there had been produced, not simply a large number of apostates, but also a large number of confessors not actually finally killed. The latter were presumably released, bearing physical scars, because the torturer had simply despaired of their obstinacy, considered that they had suffered enough for the moment, and perhaps left then to consider their position. Large numbers could be found still in prison, where the faithful could visit them.

This sizeable and highly respected group evolved a novel solution in prison visits when they confronted their weaker brethren who had apostatized. Since the fallen brethren had done so through obtaining a *libellus* certifying their pagan sacrifice, the confessors who were standing fast would issue to the fallen a 'certificate of reconciliation (*libellus pacis*)'. By presenting this to the presbyter or bishop at the Eucharist, they could thus be readmitted to communion. Though Cyprian constantly misrepresents this act as a kind of letter of advice

66. *Ap. Trad.*, 9.
67. *C.A.*, VIII.23.4.

to bishops, who may or may not act upon it, undoubtedly a confessor released from prison could themselves give communion from the Eucharist that they themselves had the power by their confession to consecrate.

Celerinus, one such confessor who had been released after physical suffering, was to make his peace with Cyprian. Previously, he had been associated with the group of confessors around Lucianus, from whom he had sought absolution for his fallen sisters. Significantly he addresses Lucianus as 'bishop (high priest) and minister (*antistes et minister*)' of his group. It is the same Lucianus who was to write his letter of instruction to Cyprian as 'pope' or 'archbishop' of Carthage and of Roman Africa, instructing him to give general absolution to those who had fallen in the persecution:

> Be it known to you that we all together have granted reconciliation to those for whom the balance of the account has been drawn up for what they are urging on you following our verdict, and we wish that this decree be brought by you to the notice of other bishops. We pray you to be reconciled with the holy martyrs. Lucianus has signed in the presence of an exorcist and a reader from the clergy.[68]

The conclusion seems to me unescapable that we have in Lucianus someone who was *antistes* and *minister* by virtue of his sufferings alone, exercising the prerogative of Eucharistic presidency that the *Apostolic Tradition* has given him. We have here a 'church of the martyrs', a veritable ecclesial body claiming sacramental authority. It is the archbishop, and other bishops under his authority to whom he is to write, that are to 'be reconciled with the holy martyrs'. It is the hierarchy that needs to submit to their authority, the authority of the suffering and absolving Christ truly and really present in the confessors' scars.[69]

Cyprian, with his pagan legal formation, could not endure such a divided authority within his community. His justification for opposing the 'church of the martyrs' was that their free absolution was likely to achieve Decius' objectives, and reabsorb into paganism the community that had renounced paganism and been cleansed in the font of baptismal regeneration. To Cornelius he writes, regarding the activity of Felicissimus and his group demanding readmission to communion at Rome:

> Is rather, dearest brother, the Catholic Church to be stripped of its status, as well as the faithful and uncorrupted grandeur of its laity found within it, along with the authority and power of its sacred bishop? That is what will be the case if those who have been found in the position of being outside the Church can keep on saying, as heretics,

---

68. Cyprian (Lucianus), *Ep.*, XXIII.1–7.
69. A. Brent, 'Cyprian and the question of ordinatio per confessionem', *StPat.*, 36 (2001), pp. 323–37.

that they wish to make a judgment on the bishop who is placed over the Church . . . They are the fallen judging the one who has stood his ground, the guilty about their judge, those who have committed sacrilege about their priest. All that is left is for the Church to yield to the Capitol. Pagan images and statues with their altars should move into the sacred and venerable assembly of our clergy, while the priests depart, removing the altar of the Lord. It is not merely a question of allowing the petition for readmission of those who had sacrificed and denied Christ publicly. Rather it is, in addition, their attempt to dominate us by force of their terrorism.[70]

Clearly his fundamental objection is to the challenge to episcopal authority. The lapsed can be absolved, but only on the authority of the bishop.

Cyprian was well versed in the Roman legal concept, with its huge rhetorical force, of a 'custom of the ancestors (*mos maiorum*)'. But notoriously new proposals were being advocated under the guise of a claim to antiquity of what might be of only very recent origin. Cyprian thus claims that the martyr-claim was contrary to a long-held tradition that only the bishop could reconcile an apostate by the laying on of hands:

I had trusted of course that the presbyters and deacons who were present there in prison would advise you and fully instruct you concerning the law of the gospel. Previously that had always happened in the time of our ancestors . . . But now . . . not only there in prison the consideration of the divine precepts has not been advanced, but also has been rather up to this moment in time impeded . . . Those presbyters instead, contrary to the law of the gospel, contrary even to your own honorable petition to the court, are offering the Eucharist for them and administering communion. They are doing this before performance of penitence, before confession has been made for the most serious and desperate sin, before imposition of hands, by the bishop and clergy, in recognition of penitence.[71]

Here Cyprian is at his most disingenuous as he appeals to a tradition from a 'past' that he has simply reconstructed to fit his case. Rather than face the church of the martyrs head on, he chooses here, with all the guile of a bureaucrat, to pretend that a *libellus pacis* is simply a piece of advice to a bishop presiding over a court ('your own honorable petition to the court'), and not an instruction to readmit to communion, as Lucianus was clearly shortly later to intend. Here, furthermore, he claims that only the bishop can reconcile by the imposition of hands as the final stage of the penitential process. As he also insists to his clergy, penitents 'regain the right of receiving communion through the imposition of hands of the bishop and clergy'.[72] But as Coppens, in his magisterial study on this subject established, there is no precedent before

70. Cyprian, *Ep.*, LIX.18.1 (494–507).
71. Cyprian, *Ep.*, XV.1.2 (10–27).
72. Cyprian, *Ep.*, XVI.2.2 (35–37).

Cyprian for such an exclusively episcopal rite of reconciliation for a penitent, as opposed to someone baptized in heresy.[73]

In order to establish his new *mos maiorum*, Cyprian deploys his method of Scriptural exegesis to derive a 'new law' as the Church's ruling principle. He takes two passages, Matthew 16:18–19 and John 20:21–3, where authority is granted to Peter or to the Twelve to 'bind and loose', which Cyprian takes to mean 'absolve' and 'reconcile'.[74] Thus he can conclude that the martyr's *libellus* is contrary to divine law if it is believed to effect what the bishop alone can effect:

> From this passage the ordination logically follows of each bishop in temporal succession, and thus the ruling principle of the Church, that the Church is founded on the bishops, and every movement of the Church is steered through the governance of those same presiding bishops.[75]

Thus only an episcopal absolutism that subjects all other sacramental authority to the bishop will satisfy Cyprian. But it is a conclusion derived from exegesis, and not from historical inquiry into any time-hallowed tradition.

How then was a penitent apostate to be reconciled before Cyprian's innovative rite of quasi-juridical examination of the 'offence', and imposition of hands masquerading as the practice of time-hallowed tradition? The penitent was reconciled simply by the act of the presbyter or bishop in giving communion. Dionysius of Alexandria, Cyprian's contemporary and episcopal colleague, in his letter to Fabius, bishop of Antioch, makes this quite clear. Serapion was an apostate who was reconciled to the catholic church on his death bed. The presbyter who was to come to his bedside was unwell, so he entrusted 'a fragment of the Eucharist' to Serapion's grandson, with instruction to place it in the old man's mouth. Thus 'his sin was blotted out' so that the receiving of the consecrated host itself was his absolution, and no act by his in any case absent bishop.[76]

All this took place, Dionysius boasts to his fellow bishop Cyprian, under his firm episcopal control. But it is not difficult to envisage how, when as at Carthage presbyters could offer the Eucharistic sacrifice, with episcopal ordination or without it in view of their martyr's scars, episcopal control could be severely curtailed: they could simply absolve and readmit to communion with the sacramental means that was in their hands. This was a fact to which Cyprian took personal exception, with the plea of the present 'emergency' of the Decian

---

73. J. Coppens, *L'imposition des mains et les rites connexes dans le Noveau Testament et dans l'église ancienne* (Universitas catholica lovaniensis, 15.2; Paris: J. de Meester et fils, 1925), p. 374.

74. Cyprian, *Unit.*,4.75–8 and 85–90 (TR).

75. Cyprian, *Ep.*, XXXIII.1.1 (8–11).

76. Dionysius of Alexandria *apud* Eusebius, *H.E.*, V.44.4–6.

persecution requiring strict episcopal control to stop the faithful returning to the pagan altars of sacrifice, and the church ceasing to exist for the imminent return of Jesus Christ. But there was another threat to the absolute episcopal control that Cyprian sought.

Novatian, Roman presbyter and author of a very orthodox Latin treatise *On the Trinity*, was to contend along with his group that there was no absolution possible for a mortal sin such as apostasy, any more than for adultery or for murder. Although *Hermas* was to advocate one, second chance, the stricter view, represented by Tertullian no less, was very much a 'one strike and you are out' policy. Hermas' other title was 'the Shepherd' and for his penitential leniency Tertullian was to denounce him as 'the adulterous shepherd' also to be found as a common motif on drinking cups.[77] Joined by his namesake Novatus at Carthage, Novatian sought to set up a rival church, and to this end was consecrated bishop in opposition to Cornelius, who after an interregnum had succeeded (A.D. 251) the martyred bishop Fabian (died, 20th Jan. 250).

Thus Cyprian, on his return from exile in A.D. 251 was faced with another threat to his authority from a rigorist and puritanical group that believed that the laxist group were defiling the purity of the church. How could Cyprian now respond to this further challenge to unity, in which it was possible to have two rival bishops in both Carthage and Rome, both in communion with each other and their sympathizers, but out of communion with himself and those in communion with him? Here was a new problem and one that it was difficult to resolve by the creation of a new *mos maiorum*, as he had done in the case of Felicissimus and the church of the martyrs. There was no problem for Novatian, with the notion that the bishop should have absolute control over the administration of the sacraments.

But Cyprian's problem was on what grounds was he to acknowledge Cornelius as rightful bishop of Rome and not Novatian. The test for heresy, as we have seen, was the establishment of a succession of teachers back to either Simon Magus, according to Irenaeus, or schools of philosophers, and finally worship of the snake (the Naassenes), according to the *Refutatio*. But Novatian had committed no heresy: his teaching on the Trinity was clearly in the apostolic succession.

At this point Cyprian was to fall back on his pagan formation in jurisprudence, despite his claim in his account of his baptism in which he experienced 'the corruption of my former world wiped clean with the aid of the water of regeneration'.[78] It is impossible to step completely from one social world into another, and the convert's claim to have done so is invariably based upon self-delusion. According to Roman Law, whose symbol was the bronze twelve

---

77. Tertullian, *Pudic.*, 10.12 (50–54).
78. Cyprian, *Donat.*, 4.59–67. For a discussion of the precise character of his legal training, see G. W. Clarke, 'The Secular Profession of St. Cyprian of Carthage, *Latomus*, 24 (1965)', pp. 633–38.

tables whose copy stood in the Forum of Roman Carthage, constitutional political power was always to be exercised within a defined and sanctified geographical space: that was both the scope of one's authority and its domain, its *imperium*.[79]

Thus originally Romulus, as king and augur (*rex augur*), had marked the sacred space of Rome within which legitimate political activity could be exercised by a magistrate having authority or *imperium*. At the founding of a city, along with the augural ritual, the sacrifice of a pig and a bull would take place (*suouetaurilia*) after these animals had pulled a plough around the city marking its boundary walls. Such a ceremony was performed again when a census was taken: the city boundaries and all within them must be cleansed and sanctified to be subjects of the due political authority exercised within them. Such themes were present in the frescoes of the *Ara Pacis* proclaiming Augustus' second founding of Rome and the inauguration of the 'golden age'.[80]

The principle of a geographically determined sphere of legitimate political authority thus established in Rome as a city-state became extended with the creation of the Roman Empire during the Republic. Each governor of a Roman province had *imperium* within a defined space that was his 'province'. Once one had left one's province, or one's period of command had expired, one's constitutional power lapsed: one became a private person.

This was precisely the case when Caesar, in 49 B.C., crossed the Rubicon, the border of his province, and entered Italy: he ceased to have pro-consular *imperium*, and thus was a rebel and an invader. Emperors from Augustus onwards endeavoured to give their position legitimacy by claiming a 'greater authority', a *maius imperium* by which they alone could enter constitutionally the legitimate domain of consular magistrates. The symbol of a magistrate having *imperium* was the *sella curialis*, the magistrate's chair on which he sat thus symbolized his power over his constitutionally defined, geographical domain.

Cyprian now proposes to use such a model to expose the illegitimacy of Novatian's claim to be bishop of Rome. It mattered not that Novatian's theology was orthodox: Novatian had invaded the sacred space of a bishop who thus like a magistrate sat upon an official chair:

> Cornelius was appointed bishop . . . when no one had been created bishop before him, when the place occupied by Fabian, that is to say when the position of Peter, the rank to which the sacred Chair gave entitlement (*cathedrae sacerdotalis*) was unoccupied. Once however it was filled, and confirmed by the will of God and the consent of us all, anyone who wished to be made a bishop could necessarily only be made so *outside* the Church. He who does not hold to the unity of this single number has not the Church's ordination. Whosoever this man may be, and granted that he will boast much of himself

79. Cyprian, *Donat.*, 10.196–97.
80. P. Catalano, 'Aspetti spaziali de sistema giuridico-religioso Romano', in *ANRW*, II.16.1, pp. 440–53 and Brent, *Cyprian and Roman Carthage*, chapter 2, section C.1.

and even more justify himself, he is outside the sacred precinct (*profanus*) and he is a foreigner, he is on the outside. And since after the first there cannot be a second appointment, whoever is created after the first one (of necessity the only one!) is not really the second one, but no one at all.[81]

Cornelius' 'sacred precinct' has thus been invaded by an external enemy, invading a sacred space within which sanctified legitimate power is exercised: 'he is bearing arms against the Church, he is offering resistance to God's ordered arrangement. An enemy of the altar, a rebel against Christ's sacrifice, of bad faith instead of faithfulness . . .'[82] Cornelius is already in occupancy of the *sella curialis* that Cyprian calls the 'sacred chair'. This fact alone means that Novatian's claim is utterly void.

Cyprian refers to his diocese as his 'province'.[83] His opponents, whether under Felicissimus or Novatian, are described as conducting a 'mutiny. The five presbyters, who supported the former group, are guilty of 'treachery (*perfidia*)', of forming a 'conspiracy (*coniuratio*) . . . by their constant plots continually renewing their sacrilegious designs'.[84] He clearly believes that each bishop has his own *prouincia*.[85] The notion of 'sacrilege' because of the invasion of sanctified constitutional space is clearly applied, and is connected with these political concepts of those who are opposing legitimate, constitutional authority. In order to demonstrate why, even though Novatian might claim to be in an orthodox teaching succession, his consecration as a bishop is nevertheless invalid, Cyprian is having to impose upon the concept of Church order a Roman, pagan constitutional model.

Cyprian is acutely aware, however, that he is not dealing with the organization of only the church of Carthage in isolation, as Victor and Callistus had been at Rome in the generation before. Decius' persecution had been worldwide, and so the church's response to it needed also to be worldwide. There had been an exchange of episcopal letters between himself and Dionysius of Alexandria, as well as Cornelius and many other of the North African bishops, precisely over how they should make a common response to issues of church discipline in the light of Decius' edict and its aftermath. It was here an almost republican political philosophy begins to appear in Cyprian's claims about church order.

Each bishop within his diocese is answerable to God alone. Nevertheless, each magistrate interacts with their equal within the imperial whole, holding court within their own geographical jurisdiction (diocese), but in the light of a consensus with one another that forms the basis for their intercommunion.

81. Cyprian, *Ep.*, LV.8.4 (133); 8.5 (136–45).
82. Cyprian, *Unit.*, 17.430–33.
83. Cyprian, *Ep.*, XXVII.3.1 (39–41).
84. Cyprian, *Ep.*, XLIII.1.2 (17–18).
85. Cyprian, *Ep.*, XLVIII.3.2 (26–30); LV.21.1 (346–47).

Thus, to be a member of the body of Christ, a layman must be in communion with a priest, who is in communion with a bishop, who in turn is part of the worldwide episcopal college, whose consensus is the bond of unity. To have communion with Novatian or Felicissimus is to break off from the true body of Christ, and to sunder its unity. As Cyprian says:

> Though there is one Church that comes from Christ's body, divided into many members throughout the whole world, though for precisely the same reason there is one episcopate, widely spread in a harmony of concord between many corporations, despite this, Novatian is attempting to create a Church of human origin in place of what God has handed down, in place of the unity, fastened and universally joined together, of the Catholic Church.[86]

This 'harmony of concord' between the bishops is described as 'the bond (*uinculum*)' of concord that 'inseparably sticks together' the dioceses as component parts of the whole.[87]

Cyprian, therefore, sees the unity of the church as a kind of spider's web of bishops, each with their separate jurisdiction over defined geographical space (*imperium*), forming a network by their common consent and agreement. But a new question was now to arise, particularly in the context of a pagan empire where Rome was the centre, and now with Decius organizing centrally its cult of the gods of the Roman state, including its deified emperors: did the spider's web of mutually connecting dioceses and diocesans need an episcopal centre by comparison with the imperial centre?

It was on this point that Cyprian's thinking began to search for a role for the bishop of Rome, even though his differing relations with Cornelius and Stephen was to produce some later modifications. Like the bishops, all the apostles had 'equal power', but Christ established 'one Chair. . . as the source of unity and its guiding principle', giving to Peter 'the first place (*primatus*)'. The 'one flock' thus exemplified is 'nurtured by all the apostles in unanimous agreement', that Cyprian had described as the 'bond (*uinculum*) of unity'. In his later response to pope Stephen, he was to modify his position, substituting the notion of *primatus* or 'first place' with that of *exordium* or 'starting point'. He continues:

> In order that he might reveal their unity, he ordained by his own authority, that the source of that same unity should begin from the one who began the series. The remaining Apostles were necessarily also that which Peter was, endowed with an equal partnership both of honour and of power, but the starting point (*exordium*) from which they begin is from their unity with him in order that the Church of Christ might be exemplified as one.[88]

---

86.   Cyprian, *Ep.*, LV.24.2 (427–31).
87.   Cyprian, *Unit.*, 7.163–4.
88.   Cyprian, *Unit.*, 4.88–98.

Thus the spider's web will have a centre, the 'starting point', the Latin word for which (*exordium*) can mean 'the warp set up on a loom before it is started'.[89] Even before his dispute with Stephen over the rebaptism of heretics, Cyprian had described Fortunatus and Felicissimus as daring to sail both to the chair of Peter, and to the primordial church from where the unity of the sacred bishops derived its origin.[90]

But it is at this juncture that Cyprian's eschatological concerns now come into play with his rewriting ecclesial polity in the light of his secular jurisprudence. As we have emphasized, both political and natural order must have their common origin in the metaphysical order that they will reflect. The unity of the church must, therefore, reflect the unity of the cosmos, and that unity is defined in terms primarily of Stoic metaphysics in Cyprian's general cultural background. Alexander of Aphrodisias had related the unity of the universe to the Logos thus:

> Still the *Logos* is concerned with first principles and God, it is also the unity of the universe and its sympathy with itself. For the God who permeates matter is for them the same as all existence.[91]

For Cyprian, the unity of the Church as the body of Christ who is the Logos reflects the unity of the cosmos. If that unity of the body consists of parts, of members that now configure into dioceses under bishops whose agreement is the 'bond (*uinculum*)' holding together the whole, then it reflects how the material cosmos is held together. As Cicero says:

> Thus the world is firmly established and so sticks together in order to continue in existence . . . bodies so inter-joined continue in existence, since they are bound together as if by a certain bond (*uinculum*) placed around them. This bond it effects by that nature which is outpoured throughout the whole world as it establishes all things by mind and *Logos*.[92]

Seneca might add '. . . this universe within which we are contained is both one and God, and we are its associates and physical members'.[93] Cyprian now says that it is the 'body of sacred bishops', spread throughout the world, that is 'so tightly bound together by the glue of mutual concord and by the bond (*uinculum*) of unity'.[94]

But Cyprian agrees with his pagan contemporaries, and the claims of Decius and his opponents, that the world has reached its sunset and now, unlike the unity of the golden age in the Acts of the Apostles, the unity both of the physical

---

89. A. Souter et al. (eds), *New Latin Dictionary* (Oxford: Clarendon Press 1968), p. 646, col. 1.
90. Cyprian, *Ep.*, LIX.14.1 (393–394).
91. Alexander Aphrodisias, *Mixt.* (= Arnim, II.475.14–16).
92. Cicero, *Nat. Deor.*, II.45.115 (= Arnim, II.549.8–13).
93. Seneca, *Ep.*, 92.30.
94. Cyprian, *Ep.*, LXVIII.3.2 (49–50).

and the social worlds is falling apart. Those who, like the Novatians, 'depart from the charity and unity of the catholic church' are the antichrists mentioned by John as indicative of the last times.[95] Cyprian sets their work in the context of the 'decay (*pernicies*)' that destroys the *uinculum* that binds all things together in unity:

> The same evil grows in size to threatening proportions of destructiveness. It is a poisonous decay (*pernicies*) that begins to rise up and spring forth, wrought by heretical perversity and by schisms, even as ought to happen at the world's sunset. The Holy Spirit through the Apostle forewarned with this prediction: 'In the last days . . . distressing times will come'. Whatever words were said beforehand are being fulfilled, and, with the end of the age drawing near, they will come to pass as men are searched and examined along with the times.[96]

Divisions within the body of Christ are, therefore, part of the 'old age of the world', the metaphysical collapse of the order of the world from that of the age of gold to that of iron. It is, however, Christ's Second Advent that will restore all things, and not the sacrifices at Philip's games or Decius' *supplicatio*.

The logic of a Christian discourse that availed itself of a pagan political discourse that made the ruler the channel of the Logos, or divine order of the world, into Christian society was that the divine ruler should be both priest and king. We shall see, in our next chapter, how Constantine was to wrestle with the question why this could not be the case with Christianity. For the moment, let us summarize where this chapter has taken us in answer to this question.

4. *Christian Eschatology in an Age of Iron*

An eschatology that was no longer the imminent future of apocalyptic could function to make such a case for the Christianization of Roman, pagan imperial order. Luke-Acts deals with such a realized eschatology, offering the peace of Christ and his reign as the riposte to the claim of the Principate to have realized the peace of the gods in nature and in society.

The realization of the eschatology of the return of the pagan golden age in Augustus, and the message of the *Ara Pacis*, had political consequences of making the emperor the means for that age's inauguration: emperor, augur, and *Pontifex Maximus* were to be one and the same. Why not with Christianity, once its apocalyptic was no longer in the imminent future, but now in process of realization in the present? We have seen how Justin's doctrine of the Logos, and Callistus' centralization of ecclesiastical authority in Rome, paralleled pagan developments in the ideology of power, and produced a monarchian cosmos with its monarchian Trinity.

---

95. 1 Jn 2:18-19 and Cyprian, *Ep.*, LXIX.1.3 (19–26); LXX.3.2 (85–89) (on the rebaptism of heretics).

96. Cyprian, *Unit.*, 16.392–96, in exposition of II Tim 3:1-9.

The reason why a Christian emperor was not later to become high priest, or high priest emperor has become clear in the events of Decius and Cyprian in the mid-third century. Both Decius and his pagan rivals, and the church of Cyprian, were both convinced that the golden age, or the age to come, was not available in the present. Both visions were set upon an imminent future, whether of Decius and Valerian's *nouum saeculum*, or of the kingdom of the sun promised by Uranius Antoninus, not to be found in the immediate present, but hoped for from the appropriate political messiah. In a similar vein, Cyprian had no expectation of Christianizing contemporary society, whose leaders themselves acknowledged its lost and tottering condition.

The Church in one sense was the harbinger of the world to come in that it needed to remain uncontaminated by the present age and its metaphysical defects. For that reason, it was not simply the apostates without due penance that had to be kept out of communion in the body of Christ, but those who threaten to dissolve the 'bond (*uinculum*) of unity', and thus represented the poisonous decay (*pernicies*) of the world's old age. The Christian lives in both worlds, in process of change but not yet changed:

> Thus the Spirit that we have received controls at its own pleasure what we have begun to be. Because we have not yet experienced change in our body and its members, physical change up until now appears concealed under the clouds of this carnal age . . .[97]

The believer 'had begun to be of God: the Holy Spirit was now giving life . . .'[98] To express matters once again in terms of Cyprian's Stoic background:

> For as long as our body continues here with a nature shared with the rest of mankind, it is necessary that there should be a covenant to keep us together in a common body under which it is not allowed that members of humanity should split from one another into two opposing parts without first departing hither from this age . . . until that time of this present age has been fulfilled. Then we shall be separated one from another for the dwellings of either eternal death or those of immortality.[99]

'Nature shared with mankind' and the 'common covenant' were Stoic terms expressing the Stoic belief that Spirit and matter were aspects of each other (*hylomorphism*).[100]

Clearly Cyprian did not believe in the redemption of human society, or the universal enjoyment of the return of a lost golden age:

> The kingdom of God, most beloved brothers, has begun to be imminent. The reward of life and the joy of eternal salvation, and everlasting gladness, and the gaining possession

---

97. Cyprian, *Donat.*, 5.100–103.
98. Cyprian, *Donat.*, 4.59–67.
99. Cyprian, *Demet.*, 19.368–74.
100. Cicero, *Leg.*, I.13.35; *Rep.*, I.25.39–40 (= Augustine, *Ep.*, 138.10); III.13.23.

of a paradise once lost are now coming with the passing of the world . . . Only someone
who does not believe that he is beginning to reign with Christ will be unwilling to go
to him.[101]

Those who are 'beginning to reign with Christ' will be his and the rest of
humanity will be lost. The present 'covenant' of nature that keeps Christians
and Pagans 'together in a common body' is only for 'this age', with the believers'
true nature 'concealed under the clouds of this carnal age'.

Believing, therefore, in an inaugurated eschatology, and sharing in the apocalypticism of the age of Decius, Cyprianic theology could never subscribe to
the concept of a Christian empire with a Christian emperor as representative of
the divine *logos* in human society. Eusebius was to believe this, as we shall
now see, and he, along with many Eastern Fathers, never did like apocalyptic.

101.   Cyprian, *Mort.*, 2.29–37.

Chapter 8

CONSTANTINE, THE DIVINE ORDER OF THE CHRISTIAN
EMPIRE AND ITS EUROPEAN LEGACY

In our last chapter, we saw that the pagan age of Decius as well the Christian age of Cyprian represented a rebirth of an apocalyptic vision of the political situation and its transformation. In a time of perceived, third century national and international crisis, the vision of the Republic and of Lucan had been reborn in which the present political order would be in sympathy with a natural order struggling to be reborn and reconstructed anew in an imminent future. There was no present divine order in nature to be reflected in political order: rather the natural order itself had collapsed into the chaos of the age of iron, as evidenced in the signs and portents in the heavens accompanying natural and civic woes upon earth. Cyprian produced his Christian counterpart to this revival of the apocalyptic imagination.

In times of crisis, when societies or groups within them perceive the threat of annihilation, the social-psychological phenomenon occurs in which the group develops a picture of a future to be imminently realized drawn with symbols and images taken from its mythical past: the act of creation that originally brought order out of chaos is to be repeated in a renewed world. When the threat recedes, or the present age continues beyond expectation, then 'projects' are conceived that will reinterpret future hopes in terms of what can be realized in present society. In such a context, those who have eyes to see it will see that the kingdom of God has already completely or partially come. Such, in formal terms, was the experience of the Principate under Augustus and his successors, as well as of the community of Luke-Acts, and, in more recent times, of the communism of Eastern Europe after the Marxist revolution in Russia, and of New-Labour-type 'projects' in democratic socialist movements in Western Europe.

The apocalypticism of Decius and of Cyprian lasted for comparatively short a period. Aurelian, unlike Uranius Antoninus, did not predict a coming 'kingdom of the Sun', but claimed that all deities throughout the empire were contained within the godhead of Apollo as *Sol Invictus*. Present political order, in which all things were related to the emperor as political first cause, was a reflection or incarnation of a cosmic order that at present pertained. Contemporaneously, in the reconstruction of a pagan tomb on the Vatican hillside by the

Christian family of the Julii, Christ is represented as Apollo, riding in triumph the horses and chariot of the Sun, with the orb of the world in his hand. Different theologies and cosmologies pointed to alternative political structures. And thus we return to our question, why could a Christian ruler not replace the pagan Emperor as representative of the cosmic order and its earthly incarnation? Why was Cyprian's creation of a state within a state so enduring: why could not the state within a state now simply take over the power structures of the state itself?

We saw in Chapter 6 how a monarchical Trinity in a monarchical cosmos came to be reflected in the episcopal monarchy schemed for by Callistus, and aided by the metaphysical mindset that proclaimed his Trinity, in which there could be separation of rank and order, but no separation of persons. A cosmos in which a plurality of two or three divine persons co-operated with one another in a life-giving, love-giving relation, in which no one was more powerful than another, or on a different and subordinate level of being to another, would be reflected in a quite different political structure within the community: one in which presbyter bishops, equal in power, dignity and majesty, would secure political unity on the basis of mutual consent, regard, and even love expressed in a presbytery of persons.

The tomb of the popes, and the regnal dates assigned to bishops from Pontian onward, might suggest that Callistus and his theology, both political and metaphysical, had triumphed. So far Christian cosmic order was reflected in Church order alone, and the 'catholic church', which they, in the words of the *Refutatio*, 'had the brazenness to call themselves', was the sole body with a political structure because it reflected the 'true' cosmic order. They may have been thus far a minority, whether among the Roman congregations in a loose confederation marked by the exchange of the *fermentum*, or among the many more, Gnostics, Marcionites, Valentinians, Sethites, etc. who called themselves by the name 'Christian'. But they were growing. Thus there was implicitly a political project: the ruler had been the mediator of the cosmic Logos to pagan political society, so what were the clear implications if political society became Christian: how would the cosmic Christ, as Logos, be mediated to the structure of Christian society?

Earlier Constantine, as emperor and *Pontifex Maximus* of the old religion of Aurelian and of Elagabalus, might now claim to be the *Pontifex Maximus* of the new religion, the universal bishop of those within the church and not simply those without, as he expressly had claimed. Christian sacerdotal power and imperial political power might be seen as one. In that regard a Trinity in which the Son was subordinate to the Father, a created being though not like any other created being, with the Holy Spirit proceeding from one or both, might well reflect an empire in which the church was subordinate to the emperor. Constantine could therefore hope to emerge as the sole earthly representative of *Sol Invictus*, in the pagan form of which he might once have believed, but now in the Christian form of the image of Christ Apollo, riding the chariot of the sun, holding in his hand the globe of the world, as a challenge to, and now a replacement for, Aurelian's universal, pagan solar monotheism.

All this Constantine might wish for and Eusebius seek for him, eschewing apocalypticism as the latter did. But it did not happen.

In answer to the question 'why?' we might reply with MacMillan's famous truism: 'Events, dear boy!' But although we do not believe in the Marxist dogma in which historical conditions determine systems of thought, we do not believe that historical ideas exist independently of events in some kind of a-temporal, ideational heaven: particular ideas that emerge at particular times condition, as well as being themselves conditioned, by historical events.[1] Even if we believe, as a Christian like myself believes, in a historical revelation, what is revealed is still revealed in the historical flux of things so that its form continues to appear to develop.[2] And so we may examine some of the reasons, theological as well as historical, with ideas shaping events and events shaping ideas as the history unravels.

The first reason why the project in which the cosmic order of a Christian universe was not regarded as mediated through a Christian political ruler who was also high priest was because that would require a completely realized eschatology. We have seen that the Principate subscribed to such a realized, pagan eschatology, to which the *Ara Pacis* bore witness, with its proclamation of the returning golden age. That age of peace Augustus' sacerdotal act, the *augurium pacis*, had achieved, and a Stoic philosophical theology had intellectually justified. In many respects the Lukan project had produced a Christian counterpart to such a pagan, realized eschatology, reassuring Theophilus and his circle that the faith that they had embraced would fulfil the ends of that pagan political project so much better: not the *pax deorum* but the peace of the one true God could be found, in Christ, in the angels' song at Bethlehem, and in the cries of the crowd at the Triumphal Entry on Palm Sunday. Christ's true peace would be mediated further through the apostolic ministry to the primitive church, and the concord and peace of that idyllic society, seen previously in the words of Zacharias and the picture of the future role of the infant John the Baptist.

But even Luke in such a mood still nevertheless had to represent the traditional apocalyptic expectations of early Christianity. Though the apocalyptic events were assigned to an indefinite future, they were still destined to come after the indefinite 'times of the gentiles'. Yet for the moment there was the *pax dei* of Christ in substitution for Augustus' *pax deorum*.

The effect on political ideology of the continuance of the apocalyptic tradition was effectively to rule out the placing of the final piece in the jigsaw of the

---

1. P. Berger and T. Luckmann, *The Social Construction of Reality* (Harmondsworth: Penguin, 1967), Part 1; Q. Skinner, *The Foundations of Modern Political Thought* (Cambridge: University Press, 1978).

2. J. H. Newman, *The Development of Christian Doctrine* (London: James Toovey, 1845).

Christian, Logos cosmology in contrast with the pagan version. The pagan version could have a present ruler, as mediator between the rational order of nature and civil society at peace in this time and place. The Christian version, in maintaining the apocalyptic hope, could make the focus of the promised reign of God only when Christ returned again, so that Logos and Christian ruler could not have this metaphysical bond.

Eusebius and the Eastern Fathers, as is well known, disliked apocalyptic and had great doubts about the presence of the book of Revelation in the New Testament. Indeed, for reasons that we have seen, this book directly contra-dicted the Constantinian project: 'the kingdom of our God and of his Christ' was to replace the 'kingdoms of this world': there was to be no substitution of a pagan, Augustan realized eschatology with a Christian, Lukan one.

It was such a Lukan project that Constantine, in Eusebius' eyes, was to fulfil. Certainly Constantine's religious experience as a pagan came directly from what was to become the more successful fulfilment of Elagabalus' pagan project in the reign of the emperor Aurelian (A.D. 270–275). On coins from Serdica, we find his title as: 'born god and Lord (*deus et dominus natus*)'.[3] Aurelian's god was *Sol Invictus* and was to be the supreme god of the empire, with his own priesthood.[4] He clearly saw himself as mediator of the divine power of *Sol Invictus*, since on his coins *Sol* is called by the emperor's title: 'Lord of the Roman Empire (*dominus imperii Romani*)'.[5] Uranius Antoninus, Deciuss opponent, had, in more specific terms, as we have seen, laid claim to Elagabalus' legacy.

But Aurelian's claim to a pagan monotheism, to a cosmic order of which he could be the mediator flowing through him into political order, was to be challenged by a piece of Christian iconography from this era unearthed in the Vatican excavations in the tomb of the Julii. Here, in the dome of a tomb whose walls were richly decorated with scenes of Jonah and the Great Fish and of Christ the Fisherman, we find golden mosaics into which, arising from the natural scenery of extensive clusters of green vine tendrils, emerges a figure riding a chariot with white horses, and holding in his hand a globe. Is it Apollo, as an expression of *Sol Invictus*, riding the chariots of the sun? Not juxtaposed, surely with the Jonah and Fisherman depictions? The sun's rays, with which the head of the figure is radiate has been contorted by the artist into a chi rho, the cross shaped symbol of the first two letters of 'Christ' in the Greek alpha-bet, and the original Christian 'sign of the cross'.

This was the kind of Christianity to which Constantine, until A.D. 310 still a follower of *Sol Invictus*, was converted. His conversion experience, described by Eusebius in his *Life of Constantine*, bore all the marks of a vision of *Sol Invictus* transformed into the figure of the triumphant Christ. Immediately

---

3. *RIC*, 5.1, p. 299, no. 305–306.
4. *CIL*, VIII.5143; SHA, *Aurel*. 35.3.
5. *RIC*, 5.1, p. 301, nos. 319–322.

before the battle of the Milvian bridge (A.D. 312), at which he defeated his rival Maxentius and marched victoriously into Rome, Constantine had seen in the sky 'a cross of light, brighter than the noonday sun', under which he had read in Greek the words 'By this sign conquer'. The 'sign of the cross' was the Chi Rho, and it was these two letters, as an abbreviation for 'Christ', that now was placed on the shields and banners of his legions in place of representations of pagan deities.

Constantine's coinage was still to show images of the *Sol Invictus*, which had begun before his conversion (A.D. 310–311),[6] as late as A.D. 328.[7] One of these (A.D. 316) depicts, in an image reminiscent of Christ-Apollo in the tomb of the Julii, a depiction of *Sol* radiate, with a globe in his left hand and a chlamys across his shoulder.[8] Furthermore, we have the record of the pagan panegyrist, delivered at Trier (A.D. 310) after the death of Maximian. Here Constantine entered the temple of Apollo, where he had a vision of the god:

> You saw . . . your protector Apollo, in company with Victory, offering you laurel crowns, each of which bear the presage of thirty years. For this is the span of human life owed to you, an age beyond that of Nestor . . . You really saw the god, and recognized yourself in the appearance of one to whom the prophecies of poets have declared the rule of the whole world should belong. The prophecies are to my mind fulfilled in you . . .[9]

Furthermore, we have coins of the *uota* of the legions referring to this vision, prophesying 20 or 30 years of life for Constantine, with the Latin letters XX or XXX, suggestive also of a pagan counterpart to the Chi Rho symbolism of Constantine's Christian vision. The 'kingdom of the sun' for which Uranius Antoninus sought, was now to be realized in a Christian emperor.

But what was to be the role of a Christian emperor still bearing the ancient, pagan title of *Pontifex Maximus*? Eusebius was, in a truly Lukan tradition, now to propose a kind of realized eschatology to which Constantine would be central, while retaining some concessions to traditional apocalyptic themes that he otherwise despised.

Constantine as a Christian emperor, as far as the church was concerned, was, in terms of political ideology, a problem. As we have seen, both pagan and Christian eschatology had been critical issues both for Decius and Valerian, as well as for Cyprian: the problem of metaphysical decline and collapse, as a prelude to the world's transformation, had been commonly expressed by both: it was the solution over which they had differed.

---

6. *RIC*, VI.890 (Trier).
7. *RIC*, VII.28.r3 (Thessalonica); 70.r3; 92 (Heraclea).
8. *RIC*, VII.49.r1 (Rome).
9. *Panegyrici Latini*, 6 (7).21.3–6, translated in J. Stevenson and W. H. C. Frend, *A New Eusebius. Documents Illustrating the History of the Church to A.D. 337* (London: SPCK, 1987), p. 282, no. 248.

Decius' claim, along with his rivals for the imperial purple, had been that the golden age celebrated with the millennial games was being realized in their reigns, each rival claiming to be the agent of fate in bringing back that lost age of peace and plenty. For Cyprian the 'sunset of the world', its 'old-age', could only issue in Christ's second coming in victory over Valerian as the embodi- ment of the Antichrist that was to come. The martyrs would judge both Church and the world, but the events of the Synoptic apocalypse were relevant in terms of being brought before rulers and emperors, and confessing Christ's name before men.

The problem posed now for the position of the first Christian emperor was that his victory should not have happened in terms of such apocalyptic expectation. Cyprian's own labours in response to the situation that he had confronted, in concert with Cornelius bishop of Rome, had led to a height- ened apocalyptic expectation that had remained endemic to a Christian tradi- tion that would canonize the Synoptic gospels, even without the book of Revelation. Within such a perspective, considering also that, after the brief peace under Gallienus and Aurelian, Diocletian's persecution had broken out suddenly and without warning, the next persecution was surely to be the last before Antichrist, be it Valerian or Diocletian, gave way to the second coming of Christ?

But this had not happened. Instead, not only did the emperor claim to be a Christian and to have seen the corrected, Christian version of the pagan one about the appearance of Apollo, but he was resolute against schism and heresy, clearly implying his wish for Christianity to be the faith that would unite the empire. In A.D. 313 the Donatist controversy had arisen in the church of North Africa over a number of issues over the persecution that had just ceased in the West. One issue was the perennial one in North Africa on whether apostasy in persecution could be absolved, which now included handing over sacred books and vessels, rebaptizing heretics and therefore rebaptizing those baptized in the catholic church who were held to have fallen. Another issue was whether a bishop was validly ordained if ordained by someone who had handed over sacred books (a *traditor*). Thus had arisen a duplicate succession of bishops, those in communion with the rest of the Mediterranean world including Rome, and those who had constituted themselves as the uncontaminated, 'pure' and 'true' church mainly in North Africa.

Constantine, as Christian emperor of a Rome not yet officially Christian in A.D. 313, intervened directly in church affairs by recognizing one party in the dispute. Thus he wrote to Anulinus, governor of North Africa:

> Those men who, with due holiness and constant observance of this law, bestow their
> services on the performance of divine worship, should receive the rewards of their own
> labours . . . Wherefore it is my wish that those persons who, within the province com-
> mitted unto you, in the Catholic Church *over which Caecilian presides*, bestow their

service on this holy worship – those who they are accustomed to call clerics – should once for all be kept free from all public offices . . .[10]

Thus Christian clergy were to be exempt from public offices that carried with them the onerous weight of a very high price tag. But this applied only to those clergy 'in the Catholic Church over which Caecilian presides'. Thus Constantine had defined in this situation what body was the 'true' Church and intervened in an internal ecclesiastical dispute. To the same Caecilian Constantine was to send large sums of money in support through Ursus, the finance minister of Africa, with the assurance that, if it was not enough, Heraclides, treasurer of the imperial estates, would give more.[11]

Thus the bishops of North Africa were to experience in Constantine, not Antichrist or his forerunner bringing to its height and full intensity the last persecution before Christ's second coming, but a fellow-Christian, a brother in Christ. As a self-same brother in Christ Constantine was to assemble the Council of Nicaea, granting permission for the attending bishops to use the official imperial highway, the *cursus publicus*, paying for the accommodation costs at inns on the way. Ignatius had travelled to martyrdom in chains over this route in Asia Minor, and only in irony had Ignatius regarded it as his royal highway. Nicaea itself was a council held to resolve the Arian heresy that Christ as son of God was a lesser God, a derived and subordinate being from 'the immutable Father beyond pain and death'. Many of the bishops that assembled there bore the marks in their bodies of fortitude during the most recent persecutions. Now, having stood firm against Decius, Valerian and Diocletian, they were being greeted almost unbelievably as a fellow Christian by Constantine, the successor of these persecuting emperors.

This was an event that the political ideology of early Christianity clearly had not predicted, and the challenge now to Eusebius' political theology was to explain why what ought not to have happened properly had. In consequence, as Markus has pointed out, Eusebius proposed reconstructing Christian eschatology and salvation history. It was this reconstruction that Augustine was first to accept, and then modify in his own work.[12] Basically, we might see the epochs of salvation history in terms of creation and the fall, the covenant with Noah, then Abraham, and then with Moses. Finally Christ's death and resurrection, the age of the Church, the Tribulation and apocalyptic woes, and finally Christ's second coming. Eusebius conceived an idea that the early Augustine developed, namely of a new phase in salvation history where the persecutions end, but the second coming does not immediately ensue. Instead there arises a

10. Eusebius, *H.E.*, X.7.1–2.
11. Eusebius, *H.E.*, X.6.1–3.
12. R. A. Markus, *Saeculum: History and Society in the Theology of St. Augustine* (Cambridge: University Press 1988).

universal, Christian Roman empire of peace, in which the world enjoys its long old-age, in preparation finally for Christ's second coming.

Certainly Constantine emerges in Eusebius' narrative as more than simply another Roman emperor who, remarkably, happens to be Christian. Constantine's battle and victory over Maxentius at the battle of the Milvian bridge is described in Old Testament imagery of the delivery of Israel from the Egyptians also used to describe the beginning of Jewish (and Christian in terms of antitype) epochs in salvation history. As he approached Rome, Maxentius decided not to defend the city from within, but to advance out against Constantine's forces, enlarging the Milvian bridge with a flotilla of boats bound together to enable his legion to cross in full battle line. But the current of the Tiber was flowing too strongly, and they were to collapse, with the result that his heavily armed men were to sink, and Constantine to enter Rome as victor. These events, Eusebius assures us, had been foretold and 'anciently inscribed in sacred books – disbelieved, indeed, by most as a myth, but believed by the faithful'. The confirmation was before them, found originally in the book of Exodus when Pharaoh and his chariots were drowned in the Red Sea. Maxentius, like Pharaoh, 'went down into the depths like a stone'.[13] Constantine and his men, like Moses and his, sung their triumphant song.

With these words Eusebius has taken the events of Constantine's victory out of the course of secular history, and set them firmly in the context of a new epoch in salvation history. The words of Exodus are not simply a narrative but a prophecy, originally fulfilled according to Christian tradition in Christ's death as the new Exodus of the 'Christ our Passover sacrificed for us'.[14] But for Eusebius they have now become a prophecy of Constantine, now regarded as the new Moses, creating a universal Christian Roman empire of peace, allowing the world to enjoy its *senectus*, its old age, before Christ's Second Advent. The last and final persecution had come and gone, with the Tribulation woes, all that was now left for the completion of salvation history was Christ's second coming.

Thus the scene was set to fulfil the ideological objectives of the politics of the pagan Principate founded by Augustus. Constantine, as the new Augustus, could, in Vergil's words, 'found the golden age' which was now Christian. He could thus fulfil what Decius, Valerian and Diocletian had failed to fulfil, not as an ever-turning cycle in political constitutions as in nature, but as the eternal goal of history for which the Judaeo-Christian tradition had hoped. But Eusebius is also aware that Constantine could now fulfil the Hellenistic ideal of the ruler as agent and instrument of the Logos, the ground plan of the cosmos,

13. Eusebius, *H.E.*, IX.9.4–7; Exod. 15:5-11.
14. 1 Cor. 5:7.

mediating cosmic order in Christian, imperial political order. In A.D. 336 he gave his oration on the thirtieth anniversary of the emperor's succession:

> The only begotten Logos of God reigns, from ages that had no beginning, to infinite and endless ages, the partner of his Father's kingdom. And our emperor, ever beloved by him, who derives the sources of his imperial authority from above, and is strong in the power of the sacred title, has controlled the Empire of the world for a long period of years . . . Once more, the universal Saviour opens the heavenly gates of his Father's kingdom . . . Our emperor, emulous of his divine example, having purged his earthly dominion from every stain of impious error, invited each holy and pious worshipper within his imperial mansions . . .[15]

Thus the reign of the Logos is paralleled by that of the emperor Constantine, the order of the empire his divine, cosmic order. As Eusebius continues:

> Lastly, invested as he is with a semblance of heavenly sovereignty, he directs his gaze above, and frames his earthly government according to the pattern of the divine original, feeling strength in its conformity to the monarchy of God.[16]

And in a further development of this idea that would have done justice to the Trinitarian Monarchianism of Callistus, he now states:

> And surely monarchy far transcends every other constitution and form of government: for that democratic equality of power, which is its opposite, may rather be described as anarchy and disorder. Hence there is one God, and not two, or three, or more: for to assert a plurality of gods is plainly to deny the being of God at all. There is one King, and his Logos and royal law is one . . . the living and self-subsisting Logos, who himself is divine, and administers his Father's kingdom on behalf of all who are under him and subject to his power.

Thus Eusebius firmly subscribes to the Hellenistic view characteristic of Arius and his followers that a cosmos of three persons, consubstantial and co-eternal, would be chaotic and without order: all existence must flow in a hierarchy of being from a single first principle, from which all other ruling principles are derived. Only a godhead that was hierarchical, and in which from the one unbegotten father the subordinate Son and Logos was begotten, could express the divine unity. It was thus not accidental that the Eusebian ideology that made the emperor, as representative of the Logos ruler of both spiritual and material domains, was opposed by those who believed in a godhead of two or three persons.

---

15. Eusebius, *Oration*, A.D. 336, 2.1 and 5.
16. Eusebius, *Orat.*, 3.5–7.

The designated title that enabled Augustus and his successors to so function was Pontifex Maximus, or high priest of the cults that made up the Roman pantheon. Why could not Constantine therefore now become Pontifex Maximus of the new, Christian religion, thus by some centuries claiming the title that later popes were to assume as their own? Clearly the doctrine of the Trinity is one key to that failure. But there were other, additional reasons why pagan political ideology could not now pursue the outcome that would follow from its fundamental assumptions, suitably transformed by Constantine's Christianity.

The course of human historical development is always inevitably chaotic. One answer is what we have seen to be the success of Cyprian's development of the ecclesiology of church order in the circumstances of Decius' persecution. Faced with a state commanding and enforcing a universal sacrifice to the gods of the empire, Cyprian had devised a robust ecclesial constitution, uniting all churches (dioceses) throughout the Roman world into a network of bishops in intercommunion with each other, mutually agreeing (or attempting to agree, if that is what Stephen did) on doctrine and discipline. Bishops met in council to make mutually binding decisions and judge cases.

Though there was some embryonic notion of the bishop of Rome at the centre of the interlocking network, this was not articulated in any great detail. But what Decius had thus unintentionally created, paradoxically with Cyprian's assistance, was a rival, empire-wide system of authority, a state within a state. If the emperor commanded all to sacrifice, the bishops could instruct the faithful not to obey: the choice was between torture and death in this life, or punishment in eternal fire in the next.

Constantine's claim to be bishop of those outside the Church reveals that he was unable to replace Cyprian's episcopal constitution that clearly remained robustly independent.[17] He undoubtedly did the next best thing, when he endeavoured to use the episcopal system as an instrument of imperial policy and control, as he did at Arles (A.D. 313) and at Nicaea (A.D. 325), but in both cases he was in the hands of the bishops regarding the unifying outcome that he was seeking to achieve. Both the work of Rapp and Norton have demonstrated that it would be a mistake to see any radical, post-Constantinian, reconstruction of the roles of bishops and Synods so as to imagine that these had become creatures of Constantine's empire as the result of Constantine's policies.[18] Thus Cyprian's success in creating a state within a state meant that Constantine could use bishops and councils partly as his instrument, but could not replace them.

In any case, in the West, as Ambrose's example shows, it was not possible to continue a Monarchian view of cosmic order reflected in an imperial power

---

17. Eusebius, *Vit. Const.*, 4.24.

18. C. Rapp, *Holy Bishops in Late Antiquity* (Berkeley/Los Angeles/London: University of California Press, 2005); P. Norton, *Episcopal Elections 250–600: Hierarchy and Popular Will in Late Antiquity* (Oxford: University Press, 2007).

that could control the Christian cult as it had controlled pagan ones. The events of Easter in A.D. 385 were to make the point well.[19] Theodosius was a confirmed Trinitarian, and Ambrose, bishop of Milan, had instructed Gratian, the young Western emperor, in the orthodox faith. But Gratian was murdered in A.D. 383, and his successor, the young Valentinian II, along with his mother, was an Arian. As under Roman law all religious property belonged ultimately to the emperor, Justina wanted church buildings to be handed over to Arian congregations at Milan, which at all events was a frontier citadel commanding an important pass across the Alps. There were Gothic mercenary troops stationed there, who tended to be Arians.

It was in this conflict between Ambrose and Justina that we see the new rules emerging in the relations between Church and State. The dispute began with a demand for a single basilica to be handed over to the Arians. At the beginning of Lent, at a heated meeting in Justina's palace, Ambrose had been ordered to hand over the Portian basilica just outside the gates of Milan. He had refused, with a veritable riot of the catholic faithful in support outside the palace gates. During Holy Week, a new attempt was made to seize the two prominent catholic basilicas within Milan itself, the Old and New Basilicas. Both attempts failed.

However, during that week, both basilicas had been laid siege to, with their congregations still inside praying and singing psalms. Once incident was to set the tone of the proceedings when, at the Portian basilica, also invested by Gothic troops, bishop Ambrose entered his church. During the Mass, some of the soldiers burst into the church causing consternation to the congregation, who thought that they were about to be massacred. But, far from being aggressive, they knelt at the feet of their bishop and asked for absolution. Times were changing, and with them the rules of the political ball game between Christianity and the Empire.

Valentian II could not understand why he needed to capitulate, and accused Ambrose of seeking to be a rival emperor. In dutiful support, his Grand Chamberlain, Calligonus, wrote to Ambrose: 'Do you dare to flout Valentinian while I am alive? I will take off your head'. To this the successor of St Cyprian, bishop of Carthage, executed by beheading by the act of Valerian's pro-consul for refusing the command of his lawful emperor, replied: 'May God grant you to do what you threaten! I shall suffer as bishops suffer, and you will act as eunuchs act.'[20] It was at that moment that Ambrose realized that he had won: Cyprian's heir had successfully faced down the heir of Decius, Valerian and Diocletian: times had changed!

Ambrose articulated the new set of principles reflected in these outcomes. Ambrose did not intend to deny the civil obedience of individual Christians,

19. F. Homes Dudden, *The Life and Times of St. Ambrose* (Oxford: Clarendon Press, 1935), vol. I, chapter 11.

20. Ambrose, *Ep.* 20.27–28. See also Homes Dudden, *Ambrose*, p. 279.

nor that their persons and property were at the disposal of the emperor if he should so wish, though he had no right to them under Roman law as a private individual:

> If the Emperor asks for tribute, we do not refuse it. The estates of the Church pay tribute. If he covets the estates, he has power to claim them, none of us will interfere.[21]

But a Church building and its sacred vessels a bishop cannot hand over, since the emperor has no rights to them:

> At length comes the command 'Deliver up the basilica'. . . . It is alleged that all things are lawful for the Emperor, that the whole world is his. I answer, 'Do not deceive yourself, Sir, with the fancy that you have any imperial right over divine things . . . It is written, "The things which are God's to God, and the things which are Caesar's to Caesar."' Palaces belong to the Emperor, churches to the Bishop. You can do what you please with secular buildings, but not with sacred.[22]

Thus there emerged a new concept in which there could be two spheres, the spiritual and the temporal, with bishops exercising supreme authority over the former and emperors the latter. It was a principle that Gelasius was to further articulate.

In A.D. 494, in the course of a dispute with the emperor Anastasius Ist over a heretical creed (the *Henoticon*), pope Gelasius Ist was to claim that the emperor had exceeded his authority. His grounds were:

> There are two powers, august Emperor, by which this world is chiefly ruled, namely, the sacred authority (*auctoritas*) of the priests and the royal power (*potestas*). Of these that of the priests is the more weighty, since they have to render an account for even the kings of men in the divine judgment. You are also aware, dear son, that while you are permitted honorably to rule over human kind, yet you bow your head humbly before those who preside over divine rites, and await from their hands the means of your salvation. In the reception and in the proper administration of the heavenly sacraments, you recognize that you should be subordinate rather than to preside at the level of religion, and that in these matters you depend on the judgment they pass rather than wish to subject them to your will.[23]

Here Gelasius defended two independent and co-equal powers, claiming for his own 'authority (*auctoritas*)' rather than 'power (*potestas*)', which gave the spiritual the claim to greater respect without claiming that it was a subordinating power. The argument was, after all, whether the Incarnation took place 'in two natures' as the Catholics believed, or whether it was in one nature, as the

21. Ambrose, *Serm. Contr. Auxent.*, 33.
22. Ambrose, *Ep.*, 20.15–19 and Homes Dudden, *Ambrose*, p. 277.
23. Gelasius, *Ep.*, 8.

Monophysites believed. The human and divine could coexist without one obliterating the other, or indeed subordinating it, like a puppet on a string. Here was a new version of the old Trinitarian metaphysic that had established the principle that there was not one first principle from which all others were derived and subordinate, so that, in political affairs, there need not be only one sovereign authority, one μοναρχία, from which all others were derived.

It was to prove a political principle that was extraordinarily robust through the centuries that followed, despite considerable challenges, and was to endure and flourish particularly in the West. It may be correct to see the traditional picture of the Eastern Church, as exemplified by Byzantium and Justinian and Theodora, as the empire controlling the Church and the Eastern bishops. It should be remembered that the Code of Justinian, that seeks to control the clergy along with the general population, begins with an orthodox statement of the Trinity.

Gregory Ist was to turn his mission westward, and become the father of Western Europe, converting the Gothic and Frankish tribes from both paganism and Arianism. Certainly he did not believe that the New Rome should control the Church. Thus Gelasius' principle of two powers was to become the principle of two spheres, the *sacerdotium* and the *imperium*. Certainly, with popes from Stephen II, the tendency began to move in the other way, when the latter proceeded to intervene in a political power struggle and anointed Peppin the Short. When Leo III crowned Charlemagne, an ideological assault began with the object of establishing the subordination of *imperium* to *sacerdotium*. Certainly revisions of the coronation rites, in the hands of the papacy and its liturgists, increasingly suggested that subordinate status of emperor to pope.

In the Investiture Controversy of the eleventh and twelfth centuries, the conflict between *imperium* and *sacerdotium* found a new focus in the issue of the presentation of the ring and the staff to a bishop elect. The issue at stake was whether this act had a sacramental effect, particularly when administered by a lay monarch. Was the lay claim one of sacramental and clerical status, or was it simply the expression of the transfer of the temporalities of the see, episcopal regalia, lands, properties, livestock and other forms of income from the dead bishop to his living successor? The literature of the Investiture Controversy suggest a variety of conflicting answers to this question, ranging from the ring and the staff as the essence of episcopal consecration, conveying spiritual mysteries, to the non-sacramental character of a non-verbal signification of property transfer, to the king as having received from the church the sacramental act of anointing no longer being a 'mere layman'.[24]

The unambiguously sacramental character of the transmission of the ring and the staff was finally acknowledged at the Concordat of Worms (A.D. 1124)

---

24. For discussion with bibliography, see A. Brent, 'The Investiture Controversy – an Issue in Sacramental Theology?', *ETL*, 63.1 (1987), pp. 59–89.

between pope Callistus II and the emperor Henry IV. But despite the original intentions of Gregory VII, the temporalities of the see were not inextricably bound up with that sacramental act: temporal power in one sphere and spiritual authority in another were to be kept in separate domains. Cyprian's Church as *imperium in imperio*, his 'state within a state', had survived.

It was to survive Innocent III and his successors' claims to hold the 'two swords' of temporal and spiritual jurisdiction, with the temporal sword that he placed in the hands of the lay ruler placed there at his pleasure. This had been the implied message of the legend of the Donation of Constantine, continued and further developed from earlier versions from Charlemagne's time onwards. Constantine, in repentance for his sins, had handed over to Pope Silvester and the Church the territory of Western Europe, leading the papal entourage hence-forth on foot as a subservient knight. Pope Silvester had returned his possessions to Constantine, but only, by implication, as a gracious act and on lease, so that these could always be reclaimed by their original, ecclesial owner.

Such a view could not prevail for the various reasons that we have sought to identify in this book. Christianity's original self-definition was of a group apart from the world awaiting Christ's second coming in the context of an order of nature and society in a state of collapse and yearning for its renewal. Any attempt to produce a Christian, realized eschatology, as a counterpart to the claim of Augustus and his successors to have 'founded the golden age', never succeeded in excluding the traditional future hope from its narrative. Whether in the form of a Lukan attempt to show Theophilus and his circle the realization in a church age still running throughout secular history of the true, divine 'peace', or that of Constantine inaugurating a Christian age of peace before the second coming, such an identification of the Christian society with political society was never successful.

Divinization of Christian imperial authority, with the emperor as agent of Christ the divine Logos in nature and in society proceeding from the Father, proved impossible, given the ecclesial shape of the Church created by Cyprian's ecclesiology. It also proved impossible in the light of a Trinitarian cosmos inhabited by a triune God in three persons, none of which were subordinate to the other, as pagan political theory required them to be if they were to be reflected in a political ideology that would maintain an old pagan Roman empire in a new, Christian form. It also failed because, in terms of Cyprian's ecclesiology, Christianity constituted the New Law fulfilling the Old. If the *sacerdotium* was to be the antitype of Old Testament type, then it must conform to an Old Testament polity in which kings were never priests nor priests kings: *sacerdotium* and *imperium* could never be exercised by the same persons.

But we may find a deeper reason for its failure exemplified in Augustine's experience. Markus has drawn us a portrait of the young Augustine as a sup-porter of the Eusebian ideology, and influenced by that ideology when he advocated, following the Collatio of Carthage (A.D. 410), the crushing of

Donatism by the civil power. But the events of A.D. 408, with the incursion of the Visi-Gothic tribes over the frozen waters of the Rhine and Danube, had shattered the dream of an empire of universal peace describable in Messianic terms. When he writes the *City of God*, Augustine finds no place for a Christian Rome as part of salvation history: Rome is not, as with Eusebius, part of the *praeparatio evangelica* ('preparation for the gospel'), but simply the new Babylon, the fourth empire of Daniel's prophecy.[25] Thus Rome became yet another empire to rise and fall in the tide of secular history:

> But what I say of this people and of this republic I must be understood to think and say of the Athenians, or any Greek state, of the Egyptians, of the earlier Assyria, Babylon, and of every other nation, great or small, which had a public government.[26]

The city of God is beyond history and beyond time and space: it cannot find an incarnation in any political structure. The Eusebian enterprise, as the fulfilment of the political metaphysics of Graeco-Roman philosophy, was to fail utterly in Augustine's eyes. Yet clearly the attempt was to continue both with Leo III, Gregory VII and Innocent III and their associates.

Luther, in an opposite fashion to Innocent III, was to place, in the tradition of Marsilius of Padua, both spiritual and temporal swords in the temporal ruler's hands. But in the events of the eighteenth and nineteenth centuries, once again the separation of spheres, the *sacerdotium* and the *imperium*, was to remain robust. And it still survives in the Western concept of a secular society and the separation of Church and State. Although secular humanism may greatly desire the total privatization of religious experience and practice so that this has no role in any public forum, the dismantling of the concept of a sacerdotal authority and sphere exercising influence over the *imperium* has not so far been successful.

The demand for separation of Church and State, in a secular age, may appear both obtainable and indeed rational. But we have only next to mention ethical issues such as abortion, contraception, and in vitro fertilization, stem cell cloning, etc., let alone issues of the role of the church or churches in education, the running of adoption agencies, etc., issues of gay marriage and adoption, etc. to realize how unrealizable such a separation is. But as Aquinas had always argued, the maintenance of two spheres does not imply their separation but their mutual co-operation. The abiding legacy of such a model remains the Catholic doctrine of the Trinity itself.

25. Augustine, *City of God*, XVIII.22 and XX.23. See also, Markus, *Saeculum: History and Society in the Theology of St. Augustine* (Cambridge: University Press, 1988), pp. 32–41; pp. 51–56.

26. Augustine, *City of God*, XIX.24.

BIBLIOGRAPHY

Political History

Alföldy, G., 'The Crisis of the Third Century as seen by Contemporaries', *GRBS*, 15 (1974), pp. 89–111 (= Alföldy, *Ausgewählte Beiträge*, pp. 273–94).

Anderson, G., *The Second Sophistic: A Cultural Phenomenon in the Roman Empire* (London: Routledge, 1993).

Armitage Robinson, J. (ed.), *Passio Scilitanorum*, in *The Passion of Perpetua (Passio Perpetuae)*, in *Texts and Studies: Contributions to Biblical and Patristic Literature*, No. 2 (Cambridge: University Press, 1891).

Arnim, I. von, *Stoicorum veterum fragmenta*, vol. II, *Chrysippi fragmenta logica et physica* (Leipzig: Teubner, 1903).

Aron, R., *Main Currents in Sociological Thought*, vols I–II (London: Weidenfeld and Nicolson, 1968).

Atkinson, K., *I Cried to the Lord: A Study in the Psalms of Solomon's Historical Background and Social Setting* (*Suppl. JnStJud*, 84; Leiden: Brill, 204).

Aune, D. G., 'The Influence of the Roman Imperial Court Ceremonial on the Apocalypse of John', *Papers of the Chicago Society for Biblical Research*, 28 (1983), pp. 5–26.

Babcock, C. L., 'Die "reformerten" Tetradrachmen des Uranius Antoninus', *Chiron*, 5 (1975), pp. 443–84.

—'An Inscription of Trajan Decius from Cosa', *AJP*, 83 (1962), pp. 147–58.

Baldus, H. R., 'Die 'reformerten' Tetradrachmen des Uranius Antoninus', *Chiron*, 5 (1975), pp. 452–55.

—*Uranius Antoninus: Münzprägung und Geschichte* (Antiquitas 3.11; Bonn: Habelt, 1971).

Bammel, E., 'Sukzessionsprinzip im Urchristentum', *StEphAug*, 31 (1990), pp. 63–72.

—'The Revolution Theory from Reimarus to Brandon', in Bammel, E. and Moule, C. F. D. (eds), *Jesus and Politics*, pp. 11–68.

—'The Trial before Pilate', in Bammel, E. and Moule, C. F. D. (eds), *Jesus and Politics*, pp. 415–51.

Bammel, E. and Moule, C. F. D. (eds), *Jesus and Politics of His Day* (Cambridge: University Press, 1984).

Barnard, L. W., 'St. Clement of Rome and the Persecution of Domitian', in *Studies in the Apostolic Fathers and their Background* (Oxford: Blackwell, 1966), pp. 5–15.

Barnes, T. D., 'Legislation against the Christians', *JRS*, 58 (1968), pp. 32–50.

Barrett, C. K., *The Holy Spirit in the Gospel Tradition* (London: SPCK, 1947).

Berger, K., 'Hellenistisch-heidnische Prodigien und die Vorzeichen in der jüdischen und Christlichen Apokalyptik', in *ANRW*, II.23.2, pp. 1428–69.

Berger, P., *The Social Reality of Religion* (Harmondsworth: Penguin, 1973).

Berger P. and Luckmann T., *The Social Construction of Reality* (Harmondsworth: Penguin, 1967).

Borg, M. J., *Jesus in Contemporary Scholarship* (Valley Forge, Pennsylvania: Trinity Press International, 1994).

—*Conflict, Holiness and Politics in the Teachings of Jesus* (Lampeter: Edwin Mellen, 1984).

Borgolte, M., *Petrusnachfolge und Kaiser-imitation. Die Grabliegen der Päpste, ihre Genese und Traditionsbildung* (Veröffentlichungen des Max-Planck-Instituts für Geschichte 95; Göttingen: Vandenhoeck und Ruprecht, 1989).

Borleffs, J. W. P., 'Institutum Neronianum', *VC*, 6 (1952), pp. 129–45.

Bowe, B. E., *A Church in Crisis: Ecclesiology and Paranaesis in Clement of Rome* (Harvard Dissertations in Religion 23; Minneapolis: Fortress Press, 1988).

Bradshaw, P. F., Johnson, M. E., Phillips, L. E. and Attridge H. W., *Hippolytus: The Apostolic Tradition, Translation and Commentary* (Hermeneia; Minneapolis: Fortress Press, 2002).

Brandenburg, H., *Das Grab des Papstes Cornelius und die Lucinaregion der Calixtus-Katacombe* (*JAC*, Ergänzungsreihe 11–12; Münster, Westfalen: Aschendorf, 1968–1969).

Brandon, S. G. F., *The Trial of Jesus of Nazareth* (London: Batsford, 1968).

—*Jesus and the Zealots: A Study of the Political Factor in Early Christianity* (Manchester: University Press, 1967).

Brent, A., *Cyprian and Roman Carthage in the Third Century* (Cambridge: University Press, 2009).

—*Ignatius of Antioch: A Martyr Bishop and the Origin of Episcopacy* (London: Continuum, 2007).

—*Ignatius of Antioch and the Second Sophistic* (*STAC*, 36; Tübingen: Mohr Siebeck, 2006).

—'St. Hippolytus, Biblical Exegete, Roman Bishop, and Martyr', *St Vladimir's Theological Quarterly*, 48.2–3 (2004), pp. 207–31.

—'Cyprian and the Question of Ordinatio per Confessionem', *StPat.*, 36 (2001), pp. 323–37.

—*The Imperial Cult and the Development of Church Order: Concepts and Images of Authority in Paganism and Early Christianity before the Age of Cyprian* (*VCSup*, 45; Leiden: E. J. Brill, 1999).

—'Luke-Acts and the Imperial Cult in Asia Minor', *JTS*, 48.2 (1997), pp. 411–38.

—*Hippolytus and the Roman Church in the Third Century: Communities in Tension before the Emergence of a Monarch-Bishop* (*VCSup*, 31; Leiden: E. J. Brill, 1995).

—*Cultural Episcopacy and Ecumenism: Representative Ministry in Church History from the Age of Ignatius of Antioch to the Reformation, with Special Reference to Contemporary Ecumenism* (Studies in Christian Mission, 6; Leiden: E. J. Brill, 1992).

—'Ecumenical Reconciliation and Cultural Episcopates', *ATR*, 72.3 (1990), pp. 255–79.

—'History and Eschatological Mysticism in Ignatius of Antioch', *ETL*, 65.4 (1989), pp. 309–29.

—'The Investiture Controversy – an issue in Sacramental Theology?', *ETL*, 63.1 (1987), pp. 59–89.

Brown, R. E. and Meier J.-P., *Antioch and Rome: New Testament Cradles of Catholic Christianity* (New York: Paulist Press, 1982).

Campbell, B., 'The Severan Dynasty', in *CAH²*, XII.1.1, p. 61.

Campenhausen, H. von, *Ecclesiastical Authority and Spiritual Power in the Church of the First Three Centuries*, translated by J. A. Baker (London: Adam and Charles Black, 1969).

Carleton Paget, J., *The Epistle of Barnabas: Outlook and Background* (WUNT, 2.64; Tübingen: Mohr Siebeck, 1994).

Catalano, P., 'Aspetti Spaziali de Sistema Giuridico-religioso Romano', in *ANRW*, II.16.1, pp. 440–53.

Catchpole, D. R., *The Quest for Q* (Edinburgh: T. & T. Clark, 1993).

—*The Trial of Jesus: A Study in the Gospels and Jewish Historiography from 1770 to the Present Day* (Studia post-Biblica, 18; Leiden: E. J. Brill, 1971).

Cerfaux, L. and J. Tondriau, *Le Culte des Souverains dans la Civilisation Gréco-romaine* (Bibl. de Théol., Sér. 3, 5; Paris-Tournai, 1956).

Cerrato, J. A., 'The Association of the Name Hippolytus with a Church Order now Known as *The Apostolic Tradition*', *St Vladimir's Theological Quarterly*, 48.2–3 (2004), pp. 179–94.

Chesnut, G. F., 'The Ruler and the Logos', in *ANRW*, II.16.2 (1978), pp. 1310–32.

Clarke, G., *The Letters of St. Cyprian*, vols I–IV, translation and commentary by G. W. Clarke (Ancient Christian Writers, 43, 44, 46 and 47; New York: Newman Press, 1984–1989).

Clarke, G. W., 'The Origin and Spread of Christianity', *CAH²*, XII.3.18b.

—'Some Observations on the Persecution of Decius', *Antichthon*, 3 (1969), pp. 68–73.

—'The Secular Profession of St. Cyprian of Carthage', *Latomus*, 24 (1965), pp. 633–38.

Clayton Croy, N., *3 Maccabees* (Septuagint Commentary Series; Leiden: E. J. Brill, 2006).

Cohen, H., *Description Historique des Monnaies* (Paris: Rollin and Feuardent, 1884).

Collins, J. J., The Apocalyptic Vision of the Book of Daniel (Harvard Semitic monographs 16; Missoula, Mont.: Harvard Semitic Museum, 1977), pp. 115–17.

Coppens, J., *L'imposition des mains et les rites connexes dans le Noveau Testament et dans l'église ancienne* (Universitas catholica lovaniensis, 15.2; Paris: J. de Meester et fils, 1925).

Corbier, M., 'Coinage, Society and Economy', in *CAH²*, XII.4.11, pp. 393–94.

Cox, J. E. (ed.), *Miscellaneous Writings of Thomas Cranmer* (London: Parker Society, 1844).

Cranston, M., *John Locke: A Biography* (New York: Arno Press, 1979).

Croag, E., 'Die Kaisarrede des Pseudo-Aristides', *Wiener Studien*, 40 (1918), pp. 20–45.

Crossan, J. D., *The Historical Jesus: The Life of a Mediterranean Jewish Peasant* (Edinburgh: T. & T. Clark, 1991).

Cumont, F., 'La Grande Inscription Bachique du Metropolitan Muséum, Ii: Commentaire Religieux de l'inscription', *AJA*, 37 (1933), pp. 215–63.

De Jonge, M., 'Messiah', in *ABD*, IV.777.

De Ruggiero, E., *Dizionario Epigrafico di Antichità Romane* (Rome: 'L'Erma' di Bretschneider, 1962).

De Ste. Croix, G. E. M., 'Why Were the Early Christians Persecuted?– A Rejoinder', *Past and Present*, 27 (1964), pp. 28–33.

—'Why Were the Early Christians Persecuted?' *Past and Present*, 26 (1963), pp. 6–38.

Delbrück, R., 'Uranius of Emesa', *Numismatic Chronicle*, 8 (1948), pp. 11–29.

Dieterich, A., *Die Grabschrift des Aberkios* (Leipzig: Teubner, 1896).

Downing, F. G., *Christ and the Cynics* (Sheffield: Academic Press, 1988).

Drinkwater, J., 'Maximinus to Diocletian and the "crisis"', in *CAH²*, XII.1.2, pp. 38–41.

Durkheim, E., *The Division of Labour in Society*, introduction by Lewis A. Coser; translated by W. D. Halls (New York: Free Press of Glencoe, 1997).

Ehrenberg, V. and Jones, A. H. M. (eds), *Documents Illustrating the Reigns of Augustus and Tiberius*, 2nd Edition (Oxford: Clarendon Press, 1976).

Elliott, J. K., *The Apocryphal New Testament: A Collection of Apocryphal Christian Literature in an English Translation* (Oxford: Clarendon Press, 1993).

Fears, J. R., 'The Cult of Virtues and Roman Imperial Ideology', in *ANRW*, II.17, 2 (1981), pp. 827–948.

Ferrua, A., *The Unknown Catacomb* (London: Geddes and Grosset, 1990).

Finney, P. C., *The Invisible God: The Earliest Christians on Art* (Oxford: University Press, 1994).

Foakes-Jackson, F. J., *History of the Christian Church to A.D. 461* (Cambridge: J. Hall and Son, 1909).

Foot, P., *The Politics of Harold Wilson* (Harmondsworth: Penguin, 1968).

Foucart P., 'Les certificates de sacrifice pendant la persécution de Décius (250)', *Journal des Savants*, 6 (1908), pp. 169–181.

Franke, P. R. and K Nollé M., *Die Homonoia-Münzen Kleinasiens und der Thrakischen Randgebiete* (Saarbrücker Studien zur Archäologie und alten Geschichte, 10, Hrsg Furtwängler A., Franke P. R. and Reinsberg C.; Saarbrücke: Druckerei und Verlag, 1997).

Frankfort, H., *Kingship and the Gods: A Study of the Ancient Near Eastern Religion as the Integration of Society and Nature* (Chicago: University of Chicago Press, 1978).

Frend, W. H. C., *The Rise of Christianity* (London: Darton, Longman, and Todd, 1986).

—*Martyrdom and Persecution in the Early Church* (Oxford: Blackwell, 1965).

Galinsky, K., 'Venus, Polysemy, and the Ara Pacis Augustae', *AJA*, 96, 3 (1992), pp. 457–75.

Garnsey, P., *Social Status and Legal Privilege in the Roman Empire* (Oxford: Clarendon Press, 1970).

Garnsey, P. and Saller R., *The Roman Empire: Economy, Society and Culture* (London: Duckworth, 1987).

Giordani, R., 'Novatiano beatissimo martyri Gaudentius diaconus fecit. Contributo all' identificazione del martire Novaziano della catacomba anonima sulla via Tiburtina', *RivArchCr*, 68 (1992), pp. 233–58.

Gleason, M. W., *Making Men: Sophists and Self-Representation in Ancient Rome* (New Jersey, Princeton: Princeton University Press, 1995).

Goldhill, S. (ed.), *Being Greek under Rome: Cultural Identity, the Second Sophistic, and the Development of Empire* (Cambridge: University Press, 2001).

Griffin, M., 'The Flavians', in *CAH²*, IX.1.1.

Guarducci, M., *Epigrafia Greca* IV: *Epigrafi sacre pagane e cristiane* (Rome: Istituto poligrafico dello stato, 1978).

Halsberghe, G. H., *The Cult of Sol Inuictus* (*EPRO*, 35; Leiden: E. J. Brill, 1972).

Hemer, C. J., *The Letters to the Seven Churches in their Local Setting* (JSNTSup., 11; Sheffield: Academic Press, 1986).

Hengel, M., *Victory over Violence, Jesus and the Revolutionists*, translated by David E. Green, with an introd. by Robin Scroggs (Philadelphia: Fortress Press, 1973).

Homes Dudden, F., *The Life and Times of St. Ambrose* (Oxford: Clarendon Press, 1935).

Horbury, W., *Herodian Judaism and New Testament Study* (WUNT, 193; Tübingen: Mohr Siebeck, 2006).

—*Jewish Messianism and the Cult of Christ* (London: SCM, 1998).

—'Messianic Associations of the "Son of Man"', *JTS*, 36.1 (1985), pp. 34–55.

Horsley, R., *Jesus and Empire: The Kingdom of God and the New World Disorder* (Minneapolis: Fortress, 2003).

—*Sociology and the Jesus Movement* (New York: Crossroad, 1989).

—*Jesus and the Spiral of Violence: Popular Jewish Resistance in Roman Palestine* (San Francisco: Harper and Row, 1987).

Hyldahl, N., 'Hegesipps Hypomnemata', *Studia Theologica*, 14 (1960), pp. 70–113.

Janssen, L. F., '"Superstitio" and the Persecution of the Christians', *VC*, 33, 2 (1979), pp. 131–59.

Jones, B. W., *The Emperor Domitian* (London: Routledge, 1992).

Jones, D. L., 'Christianity and the Roman Imperial Cult', in *ANRW*, II.23.2, pp. 1023–54.

Kearsley, R. A., 'The Asiarchs', in *The Book of Acts in its Graeco-Roman Setting*, edited by W. J. Gill and C. Gempf, in *The Book of Acts in its First Century Setting* (Michigan and Carlisle: Eerdmans/Paternoster Press, 1994), II, pp. 263–376.

Keresztes, P., 'Rome and the Christian Church I', in *ANRW*, II.23.1, pp. 247–315.

—'The Decian *libelli* and Contemporary Literature', *Latomus*, 34.3 (1975), pp. 761–81.

Kienast, D., 'Die Homonoia Verträge in der romischen Kaiserzeit', *JbNum*, 14 (1964), pp. 51–64.

Kinman, Brent, *Jesus' Entry into Jerusalem in the Context of Lukan Theology and the Politics of His Day* (AGJU, 27; Leiden: E. J. Brill, 1995).

Kloppenborg, J. S., *The Formation of Q: Trajectories in Ancient Wisdom Collections* (Studies in Antiquity and Christianity; Philadelphia: Fortress, 1987).

Knipfing, J. R., 'The Libelli of the Decian Persecution', *HTR*, 16 (1923), pp. 345–90.

Koester, H., *Ancient Christian Gospels: Their History and their Development* (London: SCM, 1990).

Kraybill, J. N., *Imperial Cult and Commerce in John's Apocalypse* (JSNTSup, 132; Sheffield: Academic Press, 1996).

Kuhlmann, P. A., *Die Giessener literarischen Papyri und die Caracalla-Erlasse-Edition, Übersetzung und Kommentar* (Berichte und Arbeiten aus der Universitäts-bibliothek und dem Universitätsarchiv Giessen, 46; Giessen: Universitätsbibliothek, 1994).

Lampe, P., *From Paul to Valentinus: Christians at Rome in the First Two Centuries*, translated by Michael Steinhauser, edited Marshall D. Johnson (London: T & T Clark International, 2003).

—*Die stadtrömischen Christen in den ersten beiden Jahrhunderten* (WUNT, 2.18; Tübingen: Mohr Siebeck, 1989).

Lane Fox, R., *Pagans and Christians* (Middlesex: Penguin, 1986).

Leclercq, H., 'Les certificats de sacrifice païen sous Dèce en 250', in *Bulletin d'ancienne littérature et d'archéologie chrétienne*, 4 (1914), pp. 52–60, 188–201.

Lenski G. E., *Power and Privilege: A Theory of Social Stratification* (New York: McGraw-Hill, 1966).

Locke, J., *The Second Treatise of Government (An essay concerning the true original, extent and end of civil government)*, and *A Letter concerning Toleration*, edited, with a revised introduction by J. W. Gough (Oxford: Blackwell, 1966).

Lotz, J.-P., *Ignatius and Concord: The Background and Use of the Language of Concord in the Letters of Ignatius of Antioch* (London: Peter Lang, 2007).

Lührmann, D., *Die Redaktion der Logienquelle* (*WMANT*, 33; Neukirchen: Neukirchen Verlag, 1969).

Mack, B. L., *A Myth of Innocence: Mark and Christian Origins* (Philadelphia: Fortress, 1988).

Markus, R. A., *Saeculum: History and Society in the Theology of St. Augustine* (Cambridge: University Press, 1988).

Mitchell, S., 'Festivals, Games, and Civic Life in Roman Asia Minor', *JRS*, 80 (1990), pp. 183–93.

Mommsen, T., 'Chronographer of 354', in *Chronica Minora, Saec. IV. V. VI. VII* (Monumenta Germaniae Historica IX; Berlin: Weidmann, 1892), vol. 1.13.

Moretti, G., *Ara Pacis Augustae* (Rome, 1948).

Moretti, L., 'Un nuovo proconsole d'Acaia', *ArcCl*, 5 (1953), pp. 255–59.

Mowinckel, S., *He that Cometh*, translated by G. W. Anderson (Oxford: Blackwell, 1956).

Newman, J. H., *The Development of Christian Doctrine* (London: James Toovey, 1845).

Nilsson, M. P., 'The Dionysiac Mysteries of the Hellenistic and Roman Age', *Acta Instituti Atheniensis Regni Sueciae*, 8, 5 (Lund: Gleerup, 1957).

Nollé, M. K., and J., 'Vom feinen Spiel städtischer Diplomatie zu Zeremoniell und Sinn kaiserlicher Homonoiafeste', *ZPE*, 102 (1994), pp. 241–61.

North, J., 'Diviners and Divination at Rome', in *Pagan Priests: Religion and Power in the Ancient World*, edited by M. Beard and J. North (London: Duckworth, 1990).

Norton, P., *Episcopal Elections 250–600: Hierarchy and Popular Will in Late Antiquity* (Oxford: University Press, 2007).

Peek, W., *Der Isishymnus von Andros und verwandte Texte* (Berlin: Weidmann, 1930).

Pelling, C., 'The Triumviral Period', in *CAH²*, X.1 (1996), *The Augustan Empire, 43 B.C. – A.D. 69*, pp. 1–69.

Perrin, N., *Thomas, the other Gospel* (London: SPCK, 2007).

Petersen, E., *Ara Pacis Augustae* (Wien: A. Hölder, 1902).

Pleket, H. W., 'An Aspect of the Imperial Cult: Imperial Mysteries', *HTR*, 58, 4 (1965), pp. 331–47.

Potter, D. S., *The Roman Empire at Bay, A.D. 180–395* (London: Routledge, 2004).

Poulsen, F., 'Talking, Weeping, and Bleeding Sculptures: A Chapter in the History of Religious Fraud', *Acta Archaeologica*, 16 (1945), pp. 178–95.

Preysing, K. von, 'Der Leserkreis der Philosophoumena Hippolyts', *ZKT*, 38 (1914), pp. 421–45.

Price, S. R. F., *Rituals and Power: The Roman Imperial Cult in Asia Minor* (Cambridge: University Press, 1984).

—'The Place of Religion: Rome in the Early Empire', in CAH2, X.16, pp. 832–33.

Rafferty, O. P., 'Thomas Cranmer and the Royal Supremacy', *Heythrop Journal*, 31 (1990), pp. 129–49 (134).

Rapp, C., *Holy Bishops in Late Antiquity* (Berkeley/Los Angeles/London: University of California Press, 2005).

Ratcliff, E. C., '"Apostolic Tradition": Questions Concerning the Appointment of the Bishop', in *Liturgical Studies*, edited by A. H. Couratin and D. H. Tripp (London: SPCK, 1976), pp. 156–60.

Reekmans, L., *La Tombe du Pape Corneille et sa Région Céméteriale* (Roma Sotteranea Cristiana 4; Città del Vaticano, 1964).

Rives, J. B., 'The Decree of Decius and the Religion of the Empire', *JRS*, 89 (1999), pp. 135–54.

Roasenda, P., 'Decio e i libellatici', *Didaskaleion*, 5.1 (1927), pp. 31–68.

Robert, L., 'Hellenica II, Inscription Éphébique', *R.Phil.*, 13 (1939), pp. 122–28, reprinted in *Opera Minora Epigraphie et antiquités grecques* (Amsterdam: A. M. Hakkert, 1969).

—*Études Anatoliennes* (Paris: Boccard, 1937).

Ross Taylor, L., *Party Politics in the Age of Caesar* (Berkeley and Los Angeles: University of California Press, 1964).

—*The Divinity of the Roman Emperor* (American Philological Association, Monographs, 1; Connecticut, 1931).

Rossini, O., *Ara Pacis* (Rome: Eclecta, 2006).

Rowland, C., *The Open Heaven: Study of Apocalyptic in Judaism and Early Christianity* (London: SPCK, 1985).

Sanders, E. P., *Jesus and Judaism* (London: SCM, 1985).

Schilpp, P. (ed.), *Albert Einstein: Philosopher-Scientist* (La Salle, Illinois: Open Court, 1969).

Schüssler Fiorenza, E., *In Memory of Her: A Feminist Theological Reconstruction of Christian Origins* (New York: Crossroad, 1983).

Schmithals, W., *The Office of Apostle in the Early Church*, translated by J. E. Steely (London: SPCK, 1971), pp. 32–38.

Schoedel, W., *Ignatius of Antioch: A Commentary on the Letters of Ignatius of Antioch* (Philadelphia: Fortress Press, 1985).

Schubart, W., 'Ptolemaeus Philopator und Dionysos', *Amtliche Berichte Aus Den Preussischen Königlichen Kunstsammlungen*, 38.7 (Berlin: G. Grotesche, 1917), col. 189–98.

—Ägyptische Abteilung (Papyrussammlung): Ptolemaeus Philopator und Dionysos, in *Amtliche Berichte aus den preussischen königlichen Kunstsammlungen (= Beiblatt zum Jahrbuch der preussischen königlichen Kunstsammlungen)*, 38 (1916/1917).

Schwartz, J., 'Une Déclaration de Sacrifice du Temps de Dèce', *RB*, 54 (1947), pp. 1–11.

Scullard, H. H., *From the Gracchi to Nero: A History of Rome from 133 B.C. to A.D. 68* (London: Methuen, 1982).

Sherk, R. K., *Rome and the Greek East to the Death of Augustus* (Translated Documents of Greece and Rome, 4, edited by E. Badian and R. Sherk; Cambridge: University Press, 1984).

Sherwin-White, A. N., 'The Early Persecutions and Roman Law Again', *JTS*, 3.2 (1952), pp. 211–12.

Skinner, Q., *The Foundations of Modern Political Thought* (Cambridge: University Press, 1978).

Sokolwski, F., *Lois Sacrées de lí Asie Mineure* (École Français d Athènes 9: Paris: Boccard, 1955).

Souter, A. Wyllie, J. M., Brink, C. O., Parker, E. A., Craig, J. D., Edwards, W. M., Glare, P. G. W., Bailey, C., Alford, M., Chadwick, J., Slater, B. V., Browning, D. C., Howard, C. L., Turton, G. E., Barrow, R. H., Trenkner, S., Palmer, R. C. (eds), *New Latin Dictionary* (Oxford: Clarendon Press, 1968).

Spaeth, B. S., 'The Goddess Ceres in the Ara Pacis Augustae and in the Carthage Relief', *AJA*, 77 (1994), pp. 65–100.

Stevenson, J. and Frend W. H. C., *A New Eusebius: Documents Illustrating the History of the Church to A.D. 337* (London: SPCK, 1987).

Stewart-Sykes, A., *Hippolytus, on the Apostolic Tradition, an English Translation with Introduction and Commentary* (Crestwood, NY: St Vladimir's Seminary Press, 2001).

Sweet, J., *Revelation* (SCM Pelican Commentaries; London: SCM, 1979).

Swift, L. J., 'The Anonymous Encomium of Philip the Arab', *GRBS,* 7 (1966), pp. 267–89.

Takács, S. A., *Isis and Sarapis in the Roman World* (EPRO, 124; Leiden: E. J. Brill, 1995).

Toynbee, J. and Ward Perkins J., *The Shrine of St. Peter and the Vatican Excavations* (London: Longmans Green, 1956).

Tuckett, C. M., *Q and the History of Early Christianity: Studies on Q* (Edinburgh: T. & T. Clark, 1996).

Valantasis, R., *The Gospel of Thomas* (London and New York: Routledge, 1997).

Weber, M., *The Protestant Ethic and the Spirit of Capitalism* (New York: Scribner, 1958).

—*Basic Concepts in Sociology*, translated by H. P. Secher (London: Peter Owen, 1962).

Weigand,Th., 'Siebenter vorläufiger Bericht über Ausgrabungen in Milet und Didyma', in *APAW* (1911), Anhang Abhandlungen I, pp. 1–71.

Weinstock, D. J., *Divus Julius* (Oxford: Clarendon, 1971).

Winter, P., *On the Trial of Jesus*, 2nd Edition revised and edited by T. A. Burkill and G. Vermes (Studia Judaica 1; Berlin and New York: De Gruyter, 1974).

Wittgenstein, L., *On Certainty*, edited by G. E. M. Anscombe and G. H. von Wright, translated by Denis Paul and G. E. M. Anscombe (Oxford: Blackwell, 1974).

Zanker, P., *The Power of Images in the Age of Augustus*, translated by A. Shapiro (Ann Arbor: University of Michigan Press, 1990).

INDEX

1. SCRIPTURE

2. Early Christian and Jewish Writers

Tertullian		Theophilus	
Apologia		*Ad*	
I.11–13 (57–71)	210	*Autolycum*	
5 (1–35)		3.4	211
8.3 (10–12)	38	3.6	211
8. 7–8 (28–36)	38	3.9	211
9.8 (31–36)	38	3.15	211
40.1–2 (1–9)	37		
		Traditio	
De Pudicitia		*Apostolica*	
1.6–8 (26–37)	240	2	178
10.12 (50–54)	269	9	265

3. Classical Works, Epigraphy, and Coins Works

Statius
Silvae
IV.1.3–4   138
IV.3.128–129   139

Stobaius
Eclogae
IV.7.61   120
IV.7.63   120

Suetonius
Augustus
7   254
7.60   106
52   116
94.4   112

Domitian
3.1   136
4.4   113
7.2   136
13.1   136
13.2   136

Nero
38   32

Tiberius
36   38, 126

Titus
5.3   221

Vespasian
4.5   52, 54
23.4   115

Tacitus
Annales
II.27–32   38, 126
IV.32–35   104
XII.22   144
XIV.15   158
XV.37   32
XV.44.3   37
XV.44.4–5   34
XV.44.4   36

Historiae
4.81   221
5.13   49, 54, 105
13   51

Ulpian
De officio proconsulis
VIII   38, 126

Valerius Maximus
Factorum et Dictorum Memorabilium
III.6.6   117

Velleius Paterculus
Historiae Romanae
II.82.4   118
II.89.5   90

Vergil
Aeneid
789–790   111
792–793   111
792–794   256

Eclogae
4   123
4.5–10   256

Epigraphy

CIG
5361.21   181

CIL
VI.1092   254
VIII.20487.1–3   254
VIII.5143   280
XIII.9119   254

IG
IV.1299   191

IGRR
I.1150   221
I.1480   254, 255
III.209   148
IV.39.30–31   159

4. Latin Words

5. GREEK TERMS

6. Modern Authors

7. SUBJECTS